THE PURCHASING POWER OF MONEY

THE MACMILLAN COMPANY
NEW YORK · BOSTON · CHICAGO
SAN FRANCISCO

MACMILLAN & CO., LIMITED
LONDON · BOMBAY · CALCUTTA
MELBOURNE

THE MACMILLAN CO. OF CANADA, LTD.
TORONTO

THE PURCHASING POWER OF MONEY

ITS DETERMINATION
AND RELATION TO CREDIT
INTEREST AND CRISES

BY

IRVING FISHER

PROFESSOR OF POLITICAL ECONOMY IN YALE UNIVERSITY

ASSISTED BY

HARRY G. BROWN

INSTRUCTOR IN POLITICAL ECONOMY IN YALE UNIVERSITY

New York
THE MACMILLAN COMPANY
1912

Set up and electrotyped. Published March, 1911. Reprinted February, 1912.

Norwood Press
J. S. Cushing Co. — Berwick & Smith Co.
Norwood, Mass., U.S.A.

To

THE MEMORY OF

SIMON NEWCOMB

GREAT SCIENTIST, INSPIRING FRIEND,

PIONEER IN THE STUDY

OF

"SOCIETARY CIRCULATION"

PREFACE

THE purpose of this book is to set forth the principles determining the purchasing power of money and to apply those principles to the study of historical changes in that purchasing power, including in particular the recent change in "the cost of living," which has aroused world-wide discussion.

If the principles here advocated are correct, the purchasing power of money — or its reciprocal, the level of prices — depends exclusively on five definite factors: (1) the volume of money in circulation; (2) its velocity of circulation; (3) the volume of bank deposits subject to check; (4) its velocity; and (5) the volume of trade. Each of these five magnitudes is extremely definite, and their relation to the purchasing power of money is definitely expressed by an "equation of exchange." In my opinion, the branch of economics which treats of these five regulators of purchasing power ought to be recognized and ultimately will be recognized as an exact science, capable of precise formulation, demonstration, and statistical verification.

The main contentions of this book are at bottom simply a restatement and amplification of the old "quantity theory" of money. With certain corrections in the usual statements of that theory, it may still be called fundamentally sound. What has long been needed is a candid reëxamination and revision of that venerable theory rather than its repudiation.

Yet in the voluminous literature on money, there seems to be very little that approaches accurate formulation and rigorous demonstration, — whether theoretical or statistical.

In making this attempt at reconstruction, I have the satisfaction of finding myself for once a conservative rather than a radical in economic theory. It has seemed to me a scandal that academic economists have, through outside clamor, been led into disagreements over the fundamental propositions concerning money. This is due to the confusion in which the subject has been thrown by reason of the political controversies with which it has become entangled.

As some one has said, it would seem that even the theorems of Euclid would be challenged and doubted if they should be appealed to by one political party as against another. At any rate, since the "quantity theory" has become the subject of political dispute, it has lost prestige and has even come to be regarded by many as an exploded fallacy. The attempts by promoters of unsound money to make an improper use of the quantity theory — as in the first Bryan campaign — led many sound money men to the utter repudiation of the quantity theory. The consequence has been that, especially in America, the quantity theory needs to be reintroduced into general knowledge.

Besides aiming to set forth the principles affecting the purchasing power of money, this book aims to illustrate and verify those principles by historical facts and statistics. In particular, the recent rise in prices is examined in detail and traced to its several causes.

The study of the principles and facts concerning the purchasing power of money is of far more than academic interest. Such questions affect the welfare of every inhabitant of the civilized world. At each turn of the tide of prices, millions of persons are benefited and other millions are injured.

For a hundred years the world has been suffering from periodic changes in the level of prices, producing alternate crises and depressions of trade. Only by knowledge, both of the principles and of the facts involved, can such fluctuations in future be prevented or mitigated, and only by such knowledge can the losses which they entail be avoided or reduced. It is not too much to say that the evils of a variable monetary standard are among the most serious economic evils with which civilization has to deal; and the practical problem of finding a solution of the difficulty is of international extent and importance. I have proposed, very tentatively, a remedy for the evils of monetary instability. But the time is not yet ripe for the acceptance of any working plan. What is at present most needed is a clear and general public understanding of principles and facts.

Toward such an end this book aims to contribute: —

1. A reconstruction of the quantity theory.
2. A discussion of the best form of index number.
3. Some mechanical methods of representing visually the determination of the level of prices.
4. A practical method of estimating the velocity of circulation of money.
5. The ascertainment statistically of the bank deposits in the United States which are *subject to check*, as distinct from "individual deposits," as usually published.
6. An improved statistical evaluation of the volume of trade, as well as of the remaining elements in the equation of exchange.
7. A thorough statistical verification of the (reconstructed) quantity theory of money.

As it is quite impossible to do justice to some of these subjects without the use of mathematics, these have been freely introduced, but have been relegated, so far as possible, to Appendices. This plan, which is in accordance with that previously adopted in *The Nature of Capital and Income* and *The Rate of Interest*, leaves the text almost wholly nonmathematical.

Most of the statistical results review and confirm the conclusions of Professor Kemmerer in his valuable *Money and Credit Instruments in their Relation to General Prices*, which appeared while the present book was in course of construction. I am greatly indebted to Professor Kemmerer for reading the entire manuscript and for much valuable criticism throughout.

My thanks are due to Professor F. Y. Edgeworth of All Souls' College, Oxford, and to Professor A. W. Flux of Manchester for kindly looking through the manuscript of the Appendix on index numbers and for suggestions and criticisms.

To Dr. A. Piatt Andrew, now Assistant Secretary of the Treasury, my thanks are due for his kindness, as Special Assistant to the National Monetary Commission, in putting the resources of that Commission at my disposal, and in working out, from the records of the office of the Comptroller of the Currency, the volume of deposits subject to check at various dates in the past. For coöperation in carrying out these same calculations, I am likewise indebted to Mr. Lawrence O. Murray, Comptroller of the Currency. These valuable figures are the first of their kind.

To Mr. Gilpin of the New York Clearing House, my thanks are due for his kindness in furnishing various figures asked for and cited specifically in the text.

To Mr. Richard M. Hurd, President of the Lawyers Mortgage Co., I am indebted for reading parts of the manuscript and for valuable criticism.

To Mr. John O. Perrin, President of the American National Bank of Indianapolis, I am indebted for statistics of the "activity" of bank accounts in his bank, and for similar figures I am indebted to the officers of the National New Haven Bank and the City Bank of New Haven.

My thanks are due to the *Economic Journal* for permission to use unaltered some parts of my article on "The Mechanics of Bimetallism," which first appeared in that journal in 1894.

My thanks are due to the *Journal of the Royal Statistical Society* for similar permission with reference to my article on "A Practical Method for estimating the Velocity of Circulation of Money," which appeared in December, 1909.

A number of my students have rendered valuable service in gathering and coördinating statistics. I would especially mention Mr. Seimin Inaoka, Mr. Morgan Porter, Mr. N. S. Fineberg, Mr. W. E. Lagerquist, now instructor at Cornell University, Messrs. G. S. and L. A. Dole, Dr. John Bauer, now assistant professor at Cornell University, Dr. John Kerr Towles, now instructor at the University of Illinois, Dr. A. S. Field, now instructor at Dartmouth College, Mr. A. G. Boesel, Mr. W. F. Hickernell, Mr. Yasuyiro Hayakawa, Mr. Chester A. Phillips, and Mr. R. N. Griswold. Mr. Griswold performed the lengthy calculations involved in ascertaining an index of the volume of trade.

There are two persons to whom I am more indebted than to any others. These are my brother, Mr. Herbert W. Fisher, and my colleague, Dr. Harry G. Brown.

To my brother my thanks are due for a most searching criticism of the whole book from the standpoint of pedagogical exposition, and to Mr. Brown for general criticism and suggestions as well as for detailed work throughout. In recognition of Mr. Brown's assistance, I have placed his name on the title-page.

IRVING FISHER.

YALE UNIVERSITY, February, 1911.

SUGGESTIONS TO READERS

1. The *general reader* will be chiefly interested in Chapters I–VIII.

2. The *cursory reader* will find the gist of the book in Chapter II.

3. *Objectors to the quantity theory* will find their theoretical and statistical objections discussed in Chapters VIII and XII respectively.

4. *Students of financial history* should read Chapter XII.

5. *Currency reformers* should read Chapter XIII.

6. The appendices are addressed mainly (though not exclusively) to *mathematical economists*, for whom the chief interest will probably lie with the Appendix to Chapter X, on Index Numbers, (which should be read as a whole,) and § 6 of the Appendix to Chapter XII, on the Method of Determining Velocity of Circulation.

7. The remainder of the Appendix to Chapter XII is supplied chiefly in order that *statistical critics* may be enabled to verify the processes described in the text.

8. Chapter X and its Appendix are of chief interest to *students of index numbers*, a subject as fascinating to some as it is dry to others.

9. The analytical table of contents, the index, and the running page headings have been constructed with especial reference to the varying needs of different classes of readers.

The book is, however, designed to constitute a complete whole, and it is hoped that as many as possible of those who approach it trom special viewpoints may, in the end, read it all.

SUMMARY OF CONTENTS

ANALYTICAL TABLE OF CONTENTS

CHAPTER I

Primary Definitions

CHAPTER II

Purchasing Power of Money as related to the Equation of Exchange

CHAPTER III

Influence of Deposit Currency on the Equation and therefore on Purchasing Power

CHAPTER IV

Disturbance of Equation and of Purchasing Power during Transition Periods

CHAPTER V

Indirect Influences on Purchasing Power

CHAPTER VI

Indirect Influences (*Continued*)

CHAPTER VII

Influence of Monetary Systems on Purchasing Power

CHAPTER VIII

Influence of Quantity of Money and Other Factors on Purchasing Power and on Each Other

CHAPTER IX

The Dispersion of Prices makes necessary an Index of Purchasing Power

CHAPTER X

The Best Index Numbers of Purchasing Power

CHAPTER XI

STATISTICAL VERIFICATION. GENERAL HISTORICAL REVIEW

CHAPTER XII

STATISTICAL VERIFICATION. RECENT YEARS

CHAPTER XIII

THE PROBLEM OF MAKING PURCHASING POWER MORE STABLE

APPENDICES

Appendix to Chapter II

Appendix to Chapter III

Appendix to Chapter V

Appendix to Chapter VI

Appendix to Chapter VII

Appendix to Chapter VIII

Appendix to Chapter X

Appendix to Chapter XII

ADDENDUM

Data have just become available by which to bring down through 1910 the statistics of Chapter XII. The results are as follows:

MAGNITUDES IN THE EQUATION OF EXCHANGE FOR 1910*

	M	M'	V	V'	P	T	$MV+M'V'$	PT
As first calculated	1.64	7.24	21	52.8	103.7	397	416	412
As finally adjusted	1.64	7.23	21	52.7	104.0	399	415	415

The table shows that the figures, as first calculated, conform admirably to the equation of exchange. The adjustment needed, to produce perfect conformity, in only one case reaches the half of one per cent!

From the adjusted figures we may calculate the percentages of cash and check transactions ($MV \div MV+M'V'$ and $M'V' \div MV+M'V'$). These are 8% and 92%, which may be added to the table on page 317. The ratio of deposits to money (M'/M) is 4.4, which shows

* The above figures may be inserted by the reader in the tables on pages 280, 281, 284, 285, 290, 292, 293, 304. The methods of deriving the figures are in general the same as those explained in the Appendix to Chapter XII. The antecedent figures on which the above table depends may be inserted by the reader as follows:

M. On page 432 add (to the bottom of columns 1–8 incl.) in the table the following: 1910, 3.42, 3.42, .32, 1.41, 3.3%, 1.46, 1.64.

M'. It is not necessary to complete the table on page 435, as the Comptroller's Report for 1910 (p. 54) gives for the first time deposits subject to check (7.82 billions). To this 7.82, however, three corrections are needed: (1) subtract .29 for "savings accounts" improperly included (estimated for me by the Comptroller's Office at half of the figure in note *a*, lower table, p. 54, Comptr. Rpt.); (2) subtract .54 as "exchanges for clearing house" (= ½ times those for national banks); (3) add .25

a great increase over 1909. The disproportionate growth of deposits relatively to money and the excessive velocity of circulation (52.7) of deposits, substantially equal to the unprecedented figure for 1909, are disquieting symptoms and serve only to confirm the forebodings in the text.

For aid in working out the figures in this addendum I am indebted to three of my students, Mr. H. A. W. Duckert, Mr. J. M. Shortliffe, and Mr. M. G. Hastings.

as the Comptroller's Office estimate, for me, of unreported deposits subject to check. By applying these corrections we obtain 7.24.

V. I have simply taken 21 as a safe approximate estimate on the basis of the previous statistics of *V* (p. 478) and its assumed relation to *V'*.

M'V' and *V'*. Add to columns 1–7 of table on page 448 the following: 1910, 97.3, 66.4, 429.3, .89 (by extrapolation, an unsafe guide), 382, 52.8.

P. This is obtained (on the principles of the table on page 487) from the index number 131.6 of wholesale prices for 1910 (kindly supplied in advance of publication by the Bureau of Labor) and the average price 96.2 of stocks as given by the *Commercial and Financial Chronicle*, both being compared with the respective figures for 1909, viz. 126.5 and 97.5. They are combined by "weighting" the wholesale prices 10 and the stock prices 1 and reducing the results so that the average for 1909 shall be 100.

T. This is obtained: (*a*) by continuing columns 1–5 of the table on page 479 by inserting: 1910, 160, 118, 162, 154; (the extension of column 2 for 1910 is made by means of somewhat more complete data than those enumerated on pages 480–482); (*b*) by combining the result, 154, obtained for column 5 with the figures for railway cars handled. These were 19.8 millions for 1909 and 22.3 for 1910. Column 5 being weighted 10 and the car figures 1, we get as indices of trade: for 1909, 1718, and for 1910, 1763, showing an increase of 2.6%, which, applied to the (corrected) estimate of the absolute trade of 1909, viz. 387 billions, gives 397 as the absolute trade in 1910.

(The opportunity is here taken to correct an inadvertence on pp. 480 ff. It should have been there stated that, of the 44 categories mentioned, some are *alternative* and not independent items, viz. those having the same names and differing only in the number of cities; also that the dates given do not imply that the items opposite are in all cases used for *all* the intervening time, but only for such periods as the items were actually available.)

It is noticeable that the changes in business in 1910 as compared with 1909 are somewhat irregular; the sales of stocks have declined; exports and imports (both of them) have declined about 10%.

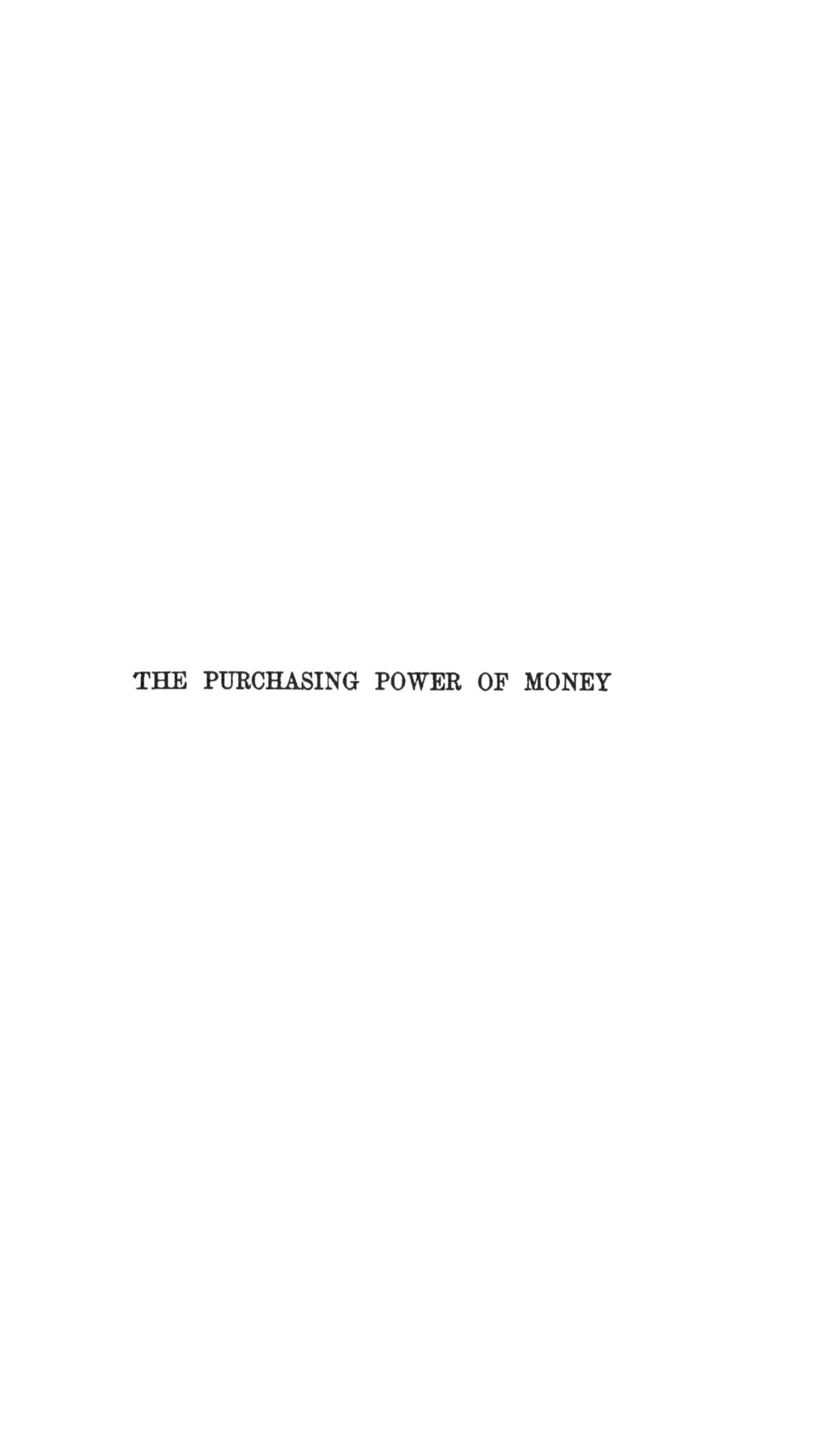

THE PURCHASING POWER OF MONEY

THE PURCHASING POWER OF MONEY

CHAPTER I[1]

PRIMARY DEFINITIONS

§ 1

In order to make clear the relation which the topic treated in this book bears to the general subject of economics, some primary definitions are necessary. In the first place, *economics* itself may be defined as the science of wealth, and *wealth* may be defined as material objects owned by human beings. Of wealth, therefore, there are two essential attributes: materiality and appropriation. For it is not all material things that are included under wealth, but only such as have been appropriated. Wealth does not include the sun, moon, and other heavenly bodies, nor even all parts of the surface of this planet, but only such parts as have been appropriated to the use of mankind. It is, then, appropriated parts of the earth's surface and the appropriated objects upon it which constitute wealth.

For convenience, wealth may be classified under three heads: real estate, commodities, and human beings. *Real estate* includes the surface of the earth and the other wealth attached thereto — improvements such as buildings, fences, drains, railways, street im-

[1] This chapter is mainly a condensation of Chapters I and II of the author's *Nature of Capital and Income*, New York (Macmillan), 1906.

provements, and so on. *Commodities* include all movable wealth (except man himself), whether raw materials or finished products. There is one particular variety of commodity — a certain finished product — which is of especial importance in the subject of which this book treats; namely, money. Any commodity to be called "money" must be *generally acceptable in exchange*, and any commodity generally acceptable in exchange should be called money. The best example of a money commodity is found to-day in gold coins.

Of all wealth, man himself is a species. Like his horses or his cattle, he is himself a material object, and like them, he is owned; for if slave, he is owned by another, and if free, by himself.[1]

But though human beings may be considered as wealth, *human qualities*, such as skill, intelligence, and inventiveness, are not wealth. Just as the hardness of steel is not wealth, but merely a quality of one particular kind of wealth, — hard steel, — so the skill of a workman is not wealth, but merely a quality of another particular kind of wealth — skilled workman. Similarly, intelligence is not wealth, but an intelligent man is wealth.

Since materiality is one of the two essential attributes of wealth, any article of wealth may be measured in physical units. Land is measured in acres; coal, in tons; milk, in quarts; and wheat, in bushels. Therefore, for estimating the quantities of different articles of wealth, all the various physical units of measurement

[1] If we wish to include only slaves as wealth and not free men, we shall have to amend our definition of wealth so as to read: Wealth consists of material objects owned by human beings and external to the owner. For the purpose of this book it makes no practical difference whether this narrower meaning or the broader one be employed.

may be employed: linear measure, square measure, cubic measure, and measure by weight.

Whenever any species of wealth is measured in its physical units, a first step is taken toward the measurement of that mysterious magnitude called "value." Sometimes value is looked upon as a psychical and sometimes as a physical phenomenon. But, although the determination of value always involves a psychical process — judgment — yet the terms in which the results are expressed and measured are physical.

It is desirable, for the sake of clearness, to lead up to the concept of value by means of three preliminary concepts; namely, transfer, exchange, and price.

A *transfer* of wealth is a change in its ownership. An *exchange* consists of two mutual and voluntary transfers, each in consideration of the other.

When a certain quantity of one kind of wealth is exchanged for a certain quantity of another kind, we may divide one of the two quantities by the other, and obtain the *price* of the latter. For instance, if two dollars of gold are exchanged for three bushels of wheat, the price of the wheat in gold is two thirds of a dollar per bushel; and the price of the gold in wheat is one and a half bushels per dollar. It is to be noticed that these are ratios of two physical quantities, the units for measuring which are quite different from each other. One commodity is measured in bushels, or units of volume of wheat, the other in dollars, or units of weight of gold. In general, a price of any species of wealth is merely the ratio of two physical quantities, in whatever way each may originally be measured.

This brings us, at last, to the concept of value. The *value* of any item of wealth is its price multiplied by its quantity. Thus, if half a dollar per bushel is the price of wheat, the value of a hundred bushels of wheat is fifty dollars.

§ 2

Hitherto we have confined our discussion to some of the consequences of the first prerequisite of wealth — that it must be material. We turn now to the second prerequisite, namely, that it must be owned. To *own* wealth is simply to have the right to benefit by it; that is, the right to enjoy its services or benefits. Thus, the owner of a loaf of bread has the right to benefit by it by eating it, by selling it, or by otherwise disposing of it. The man who owns a house has the right to benefit by enjoying its shelter, by selling it, or by renting it. This right, the right *to* or *in* the benefits of wealth—or more briefly, the right to or in the wealth itself — is called a "property right" or simply "property."

If things were always owned in fee simple, *i.e.* if there were no division of ownership,—no partnership rights, no shares, and no stock companies, — there would be little practical need to distinguish property from wealth; and as a matter of fact, in the rough popular usage, any article of wealth, and especially real estate, is often inaccurately called a "piece of property." But the ownership of wealth is frequently divided; and this fact necessitates a careful distinction between the thing owned and the rights of the owners. Thus, a railroad is wealth. Its shares and bonded debt are rights to this wealth. Each owner of shares or bonds has the right to a fractional part of the benefits from the railway. The total of these rights comprises the complete ownership of, or property in, the railway.

Like wealth, property rights also may be measured; but in units of a different character. The units of property are not physical, but consist of abstract rights to the benefits of wealth. If a man has twenty-five shares in a certain railway company, the measurement of his property is twenty-five units just as truly as though he had twenty-five bushels of wheat. What he has is twenty-five rights of a specific sort.

There exist various units of property for measuring property, as there are various units of wealth for measuring wealth; and to property may be applied precisely the same concepts of transfer, exchange, price, and value which are applied to wealth.

Besides the distinction between wealth and property rights, another distinction should here be noted. This is the distinction between property rights and certificates of those rights. The former are the rights to use wealth, the latter are merely the written evidence of those rights. Thus, the right to receive dividends from a railroad is property, but the written paper evidencing that right is a stock certificate. The right to a railway trip is a property right, the ticket evidencing that right is a certificate of property. The promise of a bank is a property right; the bank note on which that promise is engraved is a certificate of property.

Any property right which is generally acceptable in exchange may be called "money." Its printed evidence is also called money. Hence there arise three meanings of the term money, viz. its meaning in the sense of wealth; its meaning in the sense of property;[1] and its meaning in the sense of written evidence. From the standpoint of economic analysis the property sense is the most important.

[1] Cf. Menger, *Handwörterbuch der Staatswissenschaften*, Jena (Fischer), Vol. IV, 1900, Article, "Geld," pp. 69–71.

What we have been speaking of as property is the right to the services, uses, or benefits of wealth. By *benefits* of wealth is meant the desirable events which occur by means of wealth. Like wealth and property, benefits also may be measured, but in units of a still different character. Benefits are reckoned either "by time," — as the services of a gardener or of a dwelling house; or "by the piece," — as the use of a plow or a telephone. And just as the concepts of transfer, exchange, price, and value apply to wealth and property, so do they apply to benefits.

The *uses* (benefits) of wealth, with which we have been dealing, should be distinguished from the *utility* of wealth. The one means desirable events, the other, the desirability of those events. The one is usually outside of the mind, the other always inside.

Whenever we speak of rights to benefits, the benefits referred to are *future* benefits. The owner of a house owns the right to use it from the present instant onward. Its past use has perished and is no longer subject to ownership.

The term "goods" will be used in this book simply as a convenient collective term to include *wealth, property, and benefits*. The transfer, exchange, price, and value of goods take on innumerable forms. Under price alone, as thus fully applied to goods, fall rent, wages, rates of interest, prices in terms of money, and prices in terms of other goods. But we shall be chiefly concerned in this book with *prices of goods in terms of money*.

§ 3

Little has yet been said as to the relation of wealth, property and benefits to *time*. A certain quantity of goods may be either a quantity existing at a particular *instant* of time or a quantity produced, consumed, transported, or exchanged during a *period* of time. The first quantity is a *stock*, or *fund*, of goods; the second is a *flow*, or *stream*, of goods. The amount of wheat in a flour mill on any definite date is a stock of wheat, while the monthly or weekly amounts which come in or go out constitute a flow of wheat. The amount of mined coal existing in the United States at any given moment is a stock of mined coal; the weekly amount mined is a flow of coal.

There are many applications of this distinction; for instance, to capital and income. A stock of goods, whether wealth or property, existing at an instant of time is called *capital*. A flow of benefits from such capital during a period of time is called "income." Income, therefore, is one important kind of economic flow. Besides income, economic flows are of three chief classes, representing respectively changes of *condition* (such as production or consumption), changes of *position* (such as transportation, exportation, and importation), and changes of ownership, which we have already called "transfers." Trade is a flow of transfers. Whether foreign or domestic, it is simply the exchange of a stream of transferred rights in goods for an equivalent stream of transferred money or money substitutes. The second of these two streams is called the "circulation" of money. The equation between the two is called the "equation of exchange"; and it is this equation that constitutes the subject matter of the present book.

CHAPTER II

PURCHASING POWER OF MONEY AS RELATED TO THE EQUATION OF EXCHANGE

§ 1

We define money as *what is generally acceptable in exchange for goods.*[1] The facility with which it may thus be exchanged, or its general acceptability, is its distinguishing characteristic. The general acceptability may be reënforced by law, the money thus becoming what is known as "legal tender"; but such reënforcement is not essential. All that is necessary in order that any good may be money is that general acceptability attach to it. On the frontier, without any legal sanction, money is sometimes gold dust or gold nuggets. In the Colony of Virginia it was tobacco. Among the Indians in New England it was wampum. "In German New Guinea the bent tusks of a boar are used as money. In California red birds' heads have been used in the same way."[2] Stone money and shell money are so used in Melanesia.[3] "In Burmah Chinese gambling counters are used as money. Guttapercha tokens issued by

[1] For discussions on the definition of money, *see* A. Piatt Andrew, "What ought to be called Money" in *Quarterly Journal of Economics*, Vol. XIII; Jevons, *Money and the Mechanism of Exchange*, London (Kegan Paul) and New York (Appleton), 1896; Palgrave, *Dictionary of Political Economy;* Walker, *Money*, and other treatises and textbooks.

[2] Sumner, *Folkways*, Boston (Ginn), 1907, p. 147.

[3] *Ibid.*, p. 150.

street car companies in South America are said to be used in the same way."[1] Not many years ago in a town in New York state, similar tokens got into local circulation until their issue was forbidden by the United States government. In Mexico large cacao beans of relatively poor quality were used as money, and on the west coast of Africa little mats were used.[2] The list could be extended indefinitely. But whatever the substance of such a commodity, it is general exchangeability which makes it money.

On the other hand, even what is made legal tender may, by general usage, be deprived of its practical character as money. During the Civil War the government attempted to circulate fifty-dollar notes, bearing interest at 7.3 per cent, so that the interest amounted to the very easily computed amount of a cent a day. The notes, however, failed to circulate. In spite of the attempt to make their exchange easy, people preferred to keep them for the sake of the interest.[3] Money never bears interest except in the sense of creating convenience in the process of exchange. This convenience is the special service of money and offsets the apparent loss of interest involved in keeping it in one's pocket instead of investing.

There are various degrees of exchangeability which must be transcended before we arrive at real money. Of all kinds of goods, perhaps the *least* exchangeable is real estate. Only in case some person happens to be found who wants it, can a piece of real estate be traded. A mortgage on real estate is one degree more exchangeable. Yet even a mortgage is less exchangeable than a well-known and safe corporation security; and a cor-

[1] Sumner, *Folkways*, p. 148. [2] *Ibid.*
[3] See Jevons, *Money and the Mechanism of Exchange*, p. 245.

poration security is less exchangeable than a government bond. In fact persons not infrequently buy government bonds as merely temporary investments, intending to sell them again as soon as permanent investments yielding better interest are obtainable. One degree more exchangeable than a government bond is a bill of exchange; one degree more exchangeable than a bill of exchange is a sight draft; while a check is almost as exchangeable as money itself. Yet no one of these is really money for none of them is "*generally* acceptable."

If we confine our attention to present and normal conditions, and to those means of exchange which either are money or most nearly approximate it, we shall find that money itself belongs to a general class of property rights which we may call "currency" or "circulating media." Currency includes any type of property right which, whether generally acceptable or not, does actually, for its chief purpose and use, serve as a means of exchange.

Circulating media are of two chief classes: (1) money; (2) bank deposits, which will be treated fully in the next chapter. By means of checks, bank deposits serve as a means of payment in exchange for other goods. A check is the "certificate" or evidence of the transfer of bank deposits. It is acceptable to the payee only by his consent. It would not be generally accepted by strangers. Yet by checks, bank deposits even more than money do actually serve as a medium of exchange. Practically speaking, money and bank deposits subject to check are the only circulating media. If post-office orders and telegraphic transfer are to be included, they may be regarded as certificates of transfer of special deposits, the post office or telegraph company serving the purpose, for these special transactions, of a bank of deposit.

But while a bank deposit transferable by check is included as circulating media, it is not money. A bank *note*, on the other hand, is both circulating medium and money. Between these two lies the final line of distinction between what is money and what is not. True, the line is delicately drawn, especially when we come to such checks as cashier's checks or certified checks, for the latter are almost identical with bank notes. Each is a demand liability on a bank, and each confers on the holder the right to draw money. Yet while a note is *generally* acceptable in exchange, a check is *specially* acceptable only, *i.e.* only by the consent of the payee. Real money rights are what a payee accepts without question, because he is induced to do so either by "legal tender" laws or by a well-established custom.[1]

Of real money there are two kinds: primary and fiduciary. Money is called "primary" if it is a commodity which has just as much value in some use other than money as it has in monetary use. Primary money has its full value independently of any other wealth. Fiduciary money, on the other hand, is money the value of which depends partly or wholly on the confidence that the owner can exchange it for other goods, *e.g.* for primary money at a bank or government office, or at any rate for discharge of debts or purchase of goods of merchants. The chief example of primary money is gold coin; the chief example of fiduciary money is bank notes. The qualities of primary money which make for exchangeability are numerous. The most important

[1] See Francis Walker, *Money, Trade, and Industry*, New York (Holt), 1879, Chapter I.

are portability, durability, and divisibility.[1] The chief quality of fiduciary money which makes it exchangeable is its redeemability in primary money, or else its imposed character of legal tender.

Bank notes and all other fiduciary money, as well as bank deposits, circulate by certificates often called "tokens." "Token coins" are included in this description. The value of these tokens, apart from the rights they convey, is small. Thus the value of a silver dollar, as wealth, is only about forty cents; that is all that the actual silver in it is worth. Its value as property, however, is one hundred cents; for its holder has a legal right to use it in paying a debt to that amount, and a customary right to so use it in payment for goods. Likewise, the property value of a fifty-cent piece, a quarter, a ten-cent piece, a five-cent piece, or a one-cent piece is considerably greater than its value as wealth. The value of a paper dollar as wealth — for instance, a silver certificate — is almost nothing. It is worth just its value as paper, and no more. But its value as property is a hundred cents, that is, the equivalent of one gold dollar. It represents to that extent a claim of the holder on the wealth of the community.

Figure 1 indicates the classification of all circulating media in the United States. It shows that the total amount of circulating media is about 8½ billions, of which about 7 billions are bank deposits subject to check, and 1½ billions, money; and that of this 1½ billions of money, 1 billion is fiduciary money and only about ½ a billion, primary money.

In the present chapter we shall exclude the consideration of bank deposits or check circulation and confine our attention to the circulation of money, primary

[1] See Jevons, *Money and the Mechanism of Exchange*, Chapter V.

and fiduciary. In the United States, the only primary money is gold coin. The fiduciary money includes (1) token coins, viz. silver dollars, fractional silver, and minor coins ("nickels" and cents); (2) paper money, viz. (*a*) certificates for gold and silver, and (*b*) promissory notes, whether of the United States government ("greenbacks"), or of the National banks.

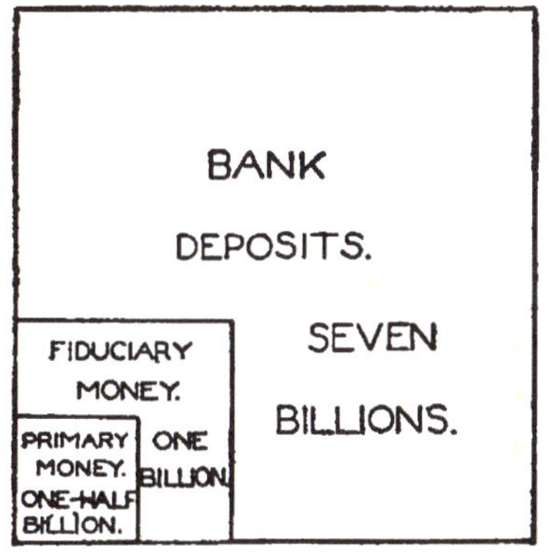

FIG. 1.

Checks aside, we may classify exchanges into three groups: the exchange of goods against goods, or barter; the exchange of money against money, or *changing* money; and the exchange of money against goods, or *purchase and sale.* Only the last-named species of exchange makes up what we call the "circulation" of money. The circulation of money signifies, therefore, the aggregate amount of its transfers against goods. All money held for circulation, *i.e.* all money, except what is in the banks and United States government's vaults, is called "money in circulation."

The chief object of this book is to explain the causes determining the purchasing power of money. The purchasing power of money is indicated by the quantities of other goods which a given quantity of money will buy. The lower we find the prices of goods, the larger the quantities that can be bought by a given amount of money, and therefore the higher the purchasing power of money. The higher we find the prices of goods, the smaller the quantities that can be bought by a given amount of money, and therefore the lower the purchasing power of money. In short, the purchasing power of money is the reciprocal of the level of prices; so that the study of the purchasing power of money is identical with the study of price levels.

§ 2

Overlooking the influence of deposit currency, or checks, the price level may be said to depend on only three sets of causes: (1) the quantity of money in circulation; (2) its "efficiency" or velocity of circulation (or the average number of times a year money is exchanged for goods); and (3) the volume of trade (or amount of goods bought by money). The so-called "quantity theory,"[1] *i.e.* that prices vary proportionately to money, has often been incorrectly formulated, but (overlooking checks) the theory is correct in the sense that the level of prices varies directly with the quantity of money in circulation, provided the velocity of circulation of that money and the volume of trade which it is obliged to perform are not changed.

The quantity theory has been one of the most bitterly contested theories in economics, largely because the recognition of its truth or falsity affected powerful

[1] This theory, though often crudely formulated, has been accepted by Locke, Hume, Adam Smith, Ricardo, Mill, Walker, Marshall, Hadley, Fetter, Kemmerer and most writers on the subject. The Roman Julius Paulus, about 200 A.D., stated his belief that the value of money depends on its quantity. See Zuckerkandl, *Theorie des Preises;* Kemmerer, *Money and Credit Instruments in their Relation to General Prices*, New York (Holt), 1909. It is true that many writers still oppose the quantity theory. See especially, Laughlin, *Principles of Money*, New York (Scribner), 1903.

interests in commerce and politics. It has been maintained — and the assertion is scarcely an exaggeration — that the theorems of Euclid would be bitterly controverted if financial or political interests were involved.

The quantity theory has, unfortunately, been made the basis of arguments for unsound currency schemes. It has been invoked in behalf of irredeemable paper money and of national free coinage of silver at the ratio of 16 to 1. As a consequence, not a few "sound money men," believing that a theory used to support such vagaries must be wrong, and fearing the political effects of its propagation, have drifted into the position of opposing, not only the unsound propaganda, but also the sound principles by which its advocates sought to bolster it up.[1] These attacks upon the quantity theory have been rendered easy by the imperfect comprehension of it on the part of those who have thus invoked it in a bad cause.

Personally, I believe that few mental attitudes are more pernicious, and in the end more disastrous, than those which would uphold sound practice by denying sound principles because some thinkers make unsound application of those principles. At any rate, in scientific study there is no choice but to find and state the unvarnished truth.

The quantity theory will be made more clear by the equation of exchange, which is now to be explained.

The equation of exchange is a statement, in math-

[1] See Scott, "It has been a most fruitful source of false doctrines regarding monetary matters, and is constantly and successfully employed in defense of harmful legislation and as a means of preventing needed monetary reforms." *Money and Banking*, New York, 1903, p. 68.

ematical form, of the total transactions effected in a certain period in a given community. It is obtained simply by adding together the equations of exchange for all individual transactions. Suppose, for instance, that a person buys 10 pounds of sugar at 7 cents per pound. This is an exchange transaction, in which 10 pounds of sugar have been regarded as equal to 70 cents, and this fact may be expressed thus: 70 cents = 10 pounds of sugar multiplied by 7 cents a pound. Every other sale and purchase may be expressed similarly, and by adding them all together we get the equation of exchange *for a certain period in a given community.* During this same period, however, the same money may serve, and usually does serve, for several transactions. For that reason the money side of the equation is of course greater than the total amount of money in circulation.

The equation of exchange relates to all the purchases made by money in a certain community during a certain time. We shall continue to ignore checks or any circulating medium not money. We shall also ignore foreign trade and thus restrict ourselves to trade within a hypothetical community. Later we shall reinclude these factors, proceeding by a series of approximations through successive hypothetical conditions to the actual conditions which prevail to-day. We must, of course, not forget that the conclusions expressed in each successive approximation are true solely on the particular hypothesis assumed.

The equation of exchange is simply the sum of the equations involved in all individual exchanges in a year. In each sale and purchase, the money and goods exchanged are *ipso facto* equivalent; for instance, the money paid for sugar is equivalent to the sugar bought.

And in the grand total of all exchanges for a year, the total money paid is equal in value to the total value of the goods bought. The equation thus has a money side and a goods side. The money side is the total money paid, and may be considered as the product of the quantity of money multiplied by its rapidity of circulation. The goods side is made up of the products of quantities of goods exchanged multiplied by their respective prices.

The important magnitude, called the velocity of circulation, or rapidity of turnover, is simply the quotient obtained by dividing the total money payments for goods in the course of a year by the average amount of money in circulation by which those payments are effected. This velocity of circulation for an entire community is a sort of average of the rates of turnover of money for different persons. Each person has his own rate of turnover which he can readily calculate by dividing the amount of money he expends per year by the average amount he carries.

Let us begin with the money side. If the number of dollars in a country is 5,000,000, and their velocity of circulation is twenty times per year, then the total amount of money changing hands (for goods) per year is 5,000,000 times twenty, or $100,000,000. This is the *money* side of the equation of exchange.

Since the money side of the equation is $100,000,000, the *goods* side must be the same. For if $100,000,000 has been spent for goods in the course of the year, then $100,000,000 worth of goods must have been sold in that year. In order to avoid the necessity of writing out the quantities and prices of the innumerable varieties of goods which are actually exchanged, let us assume for the present that there are only three kinds of goods, — bread, coal, and cloth; and that the sales are: —

200,000,000	loaves of bread at	$ .10 a loaf,
10,000,000	tons of coal at	5.00 a ton, and
30,000,000	yards of cloth at	1.00 a yard.

The value of these transactions is evidently $100,000,-000, *i.e.* $20,000,000 worth of bread plus $50,000,000 worth of coal plus $30,000,000 worth of cloth. The equation of exchange therefore (remember that the money side consisted of $5,000,000 exchanged 20 times) is as follows: —

$5,000,000 × 20 times a year
= 200,000,000 loaves × $ .10 a loaf
+ 10,000,000 tons × 5.00 a ton
+ 30,000,000 yards × 1.00 a yard.

This equation contains on the money side two magnitudes, viz. (1) the quantity of money and (2) its velocity of circulation; and on the goods side two *groups* of magnitudes in two columns, viz. (1) the quantities of goods exchanged (loaves, tons, yards), and (2) the prices of these goods. The equation shows that these four sets of magnitudes are mutually related. Because this equation must be fulfilled, the prices must bear a relation to the three other sets of magnitudes, — quantity of money, rapidity of circulation, and quantities of goods exchanged. Consequently, these prices must, as a whole, vary proportionally with the quantity of money and with its velocity of circulation, and inversely with the quantities of goods exchanged.

Suppose, for instance, that the quantity of money were doubled, while its velocity of circulation and the quantities of goods exchanged remained the same. Then it would be quite impossible for prices to remain unchanged. The money side would now be

\$10,000,000 × 20 times a year or \$200,000,000; whereas, if prices should not change, the goods would remain \$100,000,000, and the equation would be violated. Since exchanges, individually and collectively, always involve an equivalent *quid pro quo*, the two sides *must* be equal. Not only must purchases and sales be equal in amount — since every article bought by one person is necessarily sold by another — but the total value of goods sold must equal the total amount of money exchanged. Therefore, under the given conditions, prices must change in such a way as to raise the goods side from \$100,000,000 to \$200,000,000. This doubling may be accomplished by an even or uneven rise in prices, but some sort of *a rise of prices there must be.* If the prices rise evenly, they will evidently all be exactly doubled, so that the equation will read: —

\$10,000,000 × 20 times a year
= 200,000,000 loaves × \$ .20 per loaf
+ 10,000,000 tons × 10.00 per ton
+ 30,000,000 yards × 2.00 per yard.

If the prices rise unevenly, the doubling must evidently be brought about by compensation; if some prices rise by less than double, others must rise by enough more than double to exactly compensate.

But whether all prices increase uniformly, each being exactly doubled, or some prices increase more and some less (so as still to double the total money value of the goods purchased), the prices *are* doubled *on the average.*[1] This proposition is usually expressed by saying that the "general level of prices" is raised twofold. From the mere fact, therefore, that the money spent for goods

[1] This does not mean, of course, that their simple *arithmetical* average is exactly doubled. For definition of an average or "mean" in general, see § 1 of Appendix to (this) Chapter II.

must equal the quantities of those goods multiplied by their prices, it follows that the level of prices must rise or fall according to changes in the quantity of money, *unless* there are changes in its velocity of circulation or in the quantities of goods exchanged.

If changes in the quantity of money affect prices, so will changes in the other factors — quantities of goods and velocity of circulation — affect prices, and in a very similar manner. Thus a doubling in the velocity of circulation of money will double the level of prices, provided the quantity of money in circulation and the quantities of goods exchanged for money remain as before. The equation will become: —

$$
\begin{aligned}
\$5{,}000{,}000 \times 40 \text{ times a year} \\
&= 200{,}000{,}000 \text{ loaves} \times \$\ .20 \text{ a loaf} \\
&+ \ \ 10{,}000{,}000 \text{ tons} \times 10.00 \text{ a ton} \\
&+ \ \ 30{,}000{,}000 \text{ yards} \times 2.00 \text{ a yard,}
\end{aligned}
$$

or else the equation will assume a form in which some of the prices will more than double, and others less than double by enough to preserve the same total value of the sales.

Again, a doubling in the quantities of goods exchanged will not double, but halve, the height of the price level, *provided* the quantity of money and its velocity of circulation remain the same. Under these circumstances the equation will become: —

$$
\begin{aligned}
\$5{,}000{,}000 \times 20 \text{ times a year} \\
&= 400{,}000{,}000 \text{ loaves} \times \$\ .05 \text{ a loaf} \\
&+ \ \ 20{,}000{,}000 \text{ tons} \times 2.50 \text{ a ton} \\
&+ \ \ 60{,}000{,}000 \text{ yards} \times .50 \text{ a yard,}
\end{aligned}
$$

or else it will assume a form in which some of the prices are more than halved, and others less than halved, so as to preserve the equation.

Finally, if there is a simultaneous change in two or all of the three influences, *i.e.* quantity of money, velocity of circulation, and quantities of goods exchanged, the price level will be a compound or resultant of these various influences. If, for example, the quantity of money is doubled, and its velocity of circulation is halved, while the quantity of goods exchanged remains constant, the price level will be undisturbed. Likewise, it will be undisturbed if the quantity of money is doubled and the quantity of goods is doubled, while the velocity of circulation remains the same. To double the quantity of money, therefore, is not always to double prices. We must distinctly recognize that the quantity of money is only one of three factors, all equally important in determining the price level.

§ 3

The equation of exchange has now been expressed by an arithmetical illustration. It may be also represented visually, by a mechanical illustration. Such a representation is embodied in Figure 2. This represents a

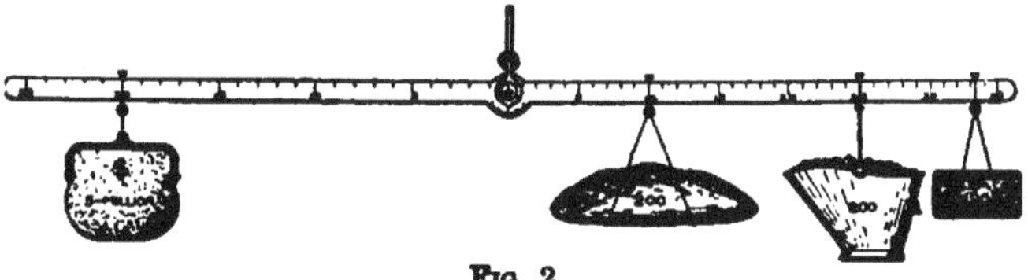

FIG. 2.

mechanical balance in equilibrium, the two sides of which symbolize respectively the money side and the goods side of the equation of exchange. The weight at the left, symbolized by a purse, represents the money in circulation; the "arm" or distance from the fulcrum at which this weight (purse) is hung represents the efficiency of this money, or its velocity of circulation. On the right side are three weights, — bread, coal, and cloth, symbolized respectively by a loaf, a coal scuttle, and a roll of cloth. The arm, or distance of each from the fulcrum, represents its price. In order that the lever arms at the right may not be inordinately long, we have found it convienient to reduce the unit of measure of coal from tons to hundredweights, and that of cloth from yards to feet, and consequently to enlarge correspondingly the numbers of units (the measure of coal changing from 10,000,000 tons to 200,000,000 hundredweights, and that of the cloth from 30,000,000 yards to 90,000,000 feet). The price of coal in the new unit per hundredweight becomes 25 cents per hundredweight, and that of cloth in feet becomes $33\frac{1}{3}$ cents per foot.

We all know that, when a balance is in equilibrium, the tendency to turn in one direction equals the tendency to turn in the other. Each weight produces on its side a tendency to turn, measured by the product of the weight by its arm. The weight on the left produces, on that side, a tendency measured by $5{,}000{,}000 \times 20$; while the weights on the right make a combined opposite tendency measured by $200{,}000{,}000 \times .10 + 200{,}000{,}000 \times .25 + 90{,}000{,}000 \times .33\frac{1}{3}$. The equality of these opposite tendencies represents the equation of exchange.

An increase in the weights or arms on one side requires, in order to preserve equilibrium, a proportional increase in the weights or arms on the other side. This simple and familiar principle, applied to the symbolism here adopted, means that if, for instance, the velocity of circulation (left arm) remains the same, and if the trade (weights at the right) remains the same, then any increase of the purse at the left will require a lengthening of one or more of the arms at the right, representing prices. If these prices increase uniformly, they will increase in the same ratio as the increase in money; if they do not increase uniformly, some will increase more and some less than this ratio, maintaining an average.

Likewise it is evident that if the arm at the left lengthens, and if the purse and the various weights on the right remain the same, there must be an increase in the arms at the right.

Again, if there is an increase in weights at the right, and if the left arm and the purse remain the same, there must be a shortening of right arms.

In general, any change among the four sets of magnitudes must be accompanied by such a change or changes in one or more of the other three as shall maintain equilibrium.

As we are interested in the average change in prices rather than in the prices individually, we may simplify this mechanical representation by hanging all the right-hand weights at one average point, so that the arm shall represent the average prices. This arm is a "weighted average" of the three original arms, the weights being literally the weights hanging at the right.

This averaging of prices is represented in Figure 3, which visualizes the fact that the average price of goods

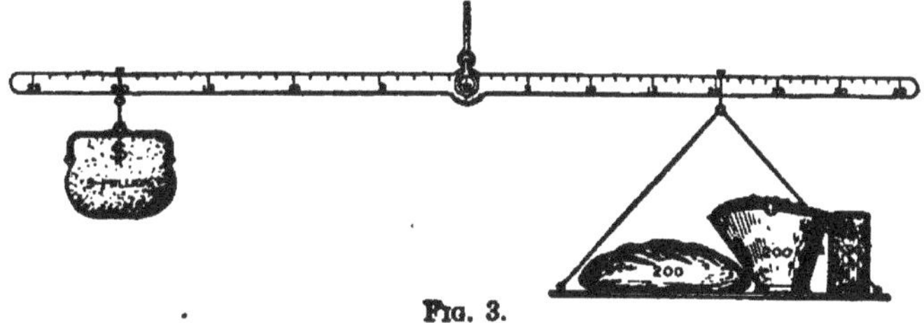

FIG. 3.

(right arm) varies directly with the quantity of money (left weight), and directly with its velocity of circulation (left arm), and inversely with the volume of trade (right weight).

§ 4

We now come to the strict algebraic statement of the equation of exchange. An algebraic statement is usually a good safeguard against loose reasoning; and loose reasoning is chiefly responsible for the suspicion under which economic theories have frequently fallen. If it is worth while in geometry to demonstrate carefully, at the start, propositions which are almost self-evident, it is a hundredfold more worth while to demonstrate with care the propositions relating to price levels, which are less self-evident; which, indeed, while confidently assumed by many, are contemptuously rejected by others.

Let us denote the total circulation of money, *i.e.* the amount of money expended for goods in a given community during a given year, by E (expenditure); and the average amount of money in circulation in the community during the year by M (money). M will be the simple arithmetical average of the amounts of money existing at successive instants separated from each other by equal intervals of time indefinitely small. If we divide the year's expenditures, E, by the average amount of money, M, we shall obtain what is called the average rate of turnover of money in its exchange for goods, $\frac{E}{M}$, that is, the velocity of circulation of money.[1] This velocity may be denoted by V, so that $\frac{E}{M} = V$; then E may be expressed as MV. In words: the total circulation of money in the sense of

[1] For discussion of the concept of velocity of circulation, see §§ 2, 4, 5 of Appendix to (this) Chapter II.

money expended is equal to the total money in circulation multiplied by its velocity of circulation or turnover. E or MV, therefore, expresses the money side of the equation of exchange. Turning to the goods side of the equation, we have to deal with the prices of goods exchanged and quantities of goods exchanged. The average[1] price of sale of any particular good, such as bread, purchased in the given community during the given year, may be represented by p (price); and the total quantity of it purchased, by Q (quantity); likewise the average price of another good (say coal) may be represented by p' and the total quantity of it exchanged, by Q'; the average price and the total quantity of a third good (say cloth) may be represented by p'' and Q'' respectively; and so on, for all other goods exchanged, however numerous. The equation of exchange may evidently be expressed as follows:[2] —

$$\begin{aligned} MV = {} & pQ \\ & + p'Q' \\ & + p''Q'' \\ & + \text{etc.} \end{aligned}$$

[1] This is an average weighted according to the quantities purchased on various occasions throughout the period and country considered. See § 3 of Appendix to (this) Chapter II.

[2] An algebraic statement of the equation of exchange was made by Simon Newcomb in his able but little appreciated *Principles of Political Economy*, New York (Harper), 1885, p. 346. It is also expressed by Edgeworth, "Report on Monetary Standard." *Report of the British Association for the Advancement of Science*, 1887, p. 293, and by President Hadley, *Economics*, New York (Putnam), 1896, p. 197. See also Irving Fisher, "The Rôle of Capital in Economic Theory," *Economic Journal*, December, 1899, pp. 515–521, and E. W. Kemmerer, *Money and Credit Instruments in their Relation to General Prices*, New York (Holt), 1907, p. 13. While thus only recently given mathematical expression, the quantity theory has long been understood as a relationship among the several fac-

The right-hand side of this equation is the sum of terms of the form pQ — a price multiplied by a quantity bought. It is customary in mathematics to abbreviate such a sum of terms (all of which are of the same form) by using "Σ" as a symbol of summation. This symbol does not signify a *magnitude* as do the symbols M, V, p, Q, etc. It signifies merely the *operation* of addition and should be read "the sum of terms of the following type." The equation of exchange may therefore be written: —

$$MV = \Sigma pQ.$$

That is, the magnitudes E, M, V, the p's and the Q's relate to the *entire* community and an *entire* year; but they are based on and related to corresponding magnitudes for the individual persons of which the community is composed and for the individual moments of time of which the year is composed.[1]

The algebraic derivation of this equation is, of course, essentially the same as the arithmetical derivation previously given. It consists simply in *adding together the equations for all individual purchases within the community during the year.*[2]

By means of this equation, $MV = \Sigma pQ$, the three theorems set forth earlier in this chapter may be now expressed as follows: —

(1) If V and the Q's remain invariable while M varies in any ratio, the money side of the equation will vary

tors: amount of money, rapidity of circulation, and amount of trade. See Mill, *Principles of Political Economy*, Book III, Chapter VIII, § 3. Ricardo probably deserves chief credit for launching the theory.

[1] For the relations subsisting between these magnitudes (as relating to the whole community and the whole year), and the corresponding elementary magnitudes relating to each individual and each moment, see § 4 of the Appendix to (this) Chapter II.

[2] See § 6 of Appendix to (this) Chapter II.

in the same ratio and therefore its equal, the goods side, must vary in that same ratio also; consequently, either the p's will all vary in that ratio or else some p's will vary more than in that ratio and others enough less to compensate and maintain the same average.[1]

(2) If M and the Q's remain invariable while V varies in any ratio, the money side of the equation will vary in the same ratio, and therefore its equal, the goods side, must vary in that ratio also; consequently, the p's will all vary in the same ratio or else some will vary more and others enough less to compensate.

(3) If M and V remain invariable, the money side and the goods side will remain invariable; consequently, if the Q's all vary in a given ratio, either the p's must all vary in the inverse ratio or else some of them will vary more and others enough less to compensate.

We may, if we wish, further simplify the right side by writing it in the form PT where P is a weighted average of all the p's, and T is the sum of all the Q's. P then represents in one magnitude the level of prices, and T represents in one magnitude the volume of trade. This simplification is the algebraic interpretation of the mechanical illustration given in Figure 3, where all the goods, instead of being hung separately, as in Figure 2, were combined and hung at an average point representing their average price.

We have derived the equation of exchange, $MV = \Sigma pQ$, by adding together, for the right side, the sums *expended* by different persons. But the same reasoning would have derived an equation of exchange by taking the sums *received* by different persons. The results of

[1] For the nature of the average here involved and for the averages involved in the other two following cases, see § 7 of Appendix to (this) Chapter II.

the two methods will harmonize if the community has no foreign trade; for, apart from foreign trade, what is expended by one person in the community is necessarily received by some other person in that community.

If we wish to extend the reasoning so as to apply to foreign trade, we shall have *two* equations of exchange, one based on money expended and the other on money *received* or accepted by members of the community. These will always be approximately equal and may or may not be exactly equal within a country according to the "balance of trade" between that country and others. The *right* side of the equation based on expenditures will include, in addition to the domestic quantities already represented there, the quantities of goods *imported* and their prices, but not those exported; while the reverse will be true of the equation based on receipts.

§ 5

This completes our statement of the equation of exchange, except for the element of check payments, which is reserved for the next chapter. We have seen that the equation of exchange has as its ultimate basis the elementary equations of exchange pertaining to given persons and given moments, in other words, the equations pertaining to individual transactions. Such elementary equations mean that the money paid in any transaction is the equivalent of the goods bought at the price of sale. From this secure and obvious premise is derived the equation of exchange $MV = \Sigma pQ$, each element in which is a sum or an average of the like elementary elements for different individuals and different moments, thus comprising all the purchases in the community during the year. Finally, from this equation we see that prices vary directly as M and V, and inversely as the Q's, provided in each case only one of these three sets of magnitudes varies, and the other two remain unchanged. Whether to change one of the three necessarily disturbs the others is a question reserved for a later chapter. Those who object to the equation of exchange as a mere truism are asked to defer judgment until they have read Chapter VIII.

To recapitulate, we find then that, under the conditions assumed, the price level varies (1) directly as the quantity of money in circulation (M), (2) directly as the velocity of its circulation (V), (3) inversely as the volume of trade done by it (T). The first of these three relations is the most important. It constitutes the "quantity theory of money."

So important is this principle, and so bitterly contested has it been, that we shall illustrate it further. As already indicated, by "the quantity of money" is meant the number of dollars (or other given monetary units) in circulation. This number may be changed in several ways, of which the following three are most important. Their statement will serve to bring home to us the conclusions we have reached and to reveal the fundamental peculiarity of money on which they rest.

As a first illustration, let us suppose the government to double the *denominations* of all money; that is, let us suppose that what has been hitherto a half dollar is henceforth called a dollar, and that what has hitherto been a dollar is henceforth called two dollars. Evidently the number of "dollars" in circulation will then be doubled; and the price level, measured in terms of the new "dollars," will be double what it would otherwise be. Every one will pay out the *same coins* as though no such law were passed. But he will, in each case, be paying twice as many "dollars." For example, if $3 formerly had to be paid for a pair of shoes, the price of this same pair of shoes will now become $6. Thus we see how the *nominal* quantity of money affects price levels.

A second illustration is found in a *debased currency*. Suppose a government cuts each dollar in two, coining the halves into new "dollars"; and, recalling all paper notes, replaces them with double the original number — two new notes for each old one of the same denomination. In short, suppose money not only to be *renamed*, as in the first illustration, but also *reissued;* prices in the debased coinage will again be doubled just as in the first illustration. The subdivision and recoinage is an immaterial circumstance, unless it be carried so far as to make counting difficult and thus to interfere with the *convenience* of money. Wherever a dollar had been paid before debasement, two dollars — *i.e.* two of the old halves coined into two of the new dollars — will now be paid instead.

In the first illustration, the increase in quantity was simply nominal, being brought about by renaming coins. In the second illustration, besides renaming, the further fact of recoining is introduced. In the first case the number of actual pieces of money of each kind was unchanged, but their denominations were doubled. In the second case, the number of pieces is also doubled by splitting each coin and reminting it into two coins, each of the same nominal denomination as the original whole of which it is the half, and by similarly redoubling the paper money.

For a third illustration, suppose that, instead of doubling the number of dollars by splitting them in two and recoining the halves, the government *duplicates* each piece of money in existence and presents the duplicate to the possessor of the original.[1] (We must in this case suppose, further, that there is some effectual bar to prevent the melting or exporting of money. Otherwise the quantity of money in circulation will not be doubled: much of the increase will escape.) If the quantity of money is thus doubled, prices will also be doubled just as truly as in the second illustration, in which there were exactly the same denominations. The only difference between the second and the third illustrations will be in the size and weight of the coins. The weights of the individual coins, instead of being reduced, will remain unchanged; but their number will be doubled. This doubling of coins must have the same effect as the 50 per cent debasement, *i.e.* it must have the effect of doubling prices.

The force of the third illustration becomes even more evident if, in accordance with Ricardo's presentation,[2] we pass back by means of a seigniorage from the third illustration to the second. That is, after duplicating all money, let the government abstract half of each coin, thereby reducing the weight to that of the debased coinage in the second illustration, and removing the only point of distinction between the two. This "seigniorage" abstracted will not affect the value of the coins, so long as their *number* remains unchanged.

In short, the quantity theory asserts that (provided velocity of circulation and volume of trade are unchanged) if we increase the *number* of dollars, whether

[1] Cf. J. S. Mill, *Principles of Political Economy*, Book III, Chapter VIII, § 2. Ricardo in his reply to Bosanquet uses an illustration similar in principle though slightly different in form. See *Works*, 2d ed., London (Murray), 1852, p. 346.

[2] *Works*, 2d ed., London (Murray), 1852, pp. 346 and 347 (reply to Bosanquet, Chapter VI); see also pp. 213 and 214.

by renaming coins, or by debasing coins, or by increasing coinage, or by any other means, prices will be increased in the same proportion. It is the number, and not the weight, that is essential. This fact needs great emphasis. It is a fact which differentiates money from all other goods and explains the peculiar manner in which its purchasing power is related to other goods. Sugar, for instance, has a specific desirability dependent on its quantity in pounds. Money has no such quality. The value of sugar depends on its *actual quantity*. If the quantity of sugar is changed from 1,000,000 pounds to 1,000,000 hundredweight, it does not follow that a hundredweight will have the value previously possessed by a pound. But if money in circulation is changed from 1,000,000 units of one weight to 1,000,000 units of another weight, the value of each unit will remain unchanged.

The quantity theory of money thus rests, ultimately, upon the fundamental peculiarity which money alone of all goods possesses, — the fact that it has no power to satisfy human wants except a power *to purchase* things which do have such power.[1]

[1] Cf. G. F. Knapp, *Staatliche Theorie des Geldes*, Leipzig, 1905; L. von Bortkiewicz, "Die geldtheoretischen und die währungspolitischen Consequenzen des 'Nominalismus,'" *Jahrbuch für Gesetzgebung, Verwaltung und Volkswirtschaft*, October, 1906; Bertrand Nogaro, "L'expérience bimétalliste du XIX siècle et la théorie générale de la monnaie," *Revue d'Économie politique*, 1908.

CHAPTER III

INFLUENCE OF DEPOSIT CURRENCY ON THE EQUATION AND THEREFORE ON PURCHASING POWER

§ 1

We are now ready to explain the nature of bank deposit currency, or circulating credit. Credit, in general, is the claim of a creditor against a debtor. Bank deposits subject to check are the claims of the creditors of a bank against the bank, by virtue of which they may, on demand, draw by check specified sums of money from the bank. Since no other kind of bank deposits will be considered by us, we shall usually refer to "bank deposits subject to check" simply as "bank deposits." They are also called "circulating credit." Bank checks, as we have seen, are merely certificates of rights to draw, *i.e.* to transfer bank deposits. The checks themselves are not the currency; the bank deposits which they represent are the currency.

It is in the connection with the transfer of bank deposits that there arises that so-called "mystery of banking" called "circulating credit." Many persons, including some economists, have supposed that credit is a special form of wealth which may be created out of whole cloth, as it were, by a bank. Others have maintained that credit has no foundation in actual wealth at all, but is a kind of unreal and inflated bubble with a precarious, if not wholly illegitimate, existence. As a matter of fact, bank deposits are as easy to understand as bank notes, and what is said in this chapter of bank deposits may in substance be taken as true also of bank notes. The chief difference is a formal one, the notes circulating from hand to hand, while the deposit currency circulates only by means of special orders called "checks."

To understand the real nature of bank deposits, let us imagine a hypothetical institution, — a kind of primitive bank existing mainly for the sake of deposits and the safe keeping of actual money. The original bank of Amsterdam was somewhat like the bank we are now imagining. In such a bank a number of people deposit $100,000 in gold, each accepting a receipt for the amount of his deposit. If this bank should issue a "capital account," or statement, it would show $100,000 in its vaults and $100,000 owed to depositors, as follows: —

Assets		*Liabilities*	
Gold	$100,000	Due depositors . .	$100,000

The right-hand side of the statement is, of course, made up of smaller amounts owed to individual depositors. Assuming that there is owed to A, $10,000, to B, $10,000, and to all others $80,000, we may write the bank statement as follows: —

Assets		*Liabilities*	
Gold	$100,000	Due depositor A . .	$10,000
		Due depositor B . .	10,000
		Due other depositors	80,000
	$100,000		$100,000

Now assume that A wishes to pay B $1000. A could go to the bank with B, present certificates or checks for $1000, obtain the gold, and hand it over to B, who might then redeposit it in the same bank, merely hand-ing it back through the cashier's window and taking a new certificate in his own name. Instead, however, of both A and B visiting the bank and handling the money, A might simply give B a check for $1000. The transfer in either case would mean that A's holding in the bank was reduced from $10,000 to $9000, and that B's was increased from $10,000 to $11,000. The statement would then read: —

Assets		*Liabilities*	
Gold	$100,000	Due depositor A . .	$ 9,000
		Due depositor B . .	11,000
		Due other depositors	80,000
	$100,000		$100,000

Thus the certificates, or checks, would circulate in place of cash among the various depositors in the bank. What really changes ownership, or "circulates," in such cases is the *right to draw* money. The check is merely the evidence of this right and of the transfer of this right from one person to another.

In the case under consideration, the bank would be conducted at a loss. It would be giving the time and labor of its clerical force for the accommodation of its depositors, without getting anything in return. But such a hypothetical bank would soon find — much as did the bank of Amsterdam[1] — that it *could* "make money" by lending at interest some of the gold on deposit. This could not offend the depositors; for they do not expect or desire to get back the identical gold they deposited. What they want is simply to be able at any time to obtain the same *amount* of gold. Since, then,

[1] See Dunbar's *Theory and History of Banking*, 2d ed., edited by O. M. W. Sprague, New York and London (G. P. Putnam's Sons), 1901, pp. 113–116.

their arrangement with the bank calls for the payment, not of any particular gold, but merely of a definite amount, and that but occasionally, the bank finds itself free to lend out part of the gold that otherwise would lie idle in its vaults. To keep it idle would be a great and needless waste of opportunity.

Let us suppose, then, that the bank decides to loan out half its cash. This is usually done in exchange for promissory notes of the borrowers. *Now a loan is really an exchange of money for a promissory note* which the lender — in this case the bank — receives in place of the gold. Let us suppose that so-called borrowers actually draw out $50,000 of gold. The bank thereby exchanges money for promises, and its books will then read: —

Assets		*Liabilities*	
Gold reserve	$50,000	Due depositor A . .	$ 9,000
Promissory notes . .	50,000	Due depositor B . .	11,000
		Due other depositors .	80,000
	$100,000		$100,000

It will be noted that now the gold in the bank is only $50,000, while the total deposits are still $100,000. In other words, the depositors now have more "money on deposit" than the bank has in its vaults! But, as will be shown, this form of expression involves a popular fallacy in the word "money." *Something* good is behind each loan, but not necessarily money.

Next, suppose that the *borrowers* become, in a sense, depositors also, by redepositing the $50,000 of cash which they borrowed, *in return for the right to draw out the same sum on demand.* In other words, suppose that after borrowing $50,000 from the bank, they lend it back to the bank. The bank's assets will thus be enlarged by $50,000, and its obligations (or credit extended) will be equally enlarged; and the balance sheet will become: —

Assets		*Liabilities*	
Gold reserve . . .	$100,000	Due depositor A . .	$ 9,000
Promissory notes . .	50,000	Due depositor B . .	11,000
		Due old depositors .	80,000
		Due new depositors, *i.e.* the borrowers .	50,000
	$150,000		$150,000

What happened in this case was the following: Gold was borrowed in exchange for a promissory note and then handed back in exchange for a right to draw. Thus the gold really did not budge; but the bank received a promissory note and the depositor a right to draw. Evidently, therefore, the same result would have followed if each borrower had merely handed in his promissory note and received, in exchange, a right to draw. As this operation most frequently puzzles the beginner in the study of banking, we repeat the tables representing the conditions before and after these "loans," *i.e.* these exchanges of promissory notes for present rights to draw.[1]

[1] In the ultimate analysis, and outside of its function of insuring credit, a bank is really an intermediary between borrowers and lenders. It is by virtue of bringing borrowers and ultimate lenders together and providing the former with a supply of loans which would not otherwise exist, that a bank simultaneously tends to lower the rate of interest and increase the supply of credit currency. See paper by Harry G. Brown, in the *Quarterly Journal of Economics*, August, 1910, on "Commercial Banking and the Rate of Interest."

BEFORE THE LOANS

Assets		*Liabilities*	
Gold reserve . . .	$100,000	Due depositors . .	$100,000

AFTER THE LOANS

Assets		*Liabilities*	
Gold reserve. . . .	$100,000	Due depositors . .	$150,000
Promissory notes . .	50,000		

Clearly, therefore, the intermediation of the money in this case is a needless complication, though it may help to a theoretical understanding of the resultant shifting of rights and liabilities. Thus the bank may receive deposits of gold or deposits of promises. In exchange for the promises it may give, or lend, either a right to draw, or gold, — the same that was deposited by another customer. Even when the borrower has only a promise, by fiction he is still held to have deposited money; and like the original cash depositors, he is given the right to make out checks. The total value of rights to draw, in whichever way arising, is termed "deposits." Banks more often lend rights to draw (or deposit rights) than actual cash, partly because of the greater convenience to borrowers, and partly because the banks wish to keep their cash reserves large, in order to meet large or unexpected demands. It is true that if a bank loans money, part of the money so loaned will be redeposited by the persons to whom the borrowers pay it in the course of business; but it will not necessarily be redeposited in the same bank. Hence the average banker prefers that the borrower should not withdraw actual cash.

Besides lending deposit rights, banks may also lend their own notes, called "bank notes." And the principle governing bank notes is the same as the principle governing deposit rights. The holder simply gets a pocketful of bank notes instead of a bank account. In either case the bank must be always ready to pay the holder — to "redeem its notes" — as well as pay its depositors, on demand, and in either case the bank exchanges a promise for a promise. In the case of the note, the bank has exchanged its bank note for a customer's promissory note. The bank note carries no interest, but is payable on demand. The customer's note bears interest, but is payable only at a definite date.

Assuming that the bank issues $50,000 of notes, the balance sheet will now become: —

Assets		*Liabilities*	
Gold reserve	$100,000	Due depositors . .	$150,000
Loans	100,000	Due note holders . .	50,000
	$200,000		$200,000

We repeat that by means of credit the deposits (and notes) of a bank may *exceed its cash.* There would be nothing mysterious or obscure about this fact, nor about credit in general, if people could be induced not to think of banking operations as money operations. To so represent them is metaphorical and misleading. They are no more money operations than they are real estate transactions. A bank depositor, A, has not ordinarily "deposited money"; and whether he has or not, he certainly cannot properly say that he "has money in the bank." What he does have is the bank's promise to pay money on demand. The bank owes him money. When a private person owes money, the creditor never thinks of saying that he has it on deposit in the debtor's pocket.

§ 2

It cannot be too strongly emphasized that, in any balance sheet, the value of the liabilities rests on that of the assets. The deposits of a bank are no exception. We must not be misled by the fact that the *cash* assets may be less than the deposits. When the uninitiated first learn that the number of dollars which note holders and depositors have the right to draw out of a bank exceeds the number of dollars in the bank, they are apt to jump to the conclusion that there is nothing behind the notes or deposit liabilities. Yet behind all these obligations there is always, in the case of a solvent bank, full value; if not actual dollars, at any rate *dollars' worth of property*. By no jugglery can the liabilities exceed the assets except in insolvency, and even in that case only nominally, for the true value of the liabilities ("bad debts") will only equal the *true* value of the assets behind them.

These assets, as already indicated, are largely the notes of merchants, although, so far as the theory of banking is concerned, they might be any property whatever. If they consisted in the ownership of real estate or other wealth in "fee simple," so that the tangible wealth which property always represents were clearly evident, all mystery would disappear. But the effect would not be different. Instead of taking grain, machines, or steel ingots on deposit, in exchange for the sums lent, banks prefer to take interest-bearing notes of corporations and individuals who own, directly or indirectly, grain, machines, and steel ingots: and by the banking laws the banks are even *compelled* to take the notes instead of the ingots. The bank finds itself with liabilities which exceed its *cash* assets;

but in either case the excess of liabilities is balanced by the possession of other assets than cash. These other assets of the bank are usually liabilities of business men. These liabilities are in turn supported by the assets of the business men. If we continue to follow up the ultimate basis of the bank's liabilities we shall find it in the visible tangible wealth of the world.

This ultimate basis of the entire credit structure is kept out of sight, but the basis exists. Indeed, we may say that banking, in a sense, causes this visible, tangible wealth to circulate. If the acres of a landowner or the iron stoves of a stove dealer cannot circulate in literally the same way that gold dollars circulate, yet the landowner or stove dealer may give to the bank a note on which the banker may base bank notes or deposits; and these bank notes and deposits will circulate like gold dollars. Through banking, he who possesses wealth difficult to exchange can create a circulating medium. He has only to give to a bank his note — for which, of course, his property is liable — get in return the right to draw, and lo! his comparatively unexchangeable wealth becomes liquid currency. To put it crudely, banking is a device for coining into dollars land, stoves, and other wealth not otherwise generally exchangeable.

It is interesting to observe that the formation of the great modern "trusts" has given a considerable impetus to deposit currency; for the securities of large corporations are more easily used as "collateral security" for bank loans than the stocks and bonds of small corporations or than partnership rights.

We began by regarding a bank as substantially a coöperative enterprise, run for the convenience and at the expense of its depositors. But, as soon as it reaches the point of lending money to *X*, *Y*, and *Z*, on time, while itself owing money on demand, it assumes toward X, Y, and Z and its cash depositors risks which the depositors would be unwilling to assume. To meet this situation, the responsibility and expense of running the bank are taken by a third class of people — stockholders — who are willing to assume the augmented risk for the sake of the chance of profit. Stockholders, in order to guarantee the depositors against loss, put in some cash of their own. Their contract is, in effect, to make good any loss to depositors. Let us suppose that the stockholders put in $50,000, viz. $40,000 in cash and $10,000 in the purchase of a bank building. The accounts now stand :—

Assets		*Liabilities*	
Cash	$140,000	Due depositors	$150,000
Loans	100,000	Due note holders	50,000
Building	10,000	Due stockholders	50,000
	$250,000		$250,000

The accounts as they now stand include the chief features of an ordinary modern bank, — a so-called "bank of deposit, issue, and discount."

§ 3

We have seen that the assets must be adequate to meet the liabilities. We now wish to point out that the form of the assets must be such as will insure meeting the liabilities promptly. Since the business of a bank is to furnish quickly available property (cash or credit) in place of the "slower" property of its depositors, it fails of its purpose when it is caught with insufficient cash. Yet it "makes money" partly by tying up its quick property, *i.e.* lending it out where it is less accessible. Its problem in policy is to tie up enough to increase its property, but not to tie up so much as to get tied up itself. So far as anything has yet been said to the contrary, a bank might increase indefinitely its loans in relation to its cash or in relation to its capital. If this were so, deposit currency could be indefinitely inflated.

There are limits, however, imposed by prudence and sound economic policy, on both these processes. Insolvency and insufficiency of cash must both be avoided. Insolvency is that condition which threatens when loans are extended with insufficient capital. Insufficiency of cash is that condition which threatens when loans are extended unduly relatively to cash. Insolvency is reached when assets no longer cover liabilities (to others than stockholders), so that the bank is unable to pay its debts. Insufficiency of cash is reached when, although the bank's total assets are fully equal to its liabilities, the actual cash on hand is insufficient to meet the needs of the instant, and the bank is unable to pay its debts *on demand*.

The less the ratio of the value of the stockholders' interests to the value of liabilities to others, the greater is the risk of insolvency; the risk of insufficiency of cash is the greater, the less the ratio of the cash to the demand liabilities. In other words, the leading safeguard against insolvency lies in a large capital and surplus, but the leading safeguard against insufficiency of cash lies in a large cash reserve. Insolvency proper may befall any business enterprise; insufficiency of cash relates especially to banks in their function of redeeming notes and deposits.

Let us illustrate insufficiency of cash. In our bank's accounts as we left them, there was a reserve of $140,000 of cash, and $200,000 of demand liabilities (deposits and notes). The managers of the bank may think this reserve of $140,000 unnecessarily large or the loans unnecessarily small. They may then extend their loans (extended to customers in the form of cash, notes or deposit accounts) until the cash reserve is reduced, say to $40,000, and the liabilities due depositors and note holders increased to $300,000. If, under these circumstances, some depositor or note holder demands $50,000 cash, immediate payment will be impossible. It is true that the assets still equal the liabilities. There is full value behind the $50,000 demanded; but the understanding was that depositors and note holders should be paid in *money* and *on demand.* Were this not a stipulation of the deposit contract, the bank might pay the claims thus made upon it by transferring to its creditors the promissory notes due it from its debtors; or it might ask the customers to wait until it could turn these securities into cash.[1]

Since a bank cannot follow either of these plans, it tries, where insufficiency of cash impends, to forestall this condition by "calling in" some of its loans, or if none can be called in, by selling some of its securities or other property for cash. But it happens unfortunately that there is a limit to the amount of cash which a bank can suddenly realize. No bank could escape failure if a large percentage of its note holders and depositors should *simultaneously* demand cash payment.[2] The paradox of a panic is well expressed by the case of the man who inquired of his bank whether it had cash available for paying the amount of his deposit, saying, "If you can pay me, I don't want it; but if you can't,

[1] See Irving Fisher, *The Nature of Capital and Income*, Chapter V.

[2] Cf. Ricardo, *Works*, 2d ed., London (Murray), 1852, p. 217 (*Principles of Political Economy and Taxation*, Chapter XXVII).

I do." Such was the situation in 1907 in Wall Street. All the depositors at one time wanted to be sure their money "was there." Yet it never *is* there all at one time.

Since, then, insufficiency of cash is so troublesome a condition, — so difficult to escape when it has arrived, and so difficult to forestall when it begins to approach, — a bank must so regulate its loans and note issues as to keep on hand a sufficient cash reserve, and thus prevent insufficiency of cash from even threatening. It can regulate the reserve by alternately selling securities for cash and loaning cash on securities. The more the loans in proportion to the cash on hand, the greater the profits, but the greater the danger also. In the long run a bank maintains its necessary reserve by means of adjusting the interest rate charged for loans. If it has few loans and a reserve large enough to support loans of much greater volume, it will endeavor to extend its loans by lowering the rate of interest. If its loans are large and it fears too great demands on the reserve, it will restrict the loans by a high interest charge. Thus, by alternately raising and lowering interest, a bank keeps its loans within the sum which the reserve can support, but endeavors to keep them (for the sake of profit) as high as the reserve will support.

If the sums owed to individual depositors are large, relatively to the total liabilities, the reserve should be proportionately large, since the action of a small number of depositors can deplete it rapidly.[1] Similarly, the reserves should be larger against fluctuating deposits (as of stock brokers) or those known to be temporary.[2]

[1] Victor Morawetz, *The Banking and Currency Problem in the United States*, New York (The North American Review Publishing Co.), 1909, pp. 36 and 37. Also Kemmerer, *Money and Prices*, 1909, p. 80. [2] *Ibid.*

The reserve in a large city of great bank activity needs to be greater in proportion to its demand liabilities than in a small town with infrequent banking transactions.

Experience dictates differently the average size of deposit accounts for different banks according to the general character and amount of their business. For every bank there is a normal ratio, and hence for a whole community there is also a normal ratio — an average of the ratios for the different banks. No absolute numerical rule can be given. Arbitrary rules are often imposed by law. National banks in the United States, for instance, are required to keep a reserve for their deposits, varying according as they are or are not situated in certain cities designated by law as "reserve" cities, *i.e.* cities where national banks hold deposits of banks elsewhere. These reserves are all in defense of deposits. In defense of notes, on the other hand, no cash reserve is required, — that is, of national banks. True, the same economic principles apply to both bank notes and deposits, but the law treats them differently. The government itself chooses to undertake to redeem the national bank notes on demand.

The state banks are subject to varying restrictions.[1] Thus the requirement as to the ratio of reserve to deposits varies from 12½ per cent to 22½ per cent, being usually between 15 per cent and 20 per cent. Of the reserve, the part which must be cash varies from 10 per cent (of the reserve) to 50 per cent, being usually 40 per cent.

Such legal regulation of banking reserves, however,

[1] "Digest of State Banking Statutes," in *Reports of the National Monetary Commission*, 61st Congress, 2d Session Senate Document, No. 353.

is not a necessary development of banking. In Canada, the law makes the notes practically coördinate with the deposits. Indeed, banking may exist without government regulations at all. "George Smith's money" furnishes an illustration. George Smith, Alexander Mitchell and others established in 1839 an Insurance Company which, though forbidden to exercise "banking privileges," issued certificates of deposit payable to bearer, and these certificates were actually circulated like bank notes.[1]

§ 4

The study of banking operations, then, discloses two species of currency: one, bank notes, belonging to the category of money; and the other, deposits, belonging outside of that category, but constituting an excellent substitute. Referring these to the larger category of goods, we have a threefold classification of goods: first, *money;* second, deposit currency, or simply *deposits;* and third, all other *goods.* And by the use of these, there are six possible types of exchange: —

(1) Money against money,
(2) Deposits against deposits,
(3) Goods against goods,
(4) Money against deposits,
(5) Money against goods,
(6) Deposits against goods.

For our purpose, only the last two types of exchange are important, for these constitute the *circulation of currency.* As regards the other four, the first and third have been previously explained as "money changing" and "barter" respectively. The second and fourth

[1] See Horace White, *Money and Banking*

are banking transactions: the second being such as the selling of drafts for checks, or the mutual cancellation of bank clearings; and the fourth being such operations as the depositing or the withdrawing of money, by depositing cash or cashing checks.

The analysis of the balance sheets of banks has prepared us for the inclusion of bank deposits or circulating credit in the equation of exchange. We shall still use M to express the quantity of actual money, and V to express the velocity of its circulation. Similarly, we shall now use M' to express the total deposits subject to transfer by check; and V' to express the average velocity of circulation. The total value of purchases in a year is therefore no longer to be measured by MV, but by $MV + M'V'$. The equation of exchange, therefore, becomes: —

$$MV + M'V' = \Sigma pQ = PT.$$ [1]

Let us again represent the equation of exchange by means of a mechanical picture. In Figure 4, trade,

FIG. 4.

as before, is represented on the right by the weight of a miscellaneous assortment of goods; and their average price by the distance to the right from the fulcrum, or

[1] The equation of exchange is also stated by Kemmerer, *Money and Credit Instruments in their Relation to General Prices*, so as to include bank credit, although in a somewhat different way. That credit acts on prices in the same manner as money is by no means a newly established principle. See, for example, Mill, *Principles of Political Economy*, Book III, Chapter XII, §§ 1, 2.

the length of the arm on which this weight hangs. Again at the left, money (M) is represented by a weight in the form of a purse, and its velocity of circulation (V) by its arm; but now we have a new weight at the left, in the form of a bank book, to represent the bank deposits (M'). The velocity of circulation (V') of these bank deposits is represented by its distance from the fulcrum or the arm at which the book hangs.

This mechanism makes clear the fact that the average price (right arm) increases with the increase of money or bank deposits and with the velocities of their circulation, and decreases with the increase in the volume of trade.

Recurring to the left side of the equation of exchange, or $MV + M'V'$, we see that in a community without bank deposits the left side of the equation reduces simply to MV, the formula used in Chapter II; for in such a community the term "$M'V'$" vanishes. The introduction of M' tends to raise prices. That is, the hanging of the bank book on the left requires a lengthening of the arm at the right.

Just as E was used to denote the total circulation of money, MV, so we may now use E' to denote the total circulation of deposits, $M'V'$.

Like E, M, and V, so also E', M', and V' are sums and averages of corresponding magnitudes pertaining to different parts of the year, or different persons.[1]

§ 5

With the extension of the equation of monetary circulation to include deposit circulation, the influence

[1] The mathematical analysis of E', M', and V' in terms of "arrays" of e''s, m''s, and v''s, etc., is precisely parallel to that of E, M, and V, given in the Appendix to Chapter II. See also §§ 1 and 2 of Appendix to (this) Chapter III.

exerted by the quantity of money on general prices becomes less direct; and the process of tracing this influence becomes more difficult and complicated. It has even been argued that this interposition of circulating credit breaks whatever connection there may be between prices and the quantity of money.[1] This would be true if circulating credit were independent of money. But the fact is that the quantity of circulating credit, M', tends to hold a definite relation to M, the quantity of money in circulation; that is, deposits are normally a more or less definite multiple of money.

Two facts normally give deposits a more or less definite ratio to money. The first has been already explained, viz. that bank reserves are kept in a more or less definite ratio to bank deposits. The second is that individuals, firms, and corporations preserve more or less definite ratios between their cash transactions and their check transactions, and also between their money and deposit balances.[2] These ratios are determined by motives of individual convenience and habit. In general, business firms use money for wage payments, and for small miscellaneous transactions included under the term "petty cash"; while for settlements with each other they usually prefer checks. These preferences are so strong that we could not imagine them overridden except tempora-

[1] An almost opposite view is that of Laughlin that normal credit cannot affect prices because it is not an offer of standard money and cannot affect the value of the standard which alone determines general prices. See the *Principles of Money*, New York (Scribner), 1903, p. 97. Both views are inconsistent with that upheld in this book.

[2] This fact is apparently overlooked by Laughlin when he argues that there is not "any reason for limiting the amount of the deposit currency, or the assumption of an absolute scarcity of specie reserves." See *Principles of Money*, p. 127.

rily and to a small degree. A business firm would hardly pay car fares with checks and liquidate its large liabilities with cash. Each person strikes an equilibrium between his use of the two methods of payment, and does not greatly disturb it except for short periods of time. He keeps his stock of money or his bank balance in constant adjustment to the payments he makes in money or by check. Whenever his stock of money becomes relatively small and his bank balance relatively large, he cashes a check. In the opposite event, he deposits cash. In this way he is constantly converting one of the two media of exchange into the other. A private individual usually feeds his purse from his bank account; a retail commercial firm usually feeds its bank account from its till. The bank acts as intermediary for both.

In a given community the quantitative relation of deposit currency[1] to money is determined by several considerations of convenience. In the first place, the more highly developed the business of a community, the more prevalent the use of checks. Where business is conducted on a large scale, merchants habitually transact their larger operations with each other by means of checks, and their smaller ones by means of cash. Again, the more concentrated the population, the more prevalent the use of checks. In cities it is more convenient both for the payer and the payee to make large payments by check; whereas, in the country, trips to a bank are too expensive in time and effort to be convenient, and therefore more money is used in proportion to the amount of business done.[2] Again,

[1] The convenient expression "deposit currency" is used by Laughlin, *The Principles of Money*, p. 118.

[2] See Kinley's "Credit Instruments," *Report of the National*

the wealthier the members of the community, the more largely will they use checks. Laborers seldom use them; but capitalists, professional and salaried men use them habitually, for personal as well as business transactions.

There is, then, a relation of convenience and custom between check and cash circulation, and a more or less stable ratio between the deposit balance of the average man or corporation and the stock of money kept in pocket or till. This fact, as applied to the country as a whole, means that by convenience a rough ratio is fixed between M and M'. If that ratio is disturbed temporarily, there will come into play a tendency to restore it. Individuals will deposit surplus cash, or they will cash surplus deposits.

Hence, both money in circulation (as shown above) and money in reserve (as shown previously) tend to keep in a fixed ratio to deposits. It follows that the two must be in a fixed ratio to each other.

It further follows that any change in M, the quantity of money in circulation, requiring as it normally does a proportional change in M', the volume of bank deposits subject to check, will result in an exactly proportional change in the general level of prices except, of course, so far as this effect be interfered with by concomitant changes in the V's or the Q's. The truth of this proposition is evident from the equation $MV + M'V' = \Sigma pQ$; for if, say, M and M' are doubled, while V and V' remain the same, the left side of the equation is doubled and therefore the right side must be doubled also. But if the Q's remain

Monetary Commission, Senate Document, 399, 61st Congress, 2d Session, 1910, p. 188.

unchanged, then evidently all the p's must be doubled, or else if some are less than doubled, others must be enough more than doubled to compensate.

§ 6

The contents of this chapter may be formulated in a few simple propositions: —

(1) Banks supply two kinds of currency, viz. bank notes — which are money; and bank deposits (or rights to draw) — which are not money.

(2) A bank check is merely a certificate of a right to draw.

(3) Behind the claims of depositors and note holders stand, not simply the cash reserve, but all the assets of the bank.

(4) Deposit banking is a device by which wealth, incapable of direct circulation, may be made the basis of the circulation of rights to draw.

(5) The basis of such circulating rights to draw or deposits must consist in part of actual money, and it *should* consist in part also of quick assets readily exchangeable for money.

(6) Six sorts of exchange exist among the three classes of goods, money, deposits, and other goods. Of these six sorts of exchange, the most important for our present purposes are the exchanges of money and deposits against goods.

(7) The equation of money circulation extended so as to include bank deposits reads thus: —

$$MV + M'V' = \Sigma pQ \text{ or } PT.$$

(8) There tends to be a normal ratio of bank deposits (M') to the quantity of money (M); because business

convenience dictates that the available currency shall be apportioned between deposits and money in a certain more or less definite, even though elastic, ratio.

(9) The inclusion of deposit currency does not normally disturb the quantitative relation between money and prices.

CHAPTER IV

DISTURBANCE OF EQUATION AND OF PURCHASING POWER DURING TRANSITION PERIODS

§ 1

In the last chapter it was shown that the quantity of bank deposits normally maintains a definite ratio to the quantity of money in circulation and to the amount of bank reserves. As long as this normal relation holds, the existence of bank deposits merely *magnifies* the effect on the level of prices produced by the quantity of money in circulation and does not in the least *distort* that effect. Moreover, changes in velocity or trade will have the same effect on prices, whether bank deposits are included or not.

But during periods of transition this relation between money (M) and deposits (M') is by no means rigid.

We are now ready to study these periods of transition. The change which constitutes a transition may be a change in the quantity of money, or in any other factor of the equation of exchange, or in all. Usually all are involved, but the chief factor which we shall select for study (together with its effect on the other factors) is quantity of money. If the quantity of money were suddenly doubled, the effect of the change would not be the same at first as later. The ultimate effect is, as we have seen, to double prices; but before this happens, the prices oscillate up and down. In this chapter we shall consider the *temporary effects during the period of transition* separately from the *permanent or ultimate effects* which were considered in the last chapter. These permanent or ultimate effects follow after a new equilibrium is established, — if, indeed, such a condition as equilibrium may be said ever to be established. What we are concerned with in this chapter is the temporary effects, *i.e.* those in the transition period.

The transition periods may be characterized either by rising prices or by falling prices. *Rising* prices must be clearly distinguished from *high* prices, and *falling* from *low.* With stationary levels, high or low, we have in this chapter nothing to do. Our concern is with rising or falling prices. Rising prices mark the transition between a low and a high level of prices, just as a hill marks the transition between flat lowlands and flat highlands.

Since the study of these acclivities and declivities is bound up with that of the adjustment of interest rates, our first task is to present a brief statement regarding the effects of rising and falling prices[1] on *the rate of interest.* Indeed, the chief object of this chapter is to show that the peculiar behavior of the rate of interest during transition periods is largely responsible for the crises and depressions in which price movements end.

It must be borne in mind that although business loans are made in the form of money, yet whenever a man borrows money, he does not do this in order to hoard the money, but to purchase goods with it. To all intents and purposes, therefore, when A borrows one hundred dollars from B in order to purchase, say, one

[1] For a fuller statement, see Irving Fisher, *The Rate of Interest,* New York (Macmillan), 1907, Chapters V, XIV.

hundred units of a given commodity at one dollar per unit, it may be said that B is virtually lending A one hundred units of that commodity. And if at the end of a year A returns one hundred dollars to B, but the price of the commodity has meanwhile advanced, then B has lost a fraction of the purchasing power originally loaned to A. For even though A should happen to return to B the identical coins in which the loan was made, these coins represent somewhat less than the original quantity of purchasable commodities. Bearing this in mind in our investigation of interest rates, let us suppose that prices are rising at the rate of 3 per cent each year. It is plain that the man who lends $100 at the beginning of the year must, in order to get 5 per cent interest in purchasing power, receive back both $103 (then the equivalent of the $100 lent) plus 5 per cent of this, or a total of $108.15. That is, in order to get 5 per cent interest in *actual purchasing power*, he must receive a little more than 8 per cent interest in *money*. The 3 per cent rise of prices thus ought to add approximately 3 per cent to the rate of interest. Rising prices, therefore, in order that the relations between creditor and debtor shall be the same during the rise as before and after, require higher money interest than stationary prices require.

Not only will lenders require, but borrowers can afford to pay higher interest in terms of money; and to some extent competition will gradually force them to do so.[1] Yet we are so accustomed in our business dealings to consider money as the one thing stable, — to think of a "dollar as a dollar" regardless of the passage of time, that we reluctantly yield to this process of readjustment, thus rendering it very slow and imperfect. When prices

[1] *Rate of Interest*, Chapter XIV.

are rising at the rate of 3 per cent a year, and the normal rate of interest — *i.e.* the rate which would exist were prices stationary — is 5 per cent, the actual rate, though it ought (in order to make up for the rising prices) to be 8.15 per cent, will not ordinarily reach that figure; but it may reach, say, 6 per cent, and later, 7 per cent. This inadequacy and tardiness of adjustment are fostered, moreover, by law and custom, which arbitrarily tend to keep down the rate of interest.

A similar inadequacy of adjustment is observed when prices are falling. Suppose that, by the end of a year, $97 will buy as much as $100 at the beginning. In that case the lender, in order to get back a purchasing power equivalent to his principal and 5 per cent interest, should get, not $105, but only $97 + 5 per cent of $97 or $101.85. Thus the rate of interest in money should in this case be 1.85 per cent, or less than 2 per cent, instead of the original 5 per cent. In other words, the 3 per cent fall of prices should reduce the rate of interest by approximately 3 per cent. But as a matter of fact, such a perfect adjustment is seldom reached, and money interest keeps far above 2 per cent for a considerable time.[1]

§ 2

We are now ready to study temporary or transitional changes in the factors of our equation of exchange. Let us begin by assuming a slight initial disturbance, such as would be produced, for instance, by an increase in the quantity of gold. This, through the equation of exchange, will cause a rise in prices. As prices rise, profits of business men, measured in money, will rise also, even if the costs of business were to rise in the same

[1] *Rate of Interest, loc. cit.*

proportion. Thus, if a man who sold $10,000 of goods at a cost of $6000, thus clearing $4000, could get double prices at double cost, his profit would be double also, being $20,000 – $12,000, which is $8000. Of course such a rise of prices would be purely nominal, as it would merely keep pace with the rise in price level. The business man would gain no advantage, for his larger money profits would buy no more than his former smaller money profits bought before. But, as a matter of fact, the business man's profits will rise more than this because the rate of interest he has to pay will not adjust itself immediately. Among his costs is interest, and this cost will not, at first, rise. Thus the profits *will* rise faster than prices. Consequently, he will find himself making greater profits than usual, and be encouraged to expand his business by increasing his borrowings. These borrowings are mostly in the form of short-time loans from banks; and, as we have seen, short-time loans engender deposits. As is well known, the correspondence between loans and deposits is remarkably exact.[1] Therefore, deposit currency (M') will increase, but this extension of deposit currency tends further to raise the general level of prices, just as the increase of gold raised it in the first place.[2] Hence prices, which were already outstripping the rate of interest, tend to outstrip it still further, enabling borrowers,

[1] See J. Pease Norton, *Statistical Studies in the New York Money Market* (Macmillan), 1902, chart at end.

[2] See article by Knut Wicksell in the *Jahrbücher für Nationalökonomie*, 1897 (Band 68), pp. 228–243, entitled "Der Bankzins als Regulator der Warenpreise." This article, while not dealing directly with credit cycles as related to panics, points out the connection between the rate of interest on bank loans and changes in the level of prices due to the resulting expansion and contraction of such loans.

who were already increasing their profits, to increase them still further. More loans are demanded, and although nominal interest may be forced up somewhat, still it keeps lagging below the normal level. Yet nominally the rate of interest *has* increased; and hence the lenders, too, including banks, are led to become more enterprising. Beguiled by the higher nominal rates into the belief that fairly high interest is being realized, they extend their loans, and with the resulting expansion of bank loans, deposit currency (M'), already expanded, expands still more. Also, if prices are rising, the money value of collateral may be greater, making it easier for borrowers to get large credit.[1] Hence prices rise still further.[2] This sequence of events may be briefly stated as follows: —

1. Prices rise (whatever the first cause may be; but we have chosen for illustration an increase in the amount of gold).

2. The rate of interest rises, but not sufficiently.

3. Enterprisers (to use Professor Fetter's term), encouraged by large profits, expand their loans.

4. Deposit currency (M') expands relatively to money (M).

5. Prices continue to rise, that is, phenomenon No. 1 is repeated. Then No. 2 is repeated, and so on.

In other words, a slight initial rise of prices sets in motion a train of events which tends to repeat itself. Rise of prices generates rise of prices, and continues to do so as long *as the interest rate lags behind its normal figure.*

[1] See Kinley, *Money*, New York (Macmillan), 1904, p. 223.

[2] See Wicksell, *op. cit.*

§ 3

The expansion of deposit currency indicated in this cumulative movement abnormally increases the ratio of M' to M. This is evident if the rise of prices begins in a change in some element or elements in the equation other than the quantity of money; for if M remains constant and M' increases, the ratio M' to M must increase also. If M increases in any ratio, M' will increase in a greater ratio. If it increased only in the same ratio, prices would increase in that ratio (assuming velocities and quantities unchanged); and if prices increased in that ratio, loans (which being made to buy goods must be adjusted to the prices of goods) would have to be increased in that ratio in order to secure merely the same goods as before. But enterprisers, wishing to profit by the lag in interest, would extend the loans beyond this old or original point. Therefore, deposits based on loans would increase in a greater ratio. That is, the ratio M' to M would increase. In other words, during the period while M is increasing, M' increases still faster, thus disturbing the normal ratio between these two forms of currency.

This, however, is not the only disturbance caused by the increase in M. There are disturbances in the Q's (or in other words T) in V, and in V'. These will be taken up in order. Trade (the Q's) will be stimulated by the easy terms for loans. This effect is always observed during rising prices, and people note approvingly that "business is good" and "times are booming." Such statements represent the point of view of the ordinary business man who is an "enterpriser-borrower." They do not represent the sentiments of the creditor, the salaried man, or the laborer, most of whom are silent but long-suffering, — paying higher prices, but not getting proportionally higher incomes.

The first cause of the unhealthy increase in trade lies in the fact that prices, like interest, lag behind their full adjustment and have to be pushed up, so to speak, by increased purchases. This is especially true in cases where the original impetus came from an increase in money. The surplus money is first expended at nearly the old price level, but its continued expenditure gradually raises prices. In the meantime the volume of purchases will be somewhat greater than it would have been had prices risen more promptly. In fact, from the point of view of those who are selling goods, it is the possibility of a greater volume of sales at the old prices which gives encouragement to an increase of prices. Seeing that they can find purchasers for more goods than before at the previously prevailing prices, or for as many goods as before at higher prices, they will charge these higher prices.

But the amount of trade is dependent, almost entirely, on other things than the quantity of currency, so that an increase of currency cannot, even temporarily, very greatly increase trade. In ordinarily good times practically the whole community is engaged in labor, producing, transporting, and exchanging goods. The increase of currency of a "boom" period cannot, of itself, increase the population, extend invention, or increase the efficiency of labor. These factors pretty definitely limit the amount of trade which can be reasonably carried on. So, although the gains of the enterpriser-borrower may exert a psychological stimulus on trade, though a few unemployed may be employed, and some others in a few lines induced to work overtime, and although there may be some additional buying and selling which is speculative, yet almost the entire effect of an increase of deposits must be seen in a change of prices. Normally the entire effect would so express itself, but transitionally there will be also some increase in the Q's.

We next observe that the rise in prices — fall in the purchasing power of money — will accelerate the circulation of money. We all hasten to get rid of any commodity which, like ripe fruit, is spoiling on our hands.[1] Money is no exception; when it is depreciating, holders will get rid of it as fast as possible. As they view it, their motive is to buy goods which appreciate in terms of money in order to profit by the rise in their value. The inevitable result is that these goods rise in price still further. The series of changes, then, initiated by rising prices, expressed more fully than before, is as follows: —

1. Prices rise.
2. Velocities of circulation (V and V') increase; the rate of interest rises, but not sufficiently.
3. Profits increase, loans expand, and the Q's increase.
4. Deposit currency (M') expands relatively to money (M).
5. Prices continue to rise; that is, phenomenon No. 1 is repeated. Then No. 2 is repeated, and so on.

It will be noticed that these changes now involve all

[1] For statistical proof, see Pierre des Essars, *Journal de la Société de Statistique de Paris*, April, 1895, p. 143. The figures relate only to velocity of bank deposits. No corresponding figures for velocity of circulation of money exist. Pierre des Essars has shown that in European banks V' reaches a maximum in crisis years almost without fail. The same I find true in this country as shown by the ratio of clearings to deposits in New York, Boston, and Philadelphia.

the magnitudes in the equation of exchange. They are temporary changes, pertaining only to the transition period. They are like temporary increases in power and readjustments in an automobile climbing a hill.

§ 4

Evidently the expansion coming from this cycle of causes cannot proceed forever. It must ultimately spend itself. The check upon its continued operation lies in the rate of interest. It was the tardiness of the rise in interest that was responsible for the abnormal condition. But the rise in interest, though belated, is progressive, and, as soon as it overtakes the rate of rise in prices, the whole situation is changed. If prices are rising at the rate of 2 per cent per annum, the boom will continue only until interest becomes 2 per cent higher. It then offsets the rate of rise in prices. The banks are forced in self-defense to raise interest because they cannot stand so abnormal an expansion of loans relatively to reserves. As soon as the interest rate becomes adjusted, borrowers can no longer hope to make great profits, and the demand for loans ceases to expand.

There are also other forces placing a limitation on further expansion of deposit currency and introducing a tendency to contraction. Not only is the amount of deposit currency limited both by law and by prudence to a certain maximum multiple of the amount of bank reserves; but bank reserves are themselves limited by the amount of money available for use as reserves. Further, with the rise of interest, the value of certain collateral securities, such as bonds, on the basis of which loans are made, begins to fall. Such securities, being worth the discounted value of fixed sums, fall as interest rises; and therefore they cannot be used as collateral for loans as large as before. This check to loans is, as previously explained, a check to deposits also.

With the rise of interest, those who have counted on renewing their loans at the former rates and for the former amounts are unable to do so. It follows that some of them are destined to fail. The failure (or prospect of failure) of firms that have borrowed heavily from banks induces fear on the part of many depositors that the banks will not be able to realize on these loans. Hence the banks themselves fall under suspicion, and for this reason depositors demand cash. Then occur "runs on the banks," which deplete the bank reserves at the very moment they are most needed.[1] Being short of reserves, the banks have to curtail their loans. It is then that the rate of interest rises to a panic figure. Those enterprisers who are caught *must* have currency[2] to liquidate their obligations, and to get it are willing to pay high interest. Some of them are destined to become bankrupt, and, with their failure, the demand for loans is correspondingly reduced. This culmination of an upward price movement is what is called a crisis,[3]— a condition characterized by bankruptcies, and the bank-

[1] A part of the theory of crises here presented is similarly explained in a paper by Harry G. Brown, *Yale Review*, August, 1910, entitled "Typical Commercial Crises *versus* a Money Panic."

[2] Irving Fisher, *Rate of Interest*, pp. 325, 326.

[3] This is the definition of a crisis given by Juglar and the history of crises which he gives in detail corresponds to the description. See Juglar, *Des Crises Commerciales et de leur retour périodique en France en Angleterre et aux États-Unis.* 2d ed., Paris (Guillaumin), 1889, pp. 4 and 5. See also translation of part dealing with the United States, by De Courcey W. Thom, *A Brief History of Panics in the United States*, New York (Putnam), 1893, pp. 7–10.

ruptcies being due to a lack of cash when it is most needed.

It is generally recognized that the collapse of bank credit brought about by loss of confidence is the essential fact of every crisis, be the cause of the loss of confidence what it may. What is not generally recognized, and what it is desired in this chapter to emphasize, is that this loss of confidence (in the typical commercial crisis here described) is a consequence of a belated adjustment in the interest rate.

It is not our purpose here to discuss nonmonetary causes of crises, further than to say that the monetary causes are the most important *when taken in connection with the maladjustments in the rate of interest.* The other factors often emphasized are merely effects of this maladjustment. "Overconsumption" and "overinvestment" are cases in point. The reason many people spend more than they can afford is that they are relying on the dollar as a stable unit when as a matter of fact its purchasing power is rapidly falling. The bondholder, for instance, is beguiled into trenching on his capital. He never dreams that he ought to lay by a sinking fund because the decrease in purchasing power of money is reducing the real value of his principal. Again, the stockholder and enterpriser generally are beguiled by a vain reliance on the stability of the rate of interest, and so they overinvest. It is true that for a time they are gaining what the bondholder is losing and are therefore justified in both spending and investing more than if prices were not rising; and at first they prosper. But sooner or later the rate of interest rises above what they had reckoned on, and they awake to the fact that they have embarked on enterprises which cannot pay these high rates.

Then a curious thing happens: borrowers, unable to get easy loans, blame the high rate of interest for conditions which were really due to the fact that the previous rate of interest was not high enough. Had the previous rate been high enough, the borrowers never would have overinvested.

§ 5

The contraction of loans and deposits is accompanied by a decrease in velocities, and these conspire to prevent a further rise of prices and tend toward a fall. The crest of the wave is reached and a reaction sets in. Since prices have stopped rising, the rate of interest, which has risen to compensate the rise of prices, *should* fall again. But just as at first it was slow to rise, so now it is slow to fall. In fact, it tends for a time to rise still further.

The mistakes of the past of overborrowing compel the unfortunate victims of these mistakes to borrow still further to protect their solvency. It is this special abnormality which marks the period as a "crisis." Loans are wanted to continue old debts or to pay these debts by creating new ones. They are not wanted because of new investments but because of obligations connected with old (and ill-fated) investments. The problem is how to get extricated from the meshes of past commitments. It is the problem of liquidation. Even when interest begins to fall, it falls slowly, and failures continue to occur. Borrowers now find that interest, though nominally low, is still hard to meet. Especially do they find this true in the case of contracts made just before prices ceased rising or just before they began to fall. The rate of interest in these cases is agreed upon before the change in conditions takes place.

There will, in consequence, be little if any adjustment in lowering nominal interest. Because interest is hard to pay, failures continue to occur. There comes to be a greater hesitation in lending on any but the best security, and a hesitation to borrow save when the prospects of success are the greatest. Bank loans tend to be low, and consequently deposits (M') are reduced. The contraction of deposit currency makes prices fall still more. Those who have borrowed for the purpose of buying stocks of goods now find they cannot sell them for enough even to pay back what they have borrowed. Owing to this tardiness of the interest rate in falling to a lower and a normal level, the sequence of events is now the opposite of what it was before: —

1. Prices fall.
2. The rate of interest falls, but not sufficiently.
3. Enterpriser-borrowers, discouraged by small profits, contract their borrowings.
4. Deposit currency (M') contracts relatively to money (M).
5. Prices continue to fall; that is, phenomenon No. 1 is repeated. Then No. 2 is repeated, and so on.

Thus a fall of prices generates a further fall of prices. The cycle evidently repeats itself as long as the rate of interest lags behind. The man who loses most is the business man in debt. He is the typical business man, and he now complains that "business is bad." There is a "depression of trade."

During this depression, velocities (V and V') are abnormally low. People are less hasty to spend money or checks when the dollars they represent are rising in purchasing power. The Q's (or quantities in trade) decline because (1) the initiators of trade — the enterpriser-borrowers — are discouraged; (2) the inertia of high prices can be overcome only by a falling off of expenditures; (3) trade against money which alone the Q's represent gives way somewhat to barter. For a time there is not enough money to do the business which has to be done at existing prices, for these prices are still high and will not immediately adjust themselves to the sudden contraction. When such a "money famine" exists, there is no way of doing all the business except by eking out money transactions with barter. But while recourse to barter eases the first fall of prices, the inconvenience of barter immediately begins to operate as an additional force tending to reduce prices by inducing sellers to sell at a sacrifice if only money can be secured and barter avoided; although this effect is partly neutralized for a time by a decrease in the amount of business which people will attempt under such adverse conditions. A statement including these factors is: —

1. Prices fall.
2. Velocities of circulation (V and V') fall; the rate of interest falls, but not sufficiently.
3. Profits decrease; loans and the Q's decrease.
4. Deposit currency (M') contracts relatively to money (M).

Prices continue to fall; that is, phenomenon No. 1 is repeated. Then No. 2 is repeated, and so on.

The contraction brought about by this cycle of causes becomes self-limiting as soon as the rate of interest overtakes the rate of fall in prices. After a time, normal conditions begin to return. The weakest producers have been forced out, or have at least been prevented from expanding their business by increased loans. The strongest firms are left to build up a new credit structure. The continuous fall of prices has made it impossible for most borrowers to pay the old high rates of interest; the demand for loans diminishes, and interest falls to a point such that borrowers can at last pay it. Borrowers again become willing to take ventures; failures decrease in number; bank loans cease to decrease; prices cease to fall; borrowing and carrying on business become profitable; loans are again demanded; prices again begin to rise, and there occurs a repetition of the upward movement already described.

We have considered the rise, culmination, fall, and recovery of prices. These changes are abnormal oscillations, due to some initial disturbance. The upward and downward movements taken together constitute a complete credit cycle, which resembles the forward and backward movements of a pendulum.[1] In most cases the time occupied by the swing of the commercial pendulum to and fro is about ten years. While the pendulum is continually seeking a stable position, practically there is almost always some occurrence to prevent perfect equilibrium. Oscillations are set up which, though tending to be self-corrective, are continually perpetuated by fresh disturbances. Any cause which disturbs equilibrium will suffice to set up oscillations. One of the most common of such causes is an increase in the quantity of money.[2] Another is a shock to business confidence (affecting enterprise, loans, and deposits). A third is short crops, affecting the Q's. A fourth is invention.

The factors in the equation of exchange are there-

[1] For a mathematical treatment of this analogy, see Pareto, *Cours d'économie politique*, Lausanne, 1897, pp. 282–284.

[2] Such would seem to be the explanation of the panic of 1907. Cf. Irving Fisher, *Rate of Interest*, p. 336.

fore continually seeking normal adjustment. A ship in a calm sea will "pitch" only a few times before coming to rest, but in a high sea the pitching never ceases. While continually seeking equilibrium, the ship continually encounters causes which accentuate the oscillation. The factors seeking mutual adjustment are money in circulation, deposits, their velocities, the Q's and the p's. These magnitudes must always be linked together by the equation $MV + M'V' = \Sigma pQ$. This represents the mechanism of exchange. But in order to conform to such a relation the displacement of any one part of the mechanism spreads its effects during the transition period over all parts. Since periods of transition are the rule and those of equilibrium the exception, the mechanism of exchange is almost always in a dynamic rather than a static condition.

It must not be assumed that every credit cycle is so marked as to produce artificially excessive business activity at one time and "hard times" at another. The rhythm may be more or less extreme in the width of its fluctuations. If banks are conservative in making loans during the periods of rising prices, and the expansion of credit currency is therefore limited, the rise of prices is likewise limited, and the succeeding fall is apt to be less and to take place more gradually. If there were a better appreciation of the meaning of changes in the price level and an endeavor to balance these changes by adjustment in the rate of interest, the oscillations might be very greatly mitigated. It is the lagging behind of the rate of interest which allows the oscillations to reach so great proportions. On this point Marshall well says: "The cause of alternating periods of inflation and depression of commercial activity . . . is intimately connected with those variations in the real rate of interest which are caused by changes in the purchasing power of money. For when prices are likely to rise, people rush to borrow money and buy goods, and thus help prices to rise; business is inflated, and is managed recklessly and wastefully; those working on borrowed capital pay back less real value than they borrowed, and enrich themselves at the expense of the community. When afterwards credit is shaken and prices begin to fall, every one wants to get rid of commodities which are falling in value and to get hold of money which is rapidly rising; this makes prices fall all the faster, and the further fall makes credit shrink even more, and thus for a long time prices fall because prices have fallen." [1]

A somewhat different sort of cycle is the seasonal fluctuation which occurs annually. Such fluctuations, for the most part, are due, not to the departure from a state of equilibrium, but rather to a continuous adjustment to conditions, which, though changing, are normal and expected. As the autumn periods of harvesting and crop moving approach, there is a tendency toward a lower level of prices, followed after the passing of this period and the approach of winter by a rise of prices.

§ 6

In the present chapter we have analyzed the phenomena characteristic of periods of transition. We have found that one such "boom" period leads to a reaction, and that the action and reaction complete a cycle of "prosperity" and "depression."

It has been seen that rising prices tend towards a

[1] Marshall, *Principles of Economics*, 5th ed., London (Macmillan), 1907, Vol. I, p. 594.

higher nominal interest, and falling prices tend towards a lower, but that in general the adjustment is incomplete. With any initial rise of prices comes an expansion of loans, owing to the fact that interest does not at once adjust itself. This produces profits for the enterpriser-borrower, and his demand for loans further extends deposit currency. This extension still further raises prices, a result accentuated by a rise in velocities though somewhat mitigated by an increase in trade. When interest has become adjusted to rising prices, and loans and deposits have reached the limit set for them by the bank reserves and other conditions, the fact that prices no longer are rising necessitates a new adjustment. Those whose business has been unduly extended now find the high rates of interest oppressive. Failures result, constituting a commercial crisis. A reaction sets in; a reverse movement is initiated. A fall of prices, once begun, tends to be accelerated for reasons exactly corresponding to those which operate in the opposite situation.

CHAPTER V

INDIRECT INFLUENCES ON PURCHASING POWER

§ 1

Thus far we have considered the level of prices as affected by the volume of trade, by the velocities of circulation of money and of deposits, and by the quantities of money and of deposits. These are the only influences which can *directly* affect the level of prices. Any other influences on prices must act through these five. There are myriads of such influences (outside of the equation of exchange) that affect prices through these five. It is our purpose in this chapter to note the chief among them, excepting those that affect the volume of money (M); the latter will be examined in the two following chapters.

We shall first consider the outside influences that affect the volume of trade and, through it, the price level. The conditions which determine the extent of trade are numerous and technical. The most important may be classified as follows: —

1. *Conditions affecting producers.*
   (*a*) Geographical differences in natural resources.
   (*b*) The division of labor.
   (*c*) Knowledge of the technique of production.
   (*d*) The accumulation of capital.
2. *Conditions affecting consumers.*
   (*a*) The extent and variety of human wants.

3. *Conditions connecting producers and consumers.*
   (*a*) Facilities for transportation.
   (*b*) Relative freedom of trade.
   (*c*) Character of monetary and banking systems.
   (*d*) Business confidence.

1 (*a*). It is evident that if all localities were exactly alike in their natural resources, in other words, in their comparative costs of production, no trade would be set up between them. It is equally true that the greater the difference in the costs of production of different articles in different localities, the more likely is there to be trade between them and the greater the amount of that trade. Primitive trade had its *raison d'être* in the fact that the regions of this earth are unlike in their products. The traders were travelers between distant countries. Changes in commercial geography still produce changes in the distribution and volume of trade. The exhaustion of gold and silver mines in Nevada and of lumber in Michigan have tended to reduce the volume of trade of these regions, both external and internal. Contrariwise, cattle raising in Texas, the production of coal in Pennsylvania, of oranges in Florida, and of apples in Oregon have increased the volume of trade for these communities respectively.

1 (*b*). Equally obvious is the influence of the division of labor. Division of labor is based in part on differences in comparative costs or efforts as between men, — corresponding to geographic differences as between countries. These two, combined, lead to local differentiation of labor, making, for example, the town of Sheffield famous for cutlery, Dresden for china, Venice for glass, Paterson for silks, and Pittsburg for steel.

1 (*c*). Besides local and personal differentiation, the state of knowledge of production will affect trade.

The mines of Africa and Australia were left unworked for centuries by ignorant natives but were opened by white men possessing a knowledge of metallurgy. Vast coal fields in China await development, largely for lack of knowledge of how to extract and market the coal. Egypt awaits the advent of scientific agriculture, to usher in trade expansion. Nowadays, trade schools in Germany, England, and the United States are increasing and diffusing knowledge of productive technique.

1 (*d*). But knowledge, to be of use, must be applied; and its application usually requires the aid of capital. The greater and the more productive the stock or capital in any community, the more goods it can put into the currents of trade. A mill will make a town a center of trade. Docks, elevators, warehouses and railway terminals help to transform a harbor into a port of commerce.

Since increase in trade tends to decrease the general level of prices, anything which tends to increase trade likewise tends to decrease the general level of prices. We conclude, therefore, that among the causes tending to decrease prices are increasing geographical or personal specialization, improved productive technique, and the accumulation of capital. The history of commerce shows that all these causes have been increasingly operative during a long period including the last century. Consequently, there has been a constant tendency, from these sources at least, for prices to fall.

2 (*a*). Turning to the consumers' side, it is evident that their wants change from time to time. This is true even of so-called natural wants, but more conspicuously true of acquired or artificial wants.

Wants are, as it were, the mainsprings of economic

activity which in the last analysis keep the economic world in motion. The desire to have clothes as fine as the clothes of others, or finer, or different, leads to the multiplicity of silks, satins, laces, etc.; and the same principle applies to furniture, amusements, books, works of art, and every other means of gratification.

The increase of wants, by leading to an increase in trade, tends to lower the price level. Historically, during recent times through invention, education, and the emulation coming from increased contact in centers of population, there has been a great intensification and diversification of human wants and therefore increased trade. Consequently, there has been from these causes a tendency of prices to fall.

§ 2

3 (*a*). Anything which facilitates intercourse tends to increase trade. Anything that interferes with intercourse tends to decrease trade. First of all, there are the mechanical facilities for transport. As Macaulay said, with the exception of the alphabet and the printing press, no set of inventions has tended to alter civilization so much as those which abridge distance, — such as the railway, the steamship, the telephone, the telegraph, and that conveyer of information and advertisements, the newspaper. These all tend, therefore, to decrease prices.

3 (*b*). Trade barriers are not only physical but legal. A tariff between countries has the same influence in decreasing trade as a chain of mountains. The freer the trade, the more of it there will be. In France, many communities have a local tariff (*octroi*) which tends to interfere with local trade. In the United States trade is free within the country itself, but between the

United States and other countries there is a high protective tariff. The very fact of increasing facilities for transportation, lowering or removing physical barriers, has stimulated nations and communities to erect legal barriers in their place. Tariffs not only tend to decrease the frequency of exchanges, but to the extent that they prevent international or interlocal division of labor and make countries more alike as well as less productive, they also tend to decrease the amounts of goods which can be exchanged. The ultimate effect is thus to raise prices.

3 (*c*). The development of efficient monetary and banking systems tends to increase trade. There have been times in the history of the world when money was in so uncertain a state that people hesitated to make many trade contracts because of the lack of knowledge of what would be required of them when the contract should be fulfilled. In the same way, when people cannot depend on the good faith or stability of banks, they will hesitate to use deposits and checks.

3 (*d*). Confidence, not only in banks in particular, but in business in general, is truly said to be "the soul of trade." Without this confidence there cannot be a great volume of contracts. Anything that tends to increase this confidence tends to increase trade. In South America there are many places waiting to be developed simply because capitalists do not feel any security in contracts there. They are fearful that by hook or by crook the fruit of any investments they may make will be taken from them.

We see, then, that prices will tend to fall through increase in trade, which may in turn be brought about by improved transportation, by increased freedom of trade, by improved monetary and banking systems, and by business confidence. Historically, during recent years, all of these causes have tended to grow in power, except freedom of trade. Tariff barriers, however, have only partly offset the removal of physical barriers. The net effect has been a progressive lowering of trade restrictions, and therefore the tendency, so far as this group of causes goes, has been for prices to fall.

§ 3

Having examined those causes outside the equation which affect the volume of trade, our next task is to consider the outside causes that affect the velocities of circulation of money and of deposits. For the most part, the causes affecting one of these velocities affect the other also. These causes may be classified as follows: —

1. *Habits of the individual.*
   (*a*) As to thrift and hoarding.
   (*b*) As to book credit.
   (*c*) As to the use of checks.
2. *Systems of payments in the community.*
   (*a*) As to frequency of receipts and of disbursements.
   (*b*) As to regularity of receipts and disbursements.
   (*c*) As to correspondence between times and amounts of receipts and disbursements.
3. *General Causes.*
   (*a*) Density of population.
   (*b*) Rapidity of transportation.

1 (*a*). Taking these up in order, we may first consider what influence thrift has on the velocity of circulation. Velocity of circulation of money is the same thing as its rate of turnover It is found by dividing the total payments effected by money in a year by the

amount of money in circulation in that year. It depends upon the rates of turnover of the individuals who compose the society. This velocity of circulation or rapidity of turnover of money is the greater for each individual the more he spends, with a given average amount of cash on hand; or the less average cash he keeps, with a given yearly expenditure.

The velocity of circulation of a spendthrift may be presumed to be greater than the average.[1] He is always apt to be "short" of funds, — to have a small average balance on hand. But his thrifty neighbor takes care to provide himself with cash enough to meet all contingencies. The latter tends to hoard and lay by his money, and will, therefore, have a slower velocity of circulation. When, as used to be the custom in France, people put money away in stockings and kept it there for months, the velocity of circulation must have been extremely slow. The same principle applies to deposits. In a certain university town the banks often refuse to take deposits from students of spending habits because the average balances of the latter are so low; or insist on a special stipulation that the balance shall never fall below $100.

Hoarded money is sometimes said to be withdrawn from circulation. But this is only another way of saying that hoarding tends to decrease the velocity of circulation.

A man who is thrifty is usually, to some extent, a hoarder either of money[2] or of bank deposits. Laborers who save usually keep their savings in the form of

[1] Cf. Jevons, *Money and the Mechanism of Exchange*, New York (Appleton), 1896, p. 336.

[2] Cf. Harrison H. Brace, *Gold Production and Future Prices*, New York (Bankers' Publishing Co.), 1910, p. 122.

money until enough is accumulated to be deposited in a savings bank. Those who have bank accounts will likewise accumulate considerable deposits when preparing to make an investment. Banks whose depositors are "rapidly making money" and periodically investing the same, have, it is said, less active accounts than banks whose depositors "live up to their incomes."

1 (*b*). The habit of "charging," *i.e.* using book credit, tends to *increase* the velocity of circulation of money, because the man who gets things "charged" does not need to *keep on hand* as much money as he would if he made all payments in cash. A man who pays *cash* daily needs to keep cash for daily contingencies. The system of cash payments, unlike the system of book credit, requires that money shall be kept on hand *in advance* of purchases. Evidently, if money must be provided in advance, it must be provided in larger quantities than when merely required to liquidate past debts. This is true for two reasons: First, in advance of purchases, there is always uncertainty as to when money will be needed and how much, while after bills are incurred, the exact sum needed is known. Secondly, and as a consequence of the first circumstance, money held in advance must be held a longer time than money received after a use for it has been contracted for. In short, to keep money in advance requires (*a*) a larger margin for unforeseen contingencies and (*b*) a longer period before being disbursed during which the money is idle. In the system of cash payments, a man must keep money idle *in advance* lest he be caught in the embarrassing position of lacking it when he most needs it. With book credit, he knows that even if he should be caught without a

cent in his pocket, he can still get supplies on credit. These he can pay for when money comes to hand. Moreover, this money need not lie long in his pocket. Immediately it is received, there is a use awaiting it to pay debts accumulated. Now, to shorten the period of waiting evidently decreases the average balance carried, even if in the end the same sums are received and disbursed. For instance, a laborer receiving and spending $7 a week, if he cannot "charge," must make his week's wages last through the week. If he spends $1 a day, his weekly cycle must show on successive days at least as much as $7, $6, $5, $4, $3, $2, and $1, at which time another $7 comes in. This makes an average of at least $4. But if he can charge everything and then wait until pay day to meet the resulting obligations, he need keep nothing through the week, paying out his $7 when it comes in. His weekly cycle need show no higher balances than $7, $0, $0, $0, $0, $0, $0, the average of which is only $1.

Through book credit, therefore, the average amount of money or bank deposits which each person must keep at hand to meet a given expenditure is made less. This means that the rate of turnover is increased; for if people spend the same amounts as before, but keep smaller amounts on hand, the quotient of the amount spent divided by the amount on hand must decrease.

But we have seen that to increase the rate of turnover will tend to increase the price level. Therefore, book credit tends to increase the price[1] level. Moreover, a community can to some extent cover the relative scarcity of money of a period when business is large

[1] This indirect effect on the price level must not be confused with the direct effect sometimes claimed. See § 1 of Appendix to (this) Chapter V.

with the relative surplus of a period when fewer demands are made on its supply of money. Otherwise, to maintain the same general level of prices, there would have to be considerably more money when business was large; and this money, unless it were some form of elastic bank currency which could be canceled and retired, would lie idle during those seasons when business was slack.

In short, book credit economizes *money* (M) even though it may not economize money *payments* (E) and therefore increases the velocity of circulation of money (E/M).

1 (*c*). The habit of using checks rather than money will also affect the velocity of circulation; because a depositor's surplus money will immediately be put into the bank in return for a right to draw by check.

Banks thus offer an outlet for any surplus pocket money or surplus till money, and tend to prevent the existence of idle hoards. In like manner surplus deposits may be converted into cash — that is, exchanged for cash — as desired. In short, those who make use both of cash and deposits have the opportunity, by adjusting the two, to prevent either from being idle.

We see, then, that three habits — spendthrift habits, the habit of charging, and the habit of using checks — all tend to raise the level of prices through their effects on the velocity of circulation of money, or of deposits. It is believed that these habits (except probably the first) have been increasing rapidly during modern times.

§ 4

2 (*a*). The more frequently money or checks are received and disbursed, the shorter is the average interval between the receipt and the expenditure of money

or checks and the more rapid is the velocity of circulation.

This may best be seen from an example. A change from monthly to weekly wage payments tends to increase the velocity of circulation of money. If a laborer is paid weekly $7 and reduces this evenly each day, ending each week empty-handed, his average cash, as we have seen, would be a little over half of $7 or about $4. This makes his turnover nearly twice a week. Under monthly payments the laborer who receives and spends an average of $1 a day will have to spread the $30 more or less evenly over the following 30 days. If, at the next pay day, he comes out empty-handed, his average money during the month has been about $15. This makes his turnover about twice a month. Thus the rate of turnover is more rapid under weekly than under monthly payments.

The same result would hold if we assumed that, instead of ending the cycle empty-handed, he ended it with a given fraction — say half — of his wages unspent. Under weekly payments, he would begin with $10.50, and end with $3.50, averaging about $7. Under monthly payments he would thus begin with an average of $45, and end with $15, averaging about $30. In the former case his average velocity of circulation would be once a week and in the latter once a month. The turnover will thus still be about four times as rapid under weekly as under monthly payment. Thus if the distribution of expenditure over the two cycles should have exactly the same "time shape"[1] (distribution in time), weekly payments would ac-

[1] Compare Adolphe Landry, "La Rapidité de la Circulation Monétaire," Extrait de *La Revue d'Économie politique*, Février, 1905.

celerate the velocity of circulation in the same ratio which a month bears to a week. As a matter of history, however, it is not likely that the substitution of weekly payments for monthly payments has increased the rapidity of circulation of money among workingmen fourfold, because the change in another element, book credit, would be likely to cause a somewhat compensatory decrease. Book credit is less likely to be used under weekly than under monthly payments. Where this book-credit habit or habit of "charging" is prevalent, the great bulk of money is spent on pay day. It is probable that the substitution of weekly for monthly payments, when it has taken place, has enabled many workingmen, who formerly found it necessary to trade on credit, to make their own payments in cash, thus tending to decrease the velocity of turnover of money.

Frequency of disbursements evidently has an effect similar to the effect of frequency of receipts; *i.e.* it tends to accelerate the velocity of turnover, or circulation.

2 (*b*). *Regularity* of payment also facilitates the turnover. When the workingman can be fairly certain of both his receipts and expenditures, he can, by close calculation, adjust them so precisely as safely to end each payment cycle with an empty pocket. This habit is extremely common among certain classes of city laborers. On the other hand, if the receipts and expenditures are irregular, either in amount or in time, prudence requires the worker to keep a larger sum on hand, to insure against mishaps.[1] Even when foreknown with certainty, irregular receipts require a larger average sum to be kept on hand. This state-

[1] Compare Landry, *ibid.*

ment holds, at least, if we assume that the *frequency* of payments per year is the same as in the case of regular payments, and that the "time shape" of expenditures between receipts is also the same. Thus, suppose that a workman spends at the rate of $1 a day and receives at the *average* rate of $1 a day. The average amount that he will require to keep on hand will be less if his receipts occur once every fortnight than if they occur at intervals of three weeks and one week respectively in alternation. For, supposing he tries to come out empty-handed just before each payment, in the former case he will evidently need an average sum each fortnight of $7; but in the latter case, he will need for the first period of three weeks, or twenty-one days, $10.50, and in the second period $3.50, the average of which — remembering that the $10.50 applies for three weeks and the $3.50 for one week — will be $8.75. We may, therefore, conclude that regularity, both of receipts and of payments, tends to increase velocity of circulation.

2 (*c*). Next, consider the synchronizing of receipts and disbursements, *i.e.* making payments at the same intervals as obtaining receipts. Where payments such as rent, interest, insurance and taxes occur at periods irrespective of the times of receipts of money, it is often necessary to accumulate money or deposits in advance, thus increasing the average on hand, withdrawing money from use for a time, and decreasing the velocity of circulation. This result may, however, be obviated if the individual is willing and able to borrow in order to meet his tax or other special expense, repaying the loan later at his convenience. This is one of the ways in which banking, as already explained, through loans and deposits, serves the con-

venience of the public and increases the velocity of circulation of money and deposits. Similarly book credit may obviate the inconveniences arising from the disharmony between the times of receipt and disbursement; for we have already seen that it is a great convenience to the spender of money or of deposits, if dealers to whom he is in debt will allow him to postpone payment until he has received his money or his bank deposit. This arrangement obviates the necessity of keeping much money or deposits on hand, and therefore increases their velocity of circulation.

We conclude, then, that synchronizing and regularity of payment, no less than frequency of payment, have tended to increase prices by increasing velocity of circulation.

§ 5

3 (*a*). The more densely populated a locality, the more rapid will be the velocity of circulation.[1]

There is definite evidence that this is true of bank deposits. The following figures[2] give the velocities of circulation of deposits in ten cities, arranged in order of size: —

Paris	116	Lisbon	29
Berlin	161	Indianapolis	30
Brussels	123	New Haven	16
Madrid	14	Athens	4
Rome	43	Santa Barbara	1

Madrid is the only city seriously out of its order in respect to velocity of circulation.

[1] This is pointed out by Kinley, *Money*, New York (Macmillan), 1904, p. 156.

[2] These figures are the medians of those of Pierre des Essars for European banks (*Journal de la Société de Statistique de Paris*, April, 1895) supplemented by data secured by me from a few American banks.

3 (*b*). Again, the more extensive and the speedier the transportation in general, the more rapid the circulation of money.[1] Anything which makes it easier to pass money from one person to another will tend to increase the velocity of circulation. Railways have this effect. The telegraph has increased the velocity of circulation of deposits, since these can now be transferred thousands of miles in a few minutes. Mail and express, by facilitating the transmission of bank deposits and money, have likewise tended to increase their velocity of circulation.

We conclude, then, that density of population and rapidity of transportation have tended to increase prices by increasing velocities. Historically this concentration of population in cities has been an important factor in raising prices in the United States.

Ordinarily, the velocity of circulation of money and the velocity of circulation of deposits will be similarly influenced by similar causes. In time of panics, however, if the confidence of depositors is shaken, the tendency is for deposits to be withdrawn while money is hoarded. Hence, for a time, the two velocities *may* change in opposite directions, although there are no good statistics for verifying this supposition.

§ 6

Lastly, the chief specific outside influences on the volume of deposits subject to check are:—

(1) The system of banking and the habits of the people in utilizing that system.

(2) The habit of charging.

1. It goes without saying that a banking system must

[1] Cf. Jevons, *Money and the Mechanism of Exchange*, New York (Appleton), 1896, p. 336; also Kinley, *Money*, New York (Macmillan), 1904, pp. 156 and 157.

be devised and developed before it can be used. The invention of banking has made deposit currency possible, and its adoption has undoubtedly led to a great increase in deposits and consequent rise of prices. Even in the last decade the extension in the United States of deposit banking has been an exceedingly powerful influence in that direction. In Europe deposit banking is still in its infancy.

2. "Charging" is often a preliminary to payment by check, rather than by cash. If a customer did not have his obligations "charged," he would pay in money and not by check.[1] The ultimate effect of this practice, therefore, is to increase the ratio of check payments to cash payments (E' to E) and the ratio of deposits to money carried (M' to M), and therefore to increase the amount of credit currency which a given quantity of money can sustain.

This effect, the substitution of checks for cash payments, is probably by far the most important effect of "charging," and exerts a powerful influence toward raising prices.

[1] Andrew, "Credit and the Value of Money." Reprint from *Papers and Proceedings of the Seventeenth Annual Meeting American Economic Association*, December, 1904, p. 10.

CHAPTER VI

INDIRECT INFLUENCES (*continued*)

§ 1

WE have now considered those influences outside the equation of exchange which affect the volume of trade (the Q's), the velocities of circulation of money and deposits (V and V'), and the amount of deposits (M'). We have reserved for separate treatment in this chapter and the following the outside influences that affect the quantity of money (M).

The chief of these may be classified as follows: —

1. Influences operating through the exportation and importation of money.

2. Influences operating through the melting or minting of money.

3. Influences operating through the production and consumption of money metals.

4. Influences of monetary and banking systems, to be treated in the next chapter.

The first to be considered is the influence of foreign trade. Hitherto we have confined our studies of price levels to an isolated community, having no trade relation with other communities. In the modern world, however, no such community exists, and it is important to observe that international trade gives present-day problems of money and of the price level an international character. If all countries had their irredeemable paper money, and had no money acceptable elsewhere, there could be no international adjustment of monetary matters. Price levels in different countries would have no intimate connection. Indeed, to some extent the connection is actually broken between existing countries which have different metallic standards, — for example, between a gold-basis and a silver-basis country, — although through their nonmonetary uses the two metals are still somewhat bound together. But where two or more nations trading with each other use the *same* standard, there is a tendency for the price levels of each to influence profoundly the price levels of the other.

The price level in a small country like Switzerland depends largely upon the price level in other countries. Gold, which is the primary or full weight money in most civilized nations, is constantly traveling from one country or community to another. When a single small country is under consideration, it is therefore preferable to say that the quantity of money in that country is determined by the universal price level, rather than to say that its level of prices is determined by the quantity of money within its borders. An individual country bears the same relation to the world that a lagoon bears to the ocean. The level of the ocean depends, of course, upon the quantity of water in it. But when we speak of the lagoon, we reverse the statement, and say that the quantity of water in it depends upon the level of the ocean. As the tide in the outside ocean rises and falls, the quantity of water in the lagoon will adjust itself accordingly.

To simplify the problem of the distribution of money among different communities, we shall, for the time being, ignore the fact that money consists ordinarily of a material capable of nonmonetary uses and may be melted or minted.

Let us, then, consider the causes that determine the quantity of money in a state like Connecticut. If the level of prices in Connecticut temporarily falls below that of the surrounding states, Rhode Island, Massachusetts, and New York, the effect is to cause an export of money from these states to Connecticut, because people will buy goods wherever they are cheapest and sell them wherever they are dearest. With its low prices, Connecticut becomes a good place to buy from, but a poor place to sell in. But if outsiders buy of Connecticut, they will have to bring money to buy with. There will, therefore, be a tendency for money to flow to Connecticut until the level of prices there rises to a level which will arrest the influx. If, on the other hand, prices in Connecticut are higher than in surrounding states, it becomes a good place to sell to and a poor place to buy from. But if outsiders sell to Connecticut, they will receive money in exchange. There is then a tendency for money to flow out of Connecticut until the level of prices in Connecticut is lower.

But it must not be inferred that the prices of various articles or even the general level of prices will become precisely the same in different countries. Distance, ignorance as to where the best markets are to be found, tariffs, and costs of transportation help to maintain price differences. The native products of each region tend to be cheaper in that region. They are exported as long as the excess of prices abroad is enough to more than cover the cost of transportation. Practically, a commodity will not be exported at a price which would not at least be equal to the price in the country of origin, plus the freight. Many commodities are shipped only one way. Thus, wheat is shipped from the United States to England, but not from England to the United

States. It tends to be cheaper in the United States. Large exportations raise its price in America toward the price in England, but it will usually keep below that price by the cost of transportation. Other commodities that are cheap to transport will be sent in either direction, according to market conditions.

But, although international and interlocal trade will never bring about exact uniformity of price levels, it will, to the extent that it exists, produce an adjustment of these levels toward uniformity by regulating in the manner already described the distribution of money. If one commodity enters into international trade, it alone will suffice, though slowly, to act as a regulator of money distribution; for in return for that commodity, money may flow and, as the price level rises or falls, the quantity of that commodity sold may be correspondingly adjusted. In ordinary intercourse between nations, even when a deliberate attempt is made to interfere with it by protective tariffs, there will always be a large number of commodities thus acting as outlets and inlets. And since the *quantity of money itself* affects prices for *all* sorts of commodities, the regulative effect of international trade applies, not simply to the commodities which enter into that trade, but to all others as well. It follows that nowadays international and interlocal trade is constantly regulating price levels throughout the world.

We must not leave this subject without emphasizing the effects of a tariff on the purchasing power of money. When a country adopts a tariff, the tendency is for the level of prices to rise. A tariff obviously raises the prices of the "protected" goods. But it does more than that, — it tends also to raise the prices of *un*protected goods. Thus, the tariff first causes a decrease in imports. Though in the long run this decrease in imports will lead to a corresponding decrease in exports, yet at first there will be no such adjustment. The foreigner will, for a time, continue to buy from the protected country almost as much as before. This will result temporarily in an excess of that country's exports over its imports, or a so-called "favorable" balance of trade, and a consequent inflow of money. This inflow will eventually raise the prices, not alone of protected goods, but of unprotected goods as well. The rise will continue till it reaches a point high enough to put a stop to the "favorable" balance of trade.

Although the "favorable balance" of trade created by a tariff is temporary, it leaves behind a permanent increase of money and of prices. The tariff wall is a sort of dam, causing an elevation in the prices of the goods impounded behind it.

This fact is sometimes overlooked in the theory of international trade as commonly set forth. Emphasis is laid instead on the fact that in the last analysis the trade is of goods for goods, not of money for goods, and that a tariff on imports reduces, not only imports, but exports also,—that it merely interrupts temporarily the virtual barter between nations. The effect of a tax on imports is likened to that of a tax on exports. But in respect to effects on price levels a tax on imports and a tax on exports are diametrically opposed. If we place our tax on exports, we first interfere with exports. The imports are not checked until money has flowed out and has reduced the general price level enough to destroy the "unfavorable" balance of trade first created. We conclude that the general purchasing power of money is reduced by a tariff and that it would be increased by a tax on exports.

This is, perhaps, the chief reason why a protective tariff seems to many a cause of prosperity. It furnishes a temporary stimulus, not only to protected industries, but to trade in general, which is really simply the stimulus of money inflation.

Our present interest in international trade, however, is mainly directed to its effects on international price levels. Except for the export or import of money to adjust the price levels, international trade is at bottom merely an interchange of goods. Where the price level is not concerned, the money value of the goods sold by a country will exactly equal the value of those bought. Only when there is a difference in these values, or a "balance of trade," will there be any flow of money and consequently any tendency to modify the price level.[1]

We have shown how the international and interlocal equilibrium of prices may be disturbed by differential changes in the quantity of money alone. It may also be disturbed by differential changes in the volume of bank deposits; or in the velocity of circulation of money; or in the velocity of circulation of bank deposits; or in the volume of trade. But whatever may be the source of the difference in price levels, equilibrium will eventually be restored through an international or interlocal redistribution of money and goods brought about by international and interlocal trade. Other elements in the equation of exchange than money and commodities cannot be transported from one place to another.

Except for transitional effects, then, international differences of price levels produce changes only in one

[1] For mathematical statement, see § 1 of Appendix to (this) Chapter VI.

of the elements in the equation of exchange, — the volume of money. Practically, of course, transition periods may be incessant or chronic. It seldom happens that a nation has no balance of trade. For decades Oriental nations took silver from Occidental nations even when silver was, under the bimetallic régime, at a stable ratio with gold. In Europe there was a consequent long-continued tendency for prices to fall, and in Asia a tendency to rise, with all the other transitional effects involved.

§ 2

We have seen how M in the equation of exchange is affected by the import or export of money. Considered with reference to the M in any one of the countries concerned, the M's in all the others are "outside influences."

Proceeding now one step farther, we must consider those influences on M that are not only outside of the equation of exchange for a particular country, but outside those for the whole world. Besides the monetary inflow and outflow through import and export, there is an inflow and outflow through minting and melting. In other words, not only do the stocks of money in the world connect with each other like interconnecting bodies of water, but they connect in the same way with the outside *stock of bullion.* In the modern world one of the precious metals, such as gold, usually plays the part of primary money, and this metal has two uses, — a monetary use and a commodity use. That is to say, gold is not only a money material, but a commodity as well. In their character of commodities, the precious metals are raw materials for jewelry, works of art, and other products into which they may be wrought. It is in this unmanufactured or raw state that they are called bullion.

Gold money may be changed into gold bullion, and *vice versa*. In fact, both changes are going on constantly, for if the value of gold as compared with other commodities is greater in the one use than in the other, gold will immediately flow toward whichever use is more profitable, and the market price of gold bullion will determine the direction of the flow. Since 100 ounces of gold, $\frac{9}{10}$ fine, can be transformed into $1860, the market value of so much gold bullion, $\frac{9}{10}$ fine, must tend to be $1860. If it costs nothing to have bullion coined into money, and nothing to melt money into bullion, there will be an automatic flux and reflux from money to bullion and from bullion to money that will prevent the price of bullion from varying greatly. On the one hand, if the price of gold bullion is greater than the money which could be minted from it, no matter how slight the difference may be, the users of gold who require bullion — notably jewelers — will save this difference by melting gold coin into bullion. Contrariwise, if the price of bullion is less than the value of gold coin, the owners of bullion will save the difference by taking bullion to the mint and having it coined into gold dollars, instead of selling it in the bullion market. The effect of melting coin, on the one hand, is to decrease the amount of gold money and increase the amount of gold bullion, thereby lowering the value of gold as bullion and raising the value of gold as money; thereby lowering the price level and restoring the equality between bullion and money. The effect of minting bullion into coin is, by the opposite process, to bring the value of gold as coin and the value of gold as bullion again into equilibrium. In practice, the balance is probably[1] maintained chiefly by turning newly mined gold into the one or the other use according to the market. By thus feeding the two reservoirs according to their respective needs there is saved the necessity of any great amount of interflow between money and the arts.

Where a charge — called "seigniorage" — is made for changing bullion into coin, or where the process involves expense or delay, the flow of bullion into currency will be to that extent impeded. But under a modern system of free coinage and with modern methods of metallurgy, both melting and minting may be performed so inexpensively and so quickly that there is practically no cost or delay involved. In fact, there are few instances of more exact price adjustment than the adjustment between gold bullion and gold coin. It follows that the quantity of money, and therefore its purchasing power, is directly dependent on that of gold bullion.

The stability of the price of gold bullion expressed in gold coin causes confusion in the minds of many people, giving them the erroneous impression that there is no change in the value of money. Indeed, this stability has often been cited to show that gold is a stable standard of value. Dealers in objects made of gold seem to misunderstand the significance of the fact that an ounce of gold always costs about $18.60 in the United States or £3 17*s.* 10½*d.* in England. This means nothing more than the fact that gold in one form and measured in one way will always bear a constant ratio to gold in another form and measured in another way. An ounce of gold bullion is worth a fixed number of gold dollars, for the same reason that a pound sterling of

[1] Cf. De Launay, *The World's Gold*, New York (Putnam), 1908, pp. 179–183.

gold is worth a fixed number of gold dollars, or that a gold eagle is worth a fixed number of gold dollars.

Except, then, for extremely slight and temporary fluctuations, gold bullion and gold money must always have the same value. Therefore, in the following discussion respecting the more considerable fluctuations affecting both, we shall speak of these values interchangeably as "the value of gold."

§ 3

The stock of bullion is not the ultimate outside influence on the quantity of money. As the stock of bullion and the stock of money influence each other, so the total stock of both is influenced by production and consumption. The production of gold consists of the output of the mines, which constantly tends to add to the existing stocks both of bullion and coin. The consumption of gold consists of the use of bullion in the arts by being wrought up into jewelry, gilding, etc., and of losses by abrasion, shipwreck, etc. If we consider the amount of gold coin and bullion as contained in a reservoir, production would be the inflow from the mines, and consumption the outflow to the arts and by destruction and loss. To the inflow from the mines should be added the *re*inflow from forms of art into which gold had previously been wrought, but which have grown obsolete. This is illustrated by the business of producing gold bullion by burning gold picture frames.

We shall consider first the inflow or production, and afterward the outflow or consumption. The regulator of the inflow (which practically means the production of gold from the mines) is its estimated "marginal cost of production."

Mining is a hazardous business and estimates are subject to great error. But however erroneous the estimated cost, it exerts a regulatory power over production. Wherever the estimated cost of producing a dollar of gold is less than the existing value of a dollar in gold, it will normally be produced. Wherever the cost of production exceeds the existing value of a dollar, gold will normally not be produced. In the former case the production of gold is profitable; in the latter it is unprofitable. There will be an intermediate or neutral point at which normally profitable production ceases and unprofitable production begins, a point at which the cost of producing $100 will be exactly $100. The cost at this point is called the marginal cost of production. At the richest mines, the cost of production is extremely small. From this low standard the cost gradually rises at other mines, until the marginal mine is reached, at which the cost will normally be equal to the value of the product. In fact, there exists a marginal point of production, not only as among different mines, but for each mine individually. The fact that cost tends in general to increase with increased product is due to the fact that gold is an extractive industry. It is subject to the law of increasing cost, or, as it is often expressed, "the law of decreasing returns." If a mine is only moderately worked, the cost of production per ounce of gold will be less than if it is worked at more nearly its full capacity, and there will always be a rate of working such that the cost per ounce of any extension in that rate of working will make the extension barely profitable. It will pay to extend production to the point where the additional return is just equal to the consequent additional cost, but no further. The mine operator may unintentionally or temporarily overshoot the mark or fall within it, but such errors will only stimulate him to correct them; and gold production will always tend toward an equilibrium in which the marginal cost of production will (when interest is added) be equal to the value of the product.

This holds true in whatever way cost of production is measured, whether in terms of gold itself, or in terms of some other commodity such as wheat, or of commodities in general, or of any supposed "absolute" standard of value. In gold-standard countries gold miners do actually reckon the cost of producing gold in terms of gold. From their standpoint it is a needless complication to translate the cost of production and the value of the product into some other standard than gold. They are interested in the relation between the two, and this relation will not be affected by the standard.

To translate the cost and value from gold money into wheat, it is only necessary to divide both cost and value by the price of wheat in gold money. Such a change in the method of expressing both cost and value will not affect their relation to each other.

To illustrate how the producer of gold measures everything in terms of gold, suppose that the price level rises. Assuming that the rise of prices applies to wages, machinery, fuel, and the other expenses of producing gold, he will then have to pay more dollars for wages, machinery, fuel, etc., while the prices obtained for his *product* (expressed in those same dollars) will, as always, remain unchanged. Conversely, a fall in the level will lower his cost of production (measured in dollars), while the price of his product will still remain the same.[1] Thus we have a *constant* number expressing the price of gold product and a *variable* number expressing its cost of production.

If we express the same phenomena, not in terms of gold, but in terms of wheat, or rather, let us say, in terms of goods in general, we shall have the opposite conditions. When prices rise, the purchasing power of money falls, and this purchasing power is the value of the product expressed in terms of goods in general. If the mining costs change with the general price movement, there will not occur any change in the cost of producing gold *relatively to goods*. There will, however, be a change in the value of the gold product. That is, we shall then have a *variable* number expressing the price of the gold product and a *constant* number expressing its cost of production.

Thus the comparison between price and cost of production is the same, whether we use gold or other commodities as our criterion. In the one view — *i.e.* when prices are measured in gold — a rise of prices means a rise in the gold miner's cost of production; in the other view — *i.e.* when prices are measured in other goods — the same rise in prices means a fall in the price (purchasing power) of his product. In either view he will be discouraged. *He* will look at his troubles in the former light, *i.e.* as a rise in the cost of production; but we shall find it more useful to look at them in the latter, *i.e.* as a fall in the purchasing power of the product. In either case the comparison is between the cost of the production of gold and the purchasing power of gold. If this purchasing power is above the cost of production in any particular mine, it will pay

[1] Cf. Mill, *Principles of Political Economy*, Book III, Chapter IX, § 2.

to work that mine. If the purchasing power of gold is lower than the cost of production of any particular mine, it will not pay to work that mine. Thus the production of gold increases or decreases with an increase or decrease in the purchasing power of gold.

So much for the inflow of gold and the conditions regulating it. We turn next to outflow or consumption of gold. This has two forms, viz. consumption in the arts and consumption for monetary purposes.

First we consider its consumption in the arts. If objects made of gold are cheap — that is, if the prices of other objects are relatively high — then the relative cheapness of the gold objects will lead to an increase in their use and consumption. Expressing the matter in terms of money prices, when prices of everything else are higher and people's incomes are likewise higher, while gold watches and gold ornaments generally remain at their old prices, people will use and consume more gold watches and ornaments.

These are instances of the consumption of gold in the form of commodities. The consumption and loss of gold as coin is a matter of abrasion, of loss by shipwreck and other accidents. It changes with the changes in the amount of gold in use and in its rapidity of exchange. The outlets from this reservoir represent the consumption of gold coins by loss. Just as production is regulated by marginal cost of what is produced, so is consumption regulated by marginal utility of what is consumed. This is not the place to enter into a discussion of the essential symmetry between these two marginal magnitudes, a symmetry often lost sight of because cost is usually measured objectively and utility subjectively. Both are measurable in either way. The subjective method is the more fundamental, but takes us farther away from our present discussion than is necessary or profitable.

We see then that the consumption of gold is stimulated by a fall in the value (purchasing power) of gold, while the production of gold is decreased. The purchasing power of money, being thus played upon by the opposing forces of production and consumption, is driven up or down as the case may be.[1]

§ 4

In any complete picture of the forces determining the purchasing power of money we need to keep prominently in view three groups of factors: (1) the production or the "inflow" of gold (*i.e.* from the mines); (2) the consumption or "outflow" (into the arts and by destruction and loss); and (3) the "stock" or reservoir of gold (whether coin or bullion) which receives the inflow and suffers the outflow. The relations among these three sets of magnitudes can be set forth by means of a mechanical illustration, given in Figure 5. This represents two connected reservoirs of liquid, G_b and G_m. The contents of the first reservoir represent the stock of gold bullion, and the contents of the second the stock of gold money. Since purchas-

[1] The theory here presented, that the value of gold bullion and the cost of production of gold affect prices by way of the quantity of money, is the one which economists have generally held. A different view is represented by Laughlin, who says, "the quantity of money used as the actual media of exchange no more determines price than the entries of deeds and conveyances in the county records determine the prices of the land whose sale is stated in the papers recorded," and that "price is an exchange relation between goods and the standard money commodity, whether that money commodity be used as a medium of exchange or not." See *The Principles of Money*, New York (Scribner), 1903, pp. 317 and 318.

ing power increases with scarcity, the distance from the top of the cisterns, *OO*, to the surface of the liquid, is taken to represent the purchasing power of gold over other goods. A lowering of the level of the liquid indicates an increase in the purchasing power of money, since we measure this purchasing power downward from the line *OO* to the surface of the liquid. We shall not attempt to represent other forms of currency explicitly in the diagram. We have seen that normally the quantities of other currency are proportional to

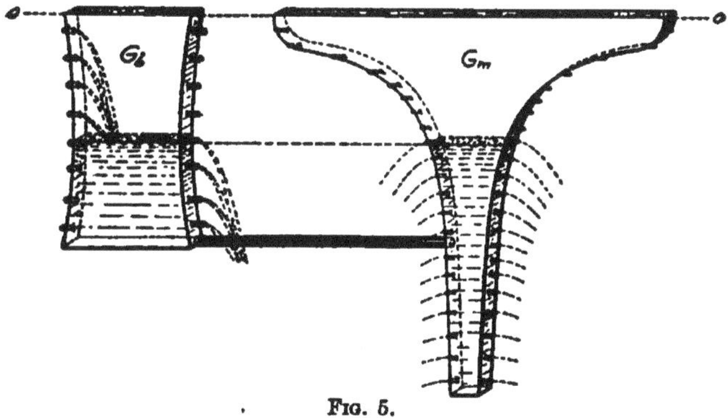

FIG. 5.

the quantity of primary money, which we are supposing to be gold. Therefore, the variation in the purchasing power of this primary money may be taken as representative of the variation of all the currency. We shall now explain the *shapes* of these cisterns. The shape of the cistern G_m must be such as will make the distance of the liquid surface below *OO* decrease with an increase of the liquid, *in exactly the same way as the purchasing power of gold decreases with an increase in its quantity.* That is, as the quantity of liquid in G_m doubles, the distance of the surface from the line

OO should decrease by one half. In a similar manner the shape of the gold bullion cistern must be such as will make the distance of the liquid surface below OO decrease with an increase of the liquid in the same way as the value of gold bullion decreases with the stock of gold bullion. The shapes of the two cisterns need not, and ordinarily will not, be the same, for we can scarcely suppose that halving the purchasing power of gold will always exactly double the amount of bullion in existence.

Both reservoirs have inlets and outlets. Let us consider these in connection with the bullion reservoir (G_b). Here each inlet represents a particular mine supplying bullion, and each outlet represents a particular use in the arts consuming gold bullion. Each mine and each use has its own distance from OO. There are, therefore, three sets of distances from OO: the inlet distances, the outlet distances, and the liquid-surface distance. Each inlet distance represents the cost of production for each mine, measured in goods; each outlet distance represents the value of gold in some particular use, likewise measured in goods. The surface distance, as we have already explained, represents the value of bullion, likewise measured in goods, — in other words, its purchasing power.

It is evident that among these three sets of levels there will be discrepancies. These discrepancies serve to interpret the relative state of things as between bullion and the various flows — in and out. If an inlet at a given moment be above the surface level, *i.e.* at a less distance from OO, the interpretation is that the cost of production is less than the purchasing power of the bullion. Hence the mine owner will turn on his spigot and keep it on until, perchance, the surface level rises to the level of his mine, — *i.e.* until the surface distance from *OO* is as small as the inlet distance, — *i.e.* until the purchasing power of bullion is as small as the cost of production. At this point there is no longer any profit in mining. So much for inlets; now let us consider the outlets. If an outlet at a given moment be below the surface level, — *i.e. at a greater distance from OO,* — the interpretation is that the value of gold in that particular use is greater than the purchasing power of bullion. Hence gold bullion will flow into these uses where its worth is greater than as bullion. That is, it will flow out of all outlets *below* the surface in the reservoir.

It is evident, therefore, that at any given moment, only the inlets above the surface level, and only the outlets below it, will be called into operation. As the surface rises, therefore, more outlets will be brought into use, but fewer inlets. That is to say, the less the purchasing power of gold as bullion, the more it will be used in the arts, but the less profitable it will be for the mines to produce it, and the smaller will be the output of the mines. As the surface falls, more inlets will come into use and fewer outlets.

We turn now to the money reservoir (G^m). The fact that gold has the same value either as bullion or as coin, because of the interflow between them, is interpreted in the diagram by connecting the bullion and coin reservoirs, in consequence of which both will (like water) have the same level. The surface of the liquid in both reservoirs will be the same distance below the line *OO*, and this distance represents the value of gold or its purchasing power. Should the inflow at any time exceed the outflow, the result will necessarily be an increase in the stock of gold in existence.

This will tend to decrease the purchasing power or value of gold. But as soon as the surface rises, fewer inlets and more outlets will operate. That is, the excessive inflow or production on the one hand will decrease, and the deficient outflow or consumption on the other hand will increase, checking the inequality between the outflow and inflow. If, on the other hand, the outflow should temporarily be greater than the inflow, the reservoir will tend to subside. The purchasing power will increase; thus the excessive outflow will be checked, and the deficient inflow stimulated, — restoring equilibrium. The exact point of equilibrium may seldom or never be realized, but as in the case of a pendulum swinging back and forth *through* a position of equilibrium, there will always be a tendency to seek it.

It need scarcely be said that our mechanical diagram is intended merely to give a picture of some of the chief variables involved in the problem under discussion. It does not of itself constitute an argument, or add any new element; nor should one pretend that it includes explicitly *all* the factors which need to be considered. But it does enable us to grasp the chief factors involved in determining the purchasing power of money. It enables us to observe and trace the following important variations and their effects: —

First, if there be an increased production of gold — due, let us suppose, to the discovery of new mines or improved methods of working old ones — this may be represented by an increase in the number or size of the inlets into the G_b reservoir. The result will evidently be an increase of "inflow" into the bullion reservoir, and from that into the currency reservoir, a consequent gradual filling up of both, and therefore a decrease in the purchasing power of money. This process will be checked finally by the increase in consumption. And when production and consumption become equal, an equilibrium will be established. An exhaustion of gold mines obviously operates in exactly the reverse manner.

Secondly, if there be an increase in the consumption of gold — as through some change of fashion — it may be represented by an increase in the number or size of the outlets of G_b. The result will be a draining out of the bullion reservoir, and consequently a decreased amount in the currency reservoir: hence an increase in the purchasing power of gold, which increase will be checked finally by an increase in the output of the mines as well as by a decrease in consumption. When the increased production and the decreased consumption become equal, equilibrium will again be reached.

If the connection between the currency reservoir and the bullion reservoir is closed by a valve, that is, if the mints are closed so that gold cannot flow from bullion into money (although it can flow in the reverse direction), then the purchasing power of the gold as money may become greater than its value as bullion. Any increase in the production of gold will then tend only to fill the bullion reservoir and decrease the distance of the surface from the line *OO*, *i.e.* lower the value of gold bullion. The surface of the liquid in the money reservoir will not be brought nearer *OO*. It may even by gradual loss be lowered farther away. In other words, the purchasing power of money will by such a valve be made entirely independent of the value of the bullion out of which it was first made.

An illustration of this principle is found in the history of the silver currency in India. After long discussion the mints of India were closed to silver in 1893. Previous to that time the value of coined silver had followed closely the value of silver bullion, but the closure produced an immediate divergence between the two. The rupee has remained independent of silver ever since; and during the first six years — until 1899 — it was independent of gold also. Its present relation to the latter metal will be discussed in the next chapter.

We have now discussed all but one of the outside influences upon the equation of exchange. That one is the character of the monetary and banking system which affects the quantity of money and deposits. This we reserve for special discussion in the following chapter. Meanwhile, it is also noteworthy that almost all of the influences affecting either the quantity or the velocities of circulation have been and are predominantly in the direction of higher prices. Almost the only opposing influence is the increased volume of trade; but this is partly neutralized by increased velocities due to the increased trade itself. We may here point out that some of those influences discussed in this and the preceding chapter operate *in more than one way*. Consider, for instance, technical knowledge and invention, which affect the equation of exchange by increasing trade. So far as these increase trade, the tendency is to decrease prices; but so far as they develop metallurgy and the other arts which increase the production and easy transportation of the precious metals, they tend to *increase* prices. So far as they make the transportation and transfer of money and deposits quicker, they also tend to increase prices. So far as they lead to the development of the art of banking, they likewise tend to increase prices, both by increasing deposit currency (M') and by increasing the velocity of circulation both of money and deposits. So far as they lead to the concentration of population in cities, they tend to increase prices by accelerating circulation.

Finally, so far as per capita trade is increased through this or any other cause, there is a tendency to decrease prices. What the net effect of the development of the arts may be during any given period will depend on the predominant direction in which the arts are developed.

CHAPTER VII

INFLUENCE OF MONETARY SYSTEMS ON PURCHASING POWER

§ 1

Thus far we have considered the influences that determine the purchasing power of money when the money in circulation is all of one kind. The illustration given in the previous chapter shows how the money mechanism operates when a single metal is used. We have now to consider the monetary systems in which more than one kind of money is used.

One of the first difficulties in the early history of money was that of keeping two (or more) metals in circulation. One of the two would become cheaper than the other, and the cheaper would drive out the dearer. This tendency was observed by Nicolas Oresme, afterwards Count Bishop of Lisieux, in a report to Charles V of France, about 1366, and by Copernicus about 1526 in a report or treatise written for Sigismund I, King of Poland.[1] Macleod in his *Elements of Political Economy*, published in 1857,[2] before he had become aware of the earlier formulations of Oresme and Copernicus,[3] gave the name "Gresham's Law" to this tendency, in honor of Sir Thomas Gresham, who stated the principle in the middle of the sixteenth cen-

[1] Henry Dunning Macleod, *The History of Economics*, New York (Putnam), 1896, pp. 37 and 38.

[2] P. 477.

[3] Macleod, *The History of Economics*, pp. 38 and 39.

tury. The tendency seems in fact, to have been recognized even among the ancient Greeks, being mentioned in the "Frogs" of Aristophanes:[1] —

"For your old and standard pieces valued and approved and tried,
Here among the Grecian nations and in all the world beside,
Recognized in every realm for trusty stamp and pure assay,
Are rejected and abandoned for the trash of yesterday,
For a vile, adulterate issue, drossy, counterfeit, and base
Which the traffic of the City passes current in their place."

Gresham's or Oresme's Law is ordinarily stated in the form, "Bad money drives out good money," for it was usually observed that the badly worn, defaced, light-weight, "clipped," "sweated," and otherwise deteriorated money tended to drive out the full-weight, freshly minted coins. This formulation, however, is not accurate. It is not true that "bad" coins, *e.g.* worn, bent, defaced, or even clipped coins, will drive out other money just because of their worn, bent, defaced, or clipped condition. Accurately stated, the Law is simply this: *Cheap money will drive out dear money.* The reason the cheaper of two moneys always prevails is that the choice of the use of money rests chiefly with the man who gives it in exchange, not with the man who receives it. When any one has the choice of paying his debts in either of two moneys, motives of economy will prompt him to use the cheaper. If the initiative and choice lay principally with the person who receives, instead of the person who pays the money, the opposite would hold true. The dearer or "good" money would then drive out the cheaper or "bad" money.

What then becomes of the dearer money? It may

[1] 893–898, Frere's translation.

be hoarded, or go into the melting pot, or go abroad,—hoarded and melted from motives of economy, and sent abroad because, where foreign trade is involved, it is the foreigner who receives the money, rather than ourselves who give it, who dictates what kind of money shall be accepted. He will take only the best, because our legal-tender laws do not bind him.

The better money might conceivably be used in exchange at a premium, *i.e.* at its bullion value; but the difficulties of arranging payments in it, which would be satisfactory to both parties, are such that in practice it is never so used in large quantities. In fact, the force of Gresham's Law is so great that it will even sacrifice the convenience of a whole nation. For instance, in Italy fifteen years ago the overissue of paper money drove not only gold across the Alps, but also silver and copper. These could circulate in Southern France at a par with corresponding coins there because France and Italy belonged to the Latin Union. Consequently, for a time there was very little small change left, below the denomination of 5 lire notes. Customers at retail stores often found it impossible to make their purchases because they lacked the small denominations necessary, and because the storekeeper lacked the same small denominations, and could not make change. To meet the difficulty, 30,000,000 of 1 lire notes were issued, and these were so much in demand that dealers paid a premium for them.

Gresham's Law applies not only to two rival moneys of the same metal; it applies to all moneys that circulate concurrently. Until "milling" the edges of coins was invented and a "limit of tolerance" of the mint (deviation from the standard weight) was adopted, much embarrassment was felt in commerce from the fact that the clipping and debasing of coin was a common practice. Nowadays, however, any coin which has been so "sweated" or clipped as to reduce its weight appreciably ceases to be legal tender, and being commonly rejected by those to whom it is offered ceases to be money. Within the customary[1] or legal limits of tolerance, however — that is, as long as the cheaper money retains the "money" power — it will drive out the dearer.

§ 2

The obvious effect of Gresham's Law is to decrease the purchasing power of money at every opportunity. The history of the world's currencies is largely a record of money debasements, often at the behest of the sovereign. Our chief purpose now, in considering Gresham's Law, is to formulate more fully the causes determining the purchasing power of money under monetary systems subject to the operation of Gresham's Law. The first application is to bimetallism.

In order to understand fully the influence of any monetary system on the purchasing power of money, we must first understand how the system works.[2] It has been denied that bimetallism ever did work or can be made to work, because the cheaper metal will drive out the dearer. Our first task is to show, quite irrespective of its desirability, that bimetallism can and does "work" under certain circumstances, but not under others. To make clear when it will work and when it will not work, we shall continue to employ the mechani-

[1] Sometimes custom is less strict than law. For instance, in California worn gold coin below the mint limit of tolerance continues to circulate. It is called "bank gold."

[2] Irving Fisher, "The Mechanics of Bimetallism," (British) *Economic Journal*, September, 1894, pp. 527–536.

cal illustration[1] of the last chapter, in which the amount of gold bullion is represented by the contents of reservoir G_b (Figs. 6, 7). Here, as before, we represent the purchasing power or value of gold by the distance of the water level below the zero level, OO. In the last chapter, our figure represented only one metal, gold, and represented that metal in two reservoirs, — the bullion reservoir and the coin reservoir. We shall now, one step at a time, elaborate that figure. First, as in Figure 6 *a*, we add a reservoir for silver bullion (S_b), a

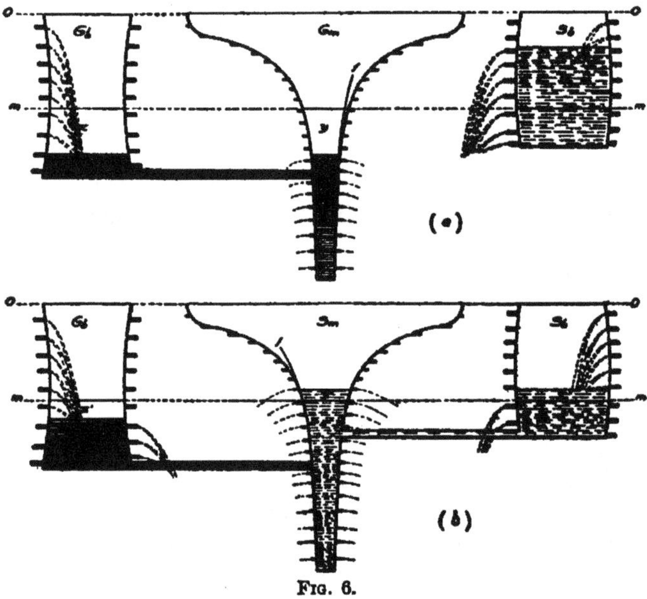

FIG. 6.

reservoir of somewhat different shape and size from G_b. This reservoir may be used to show the relation

[1] In its present application it is somewhat like a symbolism suggested by Jevons in his *Money and the Mechanism of Exchange*, New York (Appleton), 1896, p. 140.

between the value or purchasing power of silver and its quantity in the arts and as bullion. Here, then, are three reservoirs. At first the silver one is entirely isolated; but after a while we shall connect it with the middle one. For the present, let us suppose that the middle one, which contains money, is entirely filled with gold money only (Fig. 6 *a*), no silver being yet used as money. In other words, the monetary system is the same as that discussed in the last chapter. The only change we have introduced is to add to the picture another reservoir (S_b), entirely detached, showing the quantity and value of silver bullion.

We next suppose a pipe opened at the right, connecting S_b with the money reservoir; that is, we introduce bimetallism. Under bimetallism, governments open their mints to the free coinage of both metals at a fixed ratio, *i.e.* a fixed ratio between the said metals. For instance, if a silver dollar contains 16 grains of silver for every grain of gold in a gold dollar, the ratio is said to be 16 to 1. Under this system, the debtor has the option, unless otherwise bound by his contract, of making payment either in gold or in silver money. These, in fact, are the two requisites of complete bimetallism, viz. (1) the free and unlimited coinage of both metals at a fixed ratio, and (2) the unlimited legal tender of each metal at that ratio.[1] These new conditions are represented in Figure 6 *b* (and later, Fig. 7 *b*), where a pipe gives silver an entrance into the money or central reservoir.[2]

[1] The possibility of government's fixing any ratio between gold and silver to which the market ratio will conform has been so bitterly disputed that in addition to the positive argument contained in the text, a negative criticism of what are believed to be the chief fallacies underlying these disputes is inserted in § 1 of the Appendix to (this) Chapter VII.

[2] Of course a unit of water represents gold and silver at their

What we are about to represent is not the relations between mines, bullion, and arts, but the relations between bullion (two kinds) and coins. We may, therefore, disregard for the present all inlets and outlets except the connections between the bullion reservoirs and coin reservoir.

Now in these reservoirs the surface distances below *OO* represent, as we have said, purchasing power of gold and silver. But each unit of silver (say each drop of silver water, whether as money or as bullion) contains sixteen times as many grains as each unit of gold (say each drop of gold water, whether as money or as bullion). That is, a unit of water represents a dollar of gold or a dollar of silver. All we wish to represent is the relative purchasing power of corresponding units.

The waters representing gold and silver money are separated by a movable film *f*. In Figure 6 *a* this film is at the extreme right; in Figure 6 *b*, at the extreme left; in Figure 7 *a*, again at the right; and in Figure 7 *b*, midway. The *a* figures represent conditions *before* the mints are opened to silver. The *b* figures represent conditions *after* they have been opened and Gresham's Law has operated. If, just previous to the introduction of bimetallism, the silver level in S_b is below the gold level in G_b the statute introducing bimetallism will be inoperative, *i.e.* the silver bullion will not flow uphill, as it were, into the money reservoir; but if, as in Figure 6 *a* or in 7 *a*, the silver level is higher, then as

coining weights. If the bimetallic ratio is 16 to 1, the cisterns must be so constructed that a cubic inch of water shall represent an ounce of gold or 16 ounces of silver and that the number of inches separating the surfaces of liquid from *OO* shall represent the marginal utility of an ounce of gold and of 16 ounces of silver, respectively.

soon as the mints are open to silver, it will flow into circulation. Being at first cheaper than gold, it will push out the gold money through the left tube (*i.e.* by melting) into the bullion market. This expulsion of gold may be complete, as shown in Figure 6 *b*, or only partial, as shown in Figure 7 *b*. The expulsion will

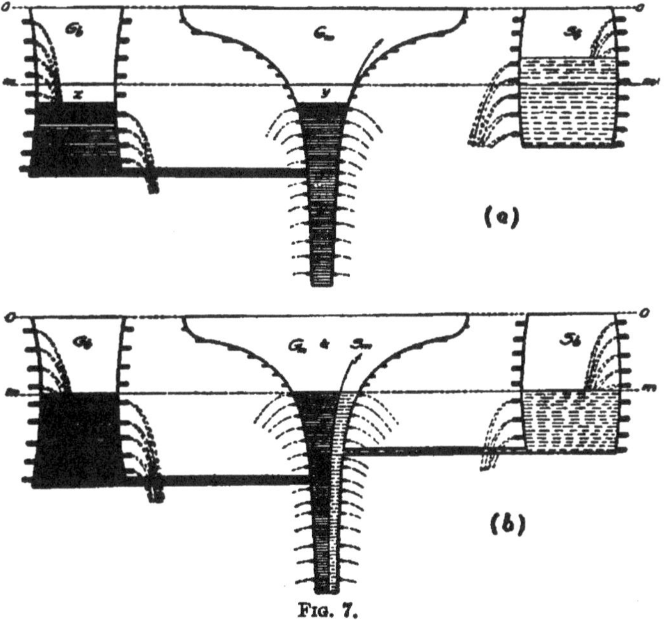

FIG. 7.

continue just as long as there is a premium on gold; that is, as long as the silver level in the bullion reservoir is above the gold level in the money reservoir; *i.e.* as long as silver bullion is cheaper than gold money.

Let *mm*, as shown in Figure 6 *a*, be the mean level; that is, a level such that the volume x above it equals the combined vacant volumes y and z below it. This line, *mm*, remains the mean level, whatever may be the distribution of the contents among the three reservoirs. As soon as the connecting pipe is inserted, silver will flow into the money reservoir and, in accordance with Gresham's Law, will displace gold.

Here we have to distinguish two cases: (1) when the silver x above the mean line, *mm, exceeds the total contents of the money reservoir below this line;* (2) when x is less than said lower contents. In the first case, it is evident that silver will sweep gold wholly out of circulation, as shown in Figure 6 *b*, where the film has moved from the extreme right to the extreme left. The contents of silver in the bullion reservoir are less than before, and the contents of gold in the bullion reservoir greater than before.

But this redistribution is only the first effect of opening the mints to silver. The balance between production and consumption has been upset both for gold and for silver. The increased value of silver (lowered level in S_b) has stimulated production, bringing into operation silver mines (uncovered inlets at right); and, on the other hand, the decreased value of gold (raised level in G_b) has discouraged gold production, shutting off gold mines (covered inlets at left). Like alterations are effected in the outflows, *i.e.* the consumption, waste, and absorption of each metal.

The result is that the levels resulting from the first redistribution will not necessarily be permanent. They may recede toward their original respective levels, and under all ordinary conditions will do so. But in any case, — and this is the point to be emphasized, — they cannot return entirely to those levels. Such a supposition would be untenable, as the following reasoning shows. Suppose, for the moment, that silver should return to its original level. Then the silver inflow (production) would also return to its original rate dependent on that level, but the silver outflow (consumption, waste, etc.) would be greater than originally. The consumption in the arts would be the same; but the waste and absorption of silver money constitute an additional drain. Therefore, consumption (equal to production before) will now exceed production, and the high original level cannot be maintained. The conclusion follows that, whatever the new level of permanent equilibrium, it lies below the old. The same argument, *mutatis mutandis*, proves that for gold the new level of permanent equilibrium lies above the old. The gap between the two original levels has therefore been reduced. Even though bimetallism has failed to bring about a concurrent circulation of both metals and a parity of values at the given coinage ratio, it has resulted in reducing the value of the dearer metal (gold) and increasing that of the cheaper (silver). This effect of mutual approach will be referred to in discussing the second case which follows.

§ 3

So much for the first case, where x is larger than the contents of the money reservoir below *mm*. In the second case, x is supposed to be smaller than the contents of the money reservoir below the line *mm*; that is, there is not enough silver to push *all* the gold out of circulation. Under these circumstances, disregarding for the moment any change in production or consumption, the opening of the pipe — the opening of the mints to silver — will bring the whole system of liquids to the common level *mm*. In other words, the premium on gold bullion will disappear (Fig. 7 *b*), and its purchasing power and the purchasing power of silver bullion will be a mean between their original purchasing powers, this mean being the distance of the mean line, *mm*, below *OO*. In other words, bimetallism in this case succeeds; that is, it will establish and maintain an equality for a time between the gold and silver dollars in the money reservoir.

But the equilibrium which we have just found is a mere equalization of levels produced by a redistribution of the *existing* stocks of gold and silver among the various reservoirs. It will be disturbed as soon as these stocks are disturbed. A permanent equilibrium requires that the stocks shall remain the same, — requires, in other words, an equality between production and consumption for each metal. After the inrush of silver from the silver bullion to the money reservoir, it is evident that the production and consumption of gold need no longer be equal to each other, nor need the production and consumption of silver be equal to each other. The same stimulation of silver production and discouragement of gold production will occur that occurred in the case considered in the last section. The result may be that silver will, in the end, entirely displace gold; or again it may fail to do so.

There may be, then, two possibilities. One possibility is obvious, namely, that gold may be completely driven out, the result being the same as already represented in the lower part of Figure 6. In the second possibility, gold will not be pushed out.

The reality of this second possibility will be clear if we attempt first to deny it. Suppose, therefore, that the film *f* be at the extreme left, and permanent equilibrium finally established. We have already seen that the gold level will be lower than before, and the silver level higher. How much lower and higher depends evidently on technical conditions of the production and consumption corresponding to the situation. It is of course not inconceivable that the gold level may be so much lower and the silver level so much higher as to make their relative positions reversed, *i.e.* to make the gold level higher than the silver level. But in this event it is quite impossible that the film *f* should be at the left. Gold, now being the cheaper, would flow into circulation and displace silver. Under the conditions we are now imagining, the film cannot stay at either extreme. If it is at the right, silver will be cheaper than gold and will move it leftward; if it is at the left, gold will be cheaper than silver and will move it rightward. Under these circumstances, evidently, equilibrium must lie between these extremes, as in Figure 7 *b*. The conditions of production and consumption under which bimetallism can succeed are therefore (1) that under silver monometallism a gold dollar would in equilibrium be cheaper than a silver dollar, and (2) that under gold monometallism silver would be cheaper than gold. A bimetallic level, therefore, when bimetallism is feasible, must always lie between the levels which the two metals would have assumed under gold monometallism, gold being currency and silver not, and for the same reasons it must lie between the levels which the two metals would have under silver monometallism, silver being currency and gold not.[1] In all our reasoning we have supposed a given legal ratio between the two metals. But bimetallism, impossible at one ratio, is always possible at

[1] But it is not necessarily between the level of the currency under gold monometallism and its level under silver monometallism.

another. There will always be two limiting ratios between which bimetallism is possible.[1]

It is easy to show that the two limiting ratios for a single nation are narrower than for a combination of nations, since the currency reservoir is, for one nation, smaller than for many, while the arts reservoirs are virtually larger by the amount of the monometallic currencies of the remaining nations. When bimetallism has broken down at one ratio, it can always be set in operation again at another, *but the transition requires a depreciation of the currency.* The only way of reintroducing the metal which has passed out of the currency reservoir is by lowering the amount of it in the monetary unit, — unless the still more drastic measure is adopted of raising the coinage weight of money already in circulation.

It should also be pointed out that two nations cannot both maintain bimetallism at two different ratios unless the difference is less than the cost of shipment. One of the two nations would lose the metal which it undervalued and find itself on a monometallic basis.

A few additional observations may now be stated. The temporary and normal equilibriums which have been considered separately are in fact quite distinctly separated in time. The time of redistributing existing stocks of metal, according to a newly enacted law, depends on the rapidity of transportation, melting, and minting, and would be measured in months or weeks. Normal equilibrium, however, depends on the slow working of changes in the rates of production and consumption, and would be measured in years. The normal equilibrium, if once established, is permanent so long as the conditions of production and consumption

[1] See § 2 of Appendix to (this) Chapter VII.

do not change. Slight alterations of these conditions — the exhaustion of mines, the discovery of new leads, etc. — will cause slight variations in the proportions of gold and silver money, that is, in the position of the film *f*. The oscillations of this film (and *not* of the price ratio as in the case of two unconnected commodities) reflect these changing conditions. But, in all probability, this film will sooner or later reach one of its limits. The probable time for such an event is, however, very long. The gold currency of the world is, roughly speaking, perhaps $5,000,000,000; the annual production of silver, reckoning at its present market price, is roughly about $100,000,000. Supposing a system of international bimetallism at, say, 36 to 1 to be initially in normal equilibrium, consider the effect of an enormous increase in the silver production, say a half, or $50,000,000. Then a hundred years would be required to push out gold without taking into account the fact that, as the pushing proceeds, the excess of production over consumption steadily declines. If this excess dwindles uniformly from $50,000,000 to zero, the period would be double, or two hundred years. When we add to these considerations the fact that, while the stimulus to the production of one metal acts quickly, the ensuing check to the production of the other acts more slowly, owing to the fixity of the "sunk" capital, and that, therefore, the volume of the currency is greater at the end than at the beginning; also the fact that the currency reservoir is itself constantly expanding; and finally the fact that fluctuations of production are likely to be in either direction, and for either metal, we may be tolerably confident that, *if initially successful with the film near the middle position*, international bimetallism would continue successful for many generations. The initial success depends, as has been seen, upon the ratio enacted.

It is to be observed that bimetallism can never avoid a *slight* premium. On the contrary, it is this difference of level which supplies the force which compells change from one point of equilibrium to another.[1]

In a series of years, the bimetallic level remains intermediate between the changing levels which the two metals would separately follow. Bimetallism spreads the effect of any single fluctuation over the combined gold and silver markets.[2] The steadying power of bimetallism depends on the breadths of the reservoirs, and not on the position of the film *f*. It remains in full force, no matter what may be the proportions

[1] As long as the premium lasts, the cheaper metal will doubtless circulate somewhat faster, and the dearer somewhat more slowly, than when there is no premium. This may, if desired, be represented by conceiving the thickness of the currency reservoir to decrease on the one side of *f* and increase on the other, making one metal "go farther" (cover more area in the diagram) than normally, and hasten the motion of *f* to the equilibrium point. Sluggishness (increase of thickness), of which "hoarding" is the chief application, is referred to below.

[2] To represent the steadying effect on a single fluctuation, we observe that under bimetallism the three reservoirs act as one. Therefore, compared with monometallism, the fluctuations are diminished in the inverse ratio of the liquid surfaces over which the fluctuations spread. Thus, if the combined breadths of the two left reservoirs at water level are two thirds of the combined breadths of the three, an influx of gold which, if distributed only over the two reservoirs, would make a layer an inch in depth, would, over the three, have a depth of two thirds of an inch. Likewise the right reservoir being one third the aggregate width, an inch fluctuation of silver, when merely merchandise, would be reduced to one third of an inch, when connection is maintained with the money reservoir. The breadths of the reservoir, which here play the important *rôle*, are the rate of increase of commodity relative to decrease of marginal utility. The law of inverse breadth applies with exactness only to static, or short-time readjustments.

of gold and silver money, and is as great when only one nation is bimetallic as when the whole world adopts the system. Even if only Switzerland had a system of bimetallism in successful operation, it would, until its breakdown, keep together and equalize the currencies of the whole world, wherever either gold or silver was standard. In fact, the world would have all the benefits of bimetallism enjoyed by Switzerland without its evils and dangers. This international function would cease abruptly as soon as the system of bimetallism should fail.

It should be pointed out that the equalizing effect maintained is relative only. It is conceivable that one metal would be steadier alone than when joined to the other. In a later chapter we shall consider the extent to which this equalization is an advantage. Here we confine ourselves to showing merely the mechanical *operation* of the bimetallic system.[1]

§ 4

Bimetallism is to-day a subject of historical interest only. It is no longer practiced; but its former prevalence has left behind it in many countries, including France and the United States, a monetary system which is sometimes called the "limping" standard. Such a system comes about when, in a system of bimetallism, before either metal can wholly expel the other, the mint is closed to the cheaper of them, but the coinage that has been accomplished up to date is not recalled. Suppose silver to be the metal thus excluded, as in France and the United States. Any money

[1] Cf. Leonard Darwin, *Bimetallism*, London (Murray), 1897, 341 pp.; Bertrand Nogaro, "*L'expérience bimétalliste*," *Revue d'économie politique*, 1908.

already coined in that metal and in circulation is kept in circulation at par with gold. This parity may continue even if *limited* additional amounts of silver be coined from time to time. There will then result a difference in value between silver bullion and silver coin, the silver coin being overvalued. This situation is represented in Figure 8. Here the pipe connection between the money reservoir and the silver-bullion

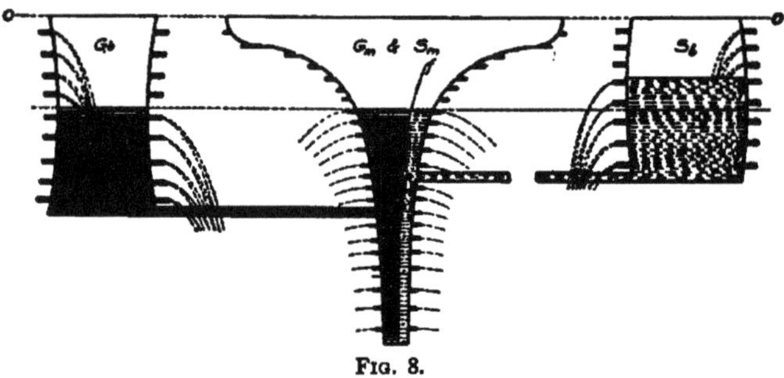

FIG. 8.

reservoir has been, as it were, cut off, or, let us say, stopped by a valve which refuses passage of silver from the money reservoir to the bullion reservoir but not the reverse (for no law ever can prevent the melting down of silver coins into bullion). Newly mined silver cannot now become money, and thus lower the purchasing power of the money.

On the other hand, new supplies of gold continue to affect the value of currency, as before,—the value, not only of the gold, but also of the concurrently circulating overvalued silver. If more gold should flow into the money reservoir, it would raise the currency level. Should this level ever become higher than the level of the silver bullion reservoir, silver would flow from the money reservoir into the bullion reservoir; for the passage *in that direction* (*i.e.* melting) is still free. So long, however, as the currency level is below the silver level, *i.e.* so long as the coined silver is worth more than the uncoined, there will be no flow of silver in either direction. The legal prohibition prevents the flow in one direction, and the laws of relative levels prevent its flow in the other.

In the case just discussed, the value of the coined silver will be equal to the value of gold at the legal ratio. Precisely the same principle applies in the case of any money, the coined value of which is greater than the value of its constituent material. Take the case, for instance, of paper money. So long as it has the distinctive characteristic of money, — general acceptability at its legal value, — and is limited in quantity, its value will ordinarily be equal to that of its legal equivalent in gold. If its quantity increases indefinitely, it will gradually push out all the gold and entirely fill the money reservoir, just as silver would do under bimetallism if produced in sufficiently large amounts. Likewise, credit money and credit in the form of bank deposits would have this effect. To the extent that they are used, they lessen the demand for gold, decrease its value as money, and cause more of it to go into the arts or to other countries.

So long as the quantity of silver or other token money, *e.g.* paper money, is too small to displace gold completely, gold will continue in circulation. The value of the other money in this case cannot fall below that of gold. For if it should, it would, by Gresham's Law, displace gold, which we have supposed it is not of sufficient quantity to do. The parity between silver coin and gold under the "limping" standard is, therefore, not necessarily dependent on any redeemability in gold, but may result merely from limitation in the amount of silver coin. Such limitation is usually sufficient to maintain parity despite irredeemability. This is not always true, however; for if the people should lose confidence in some form of irredeemable paper or token money, even though it were not overissued, it would depreciate and be nearly as cheap in money form as it is in the raw state. A man is willing to accept money at its face value so long as he has confidence that every one else is ready to do the same. But it is possible, for instance, for a *mere fear* of overissue to destroy this confidence. The payee, who, under ordinary circumstances, submits patiently to whatever money is customary or legal tender, may then take a hand and insist on "contracting out" of the offending standard.[1] That is, he may insist on making all his future contracts in terms of the better metal, — gold, for instance, — and thus contribute to the further downfall of the depreciated paper.

Irredeemable paper money, then, like our irredeemable silver dollars, may circulate at par with other money, if limited in quantity and not too unpopular. If it is gradually increased in amount, such irredeemable

[1] In the mechanical interpretation, since the law would now be inoperative, the film would no longer yield to pressure from the right, and an appreciable difference of level on its two sides would ensue. Such a mechanism would illustrate the concurrent circulation of two metals at independent valuations, but experience shows that such a condition is too full of inconveniences to be maintained long. The silver will be progressively tabooed, that is, its velocity of circulation will gradually decrease. This, as we have seen, may be figured by supposing the currency reservoir (on the right of the film only) to be thickened, thus bringing the film to the right. If the silver is completely tabooed, the film will be completely to the right, and there will be gold monometallism. The monetary result of such discrimination against silver is thus the appreciation of gold.

money may expel all metallic money and be left in undisputed possession of the field.

But though such a result — a condition of irredeemable paper money as the sole currency — is possible, it has seldom if ever proved desirable. Unless safeguarded, irredeemability is a constant temptation to abuse, and this fact alone causes business distrust and discourages long-time contracts and enterprises. Irredeemable paper money has almost invariably proved a curse to the country employing it. While, therefore, redeemability is not absolutely essential to produce parity of value with the primary money, practically it is a wise precaution. The lack of redeemability of silver dollars in the United States is one of the chief defects in our unsatisfactory monetary system, and a continuing danger.

It is possible to have various degrees of redeemability. One of the most interesting systems of partial redeemability is the system now known as the gold-exchange standard, by which countries, not themselves on a strict gold basis, nevertheless maintain substantial parity with gold through the foreign exchanges. By this system the government or its agent, while not redeeming its currency in gold, redeems it in orders on gold abroad. That is, the government sells bills of exchange on London or New York at a stated price. The currency which it thus receives, and in a sense redeems, it keeps out of circulation until the price of foreign exchange falls (*i.e.* until the demand for redemption ceases).

The gold-exchange standard may be regarded as a kind of limping standard with the added feature of partial redemption.

This added feature, however, greatly modifies the nature of the limping standard. The limping standard without the gold-exchange attachment may at any time break down, if the silver (or whatever else the over-valued money may be) should become so redundant, relatively to trade, as completely to displace gold. As soon as all gold is driven abroad, parity with gold ceases. But with the gold-exchange system this catastrophe is avoided. In fact, with this system it is not necessary to have gold in circulation at any time. The willingness of the government to sell foreign exchange at a fixed price, and to lock up the silver it receives thereby, takes that much currency out of circulation just as effectively as though the equivalent of gold had been exported. So long as the government is willing and able to maintain the price of bills of exchange with a gold country, it, *ipso facto*, maintains approximate parity with gold.[1]

§ 5

We have now to illustrate, by historical examples, the principles just explained. The first and most important case is that of France. The ratio of 15½ to 1 was adopted by France in 1785 and continued by the law of 1803. The history of France and the Latin Union during the period from 1785, and especially from 1803, to 1873 is instructive. It affords a practical illustration of the theory that when conditions are favorable, gold and silver can be kept tied together for a considerable period by means of bimetallism. During this period the public was ordinarily unconscious of any disparity of value, and only observed the changes from the relative predominance of gold to the relative predominance of silver in the currency and *vice versa*. In the wholesale bullion market, it is true, there were slight varia-

[1] Cf. Charles A. Conant, "The Gold Exchange Standard," *Economic Journal*, June, 1909, pp. 190–200.

tions from the ratio of 15½ to 1. But such variations simply supplied the force to restore equilibrium.

From 1803 until about 1850 the tendency was for silver to displace gold. In our mechanical terms there was, for the most part, an inflow on the right-hand side of the money reservoir, and the film was gradually pressed leftward. The statistics for the movements of gold and silver are not given separately and continuously before 1830. But from 1830 to 1847, inclusive, there was a net export of gold of 73,000,000 francs, although five of the years showed an import, making an average export of over 4,000,000 francs a year.[1] From 1830 until 1851 there was a net importation of silver in every year, amounting to a total for the period of 2,297,000,000 francs or an average of over 104,000,000 francs a year.[2] The statistics for silver are taken to 1851 because after that year the movement for silver was reversed, while for gold the inward flow began with 1848. Silver was displacing gold and filling up the currency reservoir. Nevertheless, the reservoir was expanding so fast, that is, trade was increasing, that there was no increase of prices, but rather a decrease. By 1850, the film had practically reached its limit. Bimetallism would have broken down and resulted in silver monometallism then and there, except for the fact that, as though to save the day, gold had just been discovered in California. The consequence of the new and increased gold production was a reverse movement, an inflow of gold into the French currency and an outflow of silver. From 1848 to 1870, inclusive, the net importation of gold amounted to 5,153,000,000 francs or over 224,000,000 francs a year, while the net exporta-

[1] W. A. Shaw, *The History of the Currency*, 3d ed., London (Clement Wilson), 1899, p. 183.
[2] *Ibid.*, p. 184.

tion of silver from 1852 to 1864, inclusive, amounted to 1,726,000,000 francs or nearly 133,000,000 francs a year.[1] Gold was displacing silver and filling the currency. It seemed probable that France would be entirely drained of her silver currency and come to a gold basis. France formed with Belgium, Italy, and Switzerland in 1865, and Greece in 1868, the Latin Monetary Union. The amount of silver in the subsidiary coins was reduced, but the standard silver coins were kept at the old ratio with gold. But the new gold mines were gradually exhausted, while silver production increased, with the consequence that there was again a reversal of the movement. From 1871 to 1873, inclusive, the exportation of gold netted 375,000,000 francs, or an average of 125,000,000 francs a year, while from 1865 to 1873, inclusive, the net importation of silver was 860,000,000 francs, or over 94,000,000 francs a year. Thus, even before the gold began to flow out, in 1871, silver had begun to flow in, *i.e.* in 1865. Silver gradually pushed gold out of circulation and, had not France and the other countries of the Latin Union successively suspended the free coinage of silver in 1873–1878, they would have found themselves on a silver, instead of a gold, basis. It has been claimed by bimetallists that this action in demonetizing silver was itself the cause of the breakdown. The truth is, that the breakdown was the cause of demonetization, although demonetization, by keeping back silver from circulation and keeping gold in circulation, did operate to widen the breach already made.

The film, in other words, was close to the left limit, and the currency reservoir was filled for the most part with

[1] W. A. Shaw, *The History of the Currency*, 3d ed., London (Clement Wilson), 1899, pp. 183 and 184.

silver. The Latin Union might conceivably have maintained bimetallism longer if other countries had joined with them. But it had to absorb, not only much of the silver provided by the mines, but also a considerable amount which had previously formed part of the monetary stock of Germany and which, at the adoption of the gold standard by that country following the Franco-Prussian War, was thrown on the market. That is, not only silver mines, but countries demonetizing silver, dumped silver on the Latin Union. Add to this the movement toward the gold standard in Scandinavia and the United States, and it becomes evident that the obstacles were many for a union comprising so few, and mostly unimportant, states.

The parity with gold of the silver remaining in circulation in the Latin Union is now preserved on the principles explained earlier in the chapter, viz. by limiting its quantity, as well as by making it full legal tender and receivable for public dues.

§ 6

It is strange that the lessons of the French and other experiments do not seem to be generally understood either by monometallists or bimetallists. For instance, uncompromising monometallists have pointed to the variation in the value of gold and silver during the three quarters of a century as disproving the possibility of maintaining a legal ratio. They might as well point to the ripples on a pond or the slight gradient of a river, as disproving the fact that water seeks a level. These ripples are really evidence of the process of seeking a level and are trifling as compared with those which in all probability would have taken place had there not been a legal ratio. The diagram and tables used in

Shaw's *History of the Currency* and the similar diagram here given show that during the period of inflowing silver, 1803 to 1850, in spite of the great increase in the quantity of silver, the ratio was changed from 15½ to 1 by at most only .75 points or slightly over 4.8 per cent in any year, and the average departure was only .29 points or 1.9 per cent. Moreover, the greater part of the deviation is explainable by the seigniorage charge then in force in France.[1] During the succeeding period from 1851 to 1870, characterized largely by an inflow of gold, the maximum departure (in the opposite direction) was .31 points or 2 per cent, with an average departure of .14 points or .9 per cent, while during the succeeding period of inflowing silver and outflowing gold, from 1871 to 1873, the ratio rose above 15½ to 1 by a maximum of .42 points or 2.7 per cent and an average of .21 points or 1.4 per cent. Contrast these figures with those since 1873.[2] The maximum departure from the ratio of 15½ to 1 since 1873 is 23.65 points, or 152.6 per cent, and the average departure 10.4 points, or 67.1 per cent.[3] The history of the ratio is shown in Figure 9.

On the other hand, bimetallists have often failed to see that this experiment illustrates the limits as well as the possibilities of bimetallism. In 1850 bimetallism had almost broken down in France and would have been succeeded by silver monometallism had not the increased production of gold reversed the flow. In 1865,

[1] Cf. J. F. Johnson, *Money and Currency*, Boston (Ginn) 1905, p. 227.

[2] Although France did not entirely suspend the coinage of the silver five-franc pieces until 1876, yet limitation began with 1874. See W. A. Shaw, *The History of the Currency*, pp. 194, 196.

[3] These figures are compiled from data given in W. A. Shaw, *The History of the Currency*, p. 159, and *Reports of the Director of the Mint*.

gold had largely driven out silver. By 1873, gold had again largely disappeared, and it seems evident that it would have disappeared entirely had not the suspension of the free coinage of silver followed. A continuance

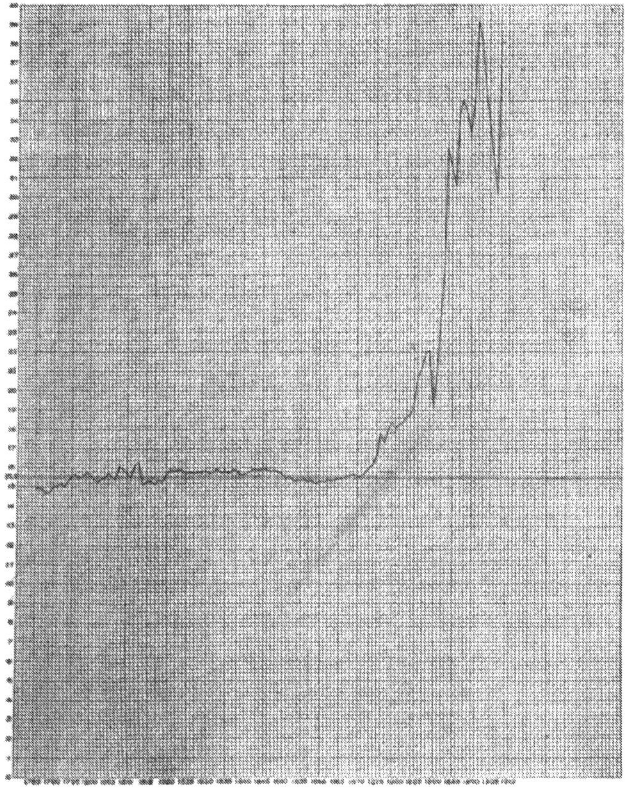

FIG. 9.

of bimetallism at a ratio of 15½ to 1 by France and the Latin Union alone would doubtless have been impossible. Yet the attempt, though a failure, would have kept the ratio nearer 15½ to 1 than it actually has been;

for the Union would have furnished a large market for silver. Possibly bimetallism could have been maintained longer, despite increased silver production, had not several other countries adopted the gold standard in these critical years. This fact helped to flood the countries of the Latin Union with silver and drain them of their gold. These countries were suffering all the expense and trouble of maintaining the ratio between gold and silver, while other countries were reaping most of the benefits. Herein lies one of the weaknesses of bimetallism as a practical political proposition, — each country prefers that some other country or countries should be the ones to adopt it. There is little prospect, therefore, in the future, of any single country taking the initiative, and still less of any international agreement.

§ 7

The system now in use in France is also employed in many other countries which, like France, have been forced to adopt it or else become silver-standard countries. After the rupture of the bimetallic tie, which until 1873 linked all gold and silver countries together, the commercial world broke into two parts, gold-standard countries and silver-standard countries; and many desiring to join the ranks of the former, but in danger of being thrust among the latter, saved themselves by closing their mints to silver and thereby adopting the limping standard. One of these countries was British India.

The case of India is interesting because it never was a bimetallic country, and at the time of the adoption of the present system, in which gold is the standard, no gold was in circulation. The mints were closed to silver in June, 1893, and the legal ratio put the rupee at 16*d*. At first, to the great discomfiture of those who had advocated the new system, this value was not maintained. But failure at first was to be expected because no gold was in circulation, and unsuspected coined stores of silver existed to swell the circulation in spite of the closure of the mints. Moreover, the government accepted from banks and others considerable amounts of silver which had been shipped to India before the closing of the mints, and coined it, and a considerable amount was withdrawn from the government reserve and put into circulation. The value of the rupee fell by 1895 to as low as 13*d*. But even from the first the value of the rupee kept above the value of its contained silver. If it fell as compared with the then appreciating gold, it rose as compared with the value of silver bullion. Surely this may be held to show that the value of money has some relation to its quantity, apart altogether from the quantity and the value of the constituent material. Furthermore, the value of the rupee rose gradually, even in relation to the gold standard, from 13*d*. in 1895 to 15½ in 1898 and to 16*d*., the legal par, by 1899, where it has since remained. As the Indian government has, during the last decade, paid out rupees for gold on demand, at this rate, the value of the rupee cannot go appreciably higher. Should it do so, gold would be presented for rupees, more rupees would have to be issued, and this would continue until their value had fallen to 16*d*. per rupee.[1]

The system of India is virtually the gold-exchange standard described in § 4. The same system is now in

[1] For a brief history and discussion of the Indian experience, see E. W. Kemmerer, *Money and Credit Instruments in their Relation to Prices*, pp. 36–39.

successful operation in the Philippines, in Mexico, and in Panama.[1] It withstood a severe test in India when, in 1908, the trade balance was "adverse" and required the sale of nearly £10,000,000 of bills on London before the Indian currency was sufficiently contracted to stem the tide.

§ 8

Among the nations which now have the limping standard is the United States. In 1792, Congress adopted complete bimetallism. Full legal-tender quality was given to both gold and silver coins; both were to be coined freely and without limit at the ratio of 15 ounces of silver to 1 of gold.

This soon came to be below the market ratio as affected by conditions abroad and especially in France. In consequence, gold tended to leave the country. It is impossible to state with exactness how soon this movement began, but Professor Laughlin sets it as early as 1810 and concludes that by 1818 little gold was in circulation.[2] America, although nominally a bimetallic country, became actually a silver country.

Influenced partly by the desire to bring gold back into circulation, and partly also, perhaps, by the supposed discoveries of gold in the South, Congress passed acts in 1834 and 1837 establishing the ratio of "16 to

[1] See Charles A. Conant, "The Gold Exchange Standard in the Light of Experience," *Economic Journal*, June, 1909, pp. 190–200; Hanna, Conant, and Jenks, *Report on the Introduction of the Gold Exchange Standard into China, the Philippine Islands, Panama, and other Silver-using Countries and on the Stability of Exchange*, Washington (Government Printing Office), 1904; Kemmerer, "Establishment of the Gold Exchange Standard in the Philippines," *Quarterly Journal of Economics*, August, 1905, pp. 600–605.

[2] *The History of Bimetallism in the United States*, New York (D. Appleton and Company), 1901, 4th ed., p. 29.

1," — or, more exactly, 16.002 to 1 in 1834 and 15.998 to 1 in 1837. Whereas silver money had been overvalued by the previous laws, by these new laws gold was overvalued. That is, the commercial ratio continued to be near 15½ to 1, while the monetary ratio was slightly greater. This remained the case up to 1850; consequently, in accordance with Gresham's Law, gold money, now the cheaper, drove out silver money, and the United States became a gold-standard country. In 1853, to prevent the exportation of our subsidiary silver coins, their weight was reduced.

The United States continued to be a gold-using country until the period of the Civil War, during which "greenbacks," or United States notes, were issued in considerable excess. Again Gresham's Law came into operation. Gold was in turn driven from the currency, and the United States came to a paper standard.[1] For some years after the close of the war the country remained on a paper standard, little gold being in circulation except on the Pacific coast, and not much silver anywhere.

In 1873 Congress passed a law (called by bimetallists the "Crime of '73") by which the standard silver dollar was entirely omitted from the list of authorized coins.

Of course this could not have had any immediate effect on the value of gold and silver, because the country was at the time on a paper basis. But when specie payments (*i.e.* gold and silver payments) were resumed in 1879, this repeal of the free coinage of silver brought the country to a gold standard, not to a silver one.

[1] See especially Wesley Clair Mitchell, *History of the Greenbacks*, Chicago (The University of Chicago Press), 1903; also his *Gold, Prices, and Wages under the Greenback Standard*, Berkeley, California (University of California Press), 1908.

Had it not been for the law of 1873, the United States, when it returned in 1879 to a metallic basis, would have been a silver country with a standard considerably below the gold standard it actually reached. Our monetary problems would then have been very different from what they actually became.

But in returning to a gold basis we reintroduced the silver dollar in a minor *rôle*. Although the free coinage of silver was not resumed, the advocates of silver, through the "Bland-Allison Act" of 1878 and the "Sherman Act" of 1890, which replaced it, succeeded in pledging the government to the purchase of large, but not unlimited, amounts of silver and the coinage of a large, but not unlimited, number of silver dollars. The Bland-Allison Act required the Secretary of the Treasury to purchase every month from $2,000,000 to $4,000,000 worth of silver and to coin it into standard silver dollars. The Sherman Act required the purchase every month of 4,500,000 ounces of silver.

Under these acts 554,000,000 silver dollars were coined, although less than 20 per cent of them have ever been in actual circulation. Silver certificates redeemable in silver dollars on demand, and, for a time treasury notes, have circulated in the place of this immense mass of silver. The silver dollars (and therefore the silver certificates) maintain their value on a parity with gold primarily because they are limited in amount. If any question were raised as to their parity with gold, the treasury would probably offer to specifically redeem them in gold. No law directly provides for the redemption of silver in gold, but it is made the duty of the Secretary of the Treasury to take such measures as will maintain its parity with gold.

In 1893 the Sherman Act was repealed, and in 1900 a law was passed specifically declaring that the United States shall be on a gold basis.

§ 9

The system of the limping standard, now obtaining in the United States, logically forms a connecting link between complete bimetallism and those "composite" systems by which *any* number of different kinds of money may be simultaneously kept in circulation. The manner in which most modern civilized states have solved the problem of concurrent circulation has been to use gold as a standard, and to use silver, nickel, and copper chiefly as subsidiary money, limited in quantity, with, in most cases, limited amounts of paper money, the latter being usually redeemable. The possible variations of this composite system are unlimited. In the United States at present we have a system which is very complicated and objectionable in many of its features — especially (as we shall presently see) in its lack of elasticity. Gold is the standard and is freely coined. A limited number of silver dollars, worth, moneywise, more than double their value bullionwise, are a heritage of former bimetallic laws long since rendered inoperative by the paper money of the Civil War and expressly repealed in 1873. The two attempts of 1878 and 1890 to return halfway to bimetallism by the purchase of silver — attempts discontinued in 1893 — have greatly swollen the volume of coined silver. The attempt to force silver dollars into circulation was not acceptable to the business world, and Congress therefore issued instead the two forms of paper mentioned. The chief form is the "silver certificate." For each silver certificate a silver dollar is kept in the vaults of the United States government.

The absurdity of the situation consists in the fiction that somehow the silver keeps paper at par with gold. The paper would keep its parity with gold just as well if there were no silver. A silver dollar as silver is worth less than a gold dollar just as truly as a paper dollar, as paper, is worth less than a gold dollar. The fact that the silver is worth more than the paper will not avail in the least to make the paper worth a whole dollar so long as the silver is not itself worth a whole dollar. A pillar which reaches only halfway to the ceiling cannot hold the ceiling up any more than a pillar an inch high.

The paper representatives of silver would continue to circulate as well as they do now, even if the "silver behind them" were nonexistent, although the absurdity of the situation would then be so apparent that they would probably be retired. Whether the half billion dollars of new currency, which came into circulation with the Bland and Sherman Acts, are of silver, overvalued to the extent of 50 per cent, or of paper, overvalued to the extent of 100 per cent, does not really affect the principle of the limping standard which keeps silver dollars at par with gold. The idle silver in the treasury vaults represents mere waste, a subsidy given by the government to encourage silver mining. Its only real effect to-day is to mislead the public into the belief that in some way it keeps or helps to keep silver certificates at par with *gold*;[1] whereas they are kept at par by the limitation on its amount. The

[1] Seager, in his *Introduction to Economics*, 3d ed., New York (Holt), 1908, p. 317, urges that the government should attempt gradually to dispose of this silver and substitute an equal value of gold.

silver and its paper representatives cannot fall below par without displacing gold, and they cannot displace gold because there are not enough of them.

Another and equally useless anomaly is the existing volume of "greenbacks." These are United States government notes. Under the law of 1875, the greenbacks were by 1879 retired in sufficient numbers to restore parity with gold; but by a counterlaw of 1878, 347,000,000 of them were kept in circulation and are in circulation now. As soon as redeemed, they must be reissued; they cannot be retired. They are a fixed ingredient in our money *pot pourri*, neither expansive nor shrinkable. They have been kept at par with gold because: (1) they are limited in amount; (2) they are redeemable in gold on demand; (3) they are receivable for taxes and are legal tender. But it is absurd to redeem but not retire — in fact, almost a contradiction in terms. This absurdity has at times seriously embarrassed the government.

The next feature of our currency to be considered is the bank note. Although the National Bank acts wiped out the old, ill-assorted state bank notes, it tied the new notes up with the war debt, and they have remained so tied ever since, in spite of the fact that the advantages of the connection have long been terminated and the disadvantages have grown acute. National bank notes cannot legally be issued in excess of the government debt, however urgent the need for them; nor can the government pay its debt without thereby compelling national banks to cancel their notes.

One of the curious anomalies of the situation is that the prices of United States bonds are so high, and therefore the rate of interest returned on these bonds so low that there is actually less inducement to issue bank notes in regions where the rate of interest is high, as in the West, than in regions where it is low, as in the East.

The result is an inelastic currency which, instead of adjusting itself to the seasonal fluctuations in trade, and thus mitigating the ensuing variations in the price level, remains a hard and solid mass to which the other elements in the equation of exchange must adapt themselves.[1]

The remaining features of our currency system, such as fractional and minor coins, adjusted to public demand, are satisfactory. The gold and currency certificates of deposit are scarcely independent features, as they are simply government receipts for public convenience representing the deposit of gold or greenbacks.

The recent status in the United States two years ago is represented in the table on the opposite page taken from Comptrollers' Reports and Treasurers' Reports. It is part of a more complete table constructed by one of my students, Mr. W. F. Hickernell.

The table omits figures for state banks and trust companies, for which only rough estimates are available. Assuming that the estimates are approximately correct, we have a currency system in which gold, the basis of it all, enters as a little over one third the circulation and a little over half the money in banks used as reserves for deposits (and bank notes, though these are guaranteed by the government). The remaining money in circulation, nearly two thirds, consists almost wholly of inelastic and almost constant elements. Consequently, a change in the quantity

[1] The Aldrich-Vreeland bill of 1908 has not changed this situation. However helpful it may be in mitigating the evils of crises, it does not give elasticity of the currency in ordinary times. At least it has thus far shown no tendency to do so.

of gold in circulation will not cause a proportional change in the quantity of all money in circulation, but only about one third as much. Since, however, almost all the money can be used as bank reserves, even bank notes being so used by state banks and trust companies, the proportionate relations between money in circulation, money in reserves, and bank deposits will hold true approximately as the normal condition of affairs. The legal requirements as to reserves strengthen the tendency to preserve such relationship.

	GOLD	SILVER	U.S. NOTES	BANK NOTES	FRAC. SILVER	MINOR COINS
In U. S. Treasury	305[1]	10[4]	4	15	9	2
In national banks . . .	312[2]	94[5]	161	0[7]	13	44
Outside both	850[3]	458[6]	181	589	109	

In the United States, then, we have a currency system in which gold, the basis of it all, constitutes directly, or by means of gold certificates, about one third of the total monetary circulation, and in which the remainder consists almost wholly of elements which are inelastic and almost unchangeable. Consequently, to meet any

[1] "Free" gold (*i.e.* exclusive of gold held in Treasury for gold certificates held by the public).

[2] Including 189 millions of gold certificates for which gold was on deposit in the United States government vaults.

[3] Including 411 millions of gold certificates for which gold was on deposit in the United States government vaults.

[4] "Free" (*i.e.* exclusive of silver held in the Treasury for silver certificates held by the public).

[5] Including 82 millions of silver certificates for which silver was on deposit in the United States government vaults.

[6] Including 388 millions of silver certificates for which silver was on deposit in the United States government vaults.

[7] The notes are not lawful bank reserves, and hence are not reported by national banks.

modification in other factors of the equation of exchange, — such, for instance, as trade, — the gold in circulation must bear the burden. As gold requires time for minting or transportation, the adjustment is slow and clumsy as compared with the prompt issue or retirement of bank notes practiced in other countries. The seasonal changes in the purchasing power of money, as well as the changes connected with crises and credit cycles, are therefore greatly and unnecessarily aggravated.

CHAPTER VIII

INFLUENCE OF QUANTITY OF MONEY AND OTHER FACTORS ON PURCHASING POWER AND ON EACH OTHER

§ 1

THE chief purpose of the foregoing chapters is to set forth the causes determining the purchasing power of money. This purchasing power has been studied as the effect of five, and only five, groups of causes. The five groups are money, deposits, their velocities of circulation, and the volume of trade. These and their effects, prices, we saw to be connected by an equation called the equation of exchange, $MV + M'V' = \Sigma pQ$. The five causes, in turn, we found to be themselves effects of antecedent causes lying entirely outside of the equation of exchange, as follows: the volume of trade will be increased, and therefore the price level correspondingly decreased by the differentiation of human wants; by diversification of industry; and by facilitation of transportation. The velocities of circulation will be increased, and therefore also the price level increased by improvident habits; by the use of book credit; and by rapid transportation. The quantity of money will be increased, and therefore the price level increased correspondingly by the import and minting of money, and, antecedently, by the mining of the money metal; by the introduction of another and initially cheaper money metal through bimetallism; and by the issue of bank notes and other paper money. The quantity of deposits will be increased, and therefore the price level increased by extension of the banking system and by the use of book credit. The reverse causes produce, of course, reverse effects.

Thus, behind the five sets of causes which alone affect the purchasing power of money, we find over a dozen antecedent causes. If we chose to pursue the inquiry to still remoter stages, the number of causes would be found to increase at each stage in much the same way as the number of one's ancestors increases with each generation into the past. In the last analysis myriads of factors play upon the purchasing power of money; but it would be neither feasible nor profitable to catalogue them. The value of our analysis consists rather in simplifying the problem by setting forth clearly the five proximate causes through which all others whatsoever must operate. At the close of our study, as at the beginning, stands forth the equation of exchange as the great determinant of the purchasing power of money. With its aid we see that normally the quantity of deposit currency varies directly with the quantity of money, and that therefore the introduction of deposits does not disturb the relations we found to hold true before. That is, it is still true that (1) prices vary directly as the quantity of money, provided the volume of trade and the velocities of circulation remain unchanged; (2) that prices vary directly as the velocities of circulation (if these velocities vary together), provided the quantity of money and the volume of trade remain unchanged; and (3) that prices vary inversely as the volume of trade, provided the quantity of money — and therefore deposits — and their velocities remain unchanged.

§ 2

It is proposed in this chapter to inquire how far these propositions are really *causal* propositions. We shall study in detail the influence of each of the six magnitudes on each of the other five. This study will afford answers to the objections which have often been raised to the quantity theory of money.

To set forth all the facts and possibilities as to causation we need to study the effects of varying, one at a time, the various magnitudes in the equation of exchange. We shall in each case distinguish between the effects during transition periods and the ultimate or normal effects after the transition periods are finished. For simplicity we shall in each case consider the normal or ultimate effects first and afterward the abnormal or transitional effects.

Since almost all of the possible effects of changes in the elements of the equation of exchange have been already set forth in previous chapters, our task in this chapter is chiefly one of review and rearrangement.

Our first question therefore is: given (say) a doubling of the quantity of money in circulation (M), what are the normal or ultimate effects on the other magnitudes in the equation of exchange, viz.: M', V, V', the p's and the Q's?

We have seen, in Chapter III, that normally the effect of doubling money in circulation (M) is to double deposits (M') because under any given conditions of industry and civilization deposits tend to hold a fixed or normal ratio to money in circulation. Hence the ultimate effect of a doubling in M is the same as that of doubling both M and M'. We propose next to show that this doubling of M and M' does not normally change V, V' or the Q's, but only the p's. The equation of exchange of itself does not affirm or deny these propositions.

For aught the equation of exchange itself tells us, the quantities of money and deposits might even vary inversely as their respective velocities of circulation. Were this true, an increase in the quantity of money would exhaust all its effects in reducing the velocity of circulation, and could not produce any effect on prices. If the opponents of the "quantity theory" could establish such a relationship, they would have proven their case despite the equation of exchange. But they have not even attempted to prove such a proposition. As a matter of fact, the velocities of circulation of money and of deposits depend, as we have seen, on technical conditions and bear no discoverable relation to the quantity of money in circulation. Velocity of circulation is the average rate of "turnover," and depends on countless individual rates of turnover. These, as we have seen, depend on individual habits. Each person regulates his turnover to suit his convenience. A given rate of turnover for any person implies a given time of turnover — that is, an average length of time a dollar remains in his hands. He adjusts this time of turnover by adjusting his average quantity of pocket money, or till money, to suit his expenditures. He will try to avoid carrying too little lest, on occasion, he be unduly embarrassed; and on the other hand to avoid encumbrance, waste of interest, and risk of robbery, he will avoid carrying too much. Each man's adjustment is, of course, somewhat rough, and dependent largely on the accident of the moment; but, in the long run and for a large number of people, the average rate of turnover, or what amounts to the same thing, the average time money remains in the same hands, will be very closely determined. It will depend on density of population, commercial customs, rapidity of transport, and other technical conditions, but not on the quantity of money and deposits nor on the price level. These may change without any effect on velocity. If the quantities of money and deposits are doubled, there is nothing, so far as velocity of circulation is concerned, to prevent the price level from doubling. On the contrary, doubling money, deposits, and prices would necessarily leave velocity quite unchanged. Each individual would need to spend more money for the same goods, and to keep more on hand. The ratio of money expended to money on hand would not vary. If the number of dollars in circulation and in deposit should be doubled and a dollar should come to have only half its former purchasing power, the change would imply merely that twice as many dollars as before were expended by each person and twice as many kept on hand. The ratio of expenditure to stock on hand would be unaffected.

If it be objected that this *assumes* that with the doubling in M and M' there would be also a doubling of prices, we may meet the objection by putting the argument in a slightly different form. Suppose, for a moment, that a doubling in the currency in circulation should not at once raise prices, but should halve the velocities instead; such a result would evidently upset for each individual the adjustment which he had made of cash on hand. Prices being unchanged, he now has double the amount of money and deposits which his convenience had taught him to keep on hand. He will then try to get rid of the surplus money and deposits by buying goods. But as somebody else must be found to take the money off his hands, its mere transfer will not diminish the amount in the community. It will simply increase somebody else's surplus. Everybody has money on his hands beyond what experience and convenience have shown to be necessary. Everybody will want to exchange this relatively useless extra money for goods, and the desire so to do must surely drive up the price of goods. No one can deny that the effect of every one's desiring to spend more money will be to raise prices. Obviously this tendency will continue until there is found another adjustment of quantities to expenditures, and the V's are the same as originally. That is, if there is no change in the quantities sold (the Q's), the only possible effect of doubling M and M' will be a doubling of the p's; for we have just seen that the V's cannot be permanently reduced without causing people to have surplus money and deposits, and there cannot be surplus money and deposits without a desire to spend it, and there cannot be a desire to spend it without a rise in prices. In short, the only way to get rid of a plethora of money is to raise prices to correspond.

So far as the surplus deposits are concerned, there might seem to be a way of getting rid of them by canceling bank loans, but this would reduce the normal ratio which M' bears to M, which we have seen tends to be maintained.

We come back to the conclusion that the velocity of circulation either of money or deposits is independent of the quantity of money or of deposits. No reason has been, or, so far as is apparent, can be assigned, to show why the velocity of circulation of money, or deposits, should be different, when the quantity of money, or deposits, is great, from what it is when the quantity is small.

There still remains one seeming way of escape from

the conclusion that the sole effect of an increase in the quantity of money in circulation will be to increase prices. It may be claimed — in fact it has been claimed — that such an increase results in an increased volume of trade. We now proceed to show that (except during transition periods) the volume of trade, like the velocity of circulation of money, is independent of the quantity of money. An inflation of the currency cannot increase the product of farms and factories, nor the speed of freight trains or ships. The stream of business depends on natural resources and technical conditions, not on the quantity of money. The whole machinery of production, transportation, and sale is a matter of physical capacities and technique, none of which depend on the quantity of money. The only way in which the quantities of trade appear to be affected by the quantity of money is by influencing trades accessory to the creation of money and to the money metal. An increase of gold money will, as has been noted, bring with it an increase in the trade in gold objects. It will also bring about an increase in the sales of gold mining machinery, in gold miners' services, in assaying apparatus and labor. These changes may entail changes in associated trades. Thus if more gold ornaments are sold, fewer silver ornaments and diamonds may be sold. Again the issue of paper money may affect the paper and printing trades, the employment of bank and government clerks, etc. In fact, there is no end to the minute changes in the Q's which the changes mentioned, and others, might bring about. But from a practical or statistical point of view they amount to nothing, for they could not add to nor subtract one tenth of 1 per cent from the general aggregate of trade. Only a very few Q's would be appreciably affected, and those few very insignificant. Probably no one will deny this, but some objectors might claim that, though technique of production and trade determine most of these things, nevertheless the Q's — the actual quantities of goods *exchanged for money and deposit currency* — might conceivably vary according as barter is or is not resorted to. If barter were as convenient as sale-and-purchase, this contention would have force. There would then be little need of distinguishing between money as the generally acceptable medium of exchange and other property as not generally acceptable. If all property were equally acceptable, all property would be equally money; or if there were many kinds of property nearly as exchangeable as money, resort to barter would be so easy that some of the goods sold for money could be almost equally well bartered for something else. But as long as there were any preference at all for the use of money, resort to barter would be reluctantly made and as a temporary expedient only. We have seen this when studying transition periods. Under normal conditions and in the long run only a negligible fraction of modern trade can be done through barter. We conclude, therefore, that a change in the quantity of money will not appreciably affect the quantities of goods sold for money.

Since, then, a doubling in the quantity of money: (1) will normally double deposits subject to check in the same ratio, and (2) will not appreciably affect either the velocity of circulation of money or of deposits or the volume of trade, it follows necessarily and mathematically that the level of prices must double. While, therefore, the equation of exchange, of itself, asserts no causal relations between quantity of money and price level, any more than it asserts a causal relation between any other two factors, yet, when we take into account conditions known quite apart from that equation, viz., that a change in M produces a proportional change in M', and no changes in V, V', or the Q's, there is no possible escape from the conclusion that a change in the quantity of money (M) must normally cause a proportional change in the price level (the p's).

One of the objectors to the quantity theory attempts to dispose of the equation of exchange as stated by Newcomb, by calling it a mere truism. While the equation of exchange is, if we choose, a mere "truism," based on the equivalence, in all purchases, of the money or checks expended, on the one hand, and what they buy, on the other, yet in view of supplementary knowledge as to the relation of M to M', and the non-relation of M to V, V', and the Q's, this equation is the means of demonstrating the fact that normally the p's vary directly as M, that is, demonstrating the quantity theory. "Truisms" should never be neglected. The greatest generalizations of physical science, such as that forces are proportional to mass and acceleration, are truisms, but, when duly supplemented by specific data, these truisms are the most fruitful sources of useful mechanical knowledge. To throw away contemptuously the equation of exchange because it is so obviously true is to neglect the chance to formulate for economic science some of the most important and exact laws of which it is capable.

We may now restate, then, in what causal sense the quantity theory is true. It is true in the sense that one of *the normal effects of an increase in the quantity of money is an exactly proportional increase in the general level of prices.*[1]

[1] Cf. Albert Aupetit, *Essai sur la théorie générale de la monnaie*, Paris (Guillaumin), 1901.

To deny this conclusion requires a denial of one or more of the following premises upon which it rests: —

(1) The equation of exchange, $MV + M'V' = \Sigma pQ$.

(2) An increase of M normally causes a proportional increase of M'.

(3) An increase of M does not normally affect V, V', or the Q's.

If these three premises be granted, the conclusion must be granted. If any of the premises be denied, the objector must show wherein the fallacy lies. Premise (1) has been justified in Chapter II and Chapter III, and mathematically demonstrated in the Appendices to Chapters II and III. Premise (2) has been shown to be true in Chapter III and premise (3) in the present chapter.

So much pains has been taken to establish these premises and to emphasize the results of the reasoning based on them because it seems nothing less than a scandal in Economic Science that there should be any ground for dispute on so fundamental a proposition.

The quantity theory as thus stated does not claim that while money is increased in quantity, *other* causes may not affect M', V, V', and the Q's, and thus aggravate or neutralize the effect of M on the p's. But these are not the effects of M on the p's. So far as M *by itself* is concerned, its effect on the p's is strictly proportional.

The importance and reality of this proposition are not diminished in the least by the fact that these other causes do not historically remain quiescent and allow the effect on the p's of an increase in M to be seen alone. The effects of M are blended with the effects of changes in the other factors in the equation of exchange just as the effects of gravity upon a falling body are blended with the effects of the resistance of the atmosphere.

Finally, it should be noted that, in accordance with principles previously explained, no great increase of money (M) in any one country or locality can occur without spreading to other countries or localities. As soon as local prices have risen enough to make it profitable to sell at the high prices in that place and buy at the low prices elsewhere, money will be exported. The production of gold in Colorado and Alaska first results in higher prices in Colorado and Alaska, then in sending gold to other sections of the United States, then in higher prices throughout the United States, then in export abroad, and finally in higher prices throughout the gold-using world.

§ 3

We have emphasized the fact that the strictly proportional effect on prices of an increase in M is only the *normal* or *ultimate* effect after transition periods are over. The proposition that prices vary with money holds true only as between two imaginary periods for each of which prices are stationary or are moving alike upward or downward and at the same rate.

As to the periods of transition, we have seen that an increase in M produces effects not only on the p's, but on all the magnitudes in the equation of exchange. We saw in Chapter IV on transition periods that it increases M' not only in its normal ratio to M, but often, temporarily, beyond that ratio. We saw that it also quickened V and V' temporarily.

As previously noted, while V and V' usually move in sympathy, they may move in opposite directions when a panic decreases confidence in bank deposits. Then people pay out deposits as rapidly as possible and money as slowly as possible — the last-named tendency being called hoarding.

We saw also that an increase of M during a period of rising prices stimulated the Q's. Finally we saw that a reduction in M caused the reverse effects of those above set forth, decreasing V and V', decreasing M' not absolutely only, but in relation to M, and decreasing the Q's partly because of the disinclination to sell at low money prices which are believed to be but temporary, partly because of a slight substitution of barter for sales; for if M should be very suddenly reduced, some way would have to be found to keep trade going, and barter would be temporarily resorted to in spite of its inconvenience. This would bring some relief, but its inconvenience would lead sellers to demand money whenever possible, and prospective buyers to supply themselves therewith. The great pressure to secure money would enhance its value — that is, would lower the prices of other things. This resultant fall of prices would make the currency more adequate to do the business required, and make less barter necessary. The fall would proceed until the abnormal pressure, due to the inconvenience of barter, had ceased. Practically, however, in the world of to-day, even such temporary resort to barter is trifling. The convenience of exchange by money is so much greater than the convenience of barter, that the price adjustment would be made almost at once. If barter needs to be seriously considered as a relief from money stringency, we shall be doing it full justice if we picture it as a safety-valve, working against a resistance so great as almost never to come into operation and then only for brief transition intervals. For all practical purposes and all normal cases, we may assume that money and checks are necessities for modern trade.

The peculiar effects during transition periods are analogous to the peculiar effects in starting or stopping a train of cars. Normally the caboose keeps exact pace with the locomotive, but when the train is starting or stopping this relationship is modified by the gradual transmission of effects through the intervening cars. Any special shock to one car is similarly transmitted to all the others and to the locomotive.

We have seen, for instance, that a sudden change in the quantity of money and deposits will temporarily affect their velocities of circulation and the volume of trade. Reversely, seasonal changes in the volume of trade will affect the velocities of circulation, and even, if the currency system is elastic, the quantity of money and deposits. In brisk seasons, as when "money is needed to move the crops," the velocity of circulation is evidently greater than in dull seasons. Money is kept idle at one time to be used at another, and such seasonal variations in velocity reduce materially the variations which otherwise would be necessary in the price level. In a similar way seasonal variations in the price level are reduced by the alternate expansion and contraction of an elastic bank currency. In this case temporarily, and to an extent limited by the amount of legal tender currency, money or deposits or both may be said to adapt themselves to the amount of trade. In these two ways, then, both the rise and fall of prices are mitigated.[1] Therefore the "quantity theory" will not hold true strictly and absolutely during transition periods.

[1] Cf. Hildebrand, *Theorie des Geldes*, Chapter XI, who, though seemingly unconscious of its bearing on the velocity of circulation, calls attention to the difference between two communities having the same expenditures, but one having a uniform trade and the other a trade "bunched" in certain seasons — say the crop seasons.

We have finished our sketch of the effects of M, and now proceed to the other magnitudes.

§ 4

As to deposits (M'), this magnitude is always dependent on M. Deposits are payable on demand in money. They require bank reserves of money, and there must be some relation between the amount of money in circulation (M), the amount of reserves (μ), and the amount of deposits (M'). Normally we have seen that the three remain in given ratios to each other. But what is a normal ratio at one state of industry and civilization may not be normal at another. Changes in population, commerce, habits of business men, and banking facilities and laws may produce great changes in this ratio. Statistically, as will be shown in Chapter XII, the ratio M'/M has changed from 3.1 to 4.1 in fourteen years.

Since M' is normally dependent on M, we need not ask what are the effects of an increase of M'; for these effects have been included under the effects of M. But, since the ratio of M' to M may change, we do need to ask what are the effects of this change.

Suppose, as has actually been the case in recent years, that the ratio of M' to M increases in the United States. If the magnitudes in the equations of exchange in other countries with which the United States is connected by trade are constant, the ultimate effect on M is to make it less than what it would otherwise have been, by increasing the exports of gold from the United States or reducing the imports. In no other way can the price level of the United States be prevented from rising above that of other nations in which we have assumed this level and the other magnitudes in the equation of exchange to be quiescent. While the ultimate effect then is to increase the volume of circulating media, this increase is spread over the whole world. Although the extension of banking is purely local, its effects are international. In fact, not only will there be a redistribution of gold money over all gold countries, but there will be a tendency to melt coin into bullion for use in the arts.

The remaining effects are the same as those of an increase in M which have already been studied. That is, there will be no (ultimate) appreciable effect on V, V', or the Q's, but only on the p's, and these will rise, relatively to what they would otherwise have been, throughout the world. In foreign countries the normal effect will be proportional to the increase of money in circulation which they have acquired through the displacement of gold in the United States. In the United States the effect will not be proportional to the increase in M', since M has moved in the opposite direction. It will be proportional to the increase in $M + M'$ if V and V' are equal, and less than in that proportion if V is less than V', as is the actual fact.

In any case the effect on prices is extremely small, being spread over the whole commercial world. Taking the world as a whole, the ultimate effect is, as we have seen, to raise world prices slightly and to melt some coin. The only appreciable ultimate effect of increasing the ratio of M' to M in one country is to expel money from that country into others. All of these effects are exactly the same as those of increasing the issue of bank notes, so long as they continue redeemable in gold or other exportable money. An issue beyond this point results in isolating the issuing country and therefore in rapidly raising prices there instead of spreading the effect over other countries. This is what happened in the United States during the Civil War.

As to transitional effects, it is evident that, before the expulsion of gold from the United States, there must be an appreciable rise in prices there, of which traders will then take advantage by selling in the United States, shipping away money, and buying abroad. During the period of rising prices all the other temporary effects peculiar to such a period, effects which have been described at length elsewhere, will be in evidence.

Exactly opposite effects of course follow a decrease of M' relatively to M.

§ 5

We come next to the effects of changes in velocities (V and V'). These effects are closely similar to those just described. The ultimate effects are on prices, and not on quantity of money or volume of trade. But a change in the velocity of circulation of money in any country, connected by international trade with other countries, will cause an opposite change in the quantity of money in circulation in that country. There will be a redistribution of money among the countries of the world and of money metal as between money and the arts.

The normal effect, then, of increasing V or V' in any country is to decrease M by export, to decrease M' proportionally, and to raise prices (p's) slightly throughout the world. There is no reason to believe that there will, normally, be any effects on the volume of trade. It is quite possible that a change in one of the two velocities will cause a corresponding change in the other, or, at any rate, that most of the causes which increase one will increase the other. Increased density of population, for instance, in all probability quickens the flow both of money and checks. Unfortunately, however, we have not sufficient empirical knowledge of the two sorts of velocity to assert, with confidence, any relations between them

During transition periods the effects of changes in velocities are doubtless the same as the effects of increased currency.

§ 6

Our next question is as to the effects of a general increase or decrease in the Q's, *i.e.* in the volume of trade.

An increase of the volume of trade in any one country, say the United States, ultimately increases the money in circulation (M). In no other way could there be avoided a depression in the price level in the United States as compared with foreign countries. The increase in M brings about a proportionate increase in M'. Besides this effect, the increase in trade undoubtedly has some effect in modifying the habits of the community with regard to the proportion of check and cash transactions, and so tends somewhat to increase M' relatively to M; as a country grows more commercial the need for the use of checks is more strongly felt.[1]

As to effects on velocity of circulation, we may distinguish three cases. The first is where the change in volume of trade corresponds to a change in popula-

[1] This is very far from asserting as Laughlin does that "The limit to the increase in legitimate credit operations is always expansible with the increase in the actual movement of goods"; see the *Principles of Money*, New York (Scribner), 1903, p. 82. We have seen, in Chapter IV, that deposit currency is proportional to the amount of money; a change in trade may indirectly, *i.e.* by changing the *habits* of the community, influence the proportion, but, except for transition periods, it cannot influence it directly.

tion, as when there is an increase in trade from the settling of new lands, without any greater concentration in previously settled areas, and without any change in the per capita trade or in the distribution of trade among the elements of the population. Under such conditions no reason has been assigned, nor apparently can be assigned, to show why the velocity of circulation of money should be other for a condition in which the volume of trade is large than for a condition in which it is small.

The second case is where the increase in volume of trade corresponds to an increased *density* of population, but no change in per capita trade. In this case, the closer settlement may facilitate somewhat greater velocity.

The third case is where the change in the volume of trade *does* affect the per capita trade or the distribution of trade in the population.

There are then several ways in which the velocity of circulation may conceivably be affected. First, any change in trade, implying a change in methods of transportation of goods, will imply a change in methods of transportation of money; quick transportation means usually more rapid circulation.

Secondly, a changed distribution of trade will alter the relative expenditures of different persons. If their rates of turnover are different, a change in their expenditures will clearly alter the relative importance or weighting of these rates in the general average, thus changing that average without necessarily changing the individual rates of turnover. For instance, an increased trade in the southern states, where the velocity of circulation of money is presumably slow, would tend to lower the average velocity in the United States, simply by giving more weight to the velocity in the slower portions of the country.

Thirdly, a change in individual expenditures, when due to a real change in the quantity of goods purchased, may cause a change in individual velocities. It seems to be a fact that, at a given price level, the greater a man's expenditures the more rapid his turnover; that is, the rich have a higher rate of turnover than the poor. They spend money faster, not only absolutely but relatively to the money they keep on hand. Statistics collected at Yale University of a number of cases of individual turnover show this clearly.[1] In other words, the man who spends much, though he needs to carry more money than the man who spends little, does not need to carry as much in proportion to his expenditure. This is what we should expect; since, in general, the larger any operation, the more economically it can be managed. Professor Edgeworth[2] has shown that the same rule holds in banking. When two banks are consolidated, the reserve needed is less than the sum of the two previous reserves.

We may therefore infer that, if a nation grows richer per capita, the velocity of circulation of money will increase. This proposition, of course, has no reference to *nominal* increase of expenditure. As we have seen, a doubling of all prices and incomes would not affect anybody's rate of turnover of money. Each person would need to make exactly twice the expenditure for the same actual result and to keep on hand exactly twice the money in order to meet the same contingencies in the same way. The determinant of velocity is real expenditure, not nominal. But a person's real expenditure is only another name for his volume of trade. We

[1] See § 1 of Appendix to (this) Chapter VIII.

[2] "Mathematical Theory of Banking," *Journal of the Royal Statistical Society*, March, 1888.

conclude, therefore, that a change in the volume of trade, when it affects the *per capita* trade, affects velocity of circulation as well.

We find then that an increase in trade, unlike an increase in currency (M and M') or velocities (V and V') has other effects than simply on prices — effects, in fact, of increasing magnitudes on the opposite side of the equation, V and V', and (though only indirectly by affecting business convenience and habit) M' relatively to M. If these effects increase the left side as much as the increase in trade itself (the Q's) directly increases the right side, the effect on prices will be *nil*. If the effect on the left side exceeds that on the right, prices will rise. Only provided the effect on the left side is less than the increase in trade will prices fall, and then not proportionately to the increase in trade.

In a former chapter, it was shown that a change in trade, *provided currency (M and M') and velocities (V and V') remained the same*, produced an inverse change in prices. But now we find that the proviso is inconsistent with the premise; currency and velocities can remain the same only by the clumsy hypothesis that the various other causes affecting them shall be so changed as exactly to neutralize the increase in trade. If these various other causes remain the same, then currency and velocities will not remain the same.

This is the first instance in our study where we have found that normally, *i.e.* apart from temporary or transitional effects, we reach different results by assuming *causes* to vary one at a time, than by assuming the algebraic *factors in the equation* to vary one at a time. The "quantity theory" still holds true — that prices (p's) vary with money (M) — when we assume that other *causes* remain the same, as well as when we assumed merely that other algebraic *factors* remain the same; and all the other theorems stated algebraically were found to hold causationally, excepting only the theorem as to variation in trade. While the main purpose of this chapter is to justify the "quantity theory" as expressing a causal as well as an algebraic relation, it is important to point out that causal and algebraic theorems are not always identical.

As to the transitional effects of a change in the volume of trade, these depend mainly on one of the two possible directions in which prices move. If they move upward, the transitional effects are similar to those we are already familiar with for periods of rising prices; if downward, they are similar to those incident to such a movement.

§ 7

We have now studied the effects of variations in each of the factors in the equation of exchange (save one) on the other factors. We have found that in each case except in the case of trade (the Q's) the ultimate effect was on prices (the p's). The only group of factors which we have not yet studied as cause are the prices (p's) themselves. Hitherto they have been regarded solely as effects of the other factors. But the objectors to the quantity theory have maintained that prices should be regarded as causes rather than as effects. Our next problem, therefore, is to examine and criticize this proposition.

So far as I can discover, *except to a limited extent during transition periods, or during a passing season* (e.g. *the fall*), there is no truth whatever in the idea that the price level is an independent cause of changes in any of the other magnitudes M, M', V, V', or the Q's. To show the untenability of such an idea let us grant for the sake of argument that — in some other way than as the effect of changes in M, M', V, V', and the Q's — the prices in (say) the United States are changed to (say) double their original level, and let us see what effect this cause will produce on the other magnitudes in the equation.

It is clear that the equality between the money side and the goods side must be maintained somehow, and that if the prices are raised the quantity of money or the quantity of deposits or their velocities must be raised, or else the volume of business must be reduced. But examination will show that none of these solutions is tenable.

The quantity of money cannot be increased. No money will come from abroad, for we have seen that a place with high prices drives money away. The consequence of the elevation of prices in the United States will be that traders will sell in the United States where prices are high, and take the proceeds in money and buy abroad where prices are low. It will be as difficult to make money flow into a country with high prices as to make water run up hill.

For similar reasons money will not come in *via* the mint. Since bullion and gold coin originally had the same value relatively to goods, after the supposed doubling of prices, gold coin has lost half its purchasing power. No one will take bullion to the mint when he thereby loses half its value. On the contrary, as we saw in a previous chapter, the result of high prices is to make men melt coin.

Finally, the high prices will not stimulate mining, but on the contrary they will discourage it, nor will high prices discourage consumption of gold, but on the contrary they will stimulate it. These tendencies have all been studied in detail. Every principle we have found regulating the distribution of money among nations (the distribution of money metal as between money and the arts or the production and consumption of metals) works exactly opposite to what would be necessary in order to bring money to fit prices instead of prices to fit money.

It is equally absurd to expect high prices to increase the quantity of deposits (M'). We have seen that the effect would be to diminish the quantity of money in circulation (M); but this money is the basis of the deposit currency (M'), and the shrinkage of the first will entail the shrinkage of the second. The reduction of M and M' will not tend to favor, but on the contrary will tend to pull down the high prices we have arbitrarily assumed.

The appeal to the velocities (V and V') is no more satisfactory. These have already been adjusted to suit individual convenience. To double them might not be a physical possibility, and would certainly be a great inconvenience.

There is left the forlorn hope that the high prices will diminish trade (the Q's). But if all prices including the prices of services are doubled, there is no reason why trade should be reduced. Since the average person will not only pay, but also receive high prices, it is evident that the high prices he gets will exactly make him able to stand the high prices he pays without having to reduce his purchases.

We conclude that the hypothesis of a doubled price level acting as an independent cause controlling the other factors in the equation of exchange and uncontrolled by them is untenable. Any attempt to maintain artificially high prices must result, as we have seen, not in adjusting the other elements in the equation of exchange to suit these high prices, but on the contrary in arousing their antagonism. Gold will go abroad and into the melting pot, will be produced less and consumed more until its scarcity as money will pull down the prices. *The price level is normally the one absolutely passive element in the equation of exchange.* It is controlled solely by the other elements and the causes antecedent to them, but exerts no control over them.

But though it is a fallacy to think that the price level in any community can, in the long run, affect the money in *that* community, it is true that the price level in one community may affect the money in *another* community. This proposition has been repeatedly made use of in our discussion, and should be clearly distinguished from the fallacy above mentioned. The price level in an outside community is an influence outside the equation of exchange of that community, and operates by affecting its money in circulation and not by directly affecting its price level. The price level outside of New York City, for instance, affects the price level in New York City only *via* changes in the money in New York City. Within New York City it is the money which influences the price level, and not the price level which influences the money. The price level is effect and not cause. Moreover, although the price level outside of New York is a proximate cause of changes of money in New York, that price level in turn is cause only in a secondary sense, being itself an effect of the other factors in the equation of exchange outside of New York City. For the world as a whole the price level is not even a secondary cause, but solely an effect — of the world's money, deposits, velocities, and trade.

We have seen that high prices in any *place* do not cause an increase of the money supply there; for money flows *away* from such a place. In the same way high prices at any *time* do not cause an increase of money at that time; for money, so to speak, flows *away* from that time. Thus if the price level is high in January as compared with the rest of the year, bank notes will not tend to be issued in large quantities then. On the contrary, people will seek to avoid paying money at the high prices and wait till prices are lower. When that time comes they may need more currency; bank notes and deposits may then expand to meet the excessive demands for loans which may ensue. Thus currency expands when prices are low and contracts when prices are high, and such expansion and contraction tend to lower the high prices and raise the low prices, thus working toward mutual equality. We see then that, so far from its being true that high prices cause increased supply of money, it is true that money avoids the place and time of high prices and seeks the place and time of low prices, thereby mitigating the inequality of price levels.

What has been said presupposes that purchasers have the option to change the place and time of their purchases. To the extent that their freedom to choose their market place or time is interfered with, the corrective adjustment of the quantity of money is prevented. The anomalous time of a panic may even be characterized by necessity to meet old contracts which afford no choice of deferring the payment. There may then be a "money famine" and a feverish demand for emergency currency needed to liquidate outstanding contracts which would never have been entered into if the situation had been foreseen. That such anomalous conditions do not negative the general thesis that prices are the effect and not the cause of currency (including deposit currency) is shown statistically by Minnie Throop England.[1]

§ 8

Were it not for the fanatical refusal of some economists to admit that the price level is in ultimate analysis effect and not cause, we should not be at so great pains to prove it beyond cavil. It is due our science to demonstrate its truths. The obligation to do this carries with it the obligation to explain if possible why so obvious a truth has not been fully accepted.

One reason has already been cited, the fear to give aid and comfort to the enemies of all sound economists, — the unsound money men. Another may now receive attention, viz. the fallacious idea that the price level cannot be determined by other factors in the equation of exchange because it is already determined by other causes, usually alluded to as "supply and demand." This vague phrase has covered multitudes of sins of slothful analysts in economics. Those who place such implicit reliance on the competency of supply and demand to fix prices, irrespective of the quantity of money, deposits, velocity, and trade, will have their confidence rudely shaken if they will follow the reasoning as to price causation of separate articles. They will find that there are always just one *too few equations* to determine the unknown quantities involved.[2] The equation of exchange is needed in each

[1] "Statistical inquiry into the influence of credit upon the level of prices," *University Studies* (University of Nebraska), January, 1907, pp. 41–83.

[2] Cf. Irving Fisher, "Mathematical Investigations in the Theory

case to supplement the equations of supply and demand.

It would take us too far afield to insert here a complete statement of price-determining principles. But the compatibility of the equation of exchange with the equations which have to deal with prices individually may be brought home to the reader sufficiently for our present purposes by emphasizing the distinction between (1) individual prices relatively to each other and (2) the price *level*. The equation of exchange determines the latter (the price level) only, and the latter only is the subject of this book. It will not help, but only hinder the reader to mix with the discussion of price levels the principles determining individual prices relatively to each other. It is amazing how tenaciously many people cling to the mistaken idea that an individual price, though expressed in money, may be determined wholly without reference to money. Others, more open-minded but almost equally confused, see the necessity of including the quantity of money among the causes determining prices, but in the careless spirit of eclecticism simply jumble it in with a miscellaneous collection of influences affecting prices, with no regard for their mutual relations. It should be clearly recognized that price *levels* must be studied independently of individual *prices*.

The legitimacy of separating the study of price levels from that of prices will be clearly recognized, when it is seen that individual prices cannot be fully determined by supply and demand, money cost of production, etc., without surreptitiously introducing the price level itself. We can scarcely overemphasize the fact that

and Value of Prices," *Transactions of the Connecticut Academy of Arts and Sciences*, Vol. IX, 1892, p. 62.

the "supply and demand" or the "cost of production" of goods in terms of money do not and cannot completely determine prices. Each phrase, fully expressed, already implies *money*. There is always hidden somewhere the assumption of a general price level. Yet writers, like David A. Wells,[1] have seriously sought the explanation of a general change in price levels in the individual price changes of various commodities considered separately. Much of their reasoning goes no farther than to explain one price in terms of other prices. If we attempt to explain the *money* price of a finished product in terms of the *money* prices of its raw materials and other *money* costs of prices of production, it is clear that we merely shift the problem. We have *still* to explain these antecedent prices. In elementary textbooks much emphasis is laid on the fact that "demand" and "supply" are incomplete designations and that to give them meaning it is necessary to add to each the phrase "at a price." But emphasis also needs to be laid on the fact that "demand at a price" and "supply at a price" are *still* incomplete designations, and that to give them meaning it is necessary to add "at a price level." The demand for sugar is not only relative to the price of sugar, but also to the general level of other things. Not only is the demand for sugar at ten cents a pound greater than the demand at twenty cents a pound (at a given level of prices of other things), but the demand at twenty cents *at a high level of prices* is greater than the demand at twenty cents *at a low level of prices*. In fact if the price level is doubled, the demand at twenty cents a pound will be as great as the demand was before

[1] *Recent Economic Changes*, New York (Appleton), 1890, Chapter IV.

at ten cents a pound, assuming that the doubling applies likewise to wages and incomes generally. The significance of a dollar lies in what it will buy; and the equivalence between sugar and dollars is at bottom an equivalence between sugar and *what dollars will buy.* A change in the amount of what dollars will buy is as important as a change in the amount of sugar. The price of sugar in dollars depends partly on sugar and partly on dollars, — that is, on what dollars will buy — that is, on the price level. Therefore, beneath the price of sugar in particular there lies, as one of the bases of that particular price, the general level of prices. We have more need to study the price level preparatory to a study of the price of sugar than to study the price of sugar preparatory to a study of the price level. We cannot explain the level of the sea by the height of its individual waves; rather must we explain in part the position of these waves by the general level of the sea. Each "supply curve" or "demand curve" rests upon the unconscious assumption of a price level already existing. Although the curves relate to a commodity, they relate to it only as compared with money. A price is a ratio of exchange between the commodity and money. The money side of each exchange must never be forgotten nor the fact that money already stands in the mind of the purchaser for a general purchasing power. Although every buyer and seller who bids or offers a price for a particular commodity tacitly assumes a given purchasing power of the money bid or offered, he is usually as unconscious of so doing as the spectator of a picture is unconscious of the fact that he is using the background of the picture against which to measure the figures in the foreground. As a consequence, if the general level changes, the supply and demand curves for the particular commodity considered will change accordingly. If the purchasing power of the dollar is reduced to half its former amount, these curves will be doubled in height; for each person will give or take double the former money for a given quantity of the commodity. If, through special causes affecting a special commodity, the supply and demand curves of that commodity and their intersection are raised or lowered, then the supply and demand curves of some other goods must change in the reverse direction. That is, if one commodity rises in price (without any change in the quantity of it or of other things bought and sold, and without any change in the volume of circulating medium or in the velocity of circulation), then other commodities must *fall* in price. The increased money expended for this commodity will be taken from other purchases. In other words, the waves in the sea of prices have troughs. This can be seen from the equation of exchange. If we suppose the quantity of money and its velocity of circulation to remain unaltered, the left side of the equation remains the same, and therefore the right side must remain unaltered also. Consequently, any increase in one of its many terms, due to an increase of any individual price, must occur at the expense of the remaining terms.

It is, of course, true that a decrease in the price of any particular commodity will usually be accompanied by an increase in the amount of it exchanged, so that the product of the two may not decrease and may even increase if the amount exchanged increases sufficiently. In this case, since the right side of our equation remains the same, the effect of the increase in some terms will necessarily be a decrease in others; and the remaining terms of the right side must decrease to some extent. The effect may be a general or even a universal lowering of prices. Even in this case the reduction in the price level has no direct connection with the reduction in the price of the particular commodity, but is due to the increase in the amount of it exchanged.[1]

The reactionary effect of the price of one commodity on the prices of other commodities must never be lost sight of. Much confusion will be escaped if we give up any attempt to reason directly from individual prices. Improvements in production will affect price levels simply as they affect the volume of business transacted. Any rational study of the influence of improvements in methods of production upon the level of prices should, therefore, fix attention, first, on the resulting volume of trade, and should aim to discover whether this, in turn, carries prices upwards or downwards.

One of the supposed causes of high prices to-day, much under discussion at the present time, is that of industrial and labor combinations. From what has been said, it must be evident that, other things remaining equal, trusts cannot affect the general level of prices through manipulating special commodities except as they change the amounts sold. If prices for one commodity are changed without a change in the number of sales, the effect on the price level will be neutralized by compensatory changes in other prices. If trade unions seek to raise prices of labor while trusts raise prices of commodities, the general level of everything may rise or fall; but it can rise only by a general decrease in the quantities of commodities, labor, etc., sold, or by an increase of currency, or by an increase in velocities of circulation. If there is neither an increase

[1] For further discussion, see § 2 of Appendix to (this) Chapter VIII.

nor decrease in volume of business, and if the quantity and velocity of circulation of money and its substitutes remain unchanged, the price level cannot change. Changes in some parts of the price level may occur only at the expense of opposite changes in other parts.

We have seen that the price level is not determined by individual prices, but that, on the contrary, any individual price presupposes a price level. We have seen that the complete and only explanation of a price level is to be sought in factors of the equation of exchange and whatever antecedent causes affect those factors. The terms "demand" and "supply," used in reference to particular prices, have no significance whatever in explaining a rise or fall of price *levels*. In considering the influence affecting individual prices we say that an increase in supply lowers prices, but an increase in demand raises them. But in considering the influences affecting price *levels* we enter upon an entirely different set of concepts, and must not confuse the proposition that an increase in the *trade* (the Q's) tends to lower the price *level*, with the proposition that an increase in supply tends to lower an individual price. Trade (the Q's) is not supply — in fact is no more to be associated with supply than with demand. The Q's are the quantities finally sold by those who supply, and bought by those who demand.

We may here state a paradox which will serve to bring out clearly the distinction between the causation of individual prices relatively to each other and the causation of the general level of prices. The paradox is that although an increased demand for any individual commodity results in a greater consumption *at a higher price*, yet an increased general demand for goods will result in a greater trade (the Q's) *at lower prices*.

We cannot, therefore, reason directly from particular to general prices; we can reason only indirectly by reference to the effects on quantities. Sometimes the rise in an individual price raises and at other times lowers the general price level.[1] To draw a physical parallel let us suppose that a thousand piles have been driven in a quicksand and that the owner wishes to raise their level a foot. He gets hoisting apparatus and planting it on the piles pulls one of them up a foot. He then pulls up another and continues until he has pulled up each of the thousand. But if every time he has pulled one up a foot he has pushed down 999 over $\frac{1}{999}$ of a foot, when he has finished, he will find his thousand piles lower than when he began. Each time a pile has risen, the average level of all has fallen.

The proposition that a general increase in demand, resulting in an increase in trade, tends to decrease and and not to increase the general level of prices, may be regarded as a sort of *pons asinorum* to test one's knowledge of the fundamental distinction between those influences affecting the general price level and those affecting the rise and fall of a particular price with respect to that level.

§ 9

We have seen that the various factors represented in the equation of exchange do not stand on the same causal footing. Prices are the passive element and their general level must conform to the other factors. The causal propositions we have found to be true normally, *i.e.* after transitions are completed, are in brief as follows: —

1. An increase in the quantity of money (M) tends

[1] For further discussion, see § 2 of Appendix to (this) Chapter VIII.

to increase deposits (M') proportionally, and the increase in these two (M and M') tends to increase prices proportionally.

2. An increase in the quantity of money in one country tends to spread to others using the same money metal, and to the arts, as soon as the price levels or the relative value of money and bullion differ enough to make export or melting of the money metal profitable and to raise slightly world prices.

3. An increase in deposits (M') compared with money (M) tends likewise to displace and melt coin, and to raise world prices.

4. An increase in velocities tends to produce similar effects.

5. An increase in the volume of trade (the Q's) tends, not only to decrease prices, but also to increase velocities and deposits relatively to money and through them to neutralize partly or wholly the said decrease in prices.

6. The price level is the effect and cannot be the cause of change in the other factors.

7. Innumerable causes *outside* the equation of exchange may affect M, M', V, V', and the Q's and through them affect the p's. Among these outside causes are the price levels in surrounding countries.

8. The causation of individual prices can only explain prices as compared among themselves. It cannot explain the general level of prices as compared with money.

9. Some of the foregoing propositions are subject to slight modification during transition periods. It is then true, for instance, that an increase in the quantity of money (M) besides having the effects above mentioned will change temporarily the ratio of M' to M and disturb temporarily V, V', and the Q's, making a credit cycle.

In general, then, our conclusion as to causes and effects is that normally the price level (the p's) is the effect of all the other factors in the equation of exchange (M, M', V, V', and the Q's); that among these other factors, deposits (M') are chiefly the effect of money, given the normal ratio of M' to M; that this ratio is partly the effect of trade (the Q's); that V and V' are also partly the effects of the Q's; and that all of the magnitudes, M, M', V, V', and the Q's are the effects of antecedent causes outside the equation of exchange, *ad infinitum.*

The main conclusion is that we find nothing to interfere with the truth of the quantity theory that variations in money (M) produce normally proportional changes in prices.

CHAPTER IX

THE DISPERSION OF PRICES MAKES NECESSARY AN INDEX OF PURCHASING POWER

§ 1

We have found that the general level of prices is determined by the other magnitudes in the equation of exchange. But we have not hitherto defined exactly what a "general level" may mean. There was no need of such a definition so long as we assumed, as we have usually done hitherto, that all prices move in perfect unison. But practically prices never do move in perfect unison. Their dispersion would render impossible the statistical study of general price movements were there no practical method of indicating the general movement. A simple figure indicating the general trend of thousands of prices is a great statistical convenience. It also simplifies our equation of exchange by converting the right side, which now consists of thousands of terms, into a single simple term.

Such an indication is called an "index number" of the price level. Its reciprocal indicates, of course, the purchasing power of money.

The present chapter will, then, treat of the dispersion of prices, the next chapter of index numbers which this dispersion renders a practical necessity, and the two following chapters of the practical statistical use of index numbers.

The chief conclusion of our previous study is that an increase of money, other things equal, causes a proportional increase in the level of prices. In other words, the p's in the sum ΣpQ tend to rise in proportion to the increase in money. It was noted, however, that the adjustment is not necessarily uniform, and that if some p's do not rise as much as in this proportion, others must rise more. In this connection, we observe that some prices cannot adjust themselves at once, and some not at all. This latter is true, for instance, of prices fixed by contract. A price so fixed cannot be affected by any change coming into operation between the date of the contract and that of its fulfillment. Even in the absence of explicit contracts, prices may be kept from adjustment by implied understandings and by the mere inertia of custom. Besides these restrictions on the free movement of prices, there are often legal restrictions; as, for example, when railroads are prohibited from charging over two cents per passenger per mile, or when street railways are limited to five-cent or three-cent fares.

Whatever the causes of nonadjustment, the result is that the prices which do change will have to change in a greater ratio than would be the case were there no prices which do not change. Just as an obstruction put across one half of a stream causes an increase in current in the other half, so any deficiency in the movement of some prices must cause an excess in the movement of others.

In order to picture to ourselves what are the classes of prices which rise or fall, we must survey the entire field of prices. Prices, measured as we are accustomed to measure them, in terms of money, are the ratios of exchange between other goods and money. The term "goods," as previously explained, is a collective term comprising all wealth, property, and services, these being the magnitudes designated in sales. The chief subclasses under these three groups, which occur in actual sales, may be indicated as follows: —

Wealth	Real estate
	Commodities
Property	Stocks
	Bonds
	Mortgages
	Private notes
	Time bills of exchange
Services	Of rented real estate
	Of rented commodities
	Of hired workers
	Of some or all these agencies combined.

The prices of these various classes of goods cannot all move up and down in perfect unison. Some are far more easily adjustable than others. Only by extremely violent hypotheses could we imagine perfect adjustability in all. The order of adjustability from the least to the most adjustable may be roughly indicated as follows:[1] —

1. Contract prices of properties and services, especially where the contracts are for a long time; these include bonds, mortgage notes, use of real estate by leases.

2. Contract prices of properties and services, where the contracts are for a shorter time; these include bills of exchange, use of rented real estate and commodities, services of workmen, etc.

[1] Cf. Jevons's admirable "Classification of Incomes according as they suffer from Depreciation," *Investigations in Currency and Finance*, London (Macmillan), 1884, p. 80, and after. See also *The Gold Supply and Prosperity*, edited by Byron W. Holt, New York (The Moody Corporation), 1907, especially the Conclusion or Summary by the editor, beginning on page 193.

3. Prices of commodities made of the money metal.
4. Prices of substitutes for said commodities.
5. Prices fixed by law, as court fees, postage, tolls, use of public utilities, salaries, etc.
6. Prices fixed by custom, as medical fees, teachers' salaries, etc., and to some extent wages.
7. Prices of real estate.
8. Prices of most commodities at retail.
9. Prices of most commodities at wholesale.
10. Prices of stocks.

Take, for instance, bonds and mortgages. In order that the prices of these may be perfectly adjustable, we should have to suppose, not only that there were no restraint from custom or law, but that the contracts were perfectly readjusted to each new price level. We should have to suppose, for instance, that after the price level had doubled in height, because currency had doubled, there would be a $2000 bond wherever there had been a $1000 bond. This, obviously, is not the case. The holder of a $1000 bond can receive at its maturity only $1000, besides interest payments in the interim. If, meanwhile, the price level doubles, he will receive no more. It is true that a change of price level will, in time, change the volume of new loans. A merchant, to lay in a given stock of goods, will need to borrow a larger sum if prices are high than if they are low. Personal notes and bills of exchange will be drawn for double the amount which would have obtained had the price level not doubled. Similarly, a corporation issuing bonds for new projects may have to issue a larger amount. But obligations outstanding when the price levels change cannot be thus adjusted; their prices can vary only slightly during the interim between issue and maturity. The fact that their face value is expressed in money sets very definite limits to their prices.[1] If, because of a doubling in the quantity of money, the value and profits of a railroad measured in money were doubled, the bondholder could not, on that account, realize more money for his bond. The value of the bond is not greatly affected by the valuation and profits of the railroad, so long as these are sufficient to guarantee the bond. The bond is an agreement to pay stated sums at stated times. It represents a limited money value carved out of the road. The only ways in which the money price of a bond or salable debt can vary at all are by variations in the rate of money interest and by changes in the degree of certainty of payment. Only so far as these features are affected by the changes in the volume of money will the value of bonds be affected. We have seen, for instance, that inflation, while it is taking place, raises interest.[2] It therefore lowers the price of bonds during the transition period.[3] Again if violent changes in the price level increase or decrease the number of bankruptcies, they thereby affect the degree of certainty of payment, and consequently affect the value of bonds. But these ways of affecting prices of such securities expressed in money are of less account than the ordinary effect of inflation or contraction on price levels, and of a different character.

[1] See article by Walter S. Logan on the "Duty of Gold," in *The Gold Supply and Prosperity*, edited by Byron W. Holt, New York (The Moody Corporation), 1907, p. 106. See also Ricardo, "Essay on the High Price of Bullion," *Works*, 2d ed., London (Murray), 1852, p. 287.

[2] *Supra*, Chapter IV, § 1.

[3] See article by Robert Goodbody, "More Gold means Higher 'Time' Money and Lower Bond Prices," in *The Gold Supply and Prosperity*, edited by Byron W. Holt, New York (The Moody Corporation) 1907, p. 163 and after.

The chief peculiarity of these forms of property lies, then, in the fact that they are expressed in terms of *money* and therefore are compelled to keep in certain peculiar relations to money. Being based on contracts, the money terms of which during a given period must not be changed, they are not free to be influenced in the same ways as other property. The existence of such contracts constitutes one of the chief arguments for a system of currency such that the uncertainties of its purchasing power are a minimum. An uncertain monetary standard disarranges contracts and discourages their formation.

The longer the contract, the larger the nonadjustability. A fifty-year bond usually means a relative fixity of price for half a century. Only at the end of that time, if prices have risen, can bonds, issued *de novo* for the means of purchasing goods, be correspondingly more numerous or of correspondingly larger denominations. A 30-days' bill of exchange, on the other hand, while it cannot change much in price, is canceled at the end of a month. The relative fixity of price is, therefore, of shorter duration.

A special class of goods, the prices of which cannot fluctuate greatly with other prices, are those special commodities which consist largely of the money metal. Thus, in a country employing a gold standard, the prices of gold for dentistry, of gold rings and ornaments, gold watches, gold-rimmed spectacles, gilded picture frames, etc., instead of varying in proportion to other prices, always vary in a smaller proportion. The range of variation is the narrower, the more predominantly the price of the article depends upon the gold as one of its raw materials.

From the fact that gold-made articles are thus more

or less securely tied in value to the gold standard, it follows also that the prices of substitutes for such articles will tend to vary less than prices in general. These substitutes will include silver watches, ornaments of silver, and various other forms of jewelry, whether containing gold or not. It is a fundamental principle of *relative* prices that the prices of substitutes will move in sympathy. In the case of perfect substitutes, the prices must always be equal or must bear a fixed ratio to each other.[1]

The remaining items in our list require little comment. The imperfect adjustability of prices fixed by law and custom and the perfect adjustability of wholesale prices of commodities and prices of stocks are familiar to all.

§ 2

The fact that wages, salaries, the price of gold in non-monetary forms, etc., and especially the prices of bonded securities, cannot change in proportion to monetary fluctuations, means, then, that the prices of other things, such as commodities in general and stocks, must change much more than in proportion. This supersensitiveness to the influence of the volume of currency (or its velocity of circulation or the volume of business) applies in a maximum degree to stocks. Were a railroad to double in money value, the result would be, since the money value of the bonds could not increase appreciably, that the money value of the stock would more than double. Stocks are shares in physical wealth the value of which, in money, can fluctuate. Since the money price of bonds is relatively inflexible, that of stocks will fluctuate

[1] See Irving Fisher, "Mathematical Investigations in the Theory of Value and Prices," *Transactions of the Connecticut Academy of Arts and Sciences*, 1892, p. 66 and after.

more than the price of the physical wealth as a whole. The reason is that these securities not only feel the general movement which all adjustable elements feel, but must also conform to a special adjustment to make up for the rigid nonadjustability of the bonds associated with them.

To illustrate, let us suppose the right side of the equation of exchange to consist of the following elements:—

Miscellaneous adjustable elements such as commodities, having a value of	$ 95,000,000
Five thousand shares of stock at $1000 per share, making a value of	5,000,000
Five thousand bonds on the same underlying wealth at $1000 each, making a value of	5,000,000
Miscellaneous nonadjustable elements such as other bonds, notes, government salaries, government fees, dentists' gold, etc., having a value of . . .	20,000,000
	$125,000,000

Let us suppose that, with no change in the velocities of currency circulation or in the volume of business, there is an increase of 40 per cent in the quantities of currency. Then, the total value of goods exchanged will have to increase from $125,000,000 to $175,000,000. Let us assume that the last two items are absolutely nonadjustable; then none of the increase of $50,000,000 can occur through any change in these items, which will remain at $5,000,000 and $20,000,000, respectively, or $25,000,000 in all. Consequently, the first two items must rise by the whole of the $50,000,000, that is, from $100,000,000 to $150,000,000 or 50 per cent. To distribute this increase of $50,000,000 over the first two or adjustable items, let us assume that the total $10,-000,000 worth of actual wealth, which consists half of stocks and half of bonds, will rise in the same ratio as the $95,000,000 worth of adjustable elements rise. Now the whole (comprising all three items) evidently rises from $105,000,000 to $155,000,000, making an increase of 47.6 per cent. This, therefore, is the common percentage which we are to assume applies equally to the first item and the combination of the second and third. Applied to the former it makes an increase from $95,000,000 to $140,200,000. Applied to the latter it makes an increase from $10,000,000 to $14,800,000. But since half of the property consists of bonds and cannot increase, the whole of the increase, $4,800,000, must belong to the stock alone. This will, therefore, rise from $5,000,000, to $9,800,000, a rise of 96 per cent. The four items then change as follows: —

First item — from $95,000,000 to $140,200,000, or 47.6 per cent.

Second item — from $5,000,000 to $9,800,000, or 96 per cent.

Third item and fourth item — no change.

All items combined — from $125,000,000 to $175,000,000, or 40 per cent.

Besides the dispersion of price changes produced by the fact that some prices respond more readily than others to changes in the factors determining price levels, M, M', V, V', and the Q's, a further dispersion is produced by the fact that the special forces of supply and demand are playing on each individual price, and causing relative variations among them. Although these forces do not, as we have before emphasized, necessarily affect the general price level, they do affect the number and extent of individual divergencies above and below that general level. Each individual price will have a fluctuation of its own.

Among the special factors working through supply and demand, changes in the rate of interest should be particularly mentioned. Whether or not due to monetary changes, a movement of interest will tend to make the prices of different things vary in different directions or to different extents. The prices of all goods, the benefits of which accrue in the remote future, depend on the rate of interest. The standard example is that of bonds and other securities. Another good example is that of real estate. In the case of farm lands yielding a constant rental, a reduction of interest causes an increase of value in the inverse ratio. If interest falls from 5 per cent to 4 per cent, the value will increase in the ratio 4 to 5. If the benefits or services are not constant each year, but are massed together in the remote future, the price may be still sensitive to a change in the rate of interest. In the case of land used for forest growing from which the trees are to be cut in half a century, the value will be extremely sensitive. A fall in interest from 5 per cent to 4 per cent will cause a rise of the value of the land, in the ratio not of 4 to 5, but nearly of 4 to 7.[1] On the other hand, mining land or quarries with a limited life will be less sensitive. The same is true of dwellings, machinery, fixtures, and other durable but not indestructible instruments, and so on down the scale until we reach perishable and transient commodities, such as food and clothing, which are only indirectly affected by changes in the rate of interest.

It is evident, therefore, that prices must constantly change *relatively to each other*, whatever happens to their

[1] From figures showing yield of forest of white pine in New Hampshire, *New Hampshire Forestry Commission Report*, 1905–1906, p. 246. See F. R. Fairchild, "Taxation of Timberland," *Report of the National Conservation Commission*, 60th Congress, 2d Session, Senate Document 676, vol. II, p. 624.

O

general level. It would be as idle to expect a uniform movement in prices as to expect a uniform movement for all bees in a swarm. On the other hand, it would be as idle to deny the existence of a *general* movement of prices because they do not all move alike, as to deny a general movement of a swarm of bees because the individual bees have different movements.

§ 3

Corresponding to changes in an individual price there will be changes in the *quantity* of the given commodity which is exchanged at that price. In other words, as each p changes, the Q connected with it will change also; this, because usually any influence affecting the price of a commodity will also affect the consumption of it. Changes in supply or demand or both make changes in the quantity exchanged. Otherwise expressed, the point of intersection of the supply and demand curve may move laterally as well as vertically.

This changing of the Q's introduces a new complication. We have in many of our previous discussions been assuming, as was admissible theoretically, that all the Q's remain unchanged while we investigate the changes in the p's due to changes in the currency or in velocities of circulation. But practically we can never get an opportunity to study such a case. Again, in order to show the effect of a change in "the volume of business" upon the price level, we supposed a case in which all the Q's were uniformly changed. Such a supposition is not only impossible to carry out in practice, but is difficult to conceive even in theory; because, as we have just seen, each Q is associated with a p. In showing the effect of a change in the volume of business upon the level of prices we cannot assume that all the

Q's change uniformly in one direction and all the p's uniformly in the other. If the first set change uniformly, the second cannot change uniformly. A doubling in the quantities of all commodities sold, or (what is almost the same thing), a doubling of the quantities consumed, would change their relative desirabilities and therefore their relative prices. To double the quantity of salt might make its marginal desirability zero, while to double the quantity of roses might scarcely lower their marginal desirability at all.[1]

We see, therefore, that it is well-nigh useless to speak of uniform changes in prices (p's) or of uniform changes in quantities exchanged (Q's). In place of positing such uniform changes, we must now proceed to the problem of developing some convenient method of tracing these two groups of changes. We must formulate two magnitudes, the *price level* and the *volume of trade*. This problem is especially difficult because, in measuring changes in the price level, we shall need to use the quantities (Q's) in some way as weights in our process of averaging; and we now find, not only that the prices whose average we seek are extremely variable, but that the weights by which we attempt to construct the average are variable also.

It is desired, then, in the equation of exchange, to convert the right side, ΣpQ, into a form PT where T measures the volume of trade, and P is an "index number" expressing the price level at which this trade is carried on. These magnitudes — price level (P) and volume of trade (T) — need now to be more precisely formulated. Especially does P become henceforth the focal point in our study.

[1] Cf. Jevons, *Theory of Political Economy*, London (Macmillan), 1888, pp. 155–156.

As explained in the next chapter, there are an indefinite number of ways of conceiving and forming index numbers of prices and volume of trade. We shall here mention only the simplest. T may be conceived as the sum of all the Q's, and P as the average of all the p's. This method is practically useful only provided suitable units of measure are selected. It must be remembered that the various Q's are measured in different units. Coal is sold by the ton, sugar by the pound, wheat by the bushel, etc. If we now add together these tons, pounds, bushels, etc., and call this grand total so many "units" of commodity, we shall have a very arbitrary summation. It will make a difference, for instance, whether we measure coal by tons or hundredweights. The system becomes less arbitrary if we use, as the unit for measuring any goods, not the unit in which it is commonly sold, but the amount which constitutes a "dollar's worth" at some particular year called the base year. Then every price, in the base year, is one dollar, and therefore the average of all prices in that year is also one dollar. For any other year the average price (*i.e.* the average of the prices of the newly chosen units which in the base year were worth a dollar) will be the index number representing the price level, while the number of such units will be the volume of trade.

The equation of exchange now assumes the form

$$MV + M'V' = PT$$

and its right member is the product of the index number (P) of prices multiplied by the volume of trade (T).

§ 4

In this chapter we have seen that prices do not, and in fact cannot, move in perfect unison. The reasons for dispersion are principally three: (1) Many prices are restrained by previous contract, by legal prohibition, or by force of custom. (2) Some prices are intimately related to the money metal. (3) Each individual price is subject to special variation under the influence of its particular supply and demand. There exists, however, a compensation in price movements in the sense that the failure of one set of prices to respond to any influence on the price level will necessitate a correspondingly greater change in other prices.

The quantities sold likewise vary, and their variations are bound up with those of prices.

In order to express in one figure the *general* movement of prices, an index number (P) is constructed; and in order to express in one figure the general movement of trade, an index of trade (T) is constructed. The nature of these indices will form the subject of the next chapter.

CHAPTER X

THE BEST INDEX NUMBERS OF PURCHASING POWER

§ 1

In the previous chapter the necessity for an index number (P) was shown and a particular form of index number was suggested. This form of index number had been shown in Chapter II and its appendix to meet certain conditions (of proportionality of price level to quantity of money, etc.) required by the equation of exchange, $MV+M'V'=PT$. In the present chapter, this index number will be compared with others and the general purposes of index numbers discussed, including purposes having little direct concern with the equation of exchange.

Index numbers may be compared in respect to (1) form, under which term are included methods of weighting and of determining the "base" prices; (2) the selection of elements to be included. In this section we shall consider the question of form.

The number of possible forms of index numbers is infinite. They differ enormously in complexity, in ease of calculation, and in conformity to various other tests. A few of the simplest may here be mentioned. Their discussion will be brief and will in many cases be dogmatic. Full proofs and discussions are contained in the mathematical appendix.[1]

If in 1900 the average price per pound of sugar was 6 cents, and in 1910 it was 8 cents, the ratio of the price

[1] See Appendix to (this) Chapter X, §§ 1–8, where 44 types of index numbers are compared.

in 1910 to that in 1900 must have been $\frac{8}{6}$ or $133\frac{1}{3}$ per cent. If, in the same period, the average price of coal per ton had changed from \$4 to \$6, the corresponding ratio for coal must have been $\frac{6}{4}$ or 150 per cent. If the price of a given grade of cloth, on the other hand, fell from 10 cents to 8 cents a yard, the ratio for cloth must have been $\frac{8}{10}$ or 80 per cent. P is an average of all these three price ratios and other price ratios, that is, an average of $133\frac{1}{3}$ per cent, 150 per cent, 80 per cent, etc. The simple *arithmetical* average of these three ratios specified would be $\frac{133\frac{1}{3}\% + 150\% + 80\%}{3}$, or 121 per cent. The simple *geometric* average would be $\sqrt[3]{133\frac{1}{3} \times 150 \times 80}$, or 117 per cent.

These are examples of simple or unweighted averages. Since, however, weighted averages have many advantages in theory and some advantages in practice, we shall proceed to consider them.

There are innumerable methods of weighting [1] and of averaging. None of them is perfectly satisfactory from a theoretical standpoint. We must choose what seems to be best from a practical standpoint. The effect of changed volume of currency or changed velocity of circulation on the whole series of prices is complex, and cannot, even in theory, be compressed into one figure representing all price changes, any more than a

[1] For discussions of different ways that have been proposed, see Walsh, *The Measurement of General Exchange Value*, New York and London (Macmillan), 1901; Edgeworth, "Report on Best Methods of Ascertaining and Measuring Variations in the Value of the Monetary Standard"; *Report of the British Association for the Advancement of Science for* 1887, pp. 247–301; ditto for 1888, pp. 181–209; ditto for 1889, pp. 133–164. Nitti, *La misura delle variazioni di valore della moneta*, Turin, 624 pp.; also the Appendix to (this) Chapter X.

lens can be constructed which will focus in one point all the rays of light reaching it from a given point. But, although in the science of optics we learn that a perfect lens is theoretically impossible, nevertheless, for all practical purposes lenses may be constructed so nearly perfect that it is well worth while to study and construct them. So, also, while it seems theoretically impossible to devise an index number, P, which shall satisfy all of the tests we should like to impose,[1] it is, nevertheless, possible to construct index numbers which satisfy these tests so well for practical purposes that we may profitably devote serious attention to the study and construction of index numbers.

The index number mentioned in Chapter IX may be constructed by the following process: Suppose that the year 1910 is the period to be considered in our equation of exchange $MV + M'V' = \Sigma pQ = PT$. We select another year (say 1900) and call it the "base" year. This means that the prices of 1910 are to be expressed as a percentage of the prices of the equation of exchange for 1910.

Next we obtain an expression for trade (or T). As shown in the appendix to this chapter, every form of index number, P, for prices implies a correlative form of index for trade, T, and *vice versa*. It is convenient to select T first. We observe that trade (or T) is not the value of transactions measured at the *actual* prices of the year 1910, for this value is PT or ΣpQ,

[1] Cf. Mill, *Political Economy*, Book III, Chapter XV; Sedgwick, *Principles of Political Economy*, Book I, Chapter II; "Report of Committee on Value of Monetary Standard," *Report of the British Association for the Advancement of Science*, 1887: Wesley C. Mitchell, *Gold, Prices, and Wages under the Greenback Standard*, Berkeley, 1908 (University of California Press), p. 19; and Appendix to (this) Chapter X.

that is, the entire right side of the equation. Trade (T) by itself must be divorced from the price level (P); it may be conceived as the value which the total transactions *would have had* if the actual quantities sold had been sold at the *base prices*. It is thus the sum of a number of terms, each term being the product of the quantity, or Q, pertaining to 1910 and the price, or p, pertaining to the base year 1900. Algebraically it is $p_0Q + p'_0Q' + p''_0Q''$ + etc., or, more briefly, Σp_0Q, where the prices of 1910 are expressed simply as p, p', p'', etc., and those of the base year, 1900, are expressed as p_0, p'_0, p''_0, etc.

Having defined this ideal value (T), we now define P as the ratio of the real value of transactions in 1910 (ΣpQ) to that ideal (Σp_0Q). More fully expressed, P is the ratio of a real value (the value of the trade of 1910 at the prices of 1910) to an ideal value (the value of the trade of 1910 at the prices of 1900). This ratio is really a weighted arithmetical average of price ratios.[1] The foregoing method is simple both in conception and in mathematical expression,[2] and appears to furnish, theoretically at least, the best form of P, or index number of prices. The particular form of P (viz. $\Sigma pQ \div \Sigma p_0Q$) which we have just described is, then, associated with and dependent on a particular form of T (viz. Σp_0Q). T may be called an index number *of trade*, and we may say that the particular form of T (viz. Σp_0Q) is the best form of index or barometer of trade.

Another method of conceiving the same form of index number of prices is that mentioned at the close of

[1] See Appendix to (this) Chapter X for a table and discussion of forty-four sample types of index numbers.

[2] It is formula 11 of the large table in the Appendix to (this) Chapter X.

the preceding chapter, as follows: Conceive each kind of goods to be measured in a new physical unit — viz. the amount which was worth one dollar in the base year (1900) — and let us use this unit for each other year (as 1910). Thus instead of a pound as the unit for sugar we take as the unit whatever amount of sugar was a dollar's worth in 1900. Hence the price of sugar in the base year, 1900, was $1, as of course was the price of everything else. If, now, the price of sugar in any other year (as 1910) is $1.25 in terms of the new unit (viz. the amount which was a dollar's worth in 1900), we know that the price has risen 25 per cent. In this way P may be defined simply as an average *price* instead of as an average *price ratio* and T as the total number of the new units of goods sold of all kinds. The right side of the equation is now simply the product of the total number of units sold, multiplied by their average price.

The two definitions of P which have been given (viz. the ratio of real to ideal values, and the average price in 1910 of all goods when measured in dollar's worth of 1900) are interchangeable; and both definitions of T (ideal values of transactions in 1910 at prices of 1900, and total number of units sold in 1910, the units being each a dollar's worth in 1900) are interchangeable. There are other ways of defining P and T without changing their meanings. Thus "P is the weighted arithmetical average of the ratios of prices of goods in 1910 to those of 1900, when these ratios are weighted according to the values of the goods exchanged in 1910 reckoned at the prices of 1900." Whichever of these definitions we prefer, the system of index numbers is the same and has advantages over most other systems. Above all, it enables us to say without qualification that if the quantities sold remain unchanged, T will remain unchanged, and P will vary directly as the left side of the equation of exchange.[1]

We choose, then, as one of the best index numbers of prices, the average price of the goods sold, those goods being measured in units worth a dollar in the base year; in other words, the ratio of the value of sales at actual prices to the value of the same sales if made at base prices; in still other words, the weighted arithmetical average of all price ratios, each ratio being weighted according to the values sold, reckoned at base prices.

We have still to consider the selection of the base. It makes a difference to the above index numbers, not only absolutely, but also relatively, whether the base year is, for instance, 1900 or 1860.

Excepting Jevons's index numbers, which were geometric averages, there are few index numbers which are not vitiated in some degree by having a base remote from the years for which comparisons are most needed. As Professor Marshall has maintained and as Professor Flux has emphasized, the best base for any year seems to be the previous year.

Instead, then, of employing a fixed base year for which all prices are called 100 per cent and in terms of which all other prices are expressed in percentages, each year may be taken as the base for the succeeding year. Thus we obtain a chain of index numbers, each number being connected with the preceding year instead of with a common base year.

The great advantage of this chain system is that it yields its best comparison for the cases in which comparison is most used and needed. Each year we are inter-

[1] See Appendix to Chapter II and the Appendix to (this) Chapter X, §§ 5, 6, 7.

ested in Sauerbeck's index number in order to compare it with the number of the preceding year, and only to a less extent with other years. The number, however, as actually constructed, affords something quite different. It gives us, as its best or most accurate comparison, the ratio between the current year and the years 1867–1877. This comparison is of little or no interest to any one. What all users of these statistics actually do is to compare two comparisons. The index numbers for 1909 and 1910 (each calculated in terms of 1867–1877) are compared with each other. But direct comparison between 1909 and 1910 would give a different and more valuable result. To use a common base is like comparing the relative heights of two men by measuring the height of each above the floor, instead of putting them back to back and directly measuring the difference of level between the tops of their heads. The direct comparison is more accurate, although in the case of the men's heights both methods would theoretically agree. In the case of price levels, unfortunately, few index numbers will even theoretically give consistent results when the base is shifted;[1] and those few will fail to meet other equally important tests.

It may be said that the cardinal virtue of the successive base or chain system is the facility it affords for the introduction of new commodities, the dropping out of obsolete commodities, and the continual readjustment of the system of weighting to new conditions. A fixed base system soon gets behind the times in every sense of the word.

§ 2

Our next question is: What prices should be selected in constructing an index number? The answer to this

[1] See Appendix to (this) Chapter X, § 5, test 7.

question largely depends on the *purpose* of the index number. Hitherto we have considered only one purpose of an index number, viz. to best meet the requirements of the equation of exchange. But index numbers may be used for many other purposes, of which the two chief are to measure *capital* and to measure *income*. Each of the three purposes mentioned (viz. exchange, capital, and income) may be subclassified according as the comparison desired is between *places* or *times*. Thus index numbers may be used for comparisons between *places* with respect to their exchange of goods, their capital, or their income. When, for instance, the British Board of Trade[1] tries to compare the cost of living in various towns of England, Germany, and the United States the comparison is with reference to the prices of living (or income) of the working classes.

We thus have at least six large classes of purposes for which index numbers may be used, viz. to compare the prices, in different places, of the goods exchanged; of the capital goods; and of the income goods; and of the same three groups of goods at different times.

In each of the six cases, prices of goods and quantities of goods will be associated with each other, and an index number (P) for one will imply an index number (T) for the other (we here use T in the general sense of an index of quantities of goods whether they are exchanged goods, as hitherto, or capital goods, or income goods).

Evidently there will be a great difference in the selection of the prices to be compared according to which of the six comparisions we wish to make. Suppose, for instance, that we wish to measure changes in the general

[1] See *Report* (to Parliament) *of an Enquiry by the Board of Trade into Working Class Rents, Housing and Retail Prices*, London (Darling), 1908, 1909.

level of prices of capital goods,[1] — railways, ships, real estate, etc., — and also to measure the relative changes in the amounts of those goods. The prices of some kinds of capital may have increased, and of others decreased, and some may have increased at different rates from others. How shall we measure the general change in prices of capital goods? Again, the quantity of some kinds of capital, as railroads, may have increased faster than that of other kinds, as sailing ships. Still other kinds of capital may have decreased. How shall it be determined whether capital in general has increased, and how much? These two problems (of prices of capital and quantities of capital) may be said to consist in measuring the average change in the price of the same quantity of capital, and the average change of quantity of capital taken at the same prices.

For either index (since only *capital* is under consideration), and not income or other designated goods, whether stocks or flows, the index numbers should relate, not to general prices and quantities, but only to prices and quantities of capital goods. Thus, the prices and quantities of all labor services should be omitted. The use of capital and the rents paid for that use, such as the rent paid for house shelter, should be omitted. Only capital instruments, and not the services yielded by these, should be included. We may obtain the price index first and then obtain a quantity index by dividing the value of capital in any year by the price index, or we may proceed in the reverse direction.[2] In making index numbers of prices of capital and quantities of capital, we

[1] This has been suggested by Nicholson, *Journal of the Royal Statistical Society*, March, 1887.

[2] Giffen, in his *Growth of Capital*, London (Bell & Sons), 1899, pp. 50–54, makes correction for price changes although without attempting to construct a special index number for capital.

naturally select for our list articles which are important *as capital*, and weight them accordingly.

To determine this general change in prices of capital, we should weight each ratio by the value of the particular capital to which that ratio relates. In this case each ratio should be weighted, *not* according to the annual *sales*, but according to the existing *capital*. Obviously, the difference between these two modes of weighting may be great. Thus, real estate forms a large part of all existing capital, but *sales* of real estate are a relatively unimportant part of all sales. Food products, on the other hand, contribute little to capital and much to exchange. Consequently, prices and quantities of food products would not figure in capital index numbers, but would figure largely in the index numbers relating to the equation of exchange.

Again, suppose the purpose of the index numbers of prices is to measure the quantities and prices of *income*, not of elements of capital. In this case the list of articles and their weights will be quite different from those in a *capital* index.

If the income of workingmen is under consideration, we have to deal with index numbers for prices of those goods entering into workingmen's budgets, and with index numbers of the quantities of such goods. The first will show the cost of living of the workingman, or the purchasing power of a workingman's dollar; the second will show what is called his "real wages" or "consumption." In this case the aim is to compare, not stocks existing at two points of time, but flows through two periods of time. One way to obtain an index of real wages is to correct the nominal or *money* wages by using the index number of prices of goods for which wages are spent. Thus, if money wages for

1908 were twice those for 1900, but money prices of the necessaries and comforts of life had also doubled, real wages would be unchanged.

Evidently the index numbers used in the case of quantities and prices of workmen's living are not the same as those used in the case of capital. Goods should have each an importance in the index number, dependent upon its importance in workingmen's budgets. The goods in this case are flows, while in the case of capital the goods considered were stocks. In comparing capital, the index numbers must relate to capital; and in comparing income, the index numbers must relate to income.

§ 3

Perhaps the most important purpose of index numbers is to serve as a basis of loan contracts.[1] It is

[1] An early attempt to construct a series of index numbers expressing the general change in prices was made by Sir George Shuckburgh Evelyn, Bart., F.R.S. and A.S. in 1798 in an article entitled "An Account of Some Endeavors to Ascertain a Standard of Weight and Measure," in the *Philosophical Transactions of the Royal Society of London*, Vol. LXXXVIII, pp. 133–182, inclusive.

Bishop William Fleetwood in 1707 in *Chronicon Preciosum, an Account of English Money, the Price of Corn and Other Commodities for the Last Six Hundred Years*, raises and discusses the question whether the holder of a fellowship founded between 1440 and 1460 and open only to persons having an estate of less value than £5 a year may rightly swear that he has less than that, if he has £6, the value of money, however, having meanwhile greatly depreciated.

The idea of using an index number or tabular standard of money value was later put forth by Joseph Lowe, *The Present State of England in regard to Agriculture and Finance*, London, 1822 (see pp. 261–291, Appendix, pp. 89–101), and afterwards by G. Poulett Scrope, *Principles of Political Economy . . . applied to the Present State of Britain*, London, 1833, pp. 405–408, although, as we have seen, the idea of an index number itself antedated them. See Correa Moylan Walsh, *The Measurement of General Exchange Value*, New York and London (Macmillan), 1901; Bibliography, p. 555.

desirable to determine the particular form and weighting best suited to this purpose as well as the best selection of prices to be included.

An index number which serves the purpose of measuring the appreciation or depreciation of loan contracts — or what is called "deferred payments" — evidently belongs to the *time* rather than the *place* group of comparisons. But to which if any of the three sub-groups (exchange, capital, or income) it most properly belongs is not at first clear. But, before considering this question and as a preliminary to finding the best index number for contracts between borrower and lender, we must arrive at some opinion as to what is the ideal basis for loan contracts.

In the first place, it should be pointed out that though there is a gain and loss there is not necessarily any "injustice" wrought because of a change in the level of prices. Thus, if a man borrows $1000, contracting to pay it back with $40 additional as interest at the end of five years, and meanwhile prices unexpectedly double, he is a decided gainer. Though he has to pay, to be sure, the same number of *dollars*, he needs to sell only about *half* as much of his stock of goods as he expected. He pays back, in the principal, only half of the real purchasing power borrowed. The lender, on the other hand, is a loser by the change.

Yet the contract was perfectly fair. Each party knew or should have known that the price level might change, and took the risk. There was no fraud any more than when wheat has been ordered for future delivery at a certain price and the market unexpectedly turns; or when an insurance company loses a "risk" prematurely.

Indeed, for a government to attempt by legislation

to deprive the gainer of his profit would itself be in general unfair.[1] To protect themselves from losses the risk of which they took upon themselves, the losing parties cannot justly betake themselves to legislation *after* the making of contracts.

The unfairness of so doing becomes the more manifest, when it is considered that, if the change in price level is at all expected, there is apt to be some compensation by means of an adjustment in the rate of interest.[2] If the price level is rising, the nominal rate of interest will probably be a little higher, compensating the lender somewhat for the loss of part value in his principal; while, if the price level is falling, the borrower is likely to be partly compensated for his loss by a lower nominal rate of interest. It is not right that either side should use its influence with government to impair the obligations of contracts already made.[3] It is, however, sound public policy to lessen in *advance* the risk element, as rapidly as may be, so that *future* contracts may be made by all parties on the most certain basis possible. In the problem of time contracts between borrowers and lenders, the ideal is that neither debtor nor creditor should be worse off from having been deceived by unforeseen changes. Experience shows that the rate of interest will seldom adjust itself perfectly to changes in price level, because these changes are only in part foreseen. The aim should be to make the currency as certain or dependable as possible. Practically speaking, this means that it shall be as nearly constant as possible.

[1] Cf. Irving Fisher, "Appreciation and Interest," Part 3, *Publications of the American Economic Association*, 1896.

[2] *Rate of Interest*, Chapter XIV.

[3] *Appreciation and Interest*, Part 3, § 4.

In an ideal standard of value, the index number of prices would continually register 100 per cent.[1] But as long as an absolutely stable currency does not exist, and cannot be had, the index number is itself a possible standard for long-time contracts. It is called the "tabular standard," as it depends on a table of prices. Thus, if a man borrows $1000 when the index number is 100, he might agree to pay back, not the same dollars, but the same general purchasing power, with interest. If, at the time of repayment, the index number had gone to 150, the principal of the debt would be understood to be $1500, since this represents the same purchasing power that was borrowed. If, on the other hand, the level of prices had fallen to 80, the principal would automatically become $800. Thus, both parties would be protected against fluctuations in the value of money. The same correction would apply to the interest payments, each of which would be adjusted according to the index number relating to the time of payment.

We are now ready to consider the question of what are the goods the prices of which should be included in an index number to serve the purposes of measuring changes in loan contracts.

[1] It has been argued that an ideal standard ought to be such as to keep constant not objective, but subjective, prices, so that a debt would be repaid in a given amount of "labor" or "utility." But, aside from the practical difficulties of measuring such subjective magnitudes — which are insuperable and therefore render their discussion purely academic — there are even more serious theoretical objections because of the fact that the standard would increase with some persons and decrease with others as they grow poorer or richer and that these changes are anticipated in making loan contracts — in fact, are the instigating causes of such contracts. See § 4 *infra* and Irving Fisher, "Appreciation and Interest," Chapter XII, § 2, *Publications of the American Economic Association*, 1896.

If all goods kept the same ratios of prices among themselves, it would make no difference whether a loan contract were made in terms of one index number or another or even whether it were made in terms of wheat, tons of coal, or pounds of sugar. But because prices *do not* vary in the same, but in different proportions, an index number measuring the *general level* of prices is necessary. If repayment is made in equivalent purchasing power (plus interest), over one kind of goods, this may be either more or less than equivalent purchasing power over other kinds. Hence, one party or the other is a loser according to the kind of goods he handles as a producer or prefers to use as a consumer. Even if each contracting party could arrange to receive or pay back purchasing power over an amount of goods of the kinds which most concerned him, equivalent to what he lent or borrowed, with interest, the speculative element resulting in gain or loss to one or the other, though decreased, would not be entirely removed.[1]

Suppose, for example, that a lender receives back purchasing power over an amount of goods of the kinds he wished to use, equivalent to what he lent plus interest.[2] Suppose also that, during the period of the loan, these goods appreciate relatively to others. Then the lender really gains, since he can now get more of other goods in exchange for those it was his original purpose to use, — a course which he may now be tempted to take while otherwise he would not. To the borrower, however, the appreciation of the goods on

[1] Cf. Kinley, *Money*, New York (Macmillan), 1904, p. 267.

[2] The argument of the remainder of this section is substantially the same as that in a paper by Harry G. Brown, in the *Quarterly Journal of Economics*, August, 1909, entitled, "A Problem in Deferred Payments and the Tabular Standard."

the basis of which repayment is made, relatively to the goods he is engaged in producing, might be regarded as causing him loss. The *same* purchasing power over the goods, on the basis of which he is to make payment, means in such a case, a *greater* purchasing power over the goods he is engaged in producing.

It is clear that no one kind of goods is a fair standard. An index number intended to serve as a standard for deferred payments must have a broad basis.

Were all borrowers and all lenders interested merely as consumers — lenders denying themselves in immediate consumption in order to lend, with the idea of consuming more on repayment, and borrowers planning to consume more immediately with the intention of later consuming less — an exactly satisfactory index number for each individual would seem impossible. The goods which interested a lender in any given case might not be those of most importance to the borrower. Only a rough average could be struck and an index number found to be used by all parties in their contracts. Such an average would doubtless be one in which each price ratio would be weighted according to the total consumption of the goods to which it related, — the total consumption of all borrowers and all lenders in the country considered.

The case is even more complicated, however; for many borrowers and lenders are interested less in consumption than in investment.[1] The choice is as much between lending and other investing as between lending and consuming. Similarly, the borrower may borrow to invest as well as to consume and may raise the money for repayment by curtailing investment rather than by curtailing consumption. Borrowers and lenders, in other words,

[1] Cf. Kemmerer, *Quarterly Journal of Economics*, August, 1909.

may be more interested in purchasing factories, railroads, land, durable houses, etc., which yield services during a long future, than in purchasing more or better food, shelter and entertainments, which yield immediate satisfactions. To base our index number for time contracts solely on services and immediately consumable goods would therefore be illogical. Though the practical differences may amount to little, yet, in theory at least, they are important.

Let us suppose each price ratio to be weighted by the value (at standard prices) of the services of quickly consumable goods enjoyed during a given period, purchases of durable capital being omitted. Suppose also that before the time of repayment arrives the rate of interest has risen. With higher interest, the value of land, railroads, and other durable capital will be lower because the value depends on future earnings or future services, and these are now discounted at a higher rate.[1] The borrower, in paying back an equal purchasing power over consumable goods and services, is paying back a much higher purchasing power over such things as land, houses, and factories — a much higher purchasing power over *future* income — than he borrowed. The lender is receiving back, therefore, a larger purchasing power over these durable items of capital than he loaned, though not a larger purchasing power (except for the interest) over immediately consumable goods and services. He gets back no more control over present income, but he gets a purchasing power over a greater amount of deferred income. Had he invested

[1] For a discussion of the effect of a change in the rate of interest on prices, see Irving Fisher, *Nature of Capital and Income*, New York (Macmillan), 1906, p. 227, and *Rate of Interest*, New York (Macmillan), 1907, pp. 226 and 227.

in land at the start, instead of lending, the fall of interest would have left him with the same *amount* of land, but a less value. As it is, he gets back a purchasing power over a *greater* amount and the *same* value of land. An accident has made the lender better off than he expected, and better off than he would have been had he invested instead of loaning.

If, on the other hand, the rate of interest should fall, the borrower will be benefited, and the lender injured. The value of land and of any other property, the income of which extends far into the future, would rise in comparison with the value of food, shelter, and so on. The value of a house is the discounted value of its future rent or service in affording shelter. The rate of interest having fallen, the value of the house will be higher, in comparison with the yearly rental value, than before. To repay the same amount of purchasing power over *shelter* as was borrowed is to repay less than the same amount of purchasing power over *houses*. The borrower is benefited to the extent that he has to curtail investments to repay, since he repays a less investing power although as great a spending power. He need not, therefore, curtail his investments in land and machinery quite so much as he otherwise would have to do. The lender, on the other hand, is in the same degree injured. If he wishes to invest in durable capital, such as an office building, a mine, or shares in a railroad, he cannot purchase as much of these with the returned principal as he could have borrowed with the same principal at the time of the loan. Had he foreseen the fall in interest, he might have refused to make the loan and invested instead. He would then have had, in place of interest on a loan, a return on his investment and a larger amount of capital on which to realize future income. The effect of the fall in interest would then have been, not to decrease the returns on his investment, but to increase the capitalized value of the investment.

It appears, then, that while an index number based on services and the less durable commodities may be adapted to time contracts between a borrower intending to indulge in immediate consumption, and a lender intending to postpone consumption until the repayment of the loan, such an index number is *not* entirely suited to contracts one or both parties to which are interested in more permanent investment.

Instead, therefore, of basing our index number on consumable goods and services enjoyed during a period, we ought rather to base it partly on these and partly on the amount of durable capital. Each borrower and each lender may wish to make a different distribution in *time* of his income stream.[1] One man, that he may have a large income in the future, wants to invest; another, that he may enjoy a large income soon, does not want to invest. One lender is, therefore, interested in getting back as much durable capital as he lent; another lender is interested in receiving as great purchasing power over services and consumable goods as he lent.

Now different persons, with different intentions as to the spending of their money, nevertheless make loan contracts with each other. Even if a separate index number, specially weighted, could be used for each couple, such a standard would not be equally fitted to both parties. Yet the same debt cannot be paid in two different standards. Therefore, absolute equalization is out of the question. We can mitigate

[1] *Rate of Interest*, pp. 121–125.

the evils of a fluctuating money standard, but we cannot entirely remove the element of speculation from time contracts.

Although different persons and different classes might establish different standards for special contracts, yet for the great mass of business contracts involving postponed payments, a single series of index numbers including articles used and purchased by all classes, and including also services, would probably be found advisable. This index number would be best suited to contracts between different classes, between individuals of differing habits of consumption, and to fix the money payments on bonds which are securities sold to the public in general.

Without attempting to construct index numbers which particular persons and classes might sometimes wish to take as standard, we shall merely inquire regarding the formation of such a general index number. It must, as has been pointed out, include all goods and services. But in what proportion shall these be weighted? How shall we decide how much weight should be given, in forming the index, to the *stock* of durable capital and how much weight to the *flow* of goods and services through a period of time, — the flow to individuals, which mirrors consumption? The two things are incommensurable. Shall we count the railways of the country as equally important with a month's consumption of sugar, or with a year's?

§ 4

To cut these Gordian knots, perhaps the best and most practical scheme is that which has been used in the explanation of the P in our equation of exchange, an index number in which every article and service is weighted according to the value of it *exchanged* at base prices in the year whose level of prices it is desired to find.[1] By this means, goods bought for immediate consumption are included in the weighting, as are also all durable capital goods exchanged during the period covered by the index number. What is repaid in contracts so measured is the same *general purchasing power*. This includes purchasing power over everything purchased and purchasable, including real estate, securities, labor, other services, such as the services rendered by corporations, and commodities.

There has been much discussion as to the propriety of the inclusion of services of human beings, or so-called "labor." In one way the question solves itself, since the inclusion or exclusion on the basis of *piece work* will make little or no difference to the results.

It is well known that we may measure wages either "by the piece" or by "time." In either case they enter into and affect the general index number expressing the price level, but the influence is different in the two cases. If we take hours of labor as the basis and measure the wages paid by the hour or by the day, then we are likely to find that, during a period of improvement in the arts, money wages are rising while the prices of goods are falling, or that money wages are rising faster than the prices of goods, or are falling more slowly. But if we measure wages by the piece, we shall find less inconsistency of results. If goods increase faster than currency, so that prices tend to fall, piece

[1] The same conclusion as to the best standard for deferred contracts is reached by Professor H. S. Foxwell by a somewhat different line of reasoning. See remarks of Professor F. Y. Edgeworth (as Secretary of the Committee on Variations of the Monetary Standard). *Report of the British Association for the Advancement of Science*, for 1889, pp. 134–139.

wages will tend to fall, on the average, in very much the same proportion. As improvements in machinery make the output per hour of labor, *i.e.* the piece work, increase, the price per piece may decrease.

The two methods of measurement giving these different results for price indexes make opposite differences in the volume of trade. The volume of piece work increases with progress in invention faster than the volume of time work.

In considering the index number as a standard for deferred payments, the desirability of assuming piece wages to change like commodity prices is based largely on the difficulty and consequent impracticability of including wages on a time basis. On the piece-wage basis, changes in money prices of other goods furnish an approximate measure of changes in money prices of labor.

Those who make time contracts on the basis of such an index number know that they will pay back, or receive back, purchasing power over the same quantities of goods, the purchasing power over which they borrowed or lent. This form of index number is an objective standard of goods.

If an index number were to be constructed from time wages alone (not including goods at all), debtors would pay back and creditors receive an equivalent purchasing power over hours of labor. When the time wages and prices of goods are both included, the problem is how much weight to give to each. Kemmerer weights wages 3 per cent out of a total of 100 per cent. Its influence, therefore, would in any case not be felt greatly, while, if we take piece wages, it will not be felt at all; that is, it will not greatly matter whether wages are included or not. Since practically we have no statistics of relative piece wages, and few good statistics for time wages, we may, in general, as well omit wages altogether.

This procedure has another advantage. In an index number intended to serve as a basis for deferred payments for wage earners, it is clear that wages should be excluded. A wage earner does not judge his purchasing power on the basis of how much labor he can buy.[1]

In this connection it may be well to call attention to another standard of purchasing power of money which has sometimes been suggested for adjusting contracts. This is the utility standard. According to this, each person would be expected to receive or pay back marginal utility equivalent to what he had lent or borrowed. But the marginal utility of the same goods is different for different persons and different for the same person at different periods of his life. Hence, no such standard could be practically applied.

A price is an objective datum, susceptible of measurement, and the same for all men. Marginal utilities, on the other hand, not only are impossible to measure, but are unequal and vary unequally among individuals. The purchasing power of money in the objective sense is, therefore, an ascertainable magnitude with a meaning common to all men. It is of course true that marginal utility of money is a fundamental magnitude and that it depends in part on the purchasing power of money. But it depends also on each man's income. The marginal utilities of money will vary directly with the purchasing power of money *if* all prices and *all money incomes* change in the same ratio, or

[1] Cf. Edgeworth, in Palgrave's *Dictionary of Political Economy*, "Index Numbers."

(roughly at least) if incomes change in the ratio of the average price change. Ideally, this fixed ratio between marginal utilities and purchasing power should hold true when the quantity of money varies (assuming that deposits vary equally and that velocities of circulation and volume of trade remain unchanged) after transition periods are over. Practically, however, all these elements vary, and vary unequally. Money incomes sometimes increase faster, often more slowly, than prices. The result is that changes in the purchasing power of money do not correspond to changes in marginal utilities of money.

Society may become more prosperous, or it may become less so, during the time a contract has to run. This fact, it may be thought, should influence the relation of the amount repaid to the amount borrowed. It has been claimed that the benefits of progress should be equably distributed between borrowers and lenders.[1]

But while loan contracts are made with reference to marginal utilities, it is here contended that corrections in a monetary standard not only cannot, but should not, include variations in the subjective value of money due to changes in incomes, but should be confined to variations in objective purchasing power. At any rate, to obtain a measure of objective purchasing power is

[1] See, for example, paper by Professor J. B. Clark, "The Gold Standard in Recent Theory," *Political Science Quarterly*, September, 1895. Compare with this "The Standard of Deferred Payments," by Professor Edward A. Ross, *Annals of the American Academy of Political and Social Science*, November, 1892; Lucius S. Merriam, "The Theory of Final Utility in its Relation to Money and the Standard of Deferred Payments," *ibid.*, January, 1893; Professor Frank Fetter, "The Exploitation of Theories of Value in the Discussion of the Standard of Deferred Payments," *ibid.*, May, 1895.

a step which may properly be taken by itself before any step more ambitious is considered. The search for a standard of deferred payments which shall automatically provide for the just distribution of the "benefits of progress" seems as fatuous a quest as the search for the philosopher's stone. Since we cannot measure utility statistically, we cannot measure the corrections in utility required to redistribute the "benefits of progress." In the absence of statistical measurement, any practicable correction is out of the question. The "utility standard" is therefore impracticable, even if the theory of such a standard were tenable.

Somewhat similar theories of a perfect standard of deferred payments are based on the idea that a dollar should require always the same amount of *labor* to produce it. In one sense, since marginal utility and marginal effort are normally equal, the labor standard is identical with the marginal utility standard. But in whatever sense "labor" is defined, it is an elusive magnitude, quite impracticable as a measurable basis for statistics of purchasing power. Seemingly labor may be measured in terms of *time* and, on such a basis, "a day's labor" has been suggested as a proper unit for measuring deferred payments. But even "a day's labor" is not a sufficiently definite unit in which to measure with any considerable degree of accuracy the purchasing power of money. Days' labor differ in hours, in intensity, and disagreeability of effort as well as in the quality of labor performed — whether it be manual, mental, etc. A magnitude which offers so many theoretical difficulties in measurement can never serve as a practical standard of deferred payments.

We see then that the attempt to set up a utility or labor standard is too ambitious to be practicable.[1] We should content ourselves with securing the maximum attainable improvement in the standard of deferred payments, without attempting to secure an ideal distribution of "the benefits of progress."

It will also simplify our problem if we remember that our ideal is not primarily *constancy* of the dollar but rather *dependability*. Fluctuations which can be foreseen and allowed for are not evils. Each man may presumably be depended on to allow for changes in his own fortunes, utility, and labor, and perhaps even to a large extent on the general effects of invention and progress. At any rate he should not expect the monetary unit to insure him against every wind that blows.

The manner in which each person allows for such future changes as he can foresee is by adjusting the size of loans he makes or takes and the rate of interest thereon. If the average income is rising, the borrower can afford to repay more and the lender should receive more; while, if the average income is falling, the amount paid should be less. The fact is that such are the tendencies where the rise or fall of average income is foreseen. If the average income is rising, the lender will be less anxious to deplete his present income, which is relatively meager, in order to increase his future income, which he sees will probably be larger anyway. Thus, increasing prosperity (by which is meant, not *great* prosperity, but *growing* prosperity) tends to restrict the supply of loans. At the same time, it tends to increase the demand and so raise interest. Conversely, a decreasing average income will tend to lower interest.[2]

[1] Cf. Charles A. Conant, *The Principles of Money and Banking*, Vol. II, Chapter VII.

[2] *Rate of Interest*, pp. 95–98 and 304–306. This position is taken by Correa Moylan Walsh, *The Fundamental Problem in Monetary Science*, New York (Macmillan), 1903, p. 345, footnote.

All this follows only in case the rise or fall of incomes is foreseen. If not foreseen, it can exercise no influence of importance on the interest rate. To the extent that such changes come unexpectedly after loan contracts have been entered into which take no account of them, — to that extent loan contracts are speculative. If incomes fall, the lender has gained relatively to the borrower, because he has realized a higher interest than he could have realized had the change been foreseen. The chief burden of the change falls on the borrower. If incomes experience an unexpected rise, the relative positions are reversed; the whole gain goes to the borrower. The normal effect of continuous extension of income is to raise the rate of interest.

Our present problem, however, is not to safeguard the interests of debtors and creditors against all possible elements of change, but only against those elements which are purely monetary. Industrial changes are in a class by themselves, and contracting parties must be trusted to work out their own salvation. We are merely concerned in providing them with a stable or reliable monetary standard. A secure monetary standard cannot guarantee against earthquake nor insure the equable distribution of prosperity. It can, however, mitigate the losses now suffered from changes in the relation of money to other goods.

Statistics of nominal or money interest rates and virtual or commodity interest rates prove that the latter fluctuate much more than the former.[1] The effects of this lack of compensation are evil. In the first place, the situation interferes with the normal distribution of wealth and income. If the level of prices is rising, since nominal interest does not for a con-

[1] *Rate of Interest*, Chapter XIV.

siderable time rise enough to compensate, the lender gets back a less amount of wealth or services than he might reasonably have expected. Creditors lose and debtors gain. It should be noted also that all persons with relatively fixed money salaries lose by this rise of prices. When the level of prices falls, on the other hand, creditors and persons with relatively fixed incomes gain at the expense of debtors. The distribution of wealth is changed in either case from purely monetary causes, and the change can be averted by making the standard of deferred payments more stable.

§ 5

We are brought back again, therefore, to the conclusion that on the whole the best index number for the purpose of a standard of deferred payments in business is the same index number which we found the best to indicate the changes in prices of all business done; — in other words, it is the P on the right side of the equation of exchange.[1]

It is, of course, utterly impossible to secure data for all exchanges, nor would this be advisable. Only articles which are standardized, and only those the use of which remains through many years, are available and important enough to include. These specifications exclude real estate, and to some extent wages, retail prices, and securities, thus leaving practically nothing but wholesale prices of commodities to be included in the list of goods, the prices of which are to be

[1] This is really the same conclusion as that reached by Walsh, *The Fundamental Problem in Monetary Science*, in which, after a thorough and critical review of the literature of the subject, the author concludes that the kind of stability desirable in the standard of deferred payment is "stability of exchange value."

compounded into an index number. These restrictions, however, are not as important as might be supposed. The total real estate transactions of New York City (Manhattan and the Bronx) in 1909 (an active year) measured by assessed valuations (probably $\frac{4}{5}$ of the market valuation) amounted to only $620,000,000. This is utterly insignificant if compared only with the 104 billions of bank clearings in New York City. Yet real estate transactions probably constitute a higher percentage of total transactions in New York than in the United States.[1] In the United States we feel safe, therefore, in saying that they amount only to a fraction of 1 per cent of the total transactions. As to exchanges in securities, Kemmerer estimates, on the basis of the transactions of the New York Stock Exchange, that about 8 per cent of the total transactions of the country consist in the transfer of securities.[2] As already stated, he also estimates that wages amount to about 3 per cent.[3] As to the comparative importance of retail as compared with wholesale prices, we have some figures of Professor Kinley, of the Monetary Commission.[4] On this basis, and because wholesale and retail prices roughly correspond in their move-

[1] At any rate the impression is strong that real estate is more "active" in New York than in most other cities, because of the rapid change in the character of sites on account of the narrowness of Manhattan Island and the consequent acceleration of growth in one direction (northward) and that, in general, cities have more trade in real estate than the country, not only absolutely, but relalively to other trade.

[2] *Money and Prices*, 2d ed., New York (Holt), 1909, p. 138.

[3] *Ibid.*, p. 138.

[4] *Credit Instruments*, 1910, 61st Congress, 2d Session, Senate Document 399, pp. 69, 73, 134, 136, would indicate that wholesale trade requires something like twice as much exchange work as retail trade.

ments,[1] we may omit retail prices altogether. It is true that retail prices usually lag behind wholesale prices; but part of the lagging is more apparent than real. Expert testimony of those who have collected such statistics shows that when, as at present, prices are rising rapidly, retailers obviate the necessity of confronting their customers with too frequent and rapid increases in prices by quoting the same prices and substituting inferior grades or, in some instances, smaller loaves or packages.

It is true that wholesale transactions constitute a minority of all transactions, perhaps only a fifth.[2] Nevertheless, wholesale prices are more *typical* than any other.

They are to a large extent typical of producers' prices which precede them, and of retail prices which succeed them. They are typical of many large and often nondescript groups which go to make up the total transactions, such as are classed together in Kinley's Report to the Monetary Commission under the head "other deposits," including hotel charges, fees of professional men, etc., as well as wages. Among items of which wholesale prices may not be very typical are the transactions in securities (speculative and other), railway and other transportation charges, and insurance. Latterly, prices of stock securities have advanced faster than wholesale prices, while transportation and insurance charges have not advanced as fast. The attempts

[1] The studies of the Bureau of Labor in retail prices would show a general sympathy in movement between retail or wholesale prices, as indeed might be expected.

[2] See, in *Report of National Monetary Commission on Credit Instruments*, the figures of aggregate sums deposited in banks by wholesale merchants and others. While these do not afford an exact comparison, they aid in making a rough guess.

of Kemmerer and myself (Chapter XII) to combine in one average wholesale prices *and* prices of stocks and wages yield results differing only slightly from those based on wholesale prices. From a practical standpoint, wholesale prices of commodities are the only prices which are yet sufficiently standardized, and the use of the goods sufficiently stable through a long period of time, to make them serviceable for general use.

Not only may we consider that wholesale prices roughly represent all prices, but we may, with even more confidence, confine our statistics for wholesale prices to a relatively small number. Edgeworth and others have shown, both practically and theoretically, that a large number of articles is needless and may even be detrimental. The 22 commodities employed by "The Economist" afford an index number of considerable value; the 45 of Sauerbeck have given us a standard of great value; and the 200 and more commodities used in the Aldrich Report and the bulletins of the Bureau of Labor are certainly numerous enough, if not too numerous, to give a most accurate index number of prices.

The recommendations of the Committee of the British Association for the Advancement of Science were that the index number should include six groups, comprehending twenty-seven classes of articles, and that the prices should be weighted in round numbers representing approximately the relative expenditures of the community in these objects. The groups and classes with weighting were as follows:[1] —

[1] See Report of the Committee in *Report of the British Association for the Advancement of Science*, for 1888, p. 186.

Breadstuffs (wheat 5, barley 5, oats 5, potatoes, rice, etc., 5) . . 20
Meat and dairy (meat 10, fish 2½, cheese, butter, milk, 7½) . . . 20
Luxuries (sugar 2½, tea 2½, beer 9, spirits 2½, wine 1, tobacco 2½) 20
Clothing (cotton 2½, wool 2½, silk 2½, leather 2½) 10
Minerals (coal 10, iron 5, copper 2½, lead, zinc, tin, etc., 2½) . . 20
Miscellaneous (timber 3, petroleum 1, indigo 1, flax and linseed 3, palm oil 1, caoutchouc 1) 10

This report was made after very thorough consideration by a remarkably competent committee consisting of Mr. S. Bourne, Professor F. Y. Edgeworth (Sec.), Professor H. S. Foxwell, Mr. Robert Giffen, Professor Alfred Marshall, Mr. J. B. Martin, Professor J. S. Nicholson, Mr. R. H. Inglis Palgrave, and Professor H. Sedgwick. The report also gives the precise technical description of the articles the price quotations of which are to be used (the iron, for instance, being "Scotch pig iron"), and also the price list or other source for price quotations (the wheat, for instance, being the "Gazette Average").

With slight modifications this recommendation of the British Committee could be made to apply to American figures. In America we have had a number of index numbers of wholesale prices, the most important being (1) those of Roland P. Falkner in the Aldrich Senate Report, covering a period from 1840 to 1891, in which, beginning with 1860, there were 223 commodities included. The results given in two ways, viz., weighted, the weighting being arranged according to relative expenditures on these articles or their representatives by workmen, and also unweighted; (2) those of the United States Labor Bureau for 251 to 261 commodities beginning with 1890, and since 1908, it is understood, to be continued biennially; (3) Dun's index numbers from 1860 to 1906 continued recently for Gibson by Dr. J. P. Norton; and (4) Bradstreet's index numbers since 1895 for 96 commodities.

We need not go into detailed criticism of these index numbers. On the whole they seem to include too many commodities, while they all employ the objectionable fixed-base system. It would be a great advantage if we could fix upon a system in America which would be not only authoritative, but would give out its results at least yearly and promptly.

For practical purposes the *median* is one of the best index numbers. It may be computed in a small fraction of the time required for computing the more theoretically accurate index numbers, and it meets many of the tests of a good index number remarkably well. It also has the advantage of easily exhibiting (by means of the "quartiles") the tendency to dispersion of prices (from each year as a base to the next) on either side of the median. The median should be weighted in round numbers analogously to the weighting already discussed for the more theoretically perfect index numbers.[1] The median of a series of numbers is a number such that there are as many numbers above as below it in the series. If the number of terms in the series is odd, the median is the middle term of the series of numbers arranged in the order of magnitude. If the number of terms is even, the median falls between two terms. If these are equal, the median is identical with them both; if they are unequal, the median lies between them and may then be taken as their simple arithmetical, geometric, or any other average. Practically the two middle terms are almost inevitably so close together that it would make no appreciable difference what

[1] See Appendix to (this) Chapter X, § 8.

method of averaging the two middle terms is adopted. The method of *weighting* the terms from which a median is computed consists in counting each term the number of times indicated by its weight. To illustrate these statements, it is evident that the median of the numbers 3, 4, 4, 5, 6, 6, 7, arranged in order of magnitude is 5; and the median of 3, 4, 4, 5, 6, 6 is 4½.

If the weights to be attached to these latter numbers are

for number 3 weight 1
for number 4 weight 2
for number 4 weight 3
for number 5 weight 4
for number 6 weight 2
for number 6 weight 1

the median is then found from the following: —

Series	3,	4, 4,	4, 4, 4,	5, 5, 5, 5,	6, 6,	6
The weights being	1	2	3	4	2	1

of which the median is 5. The arithmetical averages corresponding to the three medians mentioned (5, 4½ and 5) are 4.9, 4.67 and 4.54 respectively.

Practically it is not necessary to arrange the terms in exact order of size. Terms easily recognized as low can readily be paired off against those easily recognized as high and only the remaining few central terms need be arranged in exact order. The terms near the middle being usually almost or quite equal, make the selection of the median extremely easy.

In order to use the median for an index number of prices, we first arrange our *price ratios* and then select the median *ratio*.

§ 6

In this chapter we have aimed to show that an excellent form of index number of prices is the ratio of real values to ideal values at base prices; and that the elements entering into the construction of index numbers differ according to the different purposes for which they are desired. If the purpose is to measure capital, the prices of services should not be included, but only the prices of the different articles of wealth existing at any point of time. If the purpose is to obtain means to measure real wages, only those things should be included which workingmen buy; and they should be included according to the values bought during a given period, these values being measured at standard prices.

The question of justice between borrower and lender, where the purpose is to fix on the best index number as a standard for deferred payments, was also considered. It was seen to be not an infringement of justice that one man should gain from another on account of fluctuations in the money standard; for the contract is a free one in which normally each should assume whatever risk there may be of loss for the sake of whatever chance there may be of gain. It was maintained, also, that it would be wrong for the government deliberately to take his gain away from a person who had assumed a risk of loss in the first place. Nevertheless, it was urged that a means by which contracts made in the future could be made less speculative, is desirable.

It was urged that it is no part of the function of an index number of general prices to guard against rising and falling real income. The function of such an index number is to measure the change in the level of prices, in order that, in contracts involving deferred payments, there shall be no element of risk so far as money is concerned. Without the index number as a standard, such contracts are quite highly speculative. The adjustment of the rate of interest compensates to some extent, but not nearly enough, for the fluctuations in the value of money. These fluctuations influence the distribution of wealth among persons and classes, and bring about crises and business depressions. It is desirable that some basis for time contracts should be fixed upon, which will remedy these evils. It is believed that an index number expressing the price level entering into the equation of exchange might be adopted as such a basis. The ideal set forth is that neither debtor nor creditor should be the worse off by being deceived through changes in the level of prices of goods bought and sold. Some system is to be sought, therefore, by which the actual results of the contract should closely approximate the expected results in nearly all cases.

It was shown that different persons and different classes might be interested in having for their time contracts index numbers somewhat differently constructed, because different persons are interested in consuming different kinds of commodities and because they desire to invest larger or smaller proportions of their earnings. But for general purposes, as the best compromise to fit the needs of different classes, what was suggested was an index number based on the prices of all goods *exchanged* during a given period. It was pointed out, however, that the different forms of index numbers which had gained reputation lead to practically the same results.

Finally, it was shown that for rough and ready computations the median has advantages over all other forms of index numbers.

CHAPTER XI

STATISTICAL VERIFICATION. GENERAL HISTORICAL REVIEW

§ 1

Since both the level of prices and the quantity of money in circulation cannot in practice be perfectly measured, and since the level of prices depends upon other factors besides the quantity of money, — viz. the quantity of circulating credit, the velocities of circulation of that credit and of money, and the volume of business, — it would be absurd to expect any exact correspondence between variations in the quantity of circulating money and variations in the price level; and it is likewise absurd to state, as some have stated, that the absence of exact statistical correspondence proves the absence of *any* influence of quantity of money on price level. Nevertheless, when the volume of money changes greatly and quickly, the effect on prices from this cause is usually so great as to make itself manifest.

The general trend of prices has usually been upward, as Figure 10[1] shows. We may say that prices are now about ten times as high as a thousand years ago and that they are from four to six times as high as in the period between 1200 and 1500 A.D. Beginning with the last-named date, or shortly after the discovery of America, prices have almost steadily risen.

[1] This diagram shows the changes in price level according to the separate estimates of D'Avenel, Hanauer, and Leber as given in Aupetit's *Essai sur la théorie générale de la monnaie*, Paris (Guillaumin), 1901, p. 245.

The discovery of America was followed in 1519 by the invasion of Mexico under Cortez and, twenty years later, by Pizarro's conquest of Peru. From these conquests and the consequent development of New World mining of precious metals, dates the tremendous production of gold, and especially of silver, during the sixteenth century. From the discovery of America until the after effects of its discovery began to be felt,

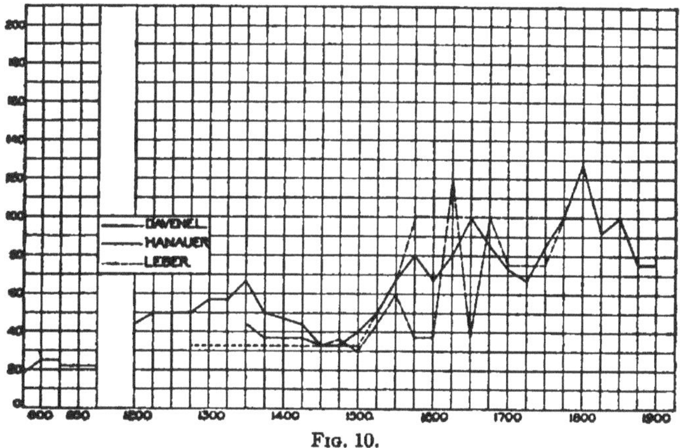

FIG. 10.

or, to be exact, through the year 1544, the average annual output of gold was less than five million dollars, and of silver about the same.[1] The rich mines of Potosi

[1] These and the following figures are from "The World's Production of Gold and Silver from 1493–1905," J. D. Magee, *Journal of Political Economy*, January, 1910, p. 50 ff. Mr. Magee's figures to 1885 are based on Soetbeer's, and since that date, on the Reports of the Director of the United States Mint. For Soetbeer's figures, see Adolf Soetbeer, *Edelmetall-Produktion und Werthverhältniss zwischen Gold und Silber seit der Entdeckung Amerika's bis zum Gegenwart*, Gotha (Justus Perthes), 1879 p. 107. These figures and others to follow are given also in the same author's *Materialen* and are quoted, and their significance discussed, in L. L. Price,

in Bolivia were discovered in 1546. From 1545 to 1560 the annual production of silver averaged eighteen millions, which was over fourfold the previous rate. The product of gold also increased, though slightly. The rates of production for both metals rose steadily (with slight interruption, 1811–1840) up to the present time.

These new world mines began to pour their product into Europe: first into Spain, the chief owner of the mines, then, by trade, into the Netherlands and other parts of Europe, and then into the Orient — that great "sink of silver." Accordingly, as Cliffe Leslie[1] has shown, prices rose first in Spain, then in the Netherlands, and then in other regions.

But, though the new supplies of the precious metals distributed themselves very gradually through Europe, and the rise of prices was consequently in some regions delayed, there can be no doubt that they rose or that the rise was great. The rise between the discovery of America and the beginning of the nineteenth century was several hundred per cent. This rise was simultaneous with an increase of the stock of the precious metals, because production outran consumption.

Although the total production of the precious metals continued to increase until 1810, the ratio of the yearly production to the existing stock became gradually less. Corresponding to this slackening of production, and presumably because of it, prices did not continue to rise at the same rapid rate as at first. Furthermore, with the development of trade with the East, more and more of the new supplies found their way thither. The most rapid rise occurred during the sixteenth century.

Money and its Relation to Prices, London (Sonnenschein), 1900, New York (Scribner's), p. 82 ff.

[1] *Essays in Political Economy*, 2d ed., No. 19.

§ 2

The stock of money metals at any time in any country is evidently the difference between the total product and the sum of the consumption and the net export. Jacob[1] has estimated roughly the stock in Europe at various dates. The following table compares the estimated metallic stocks in Europe with the estimated price levels:—

MONEY AND PRICES

Estimated Product, Consumption, and Stock of Precious Metals in Europe, expressed in Millions of Dollars, and Price Levels[2]

DATE	PRODUCT	CONSUMPTION AND EXPORT	STOCK	PRICES
1500			170	35
	670	290		
1600			550	75
	1640	740		
1700			1450	90
	4280	3880		
1800			1850	100
	13,000	8960		
1900			5890	125 (?)

[1] William Jacob, F.R.S., *An Historical Inquiry into the Production and Consumption of the Precious Metals*, 2 vols., London (Murray) 1831; Vol. II, p. 63. See also Price, *Money and its Relation to Prices*, p. 78.

[2] The estimates of the product and stock are those of Jacob and Soetbeer (*op. cit.*) and Del Mar, *History of the Precious Metals*, New York (Cambridge Encyclopaedia Co.), 1902, p. 449. The price levels (except that for 1900) are the averages of those of Vicomte D'Avenel, *Histoire Économique de la Propriété des Salaires et des Denrées*, Vol. I, pp. 27 and 32, Leber and Hanauer (see A. Aupetit, *Essai sur la théorie générale de la monnaie*, Paris (Guillaumin), 1901, p. 245, the three estimates being each reduced to 100 per cent for the last quarter of the eighteenth century, or rather 1770–1790. The figure for each century year is taken as the average of the figures given by the three authorities for the preceding and succeeding quarter century. The figure for 1900 is given as 125 as a com-

With the enormous increase in the quantity of the precious metals, small wonder if prices have risen!

We see that there has been a general increase (1) in the stock of money metals, and (2) in the price level, and that the greatest increase of each was in the sixteenth century. We find also that the prices did not increase as fast as the quantity of money. This relative slowness on the part of prices was to be expected, because of the increased volume of business. This, we know, must have come with increased population and with progress in the arts — especially the arts of trade — and with development in transportation. As to changes in the velocity of circulation of money we know absolutely nothing.

§ 3

During the last century the price movements have been more carefully recorded and show many ups and downs. The most complete statistics (those of Sauerbeck) are for England. They are represented in Figure 11.[1] As is well known, English prices were inflated by

promise between widely conflicting results. Leber, Hanauer, and D'Avenel agree fairly well and D'Avenel (writing in 1890 to 1894) finds (p. 32) the "present" price level in France to be double what it was for 1776–1790, which would make the required figure 200. The figures for England, however, of Jevons for 1782 to 1818, *Investigations in Currency and Finance*, London (Macmillan), 1884, p. 144, combined with those of Sauerbeck from 1818 to the present, *Course of Average Prices in England*, London (King), 1908, indicate an actual fall of prices, the figure for 1900 being on the above basis from 75 to 80. The English figures are so much more complete than the continental figures of D'Avenel, Leber, and Hanauer, that they are given more weight, and 125 seems a fair rough average for Europe. But the wide discrepancies between the various figures make this, or any other figure which might be chosen, extremely uncertain.

[1] The figures are taken from various numbers of the *Journal of the Royal Statistical Society*. For many years Sauerbeck has published yearly his index number in the March issue of this journal.

the issue of irredeemable paper during the Napoleonic wars. This period of the paper standard extended from 1801 to 1820. But prices in paper were only slightly higher than prices in gold, and the chief price

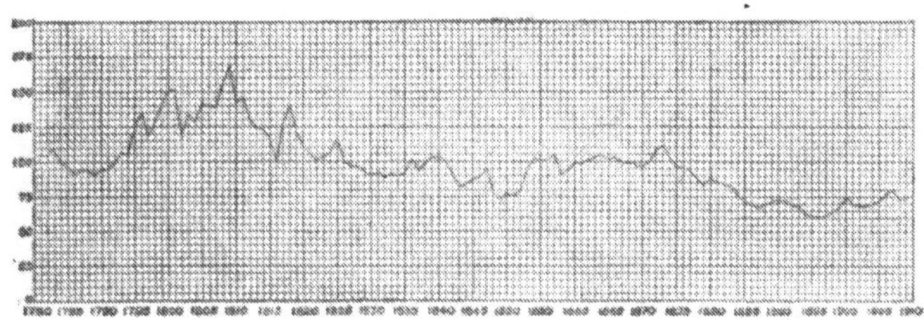

FIG. 11.

movements (except in a few years) were but slightly affected by the existence of a paper standard. The main periods of price movements in England since 1789 may be stated as follows:—

Prices rose 1789–1809, stock increasing.
Prices fell 1809–1849, stock stationary.
Prices rose 1849–1873, stock increasing.
Prices fell 1873–1896, stock increasing slightly.
Prices rose 1896–present, stock increasing.

In each case is cited the movement in the stock of money metals in Europe as given in the table of Del Mar.[1]

The only period which does not, at first glance, agree with what we might expect if our theory of price levels

[1] *History of the Precious Metals*, p. 449. The data given by Del Mar are based on the estimates of King, Humbolt, Jacob, Tooke, Newmarch, McCulloch, and himself. The dates correspond approximately with the ends of the periods of price movements as above given. The following figures summarize those of Del Mar as to stock (expressed in billions of dollars):—

1776	1.4	1870	3.6
1808	1.9	1876	3.7
1838	1.3	1893	3.7
1850	2.0	1896	4.5

in relation to money is correct, is the period 1873–1896. Of the other four periods, three are periods of rising prices and increasing stocks. The fourth is a period of a stationary stock; and since the volume of trade undoubtedly increased, a fall of prices was naturally to be expected.

The exceptional period 1873–1896 — a period of falling prices — is probably to be accounted for by the increasing volume of trade and the successive demonetization of silver by various countries.

The foregoing parallelism between monetary stocks and prices is somewhat remarkable in view of the incompleteness of the data.[1] In the table there are lacking, not only exact statistics as to the volume of trade and all statistics whatever of velocity of circulation, but also statistics of the volume of bank notes, government notes, and deposit currency. We know, however, that modern banking, which had scarcely developed at all before the French Revolution, developed rapidly throughout the nineteenth century. It is also known that banking and deposit currency developed more rapidly during the third period in the table (1849–1873) than during the fourth (1873–1896),[2] which fact contributes somewhat to explain the contrast between the price movements of these two periods.

§ 4

We may, therefore, summarize the course of price movements during the nineteenth century by the following probable statements: —

1. Between 1789 and 1809 prices rose rapidly, the

[1] Cf. Albert Aupetit, *Essai sur la théorie générale de la monnaie*, Paris (Guillaumin), 1901, pp. 271–285.

[2] See Mulhall, *Dictionary of Statistics*, article on "Banks."

index numbers of Jevons moving from 85 to 157 when prices are expressed in the gold standard, or 161 when expressed in paper.[1] That is, prices practically doubled in twenty years. This rise was due to the increased stock of gold and silver, which in turn was due to their large production during this period as compared with the periods before and after. The production of silver was especially great.[2] The Napoleonic wars with their destruction of wealth and interference with trade probably exercised some influence in the same direction.[3]

2. Between 1809 and 1849 prices fell. The fall was measured by Jevons as a fall from 157, gold (or 161, paper), to 64. That is, in forty years prices were reduced to less than half, or, to be more exact, to two fifths. This fall in prices was presumably due to the lull in the production of the precious metals, which prevented the aggregate stock from keeping pace with the volume of business. Indeed, the aggregate stock remained stationary while the volume of business increased. Even the development of bank currency was insufficient to offset the continued increase in the volume of business. It is interesting to observe that this period of falling prices was interrupted by a temporary rise after 1833, which Jevons was at a loss to account for, but which was apparently due to the inflow of Russian gold after the discoveries of gold in Siberia in 1830.[4]

3. Between 1849 and 1873 (although with two notable interruptions) prices rose. They rose, according

[1] Jevons, *Investigations in Currency and Finance*, London (Macmillan), 1884, p. 144.

[2] See Magee, "World's Production of Gold and Silver," *Journal of Political Economy*, January, 1910, pp. 54, 56.

[3] See Harrison H. Brace, *Gold Production and Future Prices*, New York (Bankers' Publishing Co.) 1910, pp. 16 and 17.

[4] Price, *Money and its Relation to Prices*, p. 112.

to Jevons's figures supplemented by Sauerbeck's,[1] from 64 to 86, and according to Sauerbeck's alone, from 74 to 111. That is, in 24 years prices increased, according to one calculation, by one third; according to another, by one half. This rise was presumably in consequence of the gold inflation following the famous California gold discoveries in 1849 and Australian discoveries in 1851 and 1852. The simultaneous rapid development of banking contributed to the same result in spite of the continued increase in trade.

4. Between 1873 and 1896 prices fell. This fall was presumably due to the slackening in the production of gold; to the adoption of the gold standard by nations previously on a silver basis, and the consequent withdrawal of gold by these new users from the old; to the arrest of the expansion of silver money consequent on the closure of mints to silver; to the slackening in the growth of banking; and to the ever present growth of trade.[2]

During the long fall of prices from 1873 to 1896, country after country adopted the gold standard. We have already seen that Germany adopted the gold standard

[1] This rise is found by adding to Jevons's table, which ends in 1865, a fictitious figure (86) for 1873, calculated to be in the ratio to the 1865 figure (78), which Sauerbeck's figure for 1873 (111) bears to his figure for 1865 (101).

[2] It is not that the left-hand side of the equation did not increase, but that it did not increase so fast as trade; therefore prices fell. Laughlin seems to think he is overthrowing Mill's position that credit acts like money on prices (an increase of credit raising prices, other things equal), by appealing to the fact of an enormous growth of deposit currency in this period which had not raised prices nor prevented their fall. But if trade increased even faster (and Laughlin himself asserts an increase of trade, though he denies that it is a satisfactory answer), then a fall of prices was not opposed to, but entirely consistent with, Mill's theory. See Laughlin, *The Principles of Money*, New York (Scribner), 1903, pp. 319 and 320.

in 1871–1873, thus helping to render impossible the maintenance of bimetallism by the Latin Union. The Scandinavian monetary union adopted the gold standard in 1873. Between that date and 1878 the countries of the Latin Union suspended the free coinage of silver and came practically to a gold basis. In the United States the legislation of 1873 signified that with resumption (which took place in 1879), the country would come to a gold basis, although no considerable amount of silver, except for small change, had been coined here for several decades previously. The Netherlands virtually adopted the gold standard in 1875–1876, Egypt in 1885, Austria in 1892, India in 1893, Chili in 1895, Venezuela and Costa Rica in 1896, Russia, Japan, and Peru in 1897, Ecuador in 1899, and Mexico in 1905. In fact, most countries of importance have now definitely adopted the gold standard.

The preceding figures apply only to gold countries. But in 1873 gold and silver countries, as it were, fell asunder. It is interesting, therefore, to inquire whether the movement of prices in gold countries was parallel or antithetical to that in silver countries. As might be expected, we find it antithetical. The demonetization of silver in gold countries made a greater amount of that metal available for silver countries. Accordingly, we find that prices rose in India from 107 in 1873 to 140 in 1896,[1] in Japan from 104 in 1873 to 133 in 1896,[2] and in

[1] F. J. Atkinson, "Silver Prices in India," *Journal of the Royal Statistical Society*, March, 1897, p. 92. The figures for 1893, 1894, 1895, and 1896 were lowered by the closure of the Indian mint to silver in 1893.

[2] The figures from 1873 to 1893 are from *Japanese Monetary Reports*, 1895, translated for me by Mr. Sakata of Yale University. The figures for 1894, 1895, 1896 were also from official Japanese sources provided by Japanese students.

China from 100 in 1874 to 109 in 1893.[1] These figures, although not as reliable and representative as the figures for gold countries, agree in indicating a rise of prices. The amount of rise is differently indicated, ranging roughly from 10 per cent to 35 per cent. The following table shows the contrast between the gold and silver countries as between 1873–1876 and 1890–1893, the last year being that of the closure of the Indian mint to silver.[2]

PRICES IN GOLD AND SILVER COUNTRIES [3]

	GOLD	SILVER
1873–1876	100	100
1890–1893	78	117

We see that gold prices fell a little more than 20 per cent and that silver prices rose a little less than 20 per cent.[4]

If some way had been contrived by which gold and silver could have been kept together (say by world-wide

[1] From the Japanese Report mentioned in the above note.

[2] The figures for prices in India are, of course, too meager and local to be of as great value as the corresponding index numbers for Europe and America. Cf. figures cited by J. Barr Robertson's article (1903), *Report of Commission on International Exchange*, 58th Congress, 2d Session, H. R. Document 144, Washington, 1903, pp. 357–378.

[3] Irving Fisher, "Prices in Silver Countries," *Yale Review*, May, 1897, p. 79. The index numbers for gold countries are based on those of Sauerbeck for England, Soetbeer, Heintz, and Conrad for Germany, and Falkner (Aldrich Report) for the United States. Those for silver countries are from Atkinson for India and the Report of the Japanese Currency Commission above referred to.

[4] We may remark in passing that this divergence between the two sets of prices is somewhat more than the divergence between gold and silver themselves.

bimetallism), prices would not have fallen so much in gold countries, or risen so much (if at all) in silver countries, but would probably have fallen in gold countries slightly — probably about 10 per cent up to 1890–1893 and more up to 1896. This is because the stocks of specie in silver countries were less than half those in gold countries [1] (including those with the "limping standard" from left-over silver); so that had there been a transfer of a given amount of silver from the silver Orient to the gold Occident, this would have affected Oriental prices about twice as much as Occidental.

The transition of India from the silver to the gold side has left about nine tenths [2] of the specie (gold and overvalued silver) in the gold column. In other words, the world is now practically on a gold basis. The result has been to make Indian prices move in sympathy with European prices,[3] instead of in opposition.

5. From 1896 to the present, prices have been rising because of the extraordinary rise in gold production and the consequent increase in money media of all kinds. The gold of South Africa combined with the gold from the rich mines of Cripple Creek and other parts of the Rocky Mountain Plateau, and reënforced by gold from the Klondike, caused, and is still causing, a repetition of the phenomenon of half a century ago.

That there has been a distinct rise in prices is evident from the figures of all index numbers. Those of *The Economist*, Sauerbeck, Dun, the Labor Bureau Reports, and Bradstreet are given on the following page.

[1] See Muhleman, *Monetary Systems of the World*, New York (Nicoll), 1897, p. 177.

[2] See Muhleman, *ibid.*

[3] See J. B. Robertson, "Variations in Indian Price Levels since 1861 expressed in Index Numbers," *Department of Commerce and Industry* (Government of India).

English			American		
Close of Dec.	Economist	Sauerbeck	Dun	Labor Bureau	Bradstreet
1896 . .	1950	61	74	90	59
1897 . .	1890	62	72	90	61
1898 . .	1918	64	77	93	66
1899 . .	2145	68	85	102	72
1900 . .	2126	75	91	111	79
1901 . .	1948	70	91	109	76
1902 . .	2003	69	102	113	79
1903 . .	2197	69	99	114	79
1904 . .	2136	70	97	113	79
1905 . .	2342	72	98	116	81
1906 . .	2499	77	105	123	84
1907 . .	2310	80		130	89
1908 . .	2197	73		123	80
1909 . .	2373	74		127	85

The high points of 1900 and 1907, as compared with the low level of 1896, must be regarded as at least partly due to expansion of credit. The fairest comparison (to eliminate the effects of undue changes in credit) is perhaps that of the years 1896, 1903, and 1909. That the rise of prices has been world wide is evidenced not only by index numbers, which are only available for a limited number of countries, but by general impressions of consumers and by special reports and investigations.[1]

The period 1896–1909 for the United States will be studied in more detail in the following chapter.

§ 5

It will be seen that the history of prices has in substance been the history of a race between the increase in media of exchange (M and M') and the increase in trade (T), while (we assume) the velocities of circulation

[1] See *Report of the Select Committee on Wages and Prices of Commodities*, Senate Report 912, 61st Congress, 2d Session, 1910.

were changing in a much less degree. Knowing little of the variations in the development of trade, we may tentatively assume a steady growth, and pay chief attention to the variations of circulating media. Sometimes the circulating media shot ahead of trade and then prices rose. This was undoubtedly the case in the periods numbered 1, 3, and 5 of the five periods just considered. Sometimes, on the other hand, circulating media lagged behind trade and then prices fell. This must have been the case in the periods numbered 2 and 4.

It is important to emphasize at this point a fact mentioned in a previous chapter; namely, that the breakdown of bimetallism and the consequent division of the world into a gold section and a silver section have made each section more sensitive than before to fluctuations in the production of the precious metals. The present flood of gold can spread itself only over the gold section of the world, and not over the whole world as was virtually the case with the Californian gold immediately after 1849. At that time gold displaced silver in bimetallic France and sent it to the Orient. In this way the Orient afforded relief for bimetallic countries by draining off silver and making room for gold; and the bimetallic countries thereby afforded relief to gold countries also.

Since 1873, therefore, the gold reservoir of Europe and America has been separated from the silver reservoir of the East, with the consequence that the European and American reservoir level has been made more sensitive to either a scarcity or a superabundance of gold. The result has been to aggravate both the fall of prices from 1873 to 1896 and the present rise, although the later effect is mitigated by the previous extension of the gold standard.

§ 6

The outlook for the future is apparently toward a continued rise of prices due to a continued increase in the gold supply. To-day almost as much gold is produced every year as was produced in the whole of the 16th century.

The most careful review of present gold-mining conditions shows that we may expect a continuance of gold inflation for a generation or more. "For at least thirty years we may count on an output of gold higher than, or at least comparable to, that of the last few years." [1] This gold will come from the United States, Alaska, Mexico, the Transvaal, and other parts of Africa and Australia, and later from Colombia, Bolivia, Chili, the Ural Province, Siberia, and Korea. It must be remembered that it is the *stock* of gold and not the annual production which influences the price level; and that the stock will probably continue to increase for many years after the production has begun to decline, — as long, in fact, as production keeps above consumption.

A lake continues to rise long after the freshet which feeds it has reached its maximum. So the stock of gold will continue to increase long after the annual production of gold has stopped increasing. Whether or not prices will continue to rise depends on whether the increase in gold and the circulating media based on gold continues to exceed the growth of trade. It is the relation of gold to trade that chiefly affects prices. Even if the stock of gold should increase for many years, prices may not rise; for trade may increase still faster.

[1] L. de Launay, *The World's Gold*, English translation, New York (Putnam), 1908, p. 227.

If the annual additions of gold to the total stock remain constant and consequently the stock continually increases, the *ratio* between the constant annual addition and the increasing stock will evidently decrease, and the increase in stock will count for less and less in raising prices.[1]

It is difficult to predict the future growth of trade and therefore impossible to say for how long gold expansion will keep ahead of trade expansion. That for many years, however, gold will outrun trade seems probable, for the reason that there is no immediate prospect of a reduction in the percentage growth of the gold stock, nor of an increase in the percentage growth of trade. Not only do mining engineers report untold workable deposits in outlying regions (for instance a full billion of dollars in one region of Colombia alone), but any long look ahead must reckon with possible and probable cheapening of gold extraction. The cyanide process has made low grade ores pay. If we let imagination run a little ahead of our times, we may expect similar improvements in the future whereby still lower grades may be worked or possibly the sea compelled to give up its gold. Like the surface of the continents, the waters of the sea contain *many thousand* times as much gold as all the gold thus far extracted in the whole history of the world. It is to be hoped that the knowledge of how to get this hidden treasure may not be secured. To whatever extent inventors and gold miners might be enriched thereby, scarcely a worse economic calamity can be imagined than the resulting

[1] Cf. Jevons, *Investigations in Currency and Finance*, London (Macmillan), 1884, pp. 64, 65, 66; also Harrison H. Brace, *Gold Production and Future Prices*, New York (Bankers' Publishing Co.), 1910, p. 113.

depreciation. It may be, however, that only by such a calamity can the nations of the world be aroused to the necessity of getting rid of metallic standards altogether.

§ 7

We have briefly summarized the history of price movements since the discovery of America and shown their relation to the stock of the precious metals. But, as we have emphasized in previous chapters, the precious metals do not include all forms of circulating media. Paper money and bank deposits have come during the nineteenth century to occupy very important places in currency systems.

We shall not attempt any complete review of the effects of paper money on prices. The best that can be done is to mention briefly the most striking cases of paper money inflation and contraction. These are all cases of irredeemable paper money. When paper money is redeemable, its possible increase is restricted by that fact and, what is more important, the effects of the increase are dissipated over so large an area as to have little perceptible effect on prices. This dissipation takes place through the export of specie from the country in which the paper issues occur. Though the paper cannot be itself exported, it can displace gold or silver, which amounts to the same thing so far as spreading out the effect on prices is concerned.

But when the paper is irredeemable, after specie has been expelled from circulation (whether by export, melting, or hoarding in anticipation of disaster) there is no such spreading-out effect. The effects on prices are then entirely local and therefore greatly magnified.[1]

[1] See Ricardo, Essay on the "High Price of Bullion," *Works*, 2d ed., London (Murray), 1852, p. 278.

The consequence is that the most striking examples of price inflation are cases of irredeemable paper money. The rise of prices is often still further aggravated by the gradual substitution of other and better money or resort to barter, which further restricts the sphere in which the paper is used and within that sphere makes it the more redundant. Where the paper money is looked upon with disfavor, for whatever reason — whether because its promised redemption has been indefinitely postponed, or simply because of the bare fact that it is depreciating, or because of any other consideration — its sphere of use is restricted.[1] Creditors and tradesmen avoid taking it if they can, by "contracting out" in advance; by barter; by fixing a double set of prices, one in paper and the other in some other money; and by outright refusal. In the end it may happen that the paper ceases to be used at all. In that case its value depreciates indefinitely and therefore prices (so far as still expressed in terms of paper) rise indefinitely.

Whatever the situation, the equation of exchange continues to hold true though its significance becomes of less importance, because T, instead of comprising practically all trade, comes to mean only that disappearing portion of trade still transacted by means of paper money.

The value of irredeemable paper money is, therefore, extremely precarious. If once it starts depreciating — from whatever cause — it is likely to depreciate further, not simply because of the ever present temptation to further issue, but also because of a growing public

[1] See Francis A. Walker, *Money*, New York (Holt), 1878, p. 199. Cf. Joseph French Johnson, *Money and Currency*, Boston (Ginn), 1906, p. 269.

sentiment against it which sooner or later restricts its use.[1] In many cases the irredeemable paper money continues to be used with sufficient acceptability to give it a virtual monopoly as a medium of exchange.

Although theoretically irredeemable paper money may be the cheapest and most easily regulated form of currency, and although, in some cases, it has remained a stable currency for a considerable period, the lesson of history is emphatically that irredeemable paper money results in monetary manipulation, business distrust, a speculative condition of trade, and all the evils which flow from these conditions.

§ 8

One of the early paper-money schemes was that of John Law, who established a bank of issue in France in 1716. Two years later (December 4, 1718), the bank was taken over by the Crown. Soon shrewd traders were acquiring specie for notes and exporting the specie secretly, although exportation of specie was illegal. May 27, 1720, only four years after its establishment, the bank stopped payment of specie. By November of the very same year the paper had fallen to one tenth of its par value, and after this it became utterly worthless.

The case of the assignats of the French Revolution is classic.[2] It was in December, 1789, that the first issue, four hundred million francs, was ordered, based ostensibly on the landed property of the nation. The notes were issued in April, 1790, and bore 3 per cent interest. According to the original plan, all of the assignats received

[1] Cf. the mention of this influence on depreciation in the Bullion Report, III.

[2] For the following facts, see Andrew D. White, *Paper Money Inflation in France*, Economic Tracts, No. VII, No. 3 of Series, 1882.

in payment for land were to be burned. But original plans seem never to be carried out with respect to paper money. Instead, a hundred millions were reissued in the form of small notes. Prices began to rise. In June of the year 1791, six hundred millions more were issued. Depreciation to the extent of 8 to 10 per cent immediately followed. Specie was rapidly disappearing. Another three hundred millions of francs were ordered in December, 1791. By February, the assignats were over 30 per cent below par. In April, 1792, came a decree for the issue of three hundred millions more, and in July for the same amount additional. Most prices were very high, but wages seem to have still remained at the level of 1788. By December 14 of 1792, thirty-four hundred million francs had been issued in assignats, of which six hundred millions had been burned, leaving twenty-eight hundred millions in circulation. Laws were enacted to fix maximum prices, but were evaded. By 1796, forty-five billion francs had been issued, of which thirty-six billions were in circulation. In February of that year the gold louis, of 25 francs, was worth 7200 francs in assignats; and the assignats were worth $\frac{1}{288}$ of par. A new kind of paper money, the mandats, was next issued, but soon fell to 5 per cent of its nominal value. In the end the twenty-five hundred million mandats and the thirty-six billion assignats were repudiated and became entirely worthless.

§ 9

England's experience with irredeemable paper money was more temperate. Under the stress of the Napoleonic wars, the Bank of England suspended cash payments in 1797. This nullified the force which automatically limited overissue. The bank resumed cash payments in 1821. During much of the intervening period of paper money, prices in paper were very high. The following table of Jevons shows the relative prices in notes and specie from 1801 to 1820:[1] —

YEAR	GOLD STANDARD	PAPER STANDARD
1801	140	153
1802	110	119
1803	125	128
1804	119	122
1805	132	136
1806	130	133
1807	129	132
1808	145	149
1809	157	161
1810	142	164
1811	136	147
1812	121	148
1813	115	149
1814	114	153
1815	109	132
1816	91	109
1817	117	120
1818	132	135
1819	112	117
1820	103	106

The causes of the rise of prices were discussed in the famous Bullion Report. The general conclusion reached was that a "rise of the market price of gold above its mint price will take place," if the local currency of any particular country, "being no longer convertible into gold, should at any time be issued to excess. That excess cannot be exported to other countries, and, not being convertible into specie, it is not necessarily returned upon those who issued it; it remains in the channel of circulation, and is gradually absorbed by

[1] *Investigations in Currency and Finance*, London (Macmillan), 1884, p. 144.

increasing the prices of all commodities. An increase in the quantity of the local currency of a particular country will raise prices in that country exactly in the same manner as an increase in the general supply of precious metals raises prices all over the world. By means of the increase of quantity, the value of a given portion of that circulating medium, in exchange for other commodities, is lowered. In other words, the money prices of all other commodities are raised — that of bullion with the rest." This is an excellent statement of the philosophy of irredeemable paper money when that money is sufficiently within bounds to remain in general use. No mention is made of partial or complete abandonment of use because of worthlessness. The reason is doubtless that in England the paper money never reached this pass, as it undoubtedly did in many instances in France, Austria, America, and elsewhere.

§ 10

Austrian experience with paper money is instructive.[1] Like so many of the European banks, that of Austria was used by the government as an instrumentality for obtaining loans. This was done by allowing the bank to issue large sums in notes. The wars with Napoleon demanded supplies, and during these wars the issue was largely increased. In 1796 the note issue was 47,000,000 gulden; in 1800 it was 200,000,000; in 1806, it was 449,000,000. The notes were much below par. In 1810 the bank notes fell successively to $\frac{1}{5}$, $\frac{1}{8}$ and about $\frac{1}{11}$ of par. In 1811 a proclamation openly valued them at one fifth of their nominal value and decreed their exchange at this rate for redemption notes, called the

[1] See W. G. Sumner, *History of American Currency*, New York (Holt), 1874, Chapter III.

Viennese legal tender, which became the Austrian legal-tender currency. But even these new issues soon fell to $\frac{1}{216}$ of their face value (May, 1812) and $\frac{1}{338}$ of their face value (June, 1812), while the bank notes were at 1690 to 100 in silver. New issues were added under a different name until, in 1816, the amount of paper money was over 638,000,000, with prices, of course, tremendously inflated. In 1816 was founded the Austrian national bank, which was intended to draw in the paper money. From time to time thereafter the amount of paper circulation was reduced, but not without occasional relapses. At the present time Austria has no paper money which is not at par.

§ 11

Many of the American colonies had experience with paper money. In fact, one of the grievances against England was the parliamentary prohibition of paper money issues! In practically all cases [1] there was over-issue and depreciation. This was true, for example, in Massachusetts, where paper money was issued to pay the expenses of the expeditions against Canada,[2] and in Rhode Island,[3] which suffered more, perhaps, from paper money than any of the others. Following are figures for Rhode Island taken from the account book of Thomas Hazard (the entries and memoranda extending from 1750 to 1785), which show the height and variability of prices.[4]

[1] Pennsylvania seems to have been an exception.

[2] W. G. Sumner, *History of American Currency*, Chapter I.

[3] *Ibid.*

[4] Rowland Hazard, *Sundry prices taken from Ye Account Book of Thomas Hazard, son of Robt.* Wakefield, R.I. (Times Print), 1892.

1755. HAY £20 PER LOAD

CORN PER BUSHEL		BUTTER PER POUND	
1751	25 s.	1751	7 s.
1758	50 s.	1760	16 s.
1762	100 s.		

WOOL PER POUND		POTATOES PER BUSHEL	
1752	8 s.	1750	10 s.
1756	12 s.	1753	20 s.
1759	28 s.	1774	35 s.
1768	32 s.		

We had also during the Revolution a national experience with Continental paper money which gave rise to the derogatory phrase, still current, "not worth a continental." Depreciation began almost from the moment of issue (1775), and finally the money was recognized by Congress itself to have reached $\frac{1}{40}$ of the nominal value.[1] All prices, of course, were tremendously high. Even the new tenor paper given for the old emissions at the rate of a dollar for forty[2] declined rapidly in value. A bushel of wheat was worth, at one time, seventy-five dollars, coffee four dollars a pound, and sugar three dollars a pound.[3] It is interesting to observe that, in this case, the depreciation seems to have been accentuated far beyond what mere overissue tended to produce, by a distrust of the money and a refusal to receive it in trade. Several classes were disinclined to receive it to begin with, and as confidence waned, the number who were unwilling to receive it increased. Barter frequently took the place of trade with money.[4]

The depreciation was doubtless much greater because

[1] See Albert S. Bolles, *Financial History of the United States*, Vol. I, from 1774 to 1789, New York (Appleton), 1879, p. 135.

[2] *Ibid.*, pp. 137 and 138. [3] *Ibid.*, p. 141. [4] *Ibid.*, Chapter IX.

the paper money of various colonies helped to overflow the circulation, competing with the congressional money and limiting its sphere of circulation.

§ 12

The effects were so disastrous that, in the Constitution of the United States, a provision was incorporated prohibiting any state from issuing "bills of credit." But, during the Civil War, the temptation again came to resort to this easy way of securing means of payment; and the federal government itself issued United States notes or "greenbacks." The banks had already suspended specie payments so that gold was at a slight premium in bank paper.[1]

These greenbacks were issued from time to time during the war with resulting depreciation as their quantity increased, — a depreciation greater or less also according as failure or success of the Union armies affected confidence in the paper money. The amounts issued were: $150,000,000 by the act of February 25, 1862; $150,000,000 by act of July 11, 1862; $150,000,000 authorized by acts of January 17 and March 3, 1863. Besides the greenbacks (issued in denominations in no case under a dollar), there was some issue of fractional currency and of interest-bearing notes running for a brief period, both of which were also made legal tender.[2] The rise in prices is shown by the following table:[3] —

[1] Davis Rich Dewey, *Financial History of the United States*, New York (Longmans), 3d ed., § 29.

[2] For a brief account of the greenbacks, see Dewey, *Financial History of the United States*, Chapter XII. The most complete account is found in Wesley Clair Mitchell, *A History of the Greenbacks*, Chicago (University of Chicago Press), 1903.

[3] Aldrich *Senate Report on Wholesale Prices and Wages*, 52d Congress, 2d Session, table 24, p. 93.

INDEX NUMBERS OF PRICES DURING GREENBACK DEPRECIATION

YEAR	PRICE OF GOLD[1] IN GREENBACKS	INDEX NOS. OF NORTHERN PRICES (1860 = 100)			
		Falkner[2]		Dun[5] in Paper	Mitchell[5] Median in Paper
		In Gold[3]	In Paper[4]		
1861 . .	100	94	94	89	96
1863 . .	144	91	132	150	134
1865 . .	163	107	232	169	158
1867 . .	138	123	166	164	150
1869 . .	136	112	152	143	158
1871 . .	112	123	136	132	130
1873 . .	114	115	129	124	130
1875 . .	115	115	129	117	121
1877 . .	105	107	114	95	100
1879 . .	100	95	95	85	85

It has been asserted that the rise of prices during the greenback depreciation was not due to the *quantity* of the greenbacks, but to the public distrust of greenbacks. The truth is probably that it was due to both. Distrust was evident and restricted the sphere of greenbacks very materially. California and, in fact, all the region west of the Rocky Mountains, made strenuous efforts to prevent the circulation of greenbacks, — efforts which were largely successful. And naturally the greenbacks could not circulate in the South. These restrictions alone would confine their circulation to a population of about 20 millions out of a total population in 1860 of 31 millions, that is, to less

[1] Average of quotations in January, April, July, October, from Wesley Clair Mitchell, *Gold Prices and Wages under the Greenback Standard*, Berkeley (University Press), March, 1908.

[2] Weighted arithmetical average of articles comprising 68.60 per cent of total expenditure. [3] *Aldrich Report*, p. 100. [4] *Ibid.*, p. 93.

[5] From Wesley Clair Mitchell, *ibid.*, p. 59.

than two thirds of the entire population. Therefore the volume of trade for which the greenbacks were used must have been greatly reduced. The total circulating currency during the war is not known with certainty; but the best estimates of the various forms of circulating media are those compiled by Mitchell.[1] Though he modestly warns the reader against any attempt to cast up sums, his results may be considered as at least of some value. The totals, omitting money in the Treasury and interest-bearing forms, which were known to have only a very sluggish circulation, we find to be as follows: —

YEAR	ROUGHLY ESTIMATED CIRCULATION IN LOYAL STATES[2]	PRICES OF ALL ARTICLES AVERAGED[3] ACCORDING TO IMPORTANCE, COMPRISING 68.60 % OF TOTAL EXPENDITURE
1860	433	100
1861	490	94
1862	360	104
1863	677	132
1864	708	172
1865	774	232
1866	759	188

Considering the unreliability of the figures for currency[4] and the lack of data as to the other magnitudes in the equation of exchange, there is here a rough correspondence between the volume of the currency and the level of prices.

[1] Wesley C. Mitchell, *History of the Greenbacks*, Chicago (University of Chicago Press), 1903, p. 179.

[2] Mitchell, *ibid.*, p. 179.

[3] Aldrich, *Report on Wholesale Prices.*

[4] The great reduction in 1862, for instance, is due to the assumption that practically all gold was withdrawn from circulation except in California. A more reasonable assumption would seem to be that it was only partially withdrawn. Much of it may have

§ 13

It is necessary to remember that the confidence with which we have to deal is not primarily confidence in redemption, but confidence in the paper money,—its purchasing power. This confidence may rest on expectation of redemption or on other conditions, particularly the expectation of further inflation or contraction. The explanation of the value of the greenbacks appears to me to be in brief as follows: —

The Redemption Act of 1875 announced the intention of our government to redeem the greenbacks on and after January 1, 1879. Each greenback being thus kept equal to the discounted value of a full dollar due January 1, 1879, they rose steadily toward par as that date approached. Some of them were withdrawn from circulation to be held for the rise. The value of a greenback dollar could not be much less than this discounted value of the gold dollar promised in 1879; otherwise speculators might withdraw the greenbacks wholly. This would pay them well provided they were certain that the government's promise would be fulfilled. On the other hand, the value of greenbacks could not, with paper money redundant for trade, be *greater* than said discounted value, because in that case speculators would return it *all* to the circulation, the prospective rise being "too small to repay the interest" lost in carrying it. Thus speculation acted as a regulator of the quantity of money.

been hoarded in coin form preparatory to export or melting. If so, it probably circulated to some extent. "Hoarding" means a longer retention in the same hands, but not necessarily failure to be exchanged at all. Gold was a valuable form of bank "reserve" at this time. While not paid out in meeting demand obligations, it was a very quick asset and could be quickly realized upon.

Thus the rise in value of the greenbacks, like other coming events, cast its shadow before. It was "discounted in advance." It is quite true that confidence in redemption was here the ultimate cause of the appreciation of the paper money; but the readjustments caused by this confidence include a reduction in the quantity of the money in circulation. Without such readjustment the appreciation would be impossible, as the equation of exchange plainly shows. We should note, however, that if the price of the currency were *already* sufficiently high, the prospect of future redemption would not further raise it. It might happen that the value of the currency was already above the discounted par value promised at the time set for redemption. In such a case there need not be any speculation or any immediate rise in value until the date of redemption drew near enough to make itself felt. On the other hand, when, during the war, the government announced a further issue of a paper currency already depreciated, the public anticipated its further depreciation by releasing such hoards and stocks as were available; in other words, by accelerating the circulation of money. Each man hastened to spend his money before an expected rise of price, and his very action hastened that rise.

Announcements of federal defeats in the war acted in the same way, being signals that further issues of greenbacks might be required; while announcement of victories acted in the opposite way, being like signals of probable redemption.

When appreciation is anticipated, there is a tendency among owners of money to hoard or hold it back, and, among owners of goods, to sell them speedily; the result being to decrease prices by reducing the velocity of circulation and increasing the volume of trade. When, on the contrary, depreciation is anticipated, there is a tendency among owners of money to spend it speedily and among owners of goods to hold them for a rise, the result being to raise prices by increasing the velocity of circulation and decreasing the volume of trade. In other words, the expectation of a future rise or fall of prices causes an immediate rise or fall of prices.

These anticipations respond so promptly to every sign or rumor that superficial observers have regarded the rise and fall of the greenbacks as related directly and solely to expected redemption and as having no relation to quantity. These observers overlook the real mechanism at work; they fail to see that these effects, though quick, are slight and limited. They are the simple adjustments of transition periods described in Chapter IV. It would be a grave mistake to reason, because the losses at Chickamauga caused greenbacks to fall 4 per cent in a single day, that their value had no relation to their volume. This fall indicated a slight acceleration in the velocity of circulation, and a slight retardation in the volume of trade; but, under ordinary circumstances, it is only slightly that the velocity of circulation can thus be accelerated; while to make trade stagnate long or completely would require a cataclysm.

§ 14

In the South it is "impossible to state even approximately how many Confederate treasury notes were outstanding at any time."[1] Professor Schwab has, however, given the value of gold in Confederate currency and index numbers of prices in the South. He concludes:[2] —

[1] J. C. Schwab, *Confederate States of America*, 1861–1865, New York (Scribner), 1901, p. 165. [2] *Ibid.*, pp. 167–169.

"This movement of the gold premium corresponds roughly with the amount of government notes outstanding in each period. The relatively rapid increase in the issue of notes after August, 1862, during the last months of 1863, and again during the last months of the war, is reflected in the rapid increase of the gold premium at those three times. When the amount of outstanding notes remained stationary at the beginning of 1863, there was a somewhat slower advance of the gold premium during those months; while the shrinking of the outstanding notes during the first half of 1864 is distinctly reflected in a temporary decline of the premium.

"In the North during the Civil War the course of gold premium only remotely suggested the amount of notes outstanding at any time. The premium rose most rapidly, or, in other words, the notes sank in value most rapidly, at the beginning of 1863, recovering again during the second quarter of that year, declining after August, 1863, to their lowest point in the summer of 1864, and rising again during the last months of the war.[1] The value of the 'greenback' was much more a barometer of popular feeling as to the eventual outcome of the war than a gauge of their amount in circulation, for the latter did not materially increase after July, 1863, and certainly not after July, 1864. In fact, the gold value of the federal 'greenback' ran closely parallel with the gold value of the federal bonds during the war. This is also true of the confederate bonds and treasury notes. These two sets of parallel fluctuations were evidently caused by the changing credit of the two governments concerned.

[1] J. C. Schwab, *Confederate States of America*, 1861–1865, New York (Scribner), 1901, table on p. 167.

"A general index number for either section, based both on a simple and a weighted average, can be constructed. The lines plotted to indicate these two sets of figures do not run parallel, but converge and diverge during different periods of the war, converging at those times when events in the military, the political, or the financial field discouraged the South, and correspondingly encouraged the North in the general belief that the war was approaching an end; diverging at those times when federal reverses, or similar events in other than the military field, raised the hopes of the South, and led to belief on both sides that the war would be protracted." [1]

We thus see that redundancy of issue produces a fall of prices, not only because of increased quantity, but because of decreased confidence,[2] which affects the sphere of use of the money and therefore the volume of trade performed by the money, and accelerates its velocity.

§ 15

We have given historical instances of the effects on prices of changes in the precious metals and in paper money.

There remain to be considered historical instances of the effects on prices of changes in deposit currency. The price movements due to changes in deposit currency usually include those culminations called crises and depressions.

The economic history of the last century has been

[1] J. C. Schwab, *ibid.*, p. 179.

[2] Cf. Wesley Clair Mitchell, *History of the Greenbacks*, pp. 208 and 210. Also Francis A. Walker, *Political Economy*, 3d ed., New York (Holt), 1888, p. 164.

characterized by a succession of crises. Juglar in his description of the conditions preceding crises mentions the signs of great prosperity, the enterprise and the speculation of all kinds, the rising prices, the demand for labor, the rising wages, the ambition to become at once rich, the increasing luxury, and the excessive expenditure.[1]

A crisis is, as Juglar in fact defines it, an arrest of the rise of prices. At higher prices than those already reached purchasers cannot be found. Those who had purchased, hoping to sell again for profit, cannot dispose of their goods.[2]

Our previous analysis has shown us that, before a crisis, while prices are ascending, there is a great increase in bank deposits; and that these, being a circulating medium, accelerate the rise.

It has been pointed out that, with trade international, the rise of prices, resulting from expansion of deposits, is also international. Even if, in some of the countries, deposits should not expand, a rise of the price level would nevertheless occur. The expansion of deposits even in one country of considerable size would, by tending to raise prices there, cause the export of gold. Thus, in other countries the supply of money would increase and prices rise also. This would tend to stimulate expansion of deposits in these other countries and bring about a further rise. Even, therefore, if credit

[1] Clément Juglar, *Des Crises Commerciales et de leur Retour Périodique en France, en Angleterre et aux États-Unis*, 2 ed., Paris (Guillaumin), 1889, pp. 4 and 5. See also translation of same dealing with United States, by De Courcy W. Thom, *A Brief History of Panics in the United States*, New York (Putnam), 1893, pp. 7–10. Juglar is mistaken in adding that interest rates *fall* during rising prices. The facts show that they rise, though not sufficiently to check the excessive lending. See Irving Fisher, *The Rate of Interest*, Chapter XIV.

[2] Juglar, *ibid.*, p. 14.

expansion did not begin at the same time in all the principal commercial countries, the beginning of it in one country would be quickly communicated to others. For the same reason the arrest of rising prices and the beginning of falling prices would occur at about the same time in most of the principal countries. As a matter of fact this is what we find to be the case. Juglar has made out a table showing the crises in England, France, and the United States from 1800 to 1882.[1] With the addition of the dates of later crises the table is as follows:—

FRANCE	ENGLAND	UNITED STATES
1804	1803	
1810	1810	
1813–1814	1815	1814
1818	1818	1818
1825	1825	1826
1830	1830	
1836–1839	1836–1839	1837–1839
1847	1847	1848
1857	1857	1857
1864	1864–1866	1864
1873	1873	1873
1882	1882	1884
1889–1890	1890–1891	1890–1891
		1893
1907	1907	1907

§ 16

A study of Juglar's or Thom's tables will show that, in general, bank note circulation and bank deposit circulation increase before a crisis and reach a maximum at the time of the crisis. Index numbers of prices show the same general trend.

[1] Juglar, *ibid.*, charts at end; Thom's translation, p. 19, brings the table to 1891.

Thus,[1] for the United States, the crisis of 1837–1839 shows that circulation of state banks increased each year from 61 millions in 1830 to 149 in 1837 and fell to 116 in the next year; that individual deposits rose each year from 55 millions in 1830 to 127 in 1837 and fell to 84 the next year; that from 1844 to 1848, the date of the next crisis, circulation rose from 75 millions to 128, falling back to 114 the next year, and that the deposits rose from 84 millions to 103, falling back to 91; that from 1851 to 1857, the date of the next crisis, circulation rose from 155 millions to 214, falling the next year to 155, and that the deposits rose from 128 millions to 230, falling the next year to 185. These facts — that prices and deposits rose, culminated, and fell together in reference to the crises of 1837, 1846, and 1857 — are confirmed by figures for per capita circulation and deposits given by Sumner.[2] These show the characteristic sharp check to expansion in the crisis years, mild in the mild crisis of 1846 and pronounced in the more pronounced crises of 1837 and 1857. Corresponding phenomena occurred at the next crisis, 1863–1864. After this time, the chief statistics are for national banks, and these show similar results. Thus, from 1868 to 1873, national bank circulation rose from 295 millions to 341 and then fell, while in the same period deposits rose from 532 millions to 656 and then fell. Similar, though less marked, movements occurred in the milder crises of 1884 and 1890, which is the last included in Thom's tables. The crisis of 1893 was exceptional and largely confined to the United States, being chiefly due to the fear as to the

[1] See Thom, tables following p. 18.

[2] *History of Banking in the United States*, Vol. I of *History of Banking in all Nations*, New York (Journal of Commerce), 1896, p. 456. The figures are taken from 37th Congress, 3d Session, 5 Ex., 210.

stability of the gold standard without much reference to currency and deposit expansion.[1] Whereas in the typical speculative cycle the ratio of deposits to reserves gradually increases until it reaches a maximum just before the crisis, as it did in 1873, 1884, and 1907, this did not happen in 1893. It is true that the deposits of national banks were larger in 1892 than in 1890 or 1891, but they were no larger relatively to reserves, though possibly this fact is to be accounted for by an increase of reserves following the slight crisis of 1890–1891. It is true, also, that the ratio of the deposits of national banks to reserves was high in 1893, but this was due, not to an expansion of deposits, for deposits decreased during that year, but to the runs on the banks and consequent depletion of their reserves.[2] The crisis of 1907, on the other hand, was, like that of 1857, typically a crisis of currency expansion. The facts in reference to this crisis will be discussed more fully in the following chapter.

In France the same tendency of circulation and deposits to reach a maximum at or about a crisis and recede immediately afterward is illustrated fairly well,[3] especially for deposits.

[1] Lauck, *Causes of the Panic of* 1893, Boston (Houghton, Mifflin), 1907, p. 118. O. M. W. Sprague, in "History of Crises under the National Banking System," *National Monetary Commission Report*, Senate Document 538 (61st Congress, 2d Session), points out that in the runs on banks there was no special demand for gold, and is inclined to think that the influence of the currency expansion has been exaggerated.

[2] For a statistical comparison of this with typical crises, see article by Harry G. Brown, "Typical Commercial Crises *versus* a Money Panic," *Yale Review*, August, 1910.

[3] Juglar, *op. cit.*, tables following p. 339 and charts at end. Juglar calls the crisis of 1873 in France political rather than commercial. The statistics of circulation and deposits and their velocity of circulation (as shown by Pierre des Essars), however, reach a maximum in 1873 and recede immediately after.

For the Bank of England we find the same general correspondence between crises, circulation, and private deposits.[1]

§ 17

Not only do money and deposit currency (M and M') rise regularly to a maximum at the time of a crisis, but their velocity of circulation, so far as statistics indicate, goes through the same cycle. Pierre des Essars has demonstrated this beyond peradventure, so far as velocity of circulation of deposits is concerned.[2]

For the United States we have scarcely any statistics of velocity of circulation of deposits, but those for two New Haven banks and for an Indianapolis bank, which I have secured for the last few years, show a maximum in the crisis year 1907.

After a crisis, a decrease occurs in M, M', V, and V'. Bank reserves are increased, and this causes a decrease in M.

Since, then, currency and velocity both increase before a crisis, reach a maximum at the crisis, and fall after the crisis, it is small wonder that prices follow the same course. That they do is the real meaning of a crisis. In fact, as we have seen, Juglar defines a crisis as an arrest of a rise of prices. The index numbers of prices show the rise, maximum, and slump for almost every crisis year for which price statistics exist.[3]

[1] Juglar, *op. cit.*, tables following p. 291.

[2] "La vitesse de la circulation," *Journal de la Société de Statistique de Paris*, April, 1895, p. 148. From 1810 to 1892 in France, taking the thirteen crisis years and the twelve years of "liquidation," Des Essars finds that, *without exception*, the velocity of circulation of deposits at the bank of France is a maximum in the crisis years and a minimum in the years of liquidation.

[3] The detailed figures will be seen in the Appendix to the next chapter (Chapter XII).

The following figures are designed to present a picture of the crisis of 1907 in the United States as illustrating the culmination of a typical credit cycle:—

Year	Deposits[1] of National Banks (billions)	Reserves[1] of National Banks (millions)	Ratio[1] of Deposits of National Banks to Reserves	Clearings[2] (billions)	$M'V'$[2] (billions)	Index[3] Number of Prices, P. (Jan.)	Per Cent[3] Rise of Prices during Year.	Money Interest[4] New York Price, m, Two-name 60-day Paper	Virtual[4] Interest
1904 .	3.31	658	5.0	113	228	113.2	.7	4.2	3.5
1905 .	3.78	649	5.8	144	279	114.0	5.3	4.3	−1.0
1906 .	4.06	651	6.2	160	315	120.0	6.6	5.7	−0.9
1907 .	4.32	692	6.2	145	323	127.9	−1.7	6.4	8.1
1908 .	4.38	849	5.1	132	294	125.7	—	4.4	—

We notice, in the first column, a steady and rapid increase in the deposits of national banks up to, and including, the crisis year. Though deposits for 1908 do not decrease, yet they remain almost stationary as

[1] The figures for deposits and reserves of national banks are those given in the *Reports of the Comptroller of the Currency*, and represent the condition of the banks at their third report to the Comptroller (generally about July 1) of each year. The ratio column explains itself.

[2] The figures for clearings are taken from the *Financial Review* for 1910, p. 33. Those for $M'V'$ are constructed from the figures for clearings by a method explained in § 5 of Appendix to Chapter XII.

[3] The index numbers of prices are those of the *Bureau of Labor* (Bulletin 81, March, 1909), and relate to January of each year in question. The next column, therefore, headed "Per cent rise of prices during year" indicates the rise from January of the year in question to January of the next.

[4] The figures for interest rates are taken from the Appendix of *The Rate of Interest*, p. 418, brought through 1908 by computations from the *Financial Review*. The per cent rise of prices is subtracted from money interest to get virtual interest.

compared with those of the previous year. The second column, that for reserves, shows, as we should expect, a large increase in the year after the crisis, the banks having fortified themselves against the decrease of business confidence. We find, then (third column), an increase in the ratio of deposits to reserves, the highest ratio being reached in 1906 and 1907, not because reserves were depleted, — on the contrary, they were expanding, — but because deposits were expanding still more rapidly. If the theory presented in Chapter IV is correct, it is precisely this high ratio of deposits to reserves, brought about by failure of interest to rise with rise of prices, which forced the banks to raise their rates of discount and so check further expansion of credit. Then came the crisis and the short succeeding depression. The next column, headed "clearings," is indicative of the volume of check transactions, the circulation of deposit currency. As a fairly constant proportion of checks is settled through the various clearing houses of the country, clearings may fairly be regarded as somewhat of a criterion of $M'V'$. The fifth column is derived from the fourth and from other data, and is intended as an estimate of $M'V'$. These two columns increase through 1906, but (since they relate to the whole year and not to a point in the middle of the year) begin to show the effects of the credit slump in the fall of 1907, and so fall off somewhat in that year, and much more in the year after. We should expect to find, then, a rise of prices reaching a maximum with 1907 and falling in 1908, and this we do find in column six. Column seven shows the per cent rise during each year. Thus, for January, 1904, the index number or P is 113.2, and for January, 1905, it is 114.0. The rise, therefore, is a little less than 1 per cent. The minus signs signify a fall.

The eighth column is for rates of interest and indicates, as we should expect, a rise, culminating in 1907. Virtual interest — that is, the interest in terms of commodities — was exceedingly low during the years immediately preceding 1907, because prices were rising so fast. This is shown in column nine, where the nominal interest (measured in money) is corrected by the rise or fall of prices to give the interest measured in actual purchasing power. With the culmination of the cycle in 1907 and the resultant fall of prices, we find virtual interest suddenly become very high. No wonder that borrowing enterprisers often found it hard to make both ends meet.

The facts as to credit cycles, then, completely confirm the analysis already given in previous chapters and indicate that prices rise and fall with cycles of currency and velocity. For the benefit of those who doubt whether the expansion of deposit currency raises prices, or whether the rise of prices creates deposit currency, it may be added that facts, as well as theory, show that the former relationship is the true one. Miss England has shown, for instance, that loans and deposits expand before prices rise, and that, though prices often fall before loans and deposits shrink, this anomalous order of events is explainable by the revival of trade following a crisis.[1]

No attempt has been made in this chapter to review all the phenomena or even all the typical phenomena of crises. We are not here concerned with crises except in relation to currency. Our concern is with the magnitudes entering the equation of exchange, es-

[1] Minnie Throop England, "Statistical Inquiry into the Influence of Credit upon the Level of Prices," *University Studies* (University of Nebraska), 1907.

pecially M, M', and V', for these are the immediate elements the variations in which affect the price level and cause it to rise and fall.

§ 18

This chapter has been devoted to an historical study of changes in the quantity of currency and of the effects of these changes on prices. We have seen that, on the whole, increases in the amount of money have tended to raise prices from century to century during the last thousand years, and especially since the discovery of America. The changes in the last century, or more exactly, from 1789 to 1909, have been considered in somewhat more detail, covering five periods of alternately rising and falling prices. We have seen evidence to connect these price movements with changes in the quantity of money and in the volume of business. The periods 1789–1809, 1849–1873, and 1896–1909 were periods of rising prices and large increases of the money supply. In the period 1809–1849 prices fell presumably because of a falling off in gold and silver production and a continuing increase of business; while between 1873 and 1896, although the world's stock of precious metals was increasing slowly, prices in gold countries fell, because in addition to the increasing volume of business there was a stampede of nations to adopt the gold standard and demonetize or limit the coinage of silver.

We have observed the recent continual increase of gold production and found reasons for the tentative prediction that the gold production of the future would continue excessive and probably cause the present rise of prices to continue for some time in the future.

We have described some of the chief examples of paper money inflation and shown that the records for circulation and price changes bear out in a general way the principles set forth in previous chapters. The paper money experiences of France during the French Revolution, of England during the Napoleonic wars, of Austria, the American colonies, the United States, and the Confederacy have been briefly reviewed. We have noted that in these cases, as in others, prices depended on the quantity of money, its velocity, and the volume of business. We have seen that the apparent exceptions due to lack of confidence in paper money are not really exceptions, because lack of confidence works itself out through the magnitudes in the equation of exchange. Distrust increases the velocity of circulation, and decreases the trade performed by the money. We have shown that the general effect of irredeemable paper money issues, which are almost always in large quantities, despite pledges to the contrary, has been to raise prices.

Finally, our study of deposit circulation and crises has afforded further illustration. Preceding a typical crisis, there is, in general, a tendency for deposits to increase and also for their velocity of circulation to increase, while prices tend to rise. Following the crisis comes a decrease in bank deposits and their velocity of circulation, an increase in bank reserves, with a corresponding tendency to diminish money in circulation, and a fall of prices. In the years of the principal crises these took place simultaneously in different countries.

CHAPTER XII

STATISTICS OF RECENT YEARS

§ 1

The last chapter was devoted to a brief sketch of price movements and their causes, in so far as the scanty data available make even a tentative interpretation possible. From this telescopic view of the past we turn to a microscopic view of the present. We shall confine it to a study of the events of the last three decades in the United States. In the study of the last chapter we found the facts of history to be in accord with the *a priori* principles already set forth in the equation of exchange. But these facts of history were too general and vague to constitute a quantitative fulfillment of the equation of exchange. We shall find, however, much fuller data in the last few decades. We shall see that the equation of exchange, which has already been proved *a priori*, may also be verified by actual statistics — within at least the limit of error to which the statistics are liable.

A good beginning of such a study is afforded by the pioneer work of Professor Kemmerer, already often referred to. He has estimated [1] roughly the chief magnitudes of the equation of exchange and found that these conform in a general way to the conditions which the equation of exchange imposes. For each year, begin-

[1] *Money and Credit Instruments in their Relation to General Prices*, New York (Holt), 1909, Book II.

ning with 1879 (the year of resumption of the gold standard), and ending with 1908, he has estimated the total monetary and check circulation (what we have called MV and $M'V'$) and the volume of trade (T), and from these has calculated[1] what the price level ought to be as determined by these factors, *i.e.* $\frac{MV + M'V'}{T}$. This calculated magnitude, which Professor Kemmerer calls the "relative circulation of money," he then compares with the actual figures for price levels as given in statistics of index numbers.

Professor Kemmerer's calculation is, I believe, the first serious attempt ever made to test statistically the so-called "quantity theory" of money. The results show a correspondence which is very surprising when we consider the exceedingly rough and fragmentary character of the data employed.

Most other writers who have attempted to test the quantity theory statistically seem to have been animated by a desire not to give it a fair test, but to disprove it. They have carefully avoided taking account of any factors except money and prices. It is not to be wondered at that they find little statistical correlation between these two factors.[2] The virtue of Professor Kemmerer's work consists in giving due attention to factors other than money.

The chief error in his investigation is the assumption of 47 as the velocity of circulation of money. The true value, as we shall see, is nearer 18 to 20. But the volume

[1] For the details of Professor Kemmerer's calculations the reader is referred to his book. A very brief summary and criticism are given in § 1 of the Appendix to (this) Chapter XII.

[2] See *e.g.* Miss S. M. Hardy, "The Quantity of Money and Prices, 1860–1891. An Inductive Study." *Journal of Political Economy*, Vol. 3, pp. 145–168.

of money payments, even with Kemmerer's exaggerated figure for velocity, is so small when compared with check payments, that this weakness does not greatly affect his final comparisons. At my request, Professor Kemmerer has recalculated his curves on the basis of 18 instead of 47 as the velocity of circulation of money. The results are given in Fig. 12. If these are compared with those contained in Professor Kemmerer's book, there will be seen to be little difference. It is interesting to observe that when minute comparison is

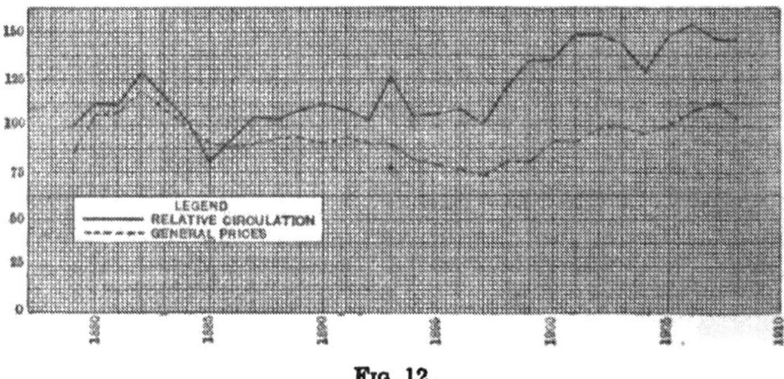

FIG. 12.

made the selection of 18 as the estimate of velocity gives a slightly better agreement between the two curves than does 47.

The "coefficient of correlation" between Professor Kemmerer's results for P, as directly shown by statistics and as indirectly calculated from the other factors in the equation of exchange, is found, by Professor Persons[1] of Dartmouth, to be only .23 (or 23 per cent of perfect correlation), with a probable error of .13. As Professor Persons says, this is a very low degree of correlation.

[1] "Quantity Theory as tested by Kemmerer," *Quarterly Journal of Economics*, February, 1908, p. 287.

But Persons's method of testing agreement by means of a coefficient of correlation is not really applicable to two curves representing magnitudes changing *in time*. For it practically ignores a most essential factor, their *order in time*. A year-to-year comparison is better. If we consider the curves of prices and of "relative circulation,"[1] we see at a glance that almost every successive change in direction in the one curve is matched by a corresponding change in direction in the other. In fact, out of 28 such possible coincidences, we find the actual number to be 16 cases of agreement in the changes of direction, 9 cases of disagreement, and 3 cases of a neutral kind (*i.e.* cases which showed no change of direction in one of the two curves).

The above figures relate to the curves in Professor Kemmerer's book. The later curves employing 18 instead of 47 for money-velocity show about the same results, there being 16 cases of agreement, 8 cases of disagreement, and 4 cases of a neutral kind. The correspondence here between prices and "relative circulation" is very slightly greater than before. In both sets of diagrams the agreements are not only much more numerous but much more pronounced than the disagreements.

Finally, some of the disagreements seem to be really agreements, disguised by being shifted forward one year. Thus, the inflections of 1899, 1900, 1901, for "relative circulation," although all counted as cases of disagreement, are strikingly similar respectively to the inflections of 1900, 1901, 1902, for "general prices." From the fact that the statistics are partly for calendar and partly for fiscal years, such one-year shifting of correspondence is to be expected, as Professor Kemmerer points out.

[1] Kemmerer, *op. cit.*, p. 149.

§ 2

I shall now attempt to make as precise statistical estimates of the magnitudes in the equation of exchange for the years 1896–1909 as the data available will allow. This period — 1896–1909 — is selected chiefly because its two end years afford the only known data making possible an estimate of velocity of circulation of money and of bank deposits.

The magnitudes will be considered in the order *M*, *M'*, *V'*, *V*, *T*, *P*. For each the figures to be used are new.

M. The following table gives the estimated amount of money in circulation in the United States. By this we mean the total amount of money (coin and paper) outside of the federal treasury and outside the banks of deposit and discount (national, state, private and trust companies). The treasury stock is excluded because it is a hoard which does not become adjusted to needs of payment in the sense — or at any rate in the degree — that the stocks in merchants' tills and in people's pockets become adjusted. The bank reserves are excluded because, as we have shown, they are used for banking operations, not commercial purchases.

ESTIMATED MONEY IN CIRCULATION IN THE UNITED STATES (*M*)
(IN BILLIONS OF DOLLARS)

Year		Year	
1896	.87	1903	1.38
1897	.88	1904	1.37
1898	.96	1905	1.45
1899	1.03	1906	1.59
1900	1.17	1907	1.63
1901	1.22	1908	1.63
1902	1.26	1909	1.63

This table is based on the official estimate of money in the United States, which includes money in banks and in the federal treasury. These official figures are then corrected by means of recent revisions of the estimates of the gold in the United States, and by deducting the money in the federal treasury and the estimate of money in banks reporting and unreporting.[1] The results differ somewhat from the official figures for so-called "money in circulation," the chief reason for the discrepancy being that these official figures include money in banks. The figures here given are probably nearly correct; the probable error may, I believe, be assumed to be within 2 or 3 per cent.

The table shows that, during the space of thirteen years between 1896 and 1909, the money in circulation has nearly doubled and that its increase has been almost uninterrupted.

M′. The following figures for *M′* are estimates of *individual deposits, subject to check.*

INDIVIDUAL DEPOSITS SUBJECT TO CHECK (*M′*)[2] (IN BILLIONS OF DOLLARS)

Year		Year	
1896	2.68	1903	5.70
1897	2.80	1904	5.80
1898	3.19	1905	6.54
1899	3.90	1906	6.84
1900	4.20	1907	7.13
1901	5.13	1908	6.57
1902	5.43	1909	6.75

These figures are based on the official figures for "individual deposits," but are much less than these, owing to the fact that the official figures include deposits in savings banks and other deposits not subject to check, as well as to several other minor causes. The estimates here given constitute the first attempt to give a series

[1] For details as to the construction of the table, see § 2 of Appendix to (this) Chapter XII.

[2] For the method of estimating these figures see § 3 of Appendix to (this) Chapter XII.

of figures for the bank deposits subject to check in the United States. It was made possible through the kind coöperation of the National Monetary Commission and its expert, Mr. A. Piatt Andrew.[1]

These figures give, therefore, the actual *deposit currency* of the United States. They show an enormous growth of bank deposit currency. In the space of thirteen years (between the beginning and the end of the table) it has nearly trebled. Moreover, each year shows an advance over the preceding year, excepting only the year 1908 following the crisis of 1907.

§ 3

Having found M and M', the circulating media, we next proceed to ascertain V and V', their velocity of circulation. We shall find it convenient to consider the latter first.

The velocity of circulation of bank deposits is found by dividing respectively the total check circulation ($M'V'$) by the bank deposits (M'). The divisor, M', has already been found. As to the dividend, $M'V'$, this is practically the total checks drawn in a year, for we may reasonably assume that, on the average, each check circulates against goods once and but once.[2]

For two years, 1896 and 1909, thanks to the efforts of Professor Kinley of the University of Illinois, we have voluminous and unique data collected originally for the purpose of calculating the ratio of money-transactions to check-transactions in the United States, *i.e.* the ratio of MV to $M'V'$. We shall see that these data, in conjunction with other official statistics, are sufficient for something more important than computing this ratio;

[1] For details see § 3 of Appendix to (this) Chapter XII.

[2] Cf. Kemmerer, *op. cit.*, p. 114.

for they enable us to calculate with a tolerable degree of exactness the magnitudes V and V' for both the years mentioned. We shall find incidentally that, with the aid of these magnitudes, it is possible to work out more exactly than in the investigations above mentioned the very magnitude for which these investigations were undertaken, viz. the ratio of money-transactions to credit-transactions.

We need first to estimate $M'V'$.

$M'V'$. Professor Kinley's special investigation of 1896 indicates that on "the settling day nearest July 1, 1896," the value of the checks deposited was about $468,000,000. If we could assume that this day was an average day for the year, we should need, in order to obtain the total year's deposits of checks, simply to multiply this by the number of settling days in 1896, which was 305.[1] But it happens that July 1 is an exceptionally heavy day in the deposit of checks. Making allowance for this fact, as indicated by the clearings of the New York clearing house, we conclude that the total year's deposits of checks in 1896 was about 97 billions, with a probable error of some 5 or 6 per cent.[2] Similar calculations for 1909 make the total check transactions of that year 364 billions.[3] We have thus the value of the total check circulation ($M'V'$) in the two years 1896 and 1909, and find them to be 97 and 364 billions respectively, indicating a prodigious growth in thirteen years. We have still to interpolate figures for intervening years. For the period between these two years, we have, unfortunately, no such data as those of

[1] This multiplication gives $143,000,000,000, which figure is used by Professor Kemmerer (*op. cit.*, pp. 110–111).

[2] The method of reaching this result is described in § 4 of Appendix to (this) Chapter XII.

[3] See § 4 of Appendix to (this) Chapter XII.

Professor Kinley for 1896 and 1909. However, we can find an excellent barometer in the clearing house transactions, — a barometer dependent partly on the clearings in New York City, but more on those outside of New York City. It is well recognized that, although the clearings in New York deserve an exceedingly large representation, their relative importance in the total clearings is exaggerated.[1]

On the question, therefore, "What relative importance should be given respectively to clearings in New York and to the outside clearings in order to get the best barometer of the check transactions for the entire country?" we conclude that, if the outside clearings be multiplied by five and the result added to the New York clearings, we shall have a good barometer of check transactions for the United States.[2]

By means of this barometer of check transactions, consisting of New York clearings plus five times the outside clearings, and our knowledge of the actual check transactions of 1896 and 1909, we may easily derive from the "barometer" an estimate of the actual check transactions. The result is as follows: —

ESTIMATED CHECK TRANSACTIONS ($M'V'$) (IN BILLIONS OF DOLLARS) 1896–1909[3]

Year		Year	
1896	97	1903	223
1897	106	1904	233
1898	127	1905	282
1899	166	1906	320
1900	165	1907	320
1901	208	1908	300
1902	222	1909	364

[1] See *e.g.* the remarks on these clearings in *Financial Review* for 1910, p. 33, and in Babson's *Business Barometers* (Wellesley Hills, Mass.), 1910, p. 188.

[2] See § 5 of Appendix to (this) Chapter XII.

[3] See § 5 of Appendix to (this) Chapter XII.

The probable error of the figures between 1896 and 1909 may be set at some 5 to 10 per cent.

V'. Having obtained estimates of $M'V'$ and having previously obtained estimates of M', it is easy, by simple division, to obtain V'. The results are as follows: —

Estimated Velocity (V') of Circulation, by Checks, of Deposits Subject to Check

1896	36	1903	39
1897	38	1904	40
1898	40	1905	43
1899	43	1906	47
1900	39	1907	45
1901	41	1908	46
1902	41	1909	54

The probable error in these figures may be set at some 5 to 10 per cent, being least for 1896 and 1909 and greatest midway between.

We note that the velocity of circulation has increased 50 per cent in thirteen years and that it has been subject to great variations from year to year. In 1899 and 1906 it reached maxima, immediately preceding crises. These results correspond to those of Pierre des Essars for the rates of turnover of deposits in continental banks already noted, except that he usually finds the maximum in the crisis year itself rather than the year before. It is to be noted that the figure for 1909 is much the highest in the table. Whether it portends an approaching crisis, time will determine.

§ 4

MV. Our next quest is for the velocity of circulation of money. The calculation of the velocity of circulation of money presents great difficulties, — difficulties which, in fact, have usually been considered insurmountable. This opinion was well expressed by Jevons,[1] who wrote:

"I have never met with any attempt to determine in any country the average rapidity of circulation, nor have I been able to think of any means whatever of approaching the investigation of the question, except in the inverse way. If we know the amount of exchanges effected, and the quantity of currency used, we might get by division the average number of times the currency is turned over; but the data, as already stated, are quite wanting."

As we shall see, however, data now exist, capable of revealing the "amount of exchanges effected," or, MV. In fact, this is equal to the total money deposited in banks, plus the total money-wages paid, plus a small miscellaneous item. From MV and M it is of course easy to obtain V by division.

The formula for obtaining MV is as simple as it may at first seem mysterious. The chief peculiarity of the method which this formula represents, and the feature which adapts it to practical use, is that it utilizes bank records and other ascertainable statistics as a means of discovering the total value of money transactions. The method is based on the idea that money in circulation and money in banks are not two independent reservoirs, but are constantly flowing from one into the other, and that the entrance and exit of money at banks, being a matter of record, may be made to reveal its circulation outside.

It is obvious how the bank-record would be read, were it true that every dollar withdrawn from banks circulated once and only once before being redeposited. Under these circumstances the annual flow of monetary circulation would exactly equal the annual withdrawal

[1] *Money and the Mechanism of Exchange* (London), p. 336.

from banks prior to circulation, as well as the annual deposits in banks subsequent to circulation.

Since we have a record of the first and last steps of the three, viz. the withdrawals and the deposits, we possess the means of knowing the intermediate step, the exchange of money for goods. The ordinary circulation of money, — excluding cases where it changes hands more than once between withdrawal and redeposit, — is equal to the money-flow through banks.

The complete facts, however, are not so simple, for the reason that money withdrawn from banks is often circulated more than once. Yet the complications involved follow definite laws. They do not destroy the value of the bank record, but merely make it somewhat more difficult to read. We propose to show (1) that in actual fact much money circulates out of bank only once, as in the hypothetical case just mentioned; (2) that when it is paid for wages, it usually circulates twice; and (3) that only rarely does it circulate three or more times before completing its circuit back to the banks.

This statement means that, like checks, money circulates in general only once outside of banks; but that when it passes through the hands of non-depositors (which practically means wage-earners) it circulates once more, thus adding the volume of wage payments to the volume of ordinary money circulation, which, as we have seen, is equal to the flow of money through banks.

We falsely picture the circulation of money in modern society when we allow ourselves to think of it as consisting of a perpetual succession of transfers from person to person. Were it such a succession, it would be, as Jevons said, beyond the reach of statistics. But we may form a truer picture by thinking of banks as the home of money, and the circulation of money as a temporary excursion from that home. If this description be true, the circulation of money is not very different from the circulation of checks. Each performs one transaction or, at most, a few transactions, outside of the bank, and then returns home to report its circuit.

As is shown in the Appendix, the total money deposited in banks in 1896 amounted to nearly 10 billions of dollars,[1] and the total expenditures of non-depositors (wage-earners) to nearly 6 billions, of which 4½ billions constituted the expenditures of non-depositors (wage-earners); the remaining item in the formula for circulation amounted to less than 1 billion, making about 16 billions for the total circulation.

For 1909 the corresponding figures are: money deposited, 21 billions; expenditures of non-depositors, 13 billions; and the remaining item about 1 billion, making 35 billions in all.

The following table summarizes these results in billions of dollars:[2] —

	1896	1909
1st term (money deposited in banks) . . .	10–	21
2d term (expenditure of "non-depositors") .	6–	13
Remaining item	1–	1
TOTAL	16+	35

[1] For a fuller account of the method of estimating the velocity of circulation of money and its statistical application, see § 6 of the Appendix to (this) Chapter XII, which consists, with revisions and additions, of an article of mine published in December, 1909, in the *Journal of the Royal Statistical Society* on "A New Method of estimating the Velocity of Circulation of Money." The additions incorporated in the Appendix (§§ 7, 8) include the statistical details of the calculations for the United States.

[2] For details as to the figures in this table, see § 7 of Appendix to (this) Chapter XII.

V. In order to obtain the velocity of circulation, the total circulation, MV (16 billions for 1896, or to be more exact, 16.2 billions), must be divided by the amount of money, M, circulating in 1896. This amount is estimated at $870,000,000. Hence the velocity is 16,200,000,000 ÷ 870,000,000 = 18.6, or about 19 times a year. In other words, money was held on the average about 365 ÷ 19, which amounts to 19 or 20 days. If I have made as full allowance for error as I believe has been made, the error in this estimate does not exceed two or three days. For 1909 the velocity of circulation is estimated as the total circulation (35.1 billions) divided by the money in circulation (1.63 billions), which is 21.5+; that is, about 22 times a year, or once in 17 days. We conclude that the velocity of circulation of money in 1896 and the velocity in 1909 were about 19 and 22 times respectively, with a probable error judged to be about 2 in 1896 and not much more than 1 in 1909.

These results would assign money a slower circulation than most of the estimates or guesses which have been made. We must remember, however, that such persons as economists, who are most apt to think about the circulation of money, have a rapid turnover. They are usually city dwellers and the comparatively well to do, who, as we know, do not keep their cash inactive long. Laborers, especially thrifty laborers and laborers paid monthly, will keep cash on hand for several weeks without spending it. Farmers and others living in sparsely settled districts will even keep it for months. Probably the velocity of circulation of money differs widely among different classes and different localities.

We may now compare the years 1896 and 1909 in respect to money in circulation, deposit currency, their velocities, and their total circulation as follows: —

(1)	(2) M	(3) M'	(4) V	(5) V'	(6) MV	(7) $M'V'$	(8) $MV+M'V'$
1896	.87	2.68	19	36	16	97	113
1909	1.63	6.75	22	54	35	364	399

Our next task is to interpolate estimates for V between 19 in 1896 and 22 in 1909. The results are given in the following table: —

ESTIMATES OF V, 1896 to 1909[1]

1896	19	1903	21
1897	19	1904	21
1898	20	1905	22
1899	22	1906	22
1900	20	1907	21
1901	22	1908	20
1902	22	1909	22

§ 5

We have now finished our statistical review of the magnitudes M, M', V, V', on the left side of the equation of exchange, and have remaining only the two magnitudes P, T, on the right side of the equation.

First we shall consider T. The results of our calculations are given in the following table, which expresses the volume of trade in billions of dollars as reckoned at the prices of 1909:—

ESTIMATED VOLUME OF TRADE (IN BILLIONS OF DOLLARS AT PRICES OF 1909)

1896	209	1903	335
1897	239	1904	324
1898	260	1905	378
1899	273	1906	396
1900	275	1907	412
1901	311	1908	381
1902	304	1909	399

[1] For the method of calculating this table see § 8 of Appendix to (this) Chapter XII.

The table is constructed by averaging the index numbers of the *quantities* (not the values) of trade in various lines. The figures representing trade are based on data for 44 articles of internal commerce, 23 articles of import and 25 of export, sales of stocks, railroad freight carried, and letters through the post office. The final figures are so adjusted that the figure for 1909 shall be 399; namely, the actual money value of transactions in that year as worked out on the other side of the equation (*i.e.* $MV + M'V'$). Relatively to each other, the numbers for T are independent of the other side of the equation.[1]

P. The only remaining factor in the equation of exchange is the index number of prices, P. Theoretically this could be calculated from the other five magnitudes already evaluated, provided all our *previous* calculations could be depended upon for absolute accuracy. But there are possible errors in all the magnitudes M, M', V, V', T, and such errors, should they exist, would be registered cumulatively in P. It is important, therefore, to check such an indirectly calculated value of P by directly calculated statistics. By so doing we are able to compare the P directly calculated and the P indirectly calculated. In like manner, we might, if desired, compare the directly and indirectly calculated values of M, M', V, V', and T. We shall confine ourselves to comparing the two values of P, since it is P which, as we have seen, is really dependent on the five other factors in the equation of exchange. The values of P (including prices of commodities, securities, and labor), directly calculated in terms of the figures for 1909, as 100 per cent, are as follows: —

[1] For the exact method (necessarily laborious) of constructing this table see § 9 of the Appendix to (this) Chapter XII.

INDEX NUMBERS OF GENERAL PRICES

Year	Index	Year	Index
1896	63	1903	87
1897	64	1904	85
1898	66	1905	91
1899	74	1906	96
1900	80	1907	97
1901	84	1908	92
1902	89	1909	100

This table is based on the figures of the Bureau of Labor for wholesale prices. It differs slightly from the Bureau of Labor figures owing to the fact that we here include prices of securities and wages.[1]

It remains to compare these actual statistics for P with P as computed indirectly from the other magnitudes in the equation of exchange. This calculation and comparison will be given in the following section.

§ 6

We have now calculated independently the six magnitudes of the equation of exchange for the fourteen years 1896–1909. But, as already stated, we know that these six magnitudes are mutually related through the equation of exchange. The question arises whether the magnitudes as calculated will actually fulfill approximately the equation of exchange.

One way of testing this question is that adopted by Professor Kemmerer; namely, to compare the statistics for any one factor (say P), as above directly calculated, with what it would be as indirectly calculated from the five other magnitudes in the equation of exchange. The following table shows the value of P as obtained in these two ways: —

[1] For the method of constructing this table see § 10 of Appendix to (this) Chapter XII.

INDEX NUMBERS OF PRICES AS CALCULATED

	DIRECTLY (P)	INDIRECTLY $\left(\frac{MV + M'V'}{T}\right)$
1896	63	54
1897	64	52
1898	66	56
1899	74	69
1900	80	68
1901	84	76
1902	89	82
1903	87	75
1904	85	81
1905	91	83
1906	97	90
1907	97	86
1908	92	87
1909	100	100

The agreement between the two sets of figures is visualized in Figure 13.

The two values as shown by the upper and lower

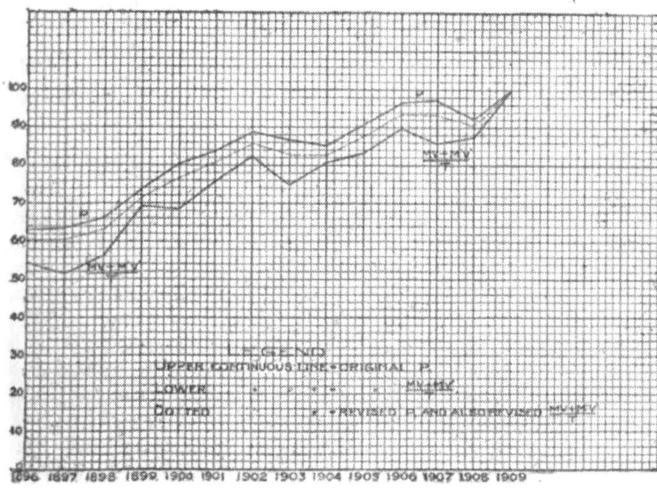

FIG. 13.

curves agree with each other remarkably well.[1] The closeness of their agreement may be expressed in several ways. One way is to count the agreements and disagreements in their changes of direction or inflections. Out of 12 inflections in each curve the two agree six times, disagree three times, and are neutral three times. Another method is that employed by Professor Pearson. This method consists in calculating what Professor Pearson calls a "correlation coefficient." It shows an agreement of 97 per cent of perfection as compared with 23 per cent which Professor Persons of Dartmouth found for Professor Kemmerer's figures[2] for 1879–1908. But, as already stated, a coefficient of correlation for *successive* data is apt to be misleading. If, in the case of Professor Kemmerer's figures, the coefficient .23 was an understatement of the parallelism between his curves, the coefficient .97 overstates the parallelism between mine. This overstatement is always likely to result when both of the curves to be compared rapidly ascend or descend.[3]

The proper method of applying a coefficient of correlation to successive data appears to be to calculate

[1] The intermediate curve will be explained later.

[2] "Quantity Theory as tested by Kemmerer," *Quarterly Journal of Economics*, 1907–1908, p. 287.

[3] *E.g.* Persons finds a coefficient of .98 for the correlation between Kemmerer's figures for bank reserves and money in circulation inclusive of bank reserves, although the two magnitudes do not show any very great agreement between fluctuations in successive years, but only a general agreement in the fact that both ascend rapidly. The coefficient for Professor Kemmerer's figures for P will be much higher, if instead of taking the period beginning with 1879, which includes many years in which prices do not greatly change, we take the period beginning at the same time as my own figures begin, viz. 1896. The correlation coefficient for Kemmerer's figures 1896–1908 is 83 per cent, which is far higher than that obtained by Persons for the period beginning in 1879.

the coefficient, not for the raw figures, but for their successive year-to-year ratios. In other words, we tabulate and compare the ratios of each year's P to the preceding year's P and of each year's $\frac{MV + M'V'}{T}$ to the preceding year's $\frac{MV + M'V'}{T}$. If the two sets of ratios should rise or fall together, the curves would show a close parallelism or agreement in their successive changes of direction. As a matter of fact, the results of this method show a coefficient of correlation of 57 per cent (or .57 ± .10, where .10 is the probable error). This figure, 57 per cent, is a moderately high coefficient of correlation.[1] We may conclude, therefore, that the "quantity theory" is statistically verified to a high degree of correlation.[2]

It is to be emphasized that the coefficients of correlation as just given compare the price level with what it should be according to the statistics of the *five* magnitudes on which, by the so-called quantity theory, it is dependent. The correlation would be less if instead of these five magnitudes only *one* were taken. Thus the coefficient of correlation for 1896–1909 as between money, M, and prices, P, by the year-to-year-ratio

[1] For instance, no one would deny that the length and breadth of nuts are highly correlated. The coefficient of their correlation is 57 per cent. The height of a man and the breadth of his face are correlated to the extent of 35 per cent.

[2] Incidentally we may here compare the relative degree of correlation of Professor Kemmerer's figures and of my own. For this purpose we take the period 1896–1908, which is the longest period common to both investigations. For these years the coefficient for my figures is 54 per cent (or .54 ± .11) as against 37 per cent (or .37 ± .14) for Kemmerer's. These are by the method of year-to-year ratios. By the method of raw figures my correlation is 95 per cent and Kemmerer's, 83 per cent.

method is 43 per cent (or $.43 \pm .13$).[1] Even this is a moderately high degree of correlation.

If the opponents of the "quantity theory" who attempt to disprove any relation between money and prices by pointing out the lack of statistical correspondence between the two mean merely that other factors besides money, M', V, V', T, change from time to time and that therefore the level of prices does not in actual fact vary exactly with the quantity of money, their contention is sound. But the proposition involved is of as little scientific consequence as the proposition that the pressure of the atmosphere does not vary from day to day in exact proportion to its density. We know that, temperature being constant, the pressure of a gas varies directly as its density; but that, as a matter of fact, temperature seldom is constant. Any critic of Boyle's law who should attempt to dispute its validity on such a ground, however, would merely betray his ignorance of the real meaning of a scientific law; and if he should seriously attempt to "disprove it statistically" by plotting daily curves of barometric pressure and atmospheric density, he would subject himself to scientific ridicule.

If any one has ever really imagined that the price level depends solely on the quantity of money, he should certainly be corrected. But the really important matter is that students of economics should appreciate the existence of a *law* of direct proportion between quantity of money and price level — a law as real, as important, and as fundamental in the economic theory of money, as Boyle's law of direct proportion between density and pressure is real, is important, and is funda-

[1] By the (misleading) direct comparison between M and P the coefficient of correlation for 1896–1909 is 97 per cent.

mental in the physical theory of gases. I believe that the frequent failure to realize the existence of this law is due largely to the lack of any clear conception of the magnitudes involved. M and P seem to be the only magnitudes which some students really understand. M, V, V', T are seldom discussed or even mentioned. But not until the subject is put on a statistical basis, — in figures which measure actual deposit currency, velocities of circulation, and volume of trade, — will these magnitudes be recognized as having a real existence and significance.

But, to a candid mind, the quantity theory, in the sense in which we have taken it, ought to appear sufficiently secure without such checking. Its best proof must always be *a priori*; not in the sense which applies to the proof of abstract mathematical propositions, but in the sense which applies to the proof of Boyle's law. Thus, it is known by induction that the pressure of a confined gas is caused by the bombardment of its molecules on the containing walls. It is likewise known by induction that the pressure must be proportional to the frequency of impact, provided the velocities of the molecules are constant. Finally, it is known that frequency of impact must be proportional to the number of molecules, *i.e.* the density of the gas, and that constancy of velocity implies constancy of temperature. Therefore, it follows that, temperature being constant, pressure is proportional to density. Thus, from knowledge gained inductively of the individual pressures of the molecules which compose the gas, we may reason out *deductively* the general pressure of a gas.

Analogously, from knowledge gained inductively of individual exchanges — molecules as it were — which compose society's exchange, we may reason out deductively the general equation of exchange.

Fortunately, just as Boyle's law has been established both deductively and inductively, we may now assert that the equation of exchange has been sufficiently established both deductively and inductively.

As previously remarked, to establish the equation of exchange is not completely to establish the quantity theory of money, for the equation does not reveal which factors are causes and which effects. But this question has been answered in Chapter VIII.

§ 7

To those who have faith in the *a priori* proof of the equation of exchange the real significance of the remarkable agreement in our statistical results should be understood as a confirmation, not of the equation by the figures, but of the figures by the equation. There are discrepancies in our inductive verification; but these are all well within the limit of errors of measurement. The discrepancies prove that slight errors exist among the figures; otherwise, they would conform exactly to the relation prescribed by the equation of exchange.

Our next task is to examine the discrepancies and locate, so far as possible, the errors involved. The degree of total mutual discrepancy between the independently calculated magnitudes is best expressed by the degree of inequality between the calculated values of $MV + M'V'$ and PT, which *should* be equal. That is, PT divided by $MV + M'V'$ should always be unity. Actual division gives the figures in the column headed "original" in the following table. The other column will be explained presently.

Ratio of PT to $MV + M'V'$ as Calculated

(1)	Original (2)	Reduced (3)
1896	1.17	1.06
1897	1.24	1.13
1898	1.18	1.07
1899	1.06	.95
1900	1.17	1.06
1901	1.11	1.00
1902	1.08	.97
1903	1.16	1.05
1904	1.06	.95
1905	1.09	.98
1906	1.08	.97
1907	1.13	1.02
1908	1.05	.94
1909	1.00	.89

The figures in column (2) show that the calculated values of PT are always larger than the calculated values of $MV + M'V'$, the excess varying from 24 per cent to 0 and averaging 11 per cent.

But these discrepancies between PT and $MV + M'V'$ can be substantially diminished merely by changing the base for measuring prices. This base we have thus far taken as the price level of 1909. But as the index numbers have only a relative significance, we are free to choose any other set of numbers so long as they maintain the same *relative* magnitudes. In accordance with this prerogative we choose to reduce all the numbers for P by 11 per cent, this being the average of the original discrepancies. The result will be to decrease PT by 11 per cent and to change the series of discrepancies from those shown in column (2) to (approximately) those shown in column (3). These numbers vary from 13 per cent above to 11 per cent below unity. These errors are very small — far smaller in fact than might have been expected in view of the incomplete and unreliable character of some of our data.

The question remains, Where shall we place the blame for the errors which the small existing discrepancies indicate? Is the fault with M, M', V, V', P, or T?

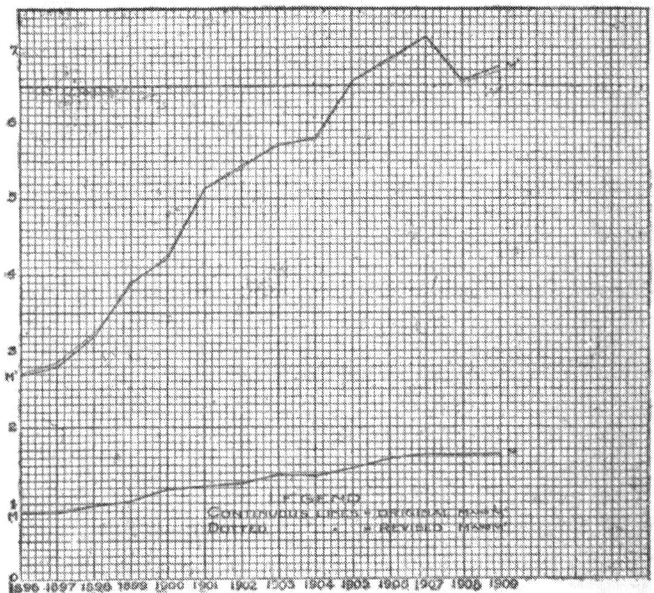

FIG. 14.

How shall we correct our calculated figures? We may conclude on general principles that the smallest corrections are the most likely to be right. The smallest corrections imply a *mutual* adjustment between the six factors, each adjustment being in the direction which will diminish the existing discrepancy. In this way each factor, as calculated, is regarded as having *some* value, and is given some influence in correcting the others; so that any one factor requires extremely little change. The changes made in the various factors are made in proportion to their assumed relative liability to error.

The results are shown in Figures 14, 15, 16, and the previous Figure 13, each of which relates to one of the factors in the equation of exchange as originally calculated and as finally adjusted (dotted lines). When they

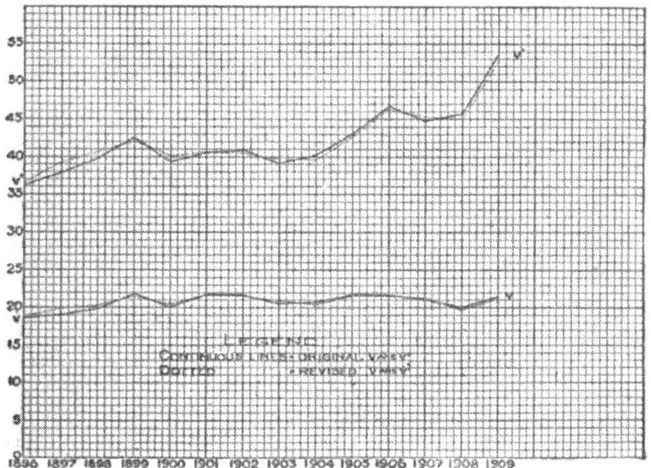

FIG. 15.

are all thus adjusted, they conform exactly to the equation of exchange.[1]

In Figure 14 we see that the alterations made in the figures for M and M' are so trifling as to be almost negligible, being usually much less than 1 per cent. The alterations in V and V', which are shown in Figure 14, though somewhat greater, are also small, being usually

[1] For the method of adjustment, see § 11 of Appendix to (this) Chapter XII.

less than 2 per cent. The alterations in T, as shown in Figure 16, though still greater than the preceding, are nevertheless so small and uniform as to preserve an almost perfect parallelism between the original and the altered curve. The differences rarely exceed 4 per cent. The alterations in P are shown in the previous Figure 13, the upper curve representing the original and the

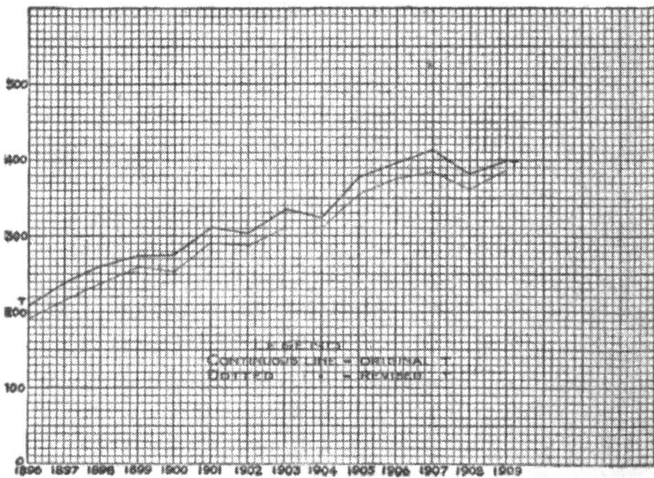

FIG. 16.

dotted, or middle, curve representing the altered figures for P. Here also an extremely close parallelism between the original and the altered curves is evident. The differences rarely exceed 3 per cent.

Certainly the most exacting of critics could not ask for any greater consistency of results and conformity to the theory of the equation of exchange than these statistics show. The corrections which have been found necessary to bring the six figures as first calculated into perfect agreement are smaller than the probable error in those figures themselves. I had — quite antecedently to any knowledge of how closely the final results would harmonize — assigned certain rough estimates of the probable errors. These are noted in the Appendix. The probable error of M is adjudged to be 2 or 3 per cent; of M', 2 or 3 per cent; of V, 5 to 10 per cent; of V', 5 to 10 per cent; of P, 5 to 10 per cent; and of T, 5 to 10 per cent. In other words, our statistical data were regarded as only rough or approximate; yet the final "doctoring" needed to make them agree with each other was, as has been seen, seldom over 2 per cent, being less than 1 per cent for M and M'; less than 2 per cent for V and V'; less than 3 per cent for P; and less than 4 per cent for T. We conclude then that the figures fit each other better than might be expected from their known lack of precision.

The corrections which we have assigned to the various factors are so insignificant that it would be hazardous to attempt to explain them specifically. The errors which they presumably represent might be due to numerous sources, such as the varying ingredient in the New York clearing house transactions of bank transfers as distinct from ordinary check transactions; or such as errors or defects in the statistics of trade in grain, etc.; or such as an over or underestimate of the deviation from normal of the particular days in 1896 and 1909 on which the statistics of deposits made in banks were gathered; or such as over or underestimates of the unreported deposits, or over or underestimates of the gold in the United States, or over or underestimates of wages and of other numerous minor though often conjectural elements in our calculations.

The sources of error just mentioned were named in the order of their probable importance. It is, perhaps, significant that the greatest discrepancies are in the years 1896–1898, whose data for T were most defective, and in 1900, 1903, and 1907, which were years of crises or of impending crises.

§ 8

After making the above named mutual adjustments among the six magnitudes in the equation of exchange, we reach the following figures, constituting our final table of values for M, M', V, V', P, and T; they are the figures plotted in the dotted curves above given: —

FINALLY ADJUSTED VALUES OF ELEMENTS OF EQUATION OF EXCHANGE

	M	M'	V	V'	P	T	MV	$M'V'$	$MV+M'V'$ & PT
1896	.88	2.71	18.8	36.6	60.3	191	16	99	115
1897	.90	2.86	19.9	39.4	60.4	215	18	112	130
1898	.97	3.22	20.2	40.6	63.2	237	20−	131−	150
1899	1.03	3.88	21.5	42.0	71.6	259	22	163	185
1900	1.18	4.24	20.4	40.1	76.5	253	24	170	194
1901	1.22	5.13	21.8	40.6	80.5	291	27	208	235
1902	1.25	5.40	21.6	40.5	85.7	287	27	219	246
1903	1.39	5.73	20.9	39.7	82.6	310	29	227	256
1904	1.36	7.77	20.4	39.6	82.6	310	28	228	256
1905	1.45	6.54	21.6	42.7	87.7	355	31+	279+	311
1906	1.58	6.81	21.5	46.3	93.2	375	34	315	349
1907	1.63	7.13	21.3	45.3	93.2	384	35	323	358
1908	1.62	6.54	19.7	45.0	90.3	361	32	294	326
1909	1.61	6.68	21.1	52.8	100.	387	34	353	387

This table, combining as it does the virtues of all the independent calculations of M, M', V, V', P, T, with the corrections of each necessary to make it conform to the others, may be considered to give the best available data concerning these magnitudes.

These figures, or the dotted curves in the preceding diagram, show that money in circulation (M) has nearly doubled in thirteen years; that its velocity of circulation (V) has increased only 10 per cent; that the deposit currency has nearly tripled and its velocity of circulation (V') has increased 50 per cent; that the volume of trade has doubled; and that prices have risen two thirds.

These results are not surprising, but are, I believe, just such as we might expect. Nevertheless, almost all are new. The figures for money in circulation (M) are not greatly different from those given in official documents and used by Professor Kemmerer. Likewise the figures for index numbers of prices are based chiefly on, and are very similar to, the index numbers for wholesale prices of the United States Labor Bureau. The statistics for volume of trade are constructed entirely anew and differ somewhat from Kemmerer's, which were their only precursors. The statistics for deposits subject to check (M') are here published for the first time. The statistics of velocities of circulation of bank deposits (V') are the first statistics of their kind, excepting the statistics for the activity of bank accounts of European banks. Finally the statistics of velocity of circulation of money (V) are the first of their kind.

With these data we are able to form a fairly correct statistical picture of the circulatory system in the United States. According to the records of 1909, the money in actual circulation (M) is 1.6 billions of dollars or $18 per capita (much less than the official figure given for circulation, $35); its velocity of circulation (V) is twenty-one times a year; the deposit currency (M') is 6.7 billions or $74 per capita — fourfold that of money; its velocity of circulation (V'), 53 times a year — two and a half times that of money; the total circulation of, or payments by, money (MV), 34 billions a year; the circulation of deposits subject to check or payments by check ($M'V'$), 353 billions — ten times as much or nearly a billion a day. This makes a grand total for business done at present prices ($MV + M'V'$ or PT) of 387 billions, or more than a billion a day. The size of this aggregate will probably astonish most readers. In the absence of actual statistics we have heretofore little realized the colossal proportions of our trade. Probably few persons outside of statisticians would have imagined that our import and export trade, which has filled so large a place in our political vision, sinks into utter insignificance as compared with the internal trade of the country. The total exports and imports amount only to a paltry 3 billions as compared with a total national trade of 387 billions.

We are now ready to represent the entire set of figures given in the last table by means of the mechanical illustration adopted in previous chapters. This is done in Figure 17, which shows at a glance the course of all the six magnitudes for fourteen years, making 84 statistical figures in all. This mechanical picture visualizes the increase in prices (lengthening in right arm) which has been going on during these fourteen years, and at the same time exhibits the changes in all the five factors on which that increase of prices depends. All of the six magnitudes represented are, of course, the *corrected* ones, so as to exactly harmonize with each other and make the two sides of the scales balance. The steady growth of the money in circulation is shown in the increase in the size of the hanging purse; the similar but more rapid growth of deposits subject to check is shown by the increase in the size of the bank book; the lesser growth in the velocities of these two media of exchange is shown by the lengthening of the two arms at the left

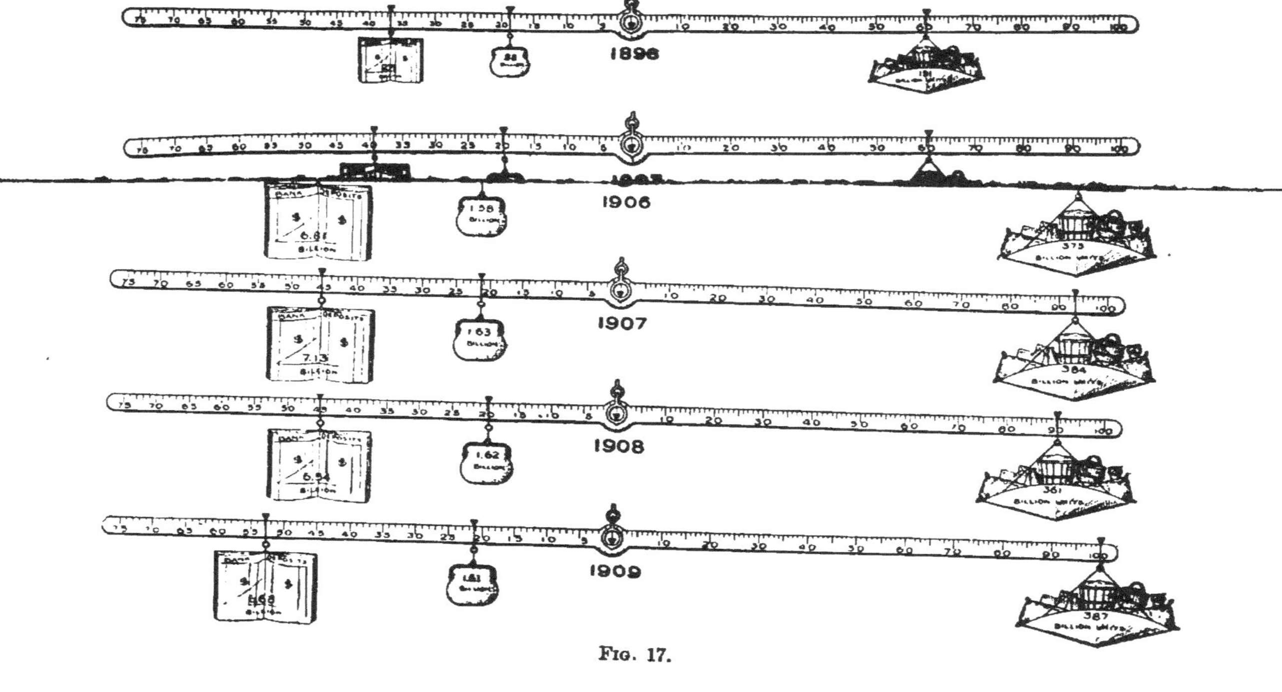
1896
1906
1.58 Billion
375 Billion units
1907
1.63 Billion
7.13 Billion
384 Billion units
1908
1.62 Billion
6.54 Billion
361 Billion units
1909
387 Billion units

Fig. 17.

of the fulcrum. These four factors have all conspired to increase prices. The only cause resisting the rise is the growth of trade, which is shown by the increasing size of the hanging tray at the right and which has tended to reduce prices.

We have here a complete quantitative picture of the causes affecting the price level during the last fourteen years, or, at any rate, of all the *proximate* causes; for, as we have noted, back of the five proximate causes lie innumerable antecedent causes.

What then, in brief, are the facts of history? They are that prices have increased by about two thirds between 1896 and 1909, that this has been *in spite of* a doubling in the volume of trade, and *because of* (1) a doubling of money, (2) a tripling of deposits, and (3 and 4) slight increases in the velocities of circulation.

§ 9

There has been much discussion as to the most important causes which have increased prices during recent years. It is, therefore, interesting to compare the four proximate causes which, as we have seen, have alone tended to increase prices in the period 1896–1909. Perhaps the simplest and best method is to compare the actual rise of prices with what it *would have been* if any one cause of that rise had been absent. That is, we test the importance of any price-raising factor by answering the question, What difference does it make to prices whether that factor is present or absent? We shall find that the growth of money is by far the most important cause. The growth of deposits is less important than appears at first glance. The growth of deposits would have to be regarded as the most important cause if deposits could be considered as independent of money.

But they are not independent. We have seen that, normally, deposits rise or fall with money in circulation. Therefore, if deposits had increased just as fast as money and no faster, we should ascribe the whole increase to money alone. In that case no part of the rise of prices would be ascribable to any increase in deposits; for there would have been no increase except what was due to the increase in money. The increase of deposits subject to check can be considered independently of the increase of money only in so far as the deposits have increased *relatively* to money. We have seen that mere increase of money would of itself normally cause a proportionate increase of deposits; only the *dis*proportionate increase of deposits should therefore be considered apart from the increase in money as a cause of rising prices. Therefore the true method of considering deposits as a separate cause appears to be to reckon them relatively to money. That is, not M', but $\frac{M'}{M}$ is the magnitude to be considered.[1]

We may therefore consider as the only causes tending to raise prices during the period 1896–1909, the following four: —

(1) The increase in money in circulation, *i.e.* the increase in M.

(2) The increase in relative deposits, *i.e.* the increase in $\frac{M'}{M}$.

(3) The increase in the velocity of circulation of money, *i.e.* the increase in V.

(4) The increase in the velocity of circulation of deposits, *i.e.* the increase in V'.

[1] See § 1 of Appendix to Chapter III, where this magnitude (*relative* deposits) is treated and represented by the letter k.

The fifth factor determining the price level, viz. the factor T has, as we have seen, tended to *lower* prices.

We shall now proceed to note what would be the *separate* effects on prices of these four price-raising causes and of the one price-depressing cause.

We wish, then, to know what the price level *would have been* in 1909 under the following five conditions : —

(1) If the money in circulation (M) had not grown at all since 1896,

(2) If the relative deposits $\frac{M'}{M}$ had not grown at all since 1896,

(3) If the velocity of circulation of money (V) had not grown at all since 1896,

(4) If the velocity of circulation of deposits (V') had not grown at all since 1896,

(5) If the volume of trade (T) had not grown at all since 1896,

assuming in each case that all the other four factors had grown in exactly the way they did grow. We have taken the actual price level in 1909 as 100 per cent and shall continue to do so, expressing on this basis what the price level *would have been* under each of the five hypotheses above named. We reach the following results :[1] —

[1] The calculations needed are obvious and simple. They consist of substituting, for all the factors but one in the right side of the equation $P = \frac{MV + M'V'}{T} = \frac{MV + M\left(\frac{M'}{M}\right)V'}{T}$, the statistics already obtained for 1909, and for that one factor remaining, the figure for 1896. This one factor remaining is, for the first hypothesis, M; for the second, M'/M; for the third, V; the fourth, V'; and the fifth T.

Were it not for the growth of

(1) Money (M), the price level of 1909 would have been 55 instead of 100;

(2) Relative deposits $\left(\frac{M'}{M}\right)$, the price level of 1909 would have been 77 instead of 100;

(3) Velocity of circulation of money (V), the price level of 1909 would have been 99 instead of 100;

(4) Velocity of circulation of deposits (V'), the price level of 1909 would have been 72 instead of 100;

(5) Volume of trade (T), the price level of 1909 would have been 206 instead of 100.

In other words, were it not for the growth of

(1) Money (M), prices would have been 45 per cent lower;

(2) Relative deposits $\left(\frac{M'}{M}\right)$, prices would have been 23 per cent lower;

(3) Velocity of money (V), prices would have been 1 per cent lower;

(4) Velocity of deposits (V'), prices would have been 28 per cent lower.

(5) Volume of trade (T), prices would have been 106 per cent higher.

The four price-raising causes may, therefore, be arranged in the following order of relative importance: —

Except for the growth of V, prices would have been 1 per cent lower than they were.

Except for the growth of $\frac{M'}{M}$, prices would have been 23 per cent lower than they were.

Except for the growth of V', prices would have been 28 per cent lower than they were.

Except for the growth of M, prices would have been 45 per cent lower than they were.

We conclude, therefore, that the growth of the velocity of circulation of money was a negligible factor in raising prices; that the relative growth of deposits and their velocity were large factors; and that the growth of money was the largest. The importance of the growth of money as a price-raising factor was, according to the above figures, almost exactly double that of relative deposits and a little over 50 per cent greater than that of their velocity of circulation.

§ 10

But the full effect of the increase in the quantity of money is really greater even than these figures indicate; for we have not included the effect of the overflow of money abroad, caused by the great increase in American bank deposits. Evidently this overflow must be taken into account; for the other three price-raising factors, by crowding out money and usurping its place, have given themselves an exaggerated appearance of importance. In other words, there has been a greater increase in money than appears from the United States figures by the amount which has overflowed into foreign lands. The United States is only a small part of the world's market, and its price level is largely determined by the world's price level. Whatever raises prices in one country tends to raise prices in all countries, and in the last analysis the only correct way to measure the relative importance of price-raising causes is to consider the world as a whole. If the statistics we have worked out for the United States were typical of the world, the resulting estimate of the relative importance of the four price-raising causes would be true of the world.

But there is strong reason to believe that the growth of deposits and of their velocity played a far greater part in raising prices in the United States than anywhere else. The reason is that banking is in its infancy in France and most other countries. It is so unimportant that even if its rate of growth there were prodigious, it would still be a relatively insignificant price-raising factor. We may therefore be certain, humanly speaking, that outside of the United States the increase of prices is even more largely due to the growth of money (gold) than in the United States.

We conclude, therefore, with much confidence, that the increase in the world's gold is chiefly responsible for the increase in the world's prices. What has been said probably explains why, in the last three years, there has been no actual increase in the quantity of money in circulation in the United States. It has been crowded out or prevented from increasing by the excessively great increase of our deposits and of their velocity of circulation.

But besides the world movements of prices there are special local movements as well. Anything which interferes with trade, like a tariff, tends to make the rise of prices unequal. We have left, therefore, the question of such *special* influences on the American price level as the tariff, — working out its effects through M.

As we have seen in a previous chapter, the effect of enacting a protective tariff is to raise the price level of the "protected" country by creating temporarily a "favorable" balance of trade and thus stimulating imports of the money metal and discouraging its export. This effect ceases as soon as the price level at home has been elevated enough, relatively to the price levels abroad, to restore the equilibrium of trade and stop the relative accumulation of gold in the protected country. Thereafter the tariff ceases to affect the price level, except as it interferes with trade and thereby prevents the price level at home from adjusting itself to the price levels abroad. This *interfering* effect may be in either direction; that is, the price level at home will be rendered more *independent* of foreign price levels than it would be if trade were free. The tariff merely *isolates* the protected country.

During the period under investigation, 1896–1909, there have been two changes in the tariff, that of 1897, and the more recent law of 1909. The first represented an advance over the rates of 1894. This law of 1897 must have tended, therefore, somewhat to restrict imports and to raise prices. So far as our prices have risen faster than prices have risen in other countries, like England, in the period here considered, it seems fair to attribute a part of this additional rise to our tariff system.

We come finally to the tariff of 1909. This act is so recent as scarcely yet to have had much perceptible influence, even if that influence be assumed to have begun as soon as the act was planned, early in 1909. There has waged a bitter political controversy over the question whether it was a revision upward or downward. The best unbiased opinion seems to be that it was slightly upward but was chiefly a mere rearrangement by which some duties were raised and others lowered. These conclusions of Professor Taussig, Professor Willis, and others are based on an intensive study of the tariff schedules.

A review of the statistics of the equation of exchange is entirely consistent with these conclusions. This consistency may not be evident at first glance. On the contrary, those who claim that duties have been greatly increased might point to the fact that since the tariff American prices have risen faster than English prices;[1] while those who claim that the revision was distinctly downward might point to the increase in our imports of commodities, and the increase in our exports of gold. But these seemingly discordant facts are reconcilable.

American statistics show that there has been an enormous expansion in bank deposits and in their velocity of circulation in 1909 as compared with 1908. This would naturally have the effect of raising American prices, displacing gold, and checking the increase of money in circulation in the United States, which would otherwise occur, and correspondingly of encouraging the import of commodities. The facts agree precisely with these known tendencies. Prices in the United States have risen more than in England, the increase in the quantity of money in circulation has been checked, the export of gold and the import of commodities have been increased. Thus we may explain all the facts without assuming the tariff as a disturbing element.[2]

It would take us too far afield to discuss all the other factors which have been held more or less responsible for the increase in prices. We have already made it clear

[1] Beyond 1909 only American figures are available. Those in the *Bulletin of the United States Bureau of Labor* show an uninterrupted rise in prices from January, 1909, to March, 1910. Between these dates the index numbers for wholesale prices rose from 124.0 to 133.8. For a good English-American comparison, see *Report of the* (Mass.) *Commission on the Cost of Living*. Boston, 1910, pp. 26, 56.

[2] But, although we cannot justly convict the tariff of raising our price level in recent years, it is of course true that *a reduction in the tariff would tend powerfully to reduce that level;* for, as we have seen, a tariff wall acts like a dam in keeping up the high level accumulated by the original imposition of duties.

that none of these could influence prices except by increasing the quantity of money in circulation, the relative deposits, or their velocities, or by decreasing trade. As trade has increased greatly, the last possibility may be ignored.

As to the causes which have increased money and deposits and their velocities, the most important seem to be the following: —

(1) The chief cause of the increase of money has been the increase in gold mining. Bank notes have only slightly more than kept pace with other money in circulation.

(2) The chief causes of the relative increase in bank deposits seem to have been those which have extended banking especially in the South. The recent banking laws, encouraging the establishment of small banks, may have had some part in this extension.

(3) The chief cause of the increase of velocity of circulation, especially of bank deposits, seems to have been the concentration of population in cities. We have seen that the larger the town the greater the velocity of circulation of bank deposits.

§ 11

Throughout this book we have aimed at explaining the *general* purchasing power of money, not its purchasing power over any particular goods or class of goods. The problem of the rise in "the cost of living" is partly a *general* problem of the purchasing power of money, and partly a *special* problem of the prices of food, clothing and other costs of "living." With the special problem we have here nothing to do. But it so happens that the special changes in the cost of living are very small as compared with the general change in prices. At any rate this is true of the wholesale prices of food. The index number of food rose between January, 1909, and March, 1910, from 122.6 to 130.9, while general wholesale prices rose from 124.0 to 133.8; that is, the special prices of food rose about evenly with the general rising tide of prices. So far as there was any difference it was such that the special prices rose slightly less than general prices. The "general prices" here referred to are only wholesale prices and do not include prices of labor and securities; but the inclusion of these elements, judging from the statistics as already given up to 1909, and market reports since that date, would not materially change the result.

We conclude that the "rise in the cost of living" is no *special* movement of food prices nor, presumably, of other particular prices, but is merely a part of the general movement of prices. The cost of living is swept along with the general rising tide of prices of all sorts. It indicates little or no special change in the supply or demand of special classes of goods, but simply reflects the fall in the general purchasing power of money. These remarks apply not simply to the months beginning w th January, 1909, but back to 1908. Back of 1908 food prices move somewhat irregularly as compared with general prices, but on the whole maintain an approximately even pace from 1897 to 1909.

The following table gives some interesting by-products of our study for the period 1896–1909.

We note from column (2) that deposits (M') have grown, not only absolutely, but relatively to money (M), changing, from a little over threefold to a little over fourfold, money in circulation. The figure for the panic year, 1907, was the highest but one, and the drop in the succeeding year was the largest drop in the table.

Column (3) shows the "virtual" velocity of money, based on the idea that the total work of exchange, even that performed by checks, is really the work, indirectly, of money. It is simply the quotient of the total exchange work done, divided by the total money in circulation *and in banks*.

(1)	(2) $\frac{M'}{M}$	(3) VIRTUAL VELOCITY	(4) $\frac{MV}{MV+M'V'}$	(5) $\frac{M'V'}{MV+M'V'}$
1896	3.1	80	.14	.86
1897	3.2	84	.14	.86
1898	3.3	89	.13	.87
1899	3.8	103	.12	.88
1900	3.6	99	.12	.88
1901	4.2	114	.11	.89
1902	4.3	115	.11	.89
1903	4.1	113	.11	.89
1904	4.2	107	.11	.89
1905	4.5	125	.10	.90
1906	4.3	132	.10	.90
1907	4.4	129	.10	.90
1908	4.0	107	.10	.90
1909	4.1	124	.09	.91

We note that this virtual ve ocity of circulation of money, or its efficiency in providing for exchanges, has grown about 50 per cent. Its growth has been interrupted by occasional slumps, but all of these were trifling excepting that following the crisis of 1907.

The fourth and fifth columns give the solution of the much mooted question of the relative importance of check transactions ($M'V'$) and money transactions (MV), — a question to which many writers, including Professor Kinley, have given much attention. We find that in 1896 about 14 per cent of the business in the United States was performed by money and in 1909 about 9 per cent. In other words, checks performed in 1896 about 86 per cent of the total exchange work, and in 1909 about 91 per cent.[1]

These figures appear to afford the first fairly precise determination of the relative importance of check and money transactions. They confirm the belief[2] that the relative part played by checks in the country's transactions has substantially increased. The prevailing impression that they constitute nine tenths of all transactions is also seen to be correct.

[1] For discussion of these figures, see § 12 of the Appendix to (this) Chapter XII, where comparison is made with Professor Kinley's results.

[2] See *e.g.* Cannon on Clearing Houses among the *Reports of the Monetary Commission*, 1910.

CHAPTER XIII

THE PROBLEM OF MAKING PURCHASING POWER MORE STABLE

§ 1

We have seen that the purchasing power of money (or its reciprocal, the level of prices) depends exclusively on five factors, viz.: the quantity of money in circulation, its velocity of circulation, the quantity of deposits subject to check, its velocity, and the volume of trade. Each of these five magnitudes depends on numerous antecedent causes, but they do not depend on each other except that:—

(1) Deposits subject to check depend on money in circulation, the two normally varying in unison.

(2) The velocities of circulation of money and deposits tend to increase with an increase in the volume of trade.

(3) Any two or more of the five factors may be *indirectly* related by virtue of being dependent on a common cause or causes. Thus, the same invention may cause an increase in both velocities, or in both money and trade, or in both deposits and their velocity. To take an historical case, we know that the growing density of population has operated to increase all of the five factors.

(4) During transition periods certain temporary disturbances or oscillations occur in all six magnitudes, the extremes of which are crises and depressions. Normally, the price level is an effect and not a cause in the equation

of exchange; but during such transition periods its fluctuations temporarily react on the other five factors, and especially on deposits. A rise will thus temporarily generate a further rise, while a fall temporarily operates in the opposite direction.

The price level, then, is the result of the five great causes mentioned, normally varying directly with the quantity of money (and with deposits which normally vary in unison with the quantity of money), provided that the velocities of circulation and the volume of trade remain unchanged, and that there be a given state of development of deposit banking. This is one of the chief propositions concerning the level of prices or its reciprocal, the purchasing power of money. It constitutes the so-called quantity theory of money. The qualifying adverb "normally" is inserted in the formulation in order to provide for the transitional periods or credit cycles. Practically, this proposition is an exact law of proportion, as exact and as fundamental in economic science as the exact law of proportion between pressure and density of gases in physics, assuming temperature to remain the same. It is, of course, true that, in practice, velocities and trade seldom remain unchanged, just as it seldom happens that temperature remains unchanged. But the *tendency* represented in the quantity theory remains true, whatever happens to the other elements involved, just as the *tendency* represented in the density theory remains true whatever happens to temperature. Only those who fail to grasp the significance of what a scientific law really is can fail to see the significance and importance of the quantitative law of money. A scientific law is not a formulation of statistics or of history. It is a formulation of what holds true under given conditions. Statistics and history can be used to illustrate and verify laws only by making suitable allowances for changed conditions. It is by making such allowances that we have pursued our study of the last ten centuries in the rough and of the last decade and a half in detail. In each case we found the facts in accord with the principles previously formulated.

From a practical point of view the most serious problem revealed by this historical and statistical study is the problem of stability and dependability in the purchasing power of money. We find that this purchasing power is subject to wide variations in two ways: (1) It oscillates up and down with the transitional periods constituting credit cycles; and (2) it is likely to suffer secular variations in either direction according to the incidents of industrial changes. The first transition is connected with the banking system; the second depends largely upon the money metal.

One method of mitigating both of these evils is the increase of knowledge as to prospective price levels. As we have seen, the real evils of changing price levels do not lie in these changes *per se*, but in the fact that they usually take us unawares. It has been shown that to be forewarned is to be forearmed, and that a foreknown change in price levels might be so taken into account in the rate of interest as to neutralize its evils. While we cannot expect our knowledge of the future ever to become so perfect as to reach this ideal, viz. compensations for every price fluctuation by corresponding adjustments in the rate of interest — nevertheless every increase in our knowledge carries us a little nearer that remote ideal. Fortunately, such increase in knowledge is now going on rapidly. The editors of trade journals to-day scan the economic horizon as weather predictors scan the physical horizon; and every indication of a change in the economic weather is noted and commented upon. Within the past year a certain firm has instituted a statistical service to supply bankers, brokers, and merchants with records, or "business barometers," and forecasts based thereon, with the avowed object of preventing panics. Yet it is probably in regard to the fundamental mechanism by which such forecasts are based that there is the greatest need of a wider diffusion of knowledge. The range of the ordinary business man's theoretical knowledge is extremely narrow. He is even apt to be suspicious of such knowledge, if not to hold it in contempt. The consequences of this narrowness are often disastrous, as, for instance, when, in pursuance of the advice of New York business men, Secretary Chase issued the greenbacks, or when the ill-advised legislation to close the Gold Room was enacted. And it is not altogether in unusual predicaments such as those brought by the Civil War that the business man's limitations in knowledge react injuriously upon him. Every day he is hampered by a lack of understanding of the principles regulating the purchasing power of money; and in proportion as he fails to understand these principles he is apt to fail in predictions. The prejudice of business men against the variability of, and especially against a rise of the rate of interest, probably stands in the way of prompt adjustment in that rate and helps to aggravate the far more harmful variability in the level of prices and its reciprocal, the purchasing power of money. The business man has, in fact, never regarded it as a part of the preparation for his work to understand the broad principles affecting money and interest. He has rather assumed that his province was confined to accumulating a technical acquaintance with the nature of the goods he handles. The sugar merchant informs himself as to sugar, the grain merchant as to grain, the real estate trader as to real estate. It scarcely occurs to any of them that he needs a knowledge as to gold; yet every bargain into which he enters depends for one of its two terms on gold. I cannot but believe that the diffusion among business men of the fuller knowledge of the equation of exchange, of the relation of money to deposits, of credit cycles and of interest, which the future is sure to bring, will pay rich returns in mitigating the evils of crises and depressions which now take them so often unawares.

§ 2

But while there is much to be hoped for from a greater foreknowledge of price changes, a lessening of the price changes themselves would be still more desirable. Various preventives of price changes have been proposed. We shall first consider those which are more particularly applicable to secular price changes, and afterward consider those more particularly applicable to the price changes involved in credit cycles. The secular price changes are, as we have seen, chiefly due to changes in money and in trade. There has been for centuries, and promises to be for centuries to come, a race between money and trade. On the results of that race depends to some extent the fate of every business man. The commercial world has become more and more committed to the gold standard through a series of historical events having little if any connection with the fitness of that or any other metal to serve as a *stable* standard. So far as the question of monetary stability is concerned, it is not too much to say that we have hit upon the gold standard by accident just as we hit on the present railway gauge by the accident of previous custom as to road carriages; and just as we hit upon the decimal notation by the accident of having had ten fingers, and quite without reference to the question of numerical convenience in which other systems of numeration would be superior. Now that we have adopted a gold standard, it is almost as difficult to substitute another as it would be to establish the Russian railway gauge or the duodecimal system of numeration. And the fact that the question of a monetary standard is to-day so much an international question makes it all the more difficult. Yet, as Professor Shaler, the geologist, has said, "It seems likely that we shall, within a few decades, contrive some other means of measuring values than by the ancient device of balancing them against a substance of which the supply is excessive."[1]

I shall not attempt to offer any *immediate* solution of this great world problem of finding a substitute for gold. Before a substitute for gold can be found, there must be much investigation and education of the public. The object here is to call attention to the necessity for this investigation and education, to examine such solutions as have been already proposed and, very tentatively, to make a suggestion which may possibly be acted upon at some future time, when, through the diffusion of knowledge, better statistics, and better government, the time shall become ripe.

One suggestion has been to readopt bimetallism. This has already been discussed in Chapter VII. We were then concerned, however, chiefly with the "mechanics

[1] *Man and the Earth*, New York (Duffield), 1906, p. 62.

of bimetallism" and not its influence on price levels. We have now to note the claim of advocates of a bimetallic standard that such a standard would tend to steady prices.[1] As we have seen, by connecting the currencies of both gold and silver countries, bimetallism, as long as it continues in working order, has the effect of spreading any variation of one particular metal over the combined area of gold, silver, and bimetallic countries. If variations occur simultaneously in both metals, they may be in opposite directions, and neutralize each other more or less completely; while, even if they happen to be in the same direction, the combined effect on the whole world united under bimetallism would be no greater than on the two halves of the world under silver and gold monometallism respectively. Even if bimetallism did not enlarge the monetary area, it might reduce monetary fluctuations. Thus a world-wide gold standard might prove more variable than bimetallism.[2] But if the amount of one metal used in coinage increases faster or more slowly than business, while the amount of the other maintains a constant ratio to business, then the use of the two metals results in less steadiness than would result from the less variable of the two, though in somewhat more steadiness than would result from the use of the more variable.

Two variable metals joined through bimetallism may be likened to two tipsy men locking arms. Together they walk somewhat more steadily than apart, although if one happens to be much more sober

[1] See Jevons, *Investigations in Currency and Finance*, London (Macmillan), 1884, pp. 331–333.

[2] Cf. F. Y. Edgeworth, "Thoughts on Monetary Reform," (British) *Economic Journal*, September, 1895, p. 449.

than the other, his own gait may be made worse by the union.[1]

The table in the footnote shows that in the seventeenth and nineteenth centuries the two metals were about equally unsteady. In the eighteenth century gold was the more steady. During the first half of the nineteenth century silver was the more steady, while for 1851–1890 gold was the more steady. Since then, silver has been the more steady. On the whole, there is not much to choose between the behaviors of the two.

Bimetallism, then, even could it be maintained, would offer but an indifferent remedy for the variations in the price level, and, moreover, there is always the objection previously noted that the system may break down. We then saw that whatever the ratio at which both metals are to circulate, one metal is likely, sometime, to be produced in such abundance as completely to fill the money reservoir, driving the other metal altogether out of circulation. Such a result may be long in coming, but eventually it is practically sure to come.

[1] The variabilities of gold and silver production have been calculated by one of my students, Mr. Morgan Porter. He finds the following mean percentage variations from the mean productions for each period named: —

		Gold	Silver
		%	%
1601–1701	5 periods of 20 years each	7.8	7.7
1701–1800	5 periods of 20 years each	15.6	27.4
1801–1900	5 periods of 20 years each	69.0	67.0
1801–1850	5 periods of 10 years each	52.4	22.3
1851–1885	7 periods of 5 years each	8.1	40.8
1886–1890	5 periods of 1 year each	5.9	10.5
1891–1895	5 periods of 1 year each	13.3	6.3
1896–1900	5 periods of 1 year each	12.3	3.4
1901–1905	5 periods of 1 year each	10.7	1.9

A more important objection remains to be noted. Since bimetallism, as usually proposed, would greatly overvalue one of the two metals, the first great effect of its adoption might be not to steady prices but to disrupt them and upset the relation of debtor and creditor. While the great overvaluation of one metal is not a necessary feature of bimetallism, it has always been the feature which has made it politically popular. Thus, the bimetallism advocated in the United States during the last twenty or thirty years has been a bimetallism which would grossly overvalue silver. It proposed that 16 ounces of silver should circulate as the equivalent of an ounce of gold, when during much of this time it really required 30 or 35 ounces of silver to be equivalent to one of gold. Such an overvaluation of silver would mean that silver would be imported from Mexico, India, China, and other silver countries, as well as mined in larger quantities and coined in the United States, thus depreciating the currency both greatly and suddenly. The proposal was well satirized by a cartoon in the "free silver" campaign of 1896 representing the United States as a ship sailing over Niagara Falls in order to reach smooth sailing below the falls, — if only it survive the shock of the fall!

Bimetallism is the only scheme of steadying the monetary standard which has ever secured political momentum; and even its popularity lay far less in its potency for ultimately steadying than in its potency for immediately unsteadying the standard. We now pass on to consider schemes which have never reached the stage of practical proposals, but are still wholly academic.

The first is polymetallism, a generalization of bimetallism. The theory of bimetallism contemplates the circulation side by side of two metals; that of polymetallism looks to the contemporaneous circulation of more than two. So long as several metals could be maintained in circulation together, the price level might fluctuate less than if one metal only were used. But all of the theoretical objections against bimetallism apply also against polymetallism. One metal would eventually drive all the others out of a country, or, — if polymetallism were international, — into the arts.

§ 3

Recognizing the force of the arguments against bimetallism (and polymetallism), Professor Marshall has suggested as a substitute a system which has been called symmetallism. Under this scheme — symmetallism — two (or more) metals would be joined together physically in the same coin or in "linked bars." Evidently any ratio could be used, and neither metal could push the other out of circulation. The value of the composite coin would be the sum of the values of its two constituents, and the fluctuations in its value would be the mean of the fluctuations of its constituents.[1]

Many other schemes for combining metals have been suggested. Among them are the "joint-metallisms" of Stokes and Hertzka, which are kinds of bimetallism at a variable instead of at a fixed ratio. Another, advocated by Walras,[2] is the gold standard with a "silver regulator," which is simply the limping standard such as now prevails in the United States, France, or India

[1] See F. Y. Edgeworth, "Thoughts on Monetary Reform," (British) *Economic Journal*, September, 1895, p. 448.

[2] "Monnaie d'or avec billon d'argent régulateur," *Revue de droit international*, December, 1884; reprinted in *Études d'Économie politique appliquée*, Lausanne (Rouge), 1898, pp. 3–19.

except that the quantity of silver in circulation, instead of being fixed, would be systematically manipulated by the government in such a manner as to keep prices steady. But these, like symmetallism and bimetallism, offer a remedy which at best is only partial. For instance, in Walras's scheme, in order to maintain prices, the amount of silver might need to be reduced to zero — after which no further regulation would be possible; or it might need to be increased so far as to expel all gold, after which the system would be no longer a gold standard, but would become an inconvertible silver standard. Worst of all, every one of these proposed remedies would be subject to the danger of unwise or dishonest political manipulation.

It is true that the level of prices might be kept almost absolutely stable merely by honest government regulation of the money supply with that specific purpose in view. One seemingly simple way by which this might be attempted would be by the issue of inconvertible paper money in quantities so proportioned to increase of business that the total amount of currency in circulation, multiplied by its rapidity, would have the same relation to the total business at one time as at any other time. If the confidence of citizens were preserved, and this relation were kept, the problem would need no further solution.

But sad experience teaches that irredeemable paper money, while theoretically capable of steadying prices, is apt in practice to be so manipulated as to produce instability. In nearly every country there exists a party, consisting of debtors and debtor-like classes, which favors depreciation. A movement is therefore at any time possible, tending to pervert any scheme for maintaining stability into a scheme for simple inflation.

As soon as any particular government controls a paper currency bearing no relation to gold or silver, excuses for its over-issue are to be feared.

Even if, in times of peace, these persistent pleas for inflation could be resisted, it is doubtful if they could be resisted in time of war. In time of war many plausible defenses can be given, notably the need of government supplies. The history of our own country in this respect is not reassuring. It is natural, therefore, that such schemes should have gotten in bad odor. Indeed, their odor has been so bad that many have impulsively concluded that the "quantity theory" which has been appealed to as making possible government manipulation of prices must be fundamentally unsound. Experience has shown, however, that the evil feared need not always be realized.

Another method by means of which government could theoretically keep the price level more stable is by confining the primary money to a precious metal, say gold, and regulating the quantity of this metal in the currency by means of a system of seigniorage. Thus, as the supply of gold from the mines increased, and gold tended to depreciate in value, the value of gold coin could be kept up by making a continuously higher charge for coinage, in the shape of seigniorage. This charge would become higher as gold bullion became cheaper, in such proportion as to keep the currency in the same relation with the volume of business, and thus to keep the level of prices stable. If, later, the annual production of gold should become very small, and gold, in consequence, should begin to appreciate in value, stability might be maintained by a reversal of this policy, *i.e.* by gradually reducing the seigniorage so as to prevent appreciation of the currency. There would, however, be a limit to the power to regulate in this direction similar to the limit we noted in the case of Walras's scheme. The seigniorage could never be reduced to less than zero. Money can never be materially cheaper than the metal composing it, since the slightest tendency in this direction will result in coin being exported or melted into bullion. In a period of rising prices, regulation would be easy; in a period of falling prices, regulation might be quite impossible.[1]

Another plan is a convertible paper currency, the paper to be redeemable on demand, — not in any required weight or coin of gold, but in a required purchasing power thereof. Under such a plan, the paper money would be redeemed by as much gold as would have the required purchasing power. Thus, the amount of gold obtainable for a paper dollar would vary inversely with its purchasing power per ounce as compared with commodities, the total purchasing power of the dollar being always the same. The fact that a paper dollar would always be redeemable in terms of purchasing power would theoretically keep the level of prices invariable. The supply of money in circulation would regulate itself automatically. Should money tend to increase fast enough to impair its purchasing power, the notes would be presented for redemption in gold; for under the arrangement assumed, the gold

[1] For the effect of the legal prohibition of exportation see Kemmerer, *Money and Credit Instruments in their Relation to General Prices*, 2d Edition, New York (Holt), 1909, p. 39 n. Cf. Kemmerer, "The Establishment of the Gold Exchange Standard in the Philippines," in the *Quarterly Journal of Economics*. Vol. XIX, 600–605 (August, 1905); *Second Annual Report of the Chief of the Division of Currency*, etc., 14, 15, 21–28; and "A Gold Standard for the Straits," II, in the *Political Science Quarterly*. Vol. XXI, p. 665–677 (December, 1906).

which would be given would always have the same purchasing power. Should the money tend to become scarce and thus to appreciate, the amount of gold having unchanged purchasing power would be exchanged for the notes.

It is true that this scheme, like a simple paper-money scheme, would be liable to abuse, — but it would have two practical advantages. Having a metallic basis, it would inspire more confidence than a pure paper-money plan, while it would offer less excuse for abuse and less chance to delude the public. Every change in the weight of the gold dollar would be definitely measurable, and would have to be justified to the public. A reduction in weight not fully explained by a fall in prices would be a clear confession of depreciation.

§ 4

The next plan to be considered is that advocated by Professor Marshall and the Committee of the British Association.[1] It is, in essence, the revival of the tabular standard proposed and discussed by Lowe,[2] Scrope,[3] Jevons,[4] and others; a standard which is relatively independent of special legislation. This involves the passing of a law — first merely permissive — by which contracts could be expressed in terms of an index number. Such a law would not be *necessary*, but it might serve to draw attention to the index method. The

[1] See *Report of the British Association for the Advancement of Science*, 1890, p. 488, containing a draft of a proposed Act of Parliament for this purpose.

[2] *Present State of England in regard to Agriculture, Trade, and Finance.* London, 1622.

[3] *Principles of Political Economy*, London, 1833, p. 406.

[4] *Investigations in Currency and Finance*, London (Macmillan), 1884, p. 122; also *Money and the Mechanism of Exchange*, London, (Kegan, Paul), 1893, Ch. XXV.

money of the country would continue to be used as a medium of exchange and as a measure of value, but not as a standard for all deferred payments. The standard of deferred payments, when advantage was taken of the law, would be the index number of general prices; and contracts involving deferred payment could, when desired, call for the exchange of a given purchasing power, or of an amount of money varying directly with the index number. To facilitate such a change, it might be well for the government to inaugurate an authorized system of index numbers, but government action would not have to go farther than this, or indeed, necessarily, so far. The aim would no longer be to keep the level of prices absolutely stable. Gold or silver or both would furnish the primary money, and their value would consequently fluctuate with that of the constituent metal or metals. But the contracts based on index numbers would not be affected because made in terms of the index number. Doubtless the plan would encounter much opposition,[1] but it would appeal strongly to certain classes.[2] For instance, those "living on their incomes" would like to be guaranteed a stable purchasing power. A widow, or a trustee, or other long-time investor, would prefer to buy bonds which guaranteed a regular yearly purchasing power over subsistence, rather than those which merely promised a given sum of money of uncertain value. A few precedents already exist, suggestive, at least, of what the new system would be. In England, the "tithe averages" have been made to vary with the value of grain, so that the tithe was in effect so much grain, not so much money;

[1] Cf. Francis Walker, *Money*, New York (Holt), 1891, pp. 157-163.

[2] See Joseph French Johnson, *Money and Currency*, Boston (Ginn), 1906, p. 175.

also the Scotch fiars prices have existed for more than two centuries for similar purposes, establishing the price of grain on the basis of which rents contracted in grain should be paid in money.[1]

As has been already indicated, government action looking to this result need not necessarily be taken. The beginnings of such a plan for "a tabular standard of value" could be made at any time by private contracting parties, some index number already in vogue, such as Sauerbeck's or the Bureau of Labor's, being used as a standard. Should the results of such experiments, on the whole, satisfy the contracting parties, others might follow their lead. At first contracts would be interpreted as having been made in terms of money except when otherwise provided. A specific proviso would therefore be required in contracts made in terms of the index number. If the latter form of contract should become more general, however, legislation could be passed, making the index number the standard in all cases, except where specifically provided that payment should be based on a different standard.

It is to be noted that such a custom, however general it might become, would not do away with the desirability of having an elastic currency to respond to seasonal variations of business. Seasonable readjustments of wages, for instance, and of many other prices, are difficult. Custom tends to establish standards holding through successive seasons. Since there is more business at some seasons than others, there will be an element of strain unless there is also an expansion of credit. An elastic banking system, facilitating credit-expansion, would, therefore, remain a desideratum.

[1] See Edgeworth, *Reports of the British Association for the Advancement of Science* for 1888, p. 182.

The system of making contracts in terms of the price level is not intended directly to prevent fluctuations in price level. Its purpose is rather to prevent these fluctuations from introducing a speculative element into business. But an incidental result of the system would be that fluctuations in the level of prices would be less than before, because credit cycles would no longer be stimulated. The alternate abnormal encouragement and discouragement of loans would cease. Hence, credit fluctuations would become less, and the level of prices would be comparatively unaffected by them.[1] Even if panics should occur, accompanied by sharp falls of prices, they would not be as severe as now. At present, loans must be liquidated in terms of a given amount of money, though that money may buy more (or less) at the time of liquidation than when the loan was contracted, and though the borrower must dispose of more (or less) commodities to raise the given amount. He is compelled to pay, when prices have fallen, on the same basis in terms of money, and a much higher value in terms of goods, than when prices ranged higher. Hence failure often results, credit currency contracts still further because of the general distrust, and depression becomes more severe. With payment in terms of purchasing power, the situation would be altogether different. Falling prices would neither injure borrowers nor benefit lenders.

On the whole, the "tabular standard" seems to have real merit.[2] Certainly there could be no material harm in trying a "permissive" law. But the tabular standard is subject to serious if not fatal objections: One is the

[1] See Jevons, *Money and the Mechanism of Exchange*, London (Kegan Paul), 1893, p. 333.

[2] See J. Allen Smith, "The Multiple Money Standard," *Annals of the American Academy of Political and Social Science*. March, 1896.

fact that it would involve the trouble of translating money into the tabular standard and would therefore fail to attract the public sufficiently to warrant its complete adoption by any government. Another objection is that its halfway adoption would really aggravate many of the evils it sought to correct, and therefore discourage, rather than encourage, its further extension. Even were the system adopted in its complete form for any one country, it would have the disadvantage of isolating that country commercially, and thus reintroducing the inconveniences of an uncertain rate of international exchange. An analogous inconvenience would arise by its partial adoption in any one country. Business men naturally and properly prefer a uniform system of accounts to two systems warring with each other. They would complain of such a double system of accounts in exactly the same way, and on exactly the same grounds, as they have always complained of the double system of accounts involved in international trade between gold and silver countries. A business man's profits constitute a narrow margin between receipts and expenses. If receipts and expenses could *both* be reckoned in the tabular standard, his profits would be more stable than if both were reckoned in money. But if he should pay some of his expenses, such as interest and wages, on a tabular basis, while his receipts remained on the gold basis, his profits would fluctuate far more than if both sides, or all items of the accounts, were in gold. In fact, his expected profits would often turn into losses by a slight deviation between the two standards, in precisely the same way as the importer or exporter of goods between China and the United States may have his profits wiped out by a slight variation in the exchange. In either case, he would prefer to have the same standard on both sides of the account, even if this standard fluctuated, rather than have two standards, only one of which fluctuated; for his profits depend more on the parallelism between the two sides of his account than on the stability of either. It was to escape the evils from having two standards that, after lengthy debate and experiment, the present gold-exchange standard was adopted in India, the Philippines, Mexico, and Panama.

§ 5

The mention of the gold-exchange standard brings us to the proposal which is here tentatively suggested, — a proposal which, it is believed, may one day be found both practicable and advisable. This plan involves a combination of the tabular standard with the principles of the gold-exchange standard.

We have already described briefly the gold-exchange standard, and given references to other and fuller sources of information. While the gold-exchange standard purports to be a system of redemption, or partial redemption in gold of the native coin, yet as a matter of fact, no gold is necessarily required in the country itself where the system is in operation. Thus, the Philippine government does not offer gold for silver pesos, even when gold is wanted for export to New York. Instead, it keeps a reserve of gold in New York, and "redeems" the Filipino's pesos in merely a draft upon this gold. As this draft may be forwarded to New York, it serves the purpose of gold redemption for export. The price of the sale includes a premium on exchange corresponding to the usual excess above the "gold point"; that is, the government charges the Filipino the equivalent of freight, insurance, and other expenses on gold to New York.

It will be evident that the gold-exchange system is only nominally a redemption system. In actual fact, it is a system of manipulating the silver currency in such a manner as to prevent its value from diverging from par with gold by more than the usual premiums on exchange between gold countries. This manipulation consists in contracting the currency when the rate of exchange reaches a certain point above par, and expanding the currency when it reaches a certain point below par. The contraction of the currency is secured by selling foreign bills of exchange and locking up the currency received therefor, while the expansion of the currency is secured by releasing this currency to circulation, or, if necessary, by coining more currency.

The successful operation of the system is not only compatible with, but actually requires, an overvaluation of the metallic content of the silver currency. In fact, in the Philippines it was found necessary to reduce the silver pesos from 374 grains to 247 grains, to prevent their disappearance. Without a margin between the coin-value and the bullion-value of the peso, the power to regulate its circulation would exist only in one direction — contraction; with such a margin, the power exists to expand as well as to contract.

After once becoming familiar, the system would operate just as successfully if the weight of the silver coins were still further reduced, or, in fact, if a paper currency were substituted instead. It will be seen, therefore, that at bottom the gold-exchange standard is practically the same standard as that which is now in operation for paper currency in Austria. In that country the paper is really irredeemable, but is kept at par by the sale of exchange on London.

The plan by which the bullion content of the coins

is kept below their value as coins not only prevents melting and exportation, and the consequent loss of control of their quantity and value, but also has the advantage of economy. The reduction of the weight of the pesos was, in fact, used as a means of defraying the expense of maintaining the gold reserve and the other expenses of inaugurating and operating the system in the Philippines.

The gold-exchange standard was at first regarded with great suspicion, and its advocates scarcely dared claim for it any better virtue than that of a practical makeshift, affording, as it did, a means of easy transition from the previously existing system to the gold standard, without shock, or introducing an unfamiliar coinage.

But the results have been so satisfactory that it may well be asked whether those who devised the gold-exchange standard did not build better than they knew. While the system bears a close, though somewhat superficial, resemblance to a fiat money system, it has now little or none of the odium or suspicion attached to it which we associate with that name. So simple are the duties of maintaining the gold-exchange par, and so unfailingly has the system been faithfully executed, that even those who at first most strenuously opposed it seem now inclined to trust it implicitly. There is, indeed, no reason why, under almost any conceivable circumstances, there should be even the fear of this system being abused.

Now that there has been actually constituted a new form of governmental machinery, which can be as fully trusted to perform its functions of regulation as the mint, there seems to be no reason why the system should not be extended. It is well known that the par of exchange which has been adopted for the gold-exchange standard is quite arbitrary, and it must be evident that this par could be changed. The par of exchange between the English and Indian system is 16*d.* per rupee. This par could be easily changed to 15*d.* or 17*d.*, and gradually changed further in either direction. By such changes of the gold par of exchange, the currency of those countries now having a gold-exchange standard could, if desired, be kept at par with a tabular standard. Thus, when it is found practicable to measure by index numbers the exact shifting of the gold standard, a corresponding shifting of the par of exchange or price of rupees in gold could be effected.

As the system is now operated, the coinage is manipulated to keep it at par with gold, that is, to follow the fluctuations of the gold standard wherever they may lead. We have, therefore, the spectacle of India, and other countries formerly having a silver standard, now clinging to the skirts, as it were, of the gold standard countries, and following that erratic standard whereever it may lead them, although it is within their power, by exactly the same machinery, to keep their course steady.

I would not, however, for a moment suggest that these countries should give up their par of exchange with gold standard countries. Although much might be said in favor of such a course, it would, to a large extent, be a step backward by again restoring the uncertainties of international exchange which have been mentioned. What is needed is to induce the entire civilized world to do what is now within the power of the gold-exchange countries to do, viz. to keep pace with a tabular standard. It is a little anomalous that these gold-exchange standard countries now have a power to regulate their price level, which is not possessed by the gold standard countries themselves. The latter are, by their present system, kept absolutely at the mercy of the accidents of gold mining and metallurgy, while the former can keep or change the par of exchange with gold countries at will.

But evidently the gold countries could do precisely what the silver countries have done, namely, inaugurate the system of a gold-exchange standard by closing their mints to gold, reducing, if need be, the weight of gold coins (although with the depreciation now going on in gold, this would probably not be necessary), and operating an exchange standard system in precisely the same way that the Philippines and the other countries mentioned now operate their gold-exchange system.

To make this clear we shall suppose, at first, that one country, say Austria, would continue on the gold standard while England, Germany, France, the United States, and the other chief countries of the world should close their mints to the free coinage of gold. They could then maintain a gold-exchange standard with a (varying) par of exchange with Austria. By suitably changing the par of exchange from time to time, the whole commercial world, excepting Austria, could then keep the purchasing power of money stable, instead of allowing it to fluctuate with gold. The same relation which India now bears toward England would then be held by both India and England toward Austria. But it would not even be necessary that one country like Austria should hold aloof in commercial isolation. The system, when put in operation, should include all the countries concerned and sufficiently interested to enter into a treaty agreement. Instead of sacrificing its own interests by serving as a gold standard country in terms of which all the other countries of the world should in common adjust their pars of exchange, Austria could itself adjust its currency by buying and selling gold. In other words, precisely the same principles which regulate the currency of India or the Philippines, by buying and selling exchange on gold abroad, could be operated more directly through buying and selling gold itself at home. Austria might be a good country in which to do this, because it has long operated substantially this system, and by it kept its irredeemable paper money at a fixed par with gold. Should suitable treaty arrangements be effected, Austria might maintain a par, not with a fixed weight of gold, but with such a weight of gold as should have a fixed purchasing power, and could do this by buying and selling gold at these adjusted prices, selling gold bullion for gulden to contract the currency, and buying gold bullion for gulden to expand the currency. All other countries could maintain their par with Austria, or each other, by the methods by which now India maintains its par with England, or, if they chose, by exactly the same process as proposed for Austria. In fact, it is evident that the method of maintaining par by selling exchange on other countries, and by exchanging currency directly for some commodity, such as gold, are at bottom much the same thing.

In order that such an international system should work, we might imagine three separate functions: (1) the function of maintaining an exchange par with the Austrian gulden to be performed by Foreign Exchange Offices exactly as at present in the Philippines under the gold-exchange system; (2) the similar function of regulating the currency in at least one country, say Austria, by a Bureau of Currency Regulation through buying or selling gold, at the option of the public, at an official price, changing from time to time according to the decisions of the Statistical Office about to be mentioned; (3) the function of fixing this official price of gold according to the price level. An international Statistical Office at, say, The Hague, could be established to do this in a purely clerical manner; its duties would consist in ascertaining the index number of prices in the usual way and then dividing the market price of gold by that number.

For instance, if, a year after the system was started, it were found by the Statistical Office that prices had risen one per cent, this Office would, in order to neutralize the rise, issue an official declaration to the Bureau of Currency Regulation fixing the official price of gold at substantially one per cent lower than the ruling market price. At this cheap price the public will buy gold bullion of the government and surrender currency in return. Therefore the currency will be contracted and general prices will fall until no more gold is called for, or until there is declared a new official gold price. Should the next official gold price be set below the market price, the government would become a buyer of gold and would thus reissue some of the currency previously called in, or if need be, issue new currency.

The plan, as above outlined, fixes a single price of gold at which the government must be ready either to buy or sell. There would be practical advantages, however, in fixing a *pair* of prices differing slightly from each other, the higher for selling and the lower for buying. The device of a pair of prices was proposed by Ricardo.[1]

[1] *Proposals for an Economical and Secure Currency*, 2d Edition, London (Murray), 1816, p. 26.

It is also employed, as we have seen, in the gold-exchange standard to simulate the "gold-points." The Austrian paper currency, although usually called irredeemable, is kept at par with gold by a similar arrangement under which the Austro-Hungarian bank stands ready to buy gold at k. 3, 278[1] per kilo and to sell gold-exchange on London at a slightly higher rate.

It will be seen that the plan here proposed requires no revolution of the world's currencies. It requires little more than to assemble, into one working whole, operations already existing separately, viz. (1) calculating Index Numbers as done at present by our Bureau of Labor; (2) buying and selling exchange, as done at present by the Philippine Government; (3) buying and selling gold, as done at present in Austria; (4) periodically readjusting the gold pars as was done at least once when the present system was inaugurated in India, the Philippines, Panama and Mexico. The readjustment of par is the only feature which could be called new, and this should not be condemned as causing fluctuations in values; for its only object is to prevent the fluctuations from which we now suffer. Neither this periodic readjustment nor any other feature of the plan would require changes in the circulating medium. Each nation would continue to use its old familiar currency, whether gold, silver, or paper. The ordinary man would be unaware of any change.

The cost of maintaining the gold-exchange system has been slight and the cost of maintaining the system here proposed, whatever it might be, could be as nothing compared with the benefits it would render the entire civilized world.

[1] See L. V. Mises, "The foreign exchange policy of the Austro-Hungarian Bank," *Economic Journal*, June, 1909, p. 201.

One incidental benefit which could easily be secured would be the oft-proposed readjustment of relative values of various coins; for the first adjustment of pars would naturally make the sovereign equivalent to five dollars, the ruble to fifty cents, the Japanese yen to fifty cents, the Dutch florin to forty cents, the mark to twenty-five cents, the franc to twenty cents, the Austrian crown to twenty cents, and the Portuguese crown to ten cents.

The plan as above outlined contemplates the regulation of the world's currencies by buying and selling gold; but of course silver or any other commodity could be used instead. The less variable the commodity relatively to commodities in general, the less would be the readjustments needed and the less active the buying or selling of that commodity by the government.

The objections which could be urged against this system are doubtless many, but they do not seem to be as serious as the objections which have already been urged against the adoption of the gold-exchange standard, and which have been satisfactorily answered by the course of events. In fact, there would seem to be no greater danger in trusting Austria, under treaty agreement, to maintain her gulden at an ideal par with commodities in accordance with an index number, than to trust her, as at present, to maintain stable exchange with London, or than to trust the Indian, Mexican, Panama or Philippine governments to maintain their overvalued silver at par with gold. The functions involved are clerical; the acts required are specific. Departures from a strict compliance with the law or treaty would be instantly recognized, and would bring upon the culprit wrath and punishment proportionate to the international gravity of the offense. The plan does not require and would not permit any experimental dosing of the circulation dependent on the judgment of an official. The official who regulates does so merely by buying and selling at specific prices fixed by others; and he must buy or sell at the pleasure of the public. He would have no more choice than a broker who is ordered to buy or sell at prices specified by his customers, or than his prototype, the present official in the Philippines, who now buys or sells foreign exchange. The danger of abuse or fraud in the Statistical Office, the work of which is based on published market prices and is necessarily done in the light of day, would seem negligible.

Not only would the scheme seem to be entirely free from the possibility of mismanagement by individual officials, but it would seem also to be fully safeguarded against the danger of inflationistic legislation. No individual nation could inflate the currency without withdrawing from the international arrangement and isolating itself accordingly, while it is quite inconceivable that all the civilized nations of the world should voluntarily and simultaneously commit the folly of inflationistic legislation.

But, before any control of the price level be undertaken, the public must learn to realize its necessity. So long as the rank and file even of business men fail to realize that they are daily gambling in changes in the value of money, a fact of which they are blissfully unaware, they will exert no demand for preventing those changes. They are the parties whose interests are chiefly involved, and the first essential step in the reform process is that they shall be made to comprehend the benefits of a stable purchasing power.[1] Until this time arrives, any political proposals will be premature.

§ 6

At the beginning of this chapter we reviewed the principles determining the purchasing power of money and the practical problems involved. We then considered the possible methods of avoiding the evils of variability in purchasing power. Among these, one of the most feasible and important was found to be an increase of knowledge, — both specific knowledge of conditions and general knowledge of principles. Next, the claims of bimetallism and polymetallism as means of maintaining a stable level of prices were considered. It was seen that there was no guarantee of keeping two or more metals in circulation indefinitely at an agreed ratio, and it was pointed out that, even could this be done, the gain in stability of prices would be likely to be inconsiderable. The latter objection was brought also against symmetallism — the proposal to have more

[1] A recent popular pamphlet by A. C. Lake, *Currency Reform the Paramount Issue*, Memphis (28 N. Front St.), Tenn., proposes to stop the free coinage of gold. As I write, other evidences of the spread beyond academic circles of the idea that gold is an unstable standard come to hand. The rapid rise in the cost of living has of course thrust the subject on the attention of the magazine and newspaper press. Mr. Edison, in a recent interview, predicts the further downfall of gold, through the discovery, — sure to be made sooner or later, — of cheap methods of extracting immense quantities of gold from some Southern clays. He asks the pertinent question: "Is it not absurd to have, as our standard of values, a substance, the only real use of which is to gild picture frames and fill teeth?" Mr. Carnegie, in his last gift of ten millions of dollars to the Carnegie Institution of Washington, stipulates that a certain part of the income shall be set aside as a sinking fund against "the diminishing purchasing power of money." This is significant as one of the first cases in which a business man has taken cognizance, in a practical way, of the instability of gold.

than one precious metal in each standard coin — as well as against joint metallism, etc.

Several methods were next considered by which a government might regulate the quantity of money relatively to business so as to keep the level of prices constant. One such method was to make inconvertible paper the standard money, and to regulate its quantity. Another was to regulate the supply of metallic money by a varying seigniorage charge. Still another was to issue paper money, redeemable on demand, not in fixed amounts of the basic precious metal, but in varying amounts, so calculated as to keep the level of prices unvarying. Lastly was considered the proposal of the writer, — to adopt the gold-exchange standard combined with a tabular standard.

It was suggested that the first step in this needed reform would be to persuade the public, and especially the business public, to study the problem of monetary stability and to realize that, at present, contracts in money are as truly speculative as the selling of futures, — are, in fact, merely a subdivision of future-selling.

The necessary education once under way, it will then be time to consider schemes for regulating the purchasing power of money in the light of public and economic conditions of the time. All this, however, is in the future. For the present there seems nothing to do but to state the problem and the principles of its solution in the hope that what is now an academic question may, in due course, become a burning issue.

APPENDIX TO CHAPTER II

§ 1 (TO CHAPTER II, § 3)

The Concept of an Average

The subject of averages or means is so important — both theoretically and practically — and so little upon it is readily available for economic readers that a short statement of its fundamental principles may be fitly inserted here.[1]

There are numerous kinds of averages or means. Among them are the arithmetical, geometrical, and harmonical; and of each of these there are many different varieties. The *simple arithmetical* mean of a specific series of terms is found by adding the terms together and dividing by their number. Thus, suppose it is desired to find a mean of 2 and 8. It is evidently $\frac{(2+8)}{2} = \frac{10}{2} = 5$. This is, as a matter of fact, the mean most commonly employed.

The *simple geometrical* mean is obtained by multiplying all the terms together and extracting that root of the product which corresponds to the number of terms. Thus, the geometrical mean of 2 and 8 is $\sqrt{2 \times 8}$ or 4.

The *simple harmonical* mean of any number of terms is the reciprocal of the arithmetical average of their reciprocals. For 2 and 8 it is $\frac{1}{\frac{\frac{1}{2}+\frac{1}{8}}{2}}$ or $3\frac{1}{5}$.

The *weighted arithmetical* mean is a modification of the simple arithmetical mean. Suppose it is desired to find the mean height of two groups of trees, one tall, the other short.

[1] For discussion of certain statistical averages, see Dr. Franz Žižek, *Die Statistischen Mittelwerte*, Leipzig (Duncker & Humblot), 1908, in which (p. 2) will be found further references.

The tall group is 8 yards high, the short, 2. The *simple* arithmetical mean as we have seen is 5. But this mean treats both groups as of equal importance. Let us suppose that there are twenty of the two-yard trees and ten of the eight-yard trees, and let us seek a mean of the two heights, such as will give equal importance to each *tree*. This will give the short group of twenty trees twice the importance of the tall group of ten trees. We shall be giving equal importance to each tree if we take the simple arithmetical mean of the thirty trees. But this *simple* mean of *thirty* trees will be a *weighted* mean of the *two* groups of trees. It is to be found by adding their heights together (twenty heights of two yards plus ten of eight) and dividing by the number of trees $(20+10)$. That is, the mean height is $\frac{20\times 2+10\times 8}{20+10}=4$, and this (considered as an average of the *two groups* instead of that of the thirty trees) is said to be the weighted arithmetical mean of 2 and 8, the 2 being weighted twenty times, and the 8, ten times. The weighted mean of the two groups means the simple mean of the thirty trees. In other words when we "weight" the various terms averaged, we no longer count these terms once each, but we count one term as though it were (say) twenty, and another as though it were (say) ten and the number of times we count a term is its "weight." In the same way we may define the weighted geometrical and weighted harmonical means. Taking the same example of the trees, we find the results to be respectively $\sqrt[30]{2^{20}\cdot 8^{10}}$ or 3.175 and $\frac{1}{\frac{20(\frac{1}{2})+10(\frac{1}{8})}{30}}$ or $2\frac{2}{3}$.

The same results would have been obtained in each case if, instead of the weights 20 and 10, we had taken, as weights, 2 and 1.

Since there are so many different kinds of means, the question arises, What is the meaning of an average or mean in general? We answer: Any mean of a series of terms must be obtainable from them by a mathematical rule such that, when applied to a series of *identical* terms, it will make their mean identical with each of them. Any rule of averaging is admissible which is consistent with this condition (that the average of identical terms must be identical with each). We know that the simple arithmetical mean A, of a, b, and c is $A = \frac{a+b+c}{3}$. It is easy to see that this formula meets the required test. Substituting A for each of the three magnitudes a, b, and c in $\frac{a+b+c}{3}$, we obtain $\frac{A+A+A}{3}$, which is evidently equal to A; thus the test is satisfied.

Again, let G be the geometrical mean of a, b, and c; so that $G = \sqrt[3]{abc}$. This formula also conforms to the definition of a mean because $G = \sqrt[3]{GGG}$.

Similarly, the harmonical average (which we may call H) of a, b, and c is $H = \frac{1}{\frac{\frac{1}{a}+\frac{1}{b}+\frac{1}{c}}{3}}$. This also conforms, because

$$H = \frac{1}{\frac{\frac{1}{H}+\frac{1}{H}+\frac{1}{H}}{3}}.$$

For a weighted arithmetical average A_w of a, b, c, the weights being α, β, γ, we have the formula $A_w = \frac{\alpha a + \beta b + \gamma c}{\alpha + \beta + \gamma}$, which conforms to our test, since evidently

$$A = \frac{\alpha A_w + \beta A_w + \gamma A_w}{\alpha + \beta + \gamma}.$$

By applying this general rule, we can make at will innumerable kinds of averages. It is only necessary to write any formula twice, once using the terms to be averaged and once using, instead, the required average, and then equate the two. Thus, let us take the complicated formula $\frac{(a + a^2 + Ka^3)\left(b + \frac{3}{ab}\right)}{c + \sqrt[3]{bc}}$. This may be employed to obtain a new species of average (x) of a, b, and c, simply by equating it with the similar form $\frac{(x+x^2+Kx^3)\left(x+\frac{3}{x^2}\right)}{x+\sqrt[3]{x^2}}$. That x as determined by this equation will conform to our definition of an average is evident, since substituting x for a, b, and c, the equation becomes a truism, showing that the proposed new average of the identical terms x is x.

A special case of the definition, requiring particular mention, is that in which two or more means (not necessarily of the same kind) are related to one another. In order that A should be a mean of $a_1, a_2, a_3, \cdots$ when we know that B is a mean of $b_1, b_2, b_3, \cdots$ it is only necessary to have a determining formula such that if $a_1 = a_2 = a_3 \cdots$ and at the same time $b_1 = b_2 = b_3 \cdots$ (each of which by hypothesis must be equal to B), then A shall also be equal to each of the magnitudes a_1, a_2, a_3, etc. Many examples of pairs of means like A and B will be given in Chapter X (on the construction of index numbers). The following is a simple example :—

Let $nAB = a_1b_1 + a_2b_2 + a_3b_3 + \cdots$ and let B be the arithmetical mean $= \frac{b_1 + b_2 + b_3 + \cdots}{n}$ (n being the number of terms). Then A is a (new) sort of mean of a_1, a_2, a_3; for, substituting A for $a_1, a_2, a_3, \cdots$ and B for b_1, b_2, b_3, in the equation $nAB = a_1b_1 + \cdots$, the equation is satisfied.

§ 2 (TO CHAPTER II, § 5)

The Concept of Velocity of Circulation

The velocity of circulation of money has been defined as a ratio of the money expended to the average money on hand, that is, as a rate of turnover. A rate of turnover differs from the popular concept of velocity. The latter regards velocity as the average number of times money changes hands from one person to another; whereas, the concept we have employed treats velocity as the average number of coins which pass through *one man's* hands, divided by the average amount held by him. The difference between the two concepts is very similar to that between two methods of obtaining the velocity of a railway train. One method is to follow the train for a certain number of miles, and note how long a time it takes to travel those miles. The other is to stand on a certain spot beside the track and note the time consumed by a given length of train in passing that spot. Following the train from place to place is like following a coin from person to person, while watching the train pass one point is like observing the rate of turnover of one person's purse. We may distinguish the two methods as the "coin-transfer" method and the "person-turnover" method. Both methods, if correctly employed, yield the same result. But in the coin-transfer method, an important distinction is usually overlooked, the distinction between the gross and net circulation of money. What is desired is the rate at which money is used for *purchasing goods*, not for "making change." The result is the difference between the number of times each piece changes hands *against* goods, and the number of times it changes hands *with* goods. If a $10 bill is transferred in purchase of goods and $2 is given back "in change," the actual money expended for goods is measured, not by $12, the gross transfer of money, nor yet by $10, the gross amount transferred against goods, but by $8, the net amount paid for goods.

If it is desired, in the coin-transfer method, to learn the average velocity of circulation of two pieces of money, such as a dollar and a ten-cent piece, we must not only find the *net* rate of turnover of each coin, but also take account of the discrepancy between the buying efficiencies of the two coins. Let it be assumed that during the year the dollar is passed 115 times against goods and 15 times with goods, so that its net velocity of circulation is 115 – 15 or 100. If we suppose the velocity of the ten-cent piece to be 290 – 90 or 200, the average velocity of the two must somehow take account of the different values of different denominations. A dollar is the equivalent of ten dimes. Its rapidity of circulation should therefore be "weighted" tenfold in order to get the real average, that is, the average of the *service* performed by the two. The net rate of circulation of 100 for the dollar is equivalent to a net velocity of circulation of 100 for each and every one of *ten* dimes. It follows that the average velocity of the two coins is $\frac{10 \times 100 + 200}{11}$, a result much closer to the velocity of the dollar than to that of the dime. With these two safeguards against error applied to the coin-transfer method, it is easy to see that the coin-transfer method will yield the same results as the person-turnover method.[1]

There is yet another magnitude which should be considered in connection with the velocity of monetary circulation. This may be called the *average time of turnover*, *i.e.* the average amount of time consumed by all the given money, in being turned over once. This is the "reciprocal" of velocity. If money changes hands twenty times in a year, it turns over, on the average, once in $\frac{1}{20}$ of a year, or once in somewhat over 18 days. This is its *average time of turnover.* If the average velocity of circulation or rate of turnover is forty times a year, then the average time of turnover is $\frac{1}{40}$ of a year or about 9 days. Or, instead of considering all the given money directly, let us come at it through a component part of it. If a man having, on the average, $10 in his pocket every day, expends on the average $1 a day, he evidently turns over $\frac{1}{10}$ of his money each day. Since to turn over $\frac{1}{10}$ of his average stock each day is to turn over the whole of it 36½ times a year or once in 10 days, the time of turnover will be 10 days. If the man under consideration had a pocketbook arranged with a series of ten one dollar bills, and every day, as one was taken from the top to be expended, another were added at the bottom, evidently any and every bill would remain in his hands just ten days traveling from the bottom to the top of the pile.

[1] For mathematical statement, see § 5 of this Appendix.

§ 3 (TO CHAPTER II, § 5)

"*Arrays*" *of p's, Q's, and pQ's*

Let us assume that the year is divided into an indefinite number of periods, or moments, and distinguish the prices and quantities relating to those successive periods by the subscripts 1, 2, 3, etc., at the left; and that we are dealing with a community of an indefinite number of persons, distinguished likewise by subscripts at the right. Thus the quantity of a particular kind of goods purchased by individual No. 1 in moment No. 3 is represented by ${}_3q_1$ and the price of the sale by ${}_3p_1$. The entire system of quantities and prices is represented by the two following "arrays."

PERSONS	PERIODS			TOTAL	PERSONS	PERIODS			AVERAGE
	1	2	3...			1	2	3...	
1	${}_1q_1$	${}_2q_1$	${}_3q_1\cdots$	Q_1	1	${}_1p_1$	${}_2p_1$	${}_3p_1\cdots$	p_1
2	${}_1q_2$	${}_2q_2$	${}_3q_2\cdots$	Q_2	2	${}_1p_2$	${}_2p_2$	${}_3p_2\cdots$	p_2
3	${}_1q_3$	${}_2q_3$	${}_3q_3\cdots$	Q_3	3	${}_1p_3$	${}_2p_3$	${}_3p_3\cdots$	p_3
—	—	—	—	—	—	—	—	—	—
—	—	—	—	—	—	—	—	—	—
Total	${}_1Q$	${}_2Q$	${}_3Q$	Q	Average	${}_1p$	${}_2p$	${}_3p\cdots$	p

We have just stated the meaning of the letters *inside* these arrays. Those outside are as follows: Q_1 is the total quantity bought by person 1 and is the sum $({}_1q_1 + {}_2q_1 + {}_3q_1 + \cdots)$ of all quantities purchased by him in all the different periods of time. Like definitions apply to Q_2, Q_3, etc. ${}_1Q$ is the total quantity purchased in moment 1 and is the sum $({}_1q_1 + {}_1q_2 + {}_1q_3 + \cdots)$ of all quantities purchased in that moment by all the different persons. Like definitions apply to ${}_2Q$, ${}_3Q$, $\cdots$. Finally Q is (as already employed in the text) the grand total of quantities bought by all persons in all periods of time. Evidently,

$$\begin{aligned} Q &= {}_1Q + {}_2Q + {}_3Q + \cdots \\ &= Q_1 + Q_2 + Q_3 + \cdots \\ &= {}_1q_1 + {}_2q_1 + \text{etc.} + {}_1q_2 + {}_2q_2 + \text{etc.} \cdots + \text{etc.} \end{aligned}$$

Like definitions apply to the letters outside the p array, but the relations to the letters inside are here averages instead of sums. We may best derive the form of these averages from a third or intermediate array for pQ indicating the money values of the purchases.

This last named array is

PERSONS	PERIODS			TOTAL
	1	2	3	
1	${}_1p_1\,{}_1q_1$	${}_2p_1\,{}_2q_1$	${}_3p_1\,{}_3q_1$	$p_1\,Q_1$
2	${}_1p_2\,{}_1q_2$	${}_2p_2\,{}_2q_2$	${}_3p_2\,{}_3q_2$	$p_2\,Q_2$
3	${}_1p_3\,{}_1q_3$	${}_2p_3\,{}_2q_3$	${}_3p_3\,{}_3q_3$	$p_3\,Q_3$
Total	${}_1p\,{}_1Q$	${}_2p\,{}_2Q$	${}_3p\,{}_3Q$	$p\,Q$

In this array the same relations must evidently hold as in the Q array. That is, pQ, the entire sum spent on the given commodity by all persons in the community during all periods of the year, must be equal to (1) the sum of the column above it, (2) the sum of the row at its left, and (3) the sum of the interior terms of the array. In other words, it must be equal to (1) the sum of the total yearly amounts spent by the many different persons, (2) the sum of the total amounts spent in the community at the many different periods of the year, and (3) the sum of the purchases of all the individuals in all the periods.

The nature of the p array is now determined by the Q and the pQ arrays. It must namely be such as to permit the summation just described for the pQ array. That is, each of the average prices (such as p_1) must conform to the type of formula:—

$$p_1\,Q_1 = {}_1p_1\,{}_1q_1 + {}_2p_1\,{}_2q_1 + \cdots, \text{ that is}$$

$$p_1 = \frac{{}_1p_1\,{}_1q_1 + {}_2p_1\,{}_2q_1 + \cdots}{Q_1}$$

$$= \frac{{}_1p_1\,{}_1q_1 + {}_2p_1\,{}_2q_1 + \cdots}{{}_1q_1 + {}_2q_1 + \cdots}.$$

Hence, p is a weighted average of ${}_1p_1$, ${}_2p_1$, etc., the weights being ${}_1q_1$, ${}_2q_1$, etc. That is, the average price paid by person No. 1 is the weighted arithmetical average of the prices paid by him at different moments through the year, the weights being the quantities bought. The same principle obtains for all other persons.

Similarly, the average price, ${}_1p$, may be shown to be

$$ {}_1p = \frac{{}_1p_1\,{}_1q_1 + {}_1p_2\,{}_1q_2 + \cdots}{{}_1Q\,(= {}_1q_1 + {}_1q_2 + \cdots)}. $$

That is, the average price in period No. 1 is the weighted arithmetical average of all prices paid by different persons at moment No. 1, the weights being the quantities bought by each. The same principles obtain at all other moments.

Finally, the average price, p, in the lower right corner of the p array, is either $p = \frac{p_1Q_1 + p_2Q_2 + \cdots}{Q\,(= Q_1 + Q_2 + \cdots)}$ (that is, p is a weighted arithmetical average of p_1, p_2, etc., the weights being Q_1, Q_2, etc.); or (using the row instead of column), p is the like weighted arithmetical average of ${}_1p$, ${}_2p$, etc., the weights being ${}_1Q$, ${}_2Q$, etc.; or lastly, either of these two expressions for p, combined with the preceding expression for p_1, p_2, etc., or with that for ${}_1p$, ${}_2p$, etc., may be used to show that p is a weighted arithmetical average of all the p's within the array, the weights being the corresponding q's. In short, the price of each commodity for the year is its average at all times and for all purchases in the year weighted according to the quantities bought.

This principle covers the method of averaging prices in different localities. Thus the average price of sugar in 1909 in the United States is the weighted arithmetical average of all prices of sales by all individuals throughout the United States, and at all moments throughout the year, the weights being the quantities bought. Thus, if there are large local or temporal variations in price, it is important to give chief weight to the largest purchases.

What has been said as to Q and p arrays relates only to one commodity. But the same principles apply to each commodity yielding separate arrays corresponding to each of the total quantities, Q, Q', Q'', etc., as well as corresponding to each of the average prices, p, p', p'', etc.

§ 4 (TO CHAPTER II, § 5)

"Arrays" of e's, m's, and V's

In the preceding section we have seen that there exists an "array" of p's, pQ's and Q's for each commodity. These relate to the right side of the equation of exchange. Similar arrays relate to the left side.

If, as before, we assume a community of any number of persons, distinguished respectively by subscripts at the right, and if we divide the year into moments, distinguished by subscripts at the left, we may designate the amount of money expended in the first moment by the first person as ${}_1e_1$, the average amount of money he has on hand at that moment as ${}_1m_1$ and his velocity of circulation at that moment (reckoned at its rate per year) as ${}_1V_1$. The expenditure in the moment being ${}_1e_1$, that moment's rate per annum is ${}_1n_1\,{}_1e_1$, there being n moments in the year, so that the velocity of circulation or rate of turnover per annum, ${}_1V_1$, is $n\frac{{}_1e_1}{{}_1m_1}$. A similar notation may be used to express the amounts expended and held and the velocity of circulation for each member of the community during each moment of the year as shown in the following three "arrays" (inside the lines).

In the first table, E_1 at the right of the first line is the sum expended by the first person, being the sum of ${}_1e_1$, ${}_2e_1$, ${}_3e_1$, $\cdots$ in the first line representing the amounts expended by him at successive moments during the year. Likewise, E_2 is the sum expended by the second person during the year, and E_3 is the sum expended by the third. ${}_1E$ at the foot of the first column is the amount expended by all persons in the first moment; that is, it is the sum of all the amounts in the column above it; $_2E$ is likewise the amount expended by all persons in the second moment; $_3E$, the amount expended in the third, etc. Finally, E, in the lower right-hand corner, is, as employed in the text, the grand total expended by *all* persons in *all* moments of the year. Evidently E can be obtained by adding the row to the left of it, or by adding the column above it. It is also the sum of all the elements inside the lines, *i.e.* $E = \Sigma_1 E = \Sigma E_1 = \Sigma_1 e_1$.

AMOUNT EXPENDED — MONEY ON HAND

PERSONS	PERIODS			TOTAL	PERSONS	PERIODS			AVERAGE
	1	2	3 ...			1	2	3 ...	
1	$_1e_1$	$_2e_1$	$_3e_1$ ...	E_1	1	$_1m_1$	$_2m_1$	$_3m_1$ ...	m_1
2	$_1e_2$	$_2e_2$	$_3e_2$ ...	E_2	2	$_1m_2$	$_2m_2$	$_3m_2$ ...	m_2
3	$_1e_3$	$_2e_3$	$_3e_3$ ...	E_3	3	$_1m_3$	$_2m_3$	$_3m_3$ ...	m_3
—	—	—	——	—	—	—	—	——	—
—	—	—	——	—	—	—	—	——	—
Total	$_1E$	$_2E$	$_3E$ ...	E	Total	$_1M$	$_2M$	$_3M$ ...	M

VELOCITY OF CIRCULATION

PERSONS	PERIODS			AVERAGE
	1	2	3	
1	$n\frac{_1e_1}{_1m_1} = {_1V_1}$	$n\frac{_2e_1}{_2m_1} = {_2V_1}$	$n\frac{_3e_1}{_3m_1} = {_3V_1}$	$\frac{E_1}{m_1} = V_1$
2	$n\frac{_1e_2}{_1m_2} = {_1V_2}$	$n\frac{_2e_2}{_2m_2} = {_2V_2}$	$n\frac{_3e_2}{_3m_2} = {_3V_2}$	$\frac{E_2}{m_2} = V_2$
3	$n\frac{_1e_3}{_1m_3} = {_1V_3}$	$n\frac{_2e_3}{_2m_3} = {_2V_3}$	$n\frac{_3e_3}{_3m_3} = {_3V_3}$	$\frac{E_3}{m_3} = V_3$
Average	$n\frac{_1E}{_1M} = {_1V}$	$n\frac{_2E}{_2M} = {_2V}$	$n\frac{_3E}{_3M} = {_3V}$	$\frac{E}{m} = V$

In the second table, M in the lower right corner is a sum of the average amounts held by the different members of the community during the year, *i.e.* it is the sum of the elements in the column above it, m_1, m_2, m_3, etc., each of which is by hypothesis a simple average of the row to its left.

Or, again, M is a simple average of the row to its left, ${}_1M$, ${}_2M$, ${}_3M$, etc., the average amounts of money in the community, in the successive moments of the year, each of which averages is in turn the sum of the column above it, *i.e.* $M = \Sigma m_1 = \frac{\Sigma {}_1M}{n}$. Thus M is both the sum of averages and the average of sums. That the two are equal follows by expressing both in terms of the elementary quantities ${}_1m_1$ by means of the equations

$$m_1 = \frac{{}_1m_1 + {}_2m_1 + {}_3m_1 + \cdots}{n}, \text{ etc.,}$$

and the equations ${}_1M = {}_1m_1 + {}_1m_2 + {}_1m_3 + \cdots$. It is, of course, easy also to express M directly in terms of ${}_1m_1$, etc., within the table. Thus expressed, it is $\frac{\Sigma {}_1m_1}{n}$.

The third table (that for velocities) is derived from the other two. As just explained, ${}_1V_1$ is the velocity of circulation (considered as a *per annum* rate) for the first person in the community in the first moment.

There remain to be shown the relations of the elements in the V table.

Evidently,

$$\begin{aligned} V &= \frac{E}{M} \\ &= \frac{E_1 + E_2 + \cdots}{m_1 + m_2 + \cdots} \\ &= \frac{m_1V_1 + m_2V_2 + \cdots}{m_1 + m_2 + \cdots} \qquad (1) \end{aligned}$$

Form (1) shows that V is a weighted average of the yearly velocities of the different persons, the velocity of each person being for the entire year and weighted according to his average amount of money on hand.

Following an analogous but slightly different sequence, we have

$$V = \frac{E}{M}$$

$$= \frac{{}_1E + {}_2E + \cdots}{\frac{{}_1M + {}_2M + \cdots}{n}}$$

$$= n\frac{{}_1E + {}_2E + \cdots}{{}_1M + {}_2M + \cdots}$$

$$= n\frac{{}_1M\frac{{}_1E}{{}_1M} + {}_2M\frac{{}_2E}{{}_2M} + \cdots}{{}_1M + {}_2M + \cdots}$$

$$= \frac{{}_1M\left(n\frac{{}_1E}{{}_1M}\right) + {}_2M\left(n\frac{{}_2E}{{}_2M}\right) + \cdots}{{}_1M + {}_2M + \cdots}$$

$$= \frac{{}_1M\,{}_1V + {}_2M\,{}_2V + \cdots}{{}_1M + {}_2M + \cdots}. \quad (2)$$

Form (2) shows that V is also the weighted average of the yearly velocities of the successive moments into which the year is divided, the velocity of each moment being for the entire community and weighted according to its average amount of money then in circulation.

Thus form (1) gives V in terms of the column above it, while form (2) gives V in terms of the row at its left. A formula similar to (1) may be constructed to express each of the magnitudes ${}_1V$, ${}_2V$, ${}_3V$, etc., in terms of the column above it, while a formula similar to (2) may be constructed to express each of the magnitudes V_1, V_2, V_3, etc., in terms of the row at its left. That is, the velocity in the entire community at any particular moment is a specific form of average of the velocities of different persons at that moment; and the velocity for the entire year of any particular person is a specific form of average of the velocities at different moments for that person.

Finally, V may be expressed, not only as an average of its column and row as in formula (1) and (2), but also as an average of the magnitudes in the interior of the table. This last result may be obtained in several ways, of which the most direct may briefly be expressed as follows: We know that E is the sum of the interior of the first or E table, that is, $E = \Sigma_1 e_1$; and that M is equal to $\frac{1}{n}\Sigma_1 m_1$. Hence, we have

$$V = \frac{E}{M}$$

$$= \frac{\Sigma_1 e_1}{\frac{1}{n}\Sigma_1 m_1}$$

$$= n\frac{\Sigma\left({}_1m_1 \frac{{}_1e_1}{{}_1m_1}\right)}{\Sigma_1 m_1}$$

$$= \frac{\Sigma_1 m_{1\,1}V_1}{\Sigma_1 m_1}.$$

That is, V is the weighted arithmetical average of the yearly velocities pertaining to different persons in different moments, each velocity being weighted by the amount of money on hand in that instance. The mathematical reader will perceive that an alternative treatment would derive the result in terms of an *harmonic* average.

§ 5 (TO CHAPTER II, § 5)

The Coin-transfer Concept of Velocity and the Concept of Time of Turnover

We now turn to the coin-transfer concept of velocity of circulation. To show what kind of an average V is of the velocity of circulation of individual coins, or rather of individual pieces of money in general, let us denote the values of the individual pieces of money circulating in the community by the letters a, b, c, d, etc., and let us denote the *net* velocity of circulation of these (the number of times exchanged *against* goods *minus* the number of times exchanged *with* goods or "in change") by h, i, j, k, respectively, etc. Then E, the total amount expended, is denoted by $ha+ib+jc+kd+\cdots$; and the amount of money, M, in the community is $a+b+c+d$.

Hence

$$\frac{E}{M}=\frac{ha+ib+jc+kd+\cdots}{a+b+c+d+\cdots}.$$

That is, $\frac{E}{M}$ is a weighted average of the net velocities of circulation of the different pieces of money, the velocity of each piece being weighted according to its denomination. But $\frac{E}{M}$ is also V, which we have already seen is the velocity of circulation in the person-turnover sense.

It is clear, therefore, that the coin-transfer method of averaging is the same in results as the person-turnover method, if all the pieces of money in the community are included.

Finally, we come to the concept of "time of turnover." If velocity of circulation is represented as V, then $\frac{1}{V}$ represents the time of turnover. Similarly, the reciprocals of ${}_1V$, ${}_2V$, $\cdots$, V_1, V_2, $\cdots$, ${}_1V_1$, ${}_1V_2$, $\cdots$, ${}_2V_1$, $\cdots$, are corresponding times of turnover. Using W for the reciprocal of V and applying the appropriate subscripts, we may write an array of W's analogous to the previous array of V's, and we may show that W is an average of W_1, W_2, or of ${}_1W$, ${}_2W$, $\cdots$ or of ${}_1W_1$, ${}_1W_2$, $\cdots$, ${}_2W_1$, $\cdots$.

But these averages are all *harmonic* averages. To see this, we need only remember that V has already been analyzed[1] as a weighted average of the elementary V's, and that W has been defined as the reciprocal of V. That is, W is the reciprocal of this weighted average of elementary V's. But the elementary W's are reciprocals of the elementary V's. In other words, W is the reciprocal of the weighted arithmetical average of the reciprocals of elementary W's. This

[1] In § 4 of this Appendix.

makes W, by definition, a weighted *harmonic* average of these elementary magnitudes.

§ 6 (TO CHAPTER II, § 5)

Algebraic Demonstration of Equation of Exchange

It is clear that the equation of exchange, $MV = \Sigma pQ$, is derived from elementary equations expressing the equivalence of purchase money and goods bought. The money expended by any particular person at any particular moment is, by the very concept of price, equal to the quantities of all commodities bought in that moment by that person multiplied by the prices, *i.e.*

$$_1e_1 = {_1p_1}\,{_1q_1} + {_1p'_1}\,{_1q'_1} + {_1p''_1}\,{_1q''_1} + \cdots.$$

From this equation and others like it, for every person in the community and for every moment in the year, simply by adding them together, we obtain, for the left side of the equation, the sum of the e's which we call E; and for the right side the sum of all the pq's. We have already seen in the text how the left side, E, may be converted (by multiplying and dividing by M) into MV, and we have also just seen (§ 3 of this Appendix) how the sum of all the terms relating to each particular commodity represented on the right side may be converted (by similar simple algebraic operations) into one term of the form pQ so that the whole sum becomes ΣpQ. The final result is, therefore, $MV = \Sigma pQ$. This reasoning constitutes, therefore, a demonstration of the truth of this formula, based on the simple elementary truth that in every exchange the money expended equals the quantity bought multiplied by the price of sale.

§ 7 (TO CHAPTER II, § 5)

P must be a Specific Form of Average in order to vary directly as M and V and inversely as the Q's

Let us assume that V and the Q's remain invariable while M changes to M_0 and p, p', p'', etc., to p_0, p'_0, p''_0, etc.

(The subscripts "0" refer to a year called the base year other than the original year.) We have for the two years respectively the two equations:—

$$MV = pQ + p'Q' + \cdots$$
$$M_0V = p_0Q + p'_0Q' + \cdots$$

whence by division, we obtain

$$\frac{M}{M_0} = \frac{pQ + p'Q' + \cdots}{p_0Q + p'_0Q' + \cdots} = \frac{\left(\frac{p}{p_0}\right)p_0Q + \left(\frac{p'}{p'_0}\right)p'_0Q' + \cdots}{p_0Q + p'_0Q'' + \cdots}.$$

The last expression is evidently a weighted arithmetical average of $\left(\frac{p}{p_0}\right)$, $\left(\frac{p'}{p'_0}\right)$, etc., the weights being p_0Q, p'_0Q', etc. We conclude that, if the velocity of circulation and the quantities of goods exchanged remain unaltered, while the quantity of money is altered in a given ratio, then prices will change in this same ratio "on the average," the average being exactly defined as a *weighted arithmetical average*, in which the weights are the *values* of goods sold, reckoned at the prices of the *base* year. The ratio may evidently also be written:—

$$\frac{M}{M_0} = \frac{pQ + p'Q' + \cdots}{p_0Q + p'_0Q' + \cdots} = \frac{1}{\frac{p_0Q + p'_0Q' + \cdots}{pQ + p'Q' + \cdots}}$$
$$= \frac{1}{\frac{\left(\frac{p_0}{p}\right)pQ + \left(\frac{p'_0}{p'}\right)p'Q' + \cdots}{pQ + p'Q' + \cdots}}$$

which is a *weighted harmonic* average of $\frac{p}{p_0}$, $\frac{p'}{p'_0}$, etc., in which the weights are pQ, $p'Q'$, etc., that is, the values, not in the base year, but the other year.

If M and the Q's remain invariable, while V changes from V to V_1, evidently the ratio $\frac{V}{V_1}$ will be expressed by precisely the same formulæ as above.

If the Q's remain invariable, while M and V both change, evidently the ratio $\frac{MV}{M_1V_1}$ will be expressed by the same formulæ.

Again the same formulæ apply if M and V remain invariable while the Q's all vary *in a given ratio*, or if the Q's all vary *in a given ratio* in combination with any variation in M or V or both. In short, the formulæ apply perfectly in all cases of variation, except when the Q's vary *relatively* to each other.

These formulæ, it should be noted, are those later discussed as the formulæ numbered (11) in the large table of formulæ in the Appendix to Chapter X.

APPENDIX TO CHAPTER III

§ 1 (TO CHAPTER III, § 2)

"Arrays" of k's and r's

Let k be the ratio of deposits to money in circulation $\left(\frac{M'}{M}\right)$ which, on the average, the public prefers to keep; k will then be derivable from the like ratios for the different persons and business firms in the community in the successive moments of the year, and we may, therefore, form an array on the analogy of previous arrays, of the form: —

PERSONS	PERIODS		AVERAGE
	1	2	
1	${}_1k_1$	${}_2k_1$	k_1
2	${}_1k_2$	${}_2k_2$	k_2
—	—	—	—
—	—	—	—
Average	${}_1k$	${}_2k$	k

Each letter outside the array is a weighted arithmetical average either of the row to its left or of the column above it. k (in the lower right corner) also is both of these as well as the weighted arithmetical average of all the elements inside the lines (the weights being in all cases the amounts of money in circulation, which are the denominators of the ratios represented in the arrays). The same proportions hold true if "harmonic" be substituted for "arithmetic" (provided the weights be changed from the denominators to the numerators of the ratios, viz. the deposits). These theorems can be easily proved analogously to those in § 7 of the Appendix to Chapter II, remembering that $k = \frac{M'}{M}$.

Similarly, we may let r stand for the average ratio, for the year, of the reserves of all banks (μ) to their deposits (M'). This ratio $\left(r, \text{ or } \frac{\mu}{M'}\right)$ is resolvable into an array expressing the ratios for different banks at different moments, viz.:—

PERSONS	PERIODS		AVERAGE
	1	2	
1	${}_1r_1$	${}_2r_1$	r_1
2	${}_1r_2$	${}_2r_2$	r_2
—	—	—	—
—	—	—	—
Average	${}_1r$	${}_2r$	r

Here each element outside the lines is a weighted arithmetic (or harmonic) average of the terms in the row to its left or the column above it, while r is both of these as well as a weighted arithmetic (or harmonic) average, the weights being (for the arithmetic average) the deposits in each case or (for the harmonic average) the money in circulation. The total currency of the community is $\mu + M + M'$, although only $M + M'$ is actually in circulation.

§ 2 (TO CHAPTER III, § 4)

Algebraic Demonstration of Equation of Exchange Including Deposit Currency

The money expended for goods by individual 1 at moment 1 is ${}_1e_1$ and his check expenditure is ${}_1e'_1$. His total expenditure for goods by money and checks is, therefore, ${}_1e_1 + {}_1e'_1 = {}_1p_1{}_1q_1 + {}_1p'_1{}_1q'_1 + \cdots$.

By adding together all such equations for all persons in the community and all moments of the year, we obtain the equation

$$E + E' = \Sigma pQ$$

which becomes

$$MV + M'V' = \Sigma pQ$$

since, by definition, $V = \frac{E}{M}$ and $V' = \frac{E'}{M'}$.

APPENDIX TO CHAPTER V

§ 1 (TO CHAPTER V, § 5)

Effect of Time Credit on Equation of Exchange

It is important to note that, though the system of book credit has a great influence on prices indirectly, it does not enter into the equation of exchange like circulation or bank credit. We may properly include in the discussion with book credit, those cases of credit where the record of the debt is not simply on the books of one of the two parties, but in which an explicit record exists in the form of a promissory note given by the purchaser to the seller. In either case, goods are bought by a *promise* to pay at a later time; in the one case, the promise is explicit; in the other, implied.

Such an exchange of goods against a later payment may be resolved into two successive exchanges. The first occurs at the start when the credit is given for the goods. The purchaser then buys goods in exchange for a promise to pay. The second exchange occurs at the close of the transaction, when the debt is liquidated. The original purchaser may then be said to *buy back* his book credit or promissory note with money. Unlike bank credit, then, time credit does not *directly* save the use of money. Its immediate effect is simply to postpone[1] that use, since, to eventually extinguish the credit, as much money or checks must be expended as though cash were paid in the first instance. Dr. Andrew, now Assistant Secretary of the Treasury, points out that if time credit is being contracted faster than it is being ex-

[1] See A. Piatt Andrew, "Credit and the Value of Money," *Proceedings Seventeenth Annual Meeting, American Economic Association*, December, 1904.

tinguished, prices tend to become higher, but that as soon as the paying of these debts becomes as rapid as the making of them, prices will fall back to their old level.[1] The *excess* of credit contracted over credit extinguished acts just as does so much money or bank deposits offered for goods.

In order to show how these considerations as to book credit affect the equation of exchange, let us denote the creation of all book credits and other time loans by the letter E'', and their extinguishment by the letter E'''. The left side of our equation of exchange — or the total of money payments, check payments, and book charges and promissory notes for goods bought in the course of the year — will now be $MV + M'V' + E''$; and the right side, including the value of (1) goods bought and (2) debts maturing and extinguished during the year by payment of money or check, will be represented by $\Sigma pQ + E'''$. Transposing for convenience E''', the equation of exchange may now be written $MV + M'V' + E'' - E''' = \Sigma pQ$. Since E'' will be approximately equal to E''', these equal and opposite terms nearly cancel, *i.e.* $E'' - E'''$ becomes zero, and the equation virtually becomes again $MV + M'V' = \Sigma pQ$.

Before leaving the subject it may be noted that book credit tends to increase prices by creating offsetting debts and thus diminishing the volume of trade which must be done by money or checks. Thus, the farmer buys on account at the village store, occasionally selling farm produce there, also on account. The account is balanced at long intervals when the difference only is paid in money.[2] And, of course, as pointed out in the text of this chapter, book credit tends also to increase velocity.[3]

[1] Andrew, *loc. cit.* [2] *Ibid*, p. 10. [3] Chapter V, § 4.

APPENDIX TO CHAPTER VI

§ 1 (TO CHAPTER VI, § 1)

Modification of Equation of Exchange required by International Trade

We have already seen that there are two equations of exchange, one for purchases, and the other for sales. In a closed community, these two are necessarily identical, for every purchase by one member of the community is a sale by another member. But in a community with international trade they will be slightly different. The equation of exchange as developed in this book relates to the *expenditure* of money for the purchase of goods, and not to the *receipt* of money for the sale of goods. This equation of exchange at its last stage of elaboration was

$$MV + M'V' + E'' - E''' = \Sigma pQ$$

where the letters have the meanings previously given to them, E'' relating to the debts contracted in the given period in book accounts and promissory notes used in purchase of goods, and E''' relating to the extinguishment of such debts during the same period. Since MV was developed from E, and $M'V'$ from E', this equation may be written as follows: —

$$E + E' + E'' - E''' = \Sigma p_b Q_b$$

where the letters E on the money side of the equations are used to indicate that the money is *expended* money and the subscripts b on the goods side are used to indicate that the goods are goods *bought*; likewise, if the letter R is used to indicate *received* money, and the subscript s to indicate that the goods are goods *sold*, the following equation expresses the receipt of money, etc., in exchange for the sale of goods: —

$$R + R' + R'' - R''' = \Sigma p_s Q_s.$$

If there is no external trade, the several magnitudes in these two equations will evidently be identical on each side. If external trade exists, each equation may be resolved into an equation in which are distinguished the home trade and the outside trade. Thus, for the first equation, relating to expenditures, the E, E', etc., may be replaced by $H + O$, $H' + O'$, etc., where the H's relate to the purchases at *home* and the O's to money spent *outward*. On the other side of the equation the $\Sigma p_b Q_b$ may be replaced by $\Sigma p_h Q_h + \Sigma p_i Q_i$ where the subscripts h relate to the goods purchased at home and the subscripts i to those coming *inward*. The equation will then become: —

$$(H + H' + H'' - H''') + (O + O' + O'' - O''') = \Sigma p_h Q_h + \Sigma p_i Q_i$$

which, for brevity, we may write $\Sigma H + \Sigma O = \Sigma p_h Q_h + \Sigma p_i Q_i$. Similarly, the second equation, relating to sales, may be written: —

$$\Sigma H + \Sigma I = \Sigma p_h Q_h + \Sigma p_o Q_o.$$

That is, the net sum of the receipts at home (of money, bank credit, and book credit) plus the sum of payments for goods coming inward, is equal to the sum of the value of the goods sold at home plus the value of those sent out of the country. The last two equations, one relating to purchases and the other to sales, may be added together so as to give in a common equation the total trade in which the given community is concerned, that is, the total sales and purchases within itself and the sales and purchases with respect to the outside world. The combined equation will be: —

$$2\,\Sigma H + \Sigma O + \Sigma I = 2\,\Sigma p_h Q_h + \Sigma P_i Q_i + \Sigma p_o Q_o.$$

Here the internal trade is counted twice, because every transaction occurs both as a sale and as a purchase. This expresses the equation of exchange for the total trade (domestic and foreign) in which the country under consideration engages. If, instead of adding, we subtract one equation from the other, we obtain the following: —

$$\Sigma O - \Sigma I = \Sigma p_i Q_i - \Sigma p_o Q_o$$

which is the equation of the *balance of trade* in its most general form, taking account, as it does, of credit as well as of money. The flow of money, as to or from a nation, depends upon this last equation.

The right-hand side of the penultimate equation, depends on three sets of prices, — the home prices (the p_h's), the prices of goods which come into the country (the p_i's), and the prices of goods which go out (the p_o's).

If, for instance, the p_h's are extremely high, the consequence will be a stimulus to goods coming in (Q_i) and a discouragement to goods going out (Q_o), thus tending to make the right side of the last equation large and, therefore, also increasing the left side. In other words, there will be a so-called unfavorable balance of trade and a tendency for media of payments to go out rather than to come in; that is, there will be an outflow of money (indicated by O), or a transfer of bank credit to foreigners (O'), or a charging on the books of the foreigners (O''), or a lessening of the liquidations of previous book accounts (O'''); or else there will be opposite changes in I, I', I'', I'''; or finally, a combination of both tendencies, while temporarily there will be fluctuations between these various magnitudes. In the long run and in the last analysis, the changes will relate largely to the actual export and import of money, that is, will concern the unprimed magnitudes O and I.

For a large country like the United States, the outside trade is so small, compared with the internal trade, as to be negligible. As we shall see in Chapter XII, the foreign trade of the United States is only a fraction of one per cent of the internal trade. And, because the export and import sides of the various magnitudes (O's, I's, Q_o's and Q_i's) nearly cancel each other, the net balance remaining on either side of the equation of exchange seldom amounts to more than one eighth of one per cent of the internal trade of the United States.

Almost equally insignificant is the difference, $E'' - E'''$, between debts annually contracted and liquidated, if we may judge from estimates of that indebtedness, such as Holmes's. We are at any rate safe in saying that the corrections to our equation of exchange which have been discussed in this and the previous section are needless complications so far as the United States is concerned. We may therefore consider the equation $MV + M'V' = \Sigma pQ$ as practically a precise form of the equation.

APPENDIX TO CHAPTER VII

§ 1 (to Chapter VII, § 2)

Money Substitutes Unlike Other Substitutes

Much reasoning has been based upon the assumption that the price determination of two commodities used as money is analogous to that of any other two commodities. It is clear, however, that two forms of money differ from a random pair of commodities in being *substitutes*.[1] Two substitutes proper are regarded by the consumer as a single commodity. This lumping together of the two commodities reduces the number of demand conditions, but does not introduce any indeterminateness into the problem because the missing conditions are at once supplied by a *fixed ratio of substitution*. Thus, if ten pounds of cane sugar serve the same purpose as eleven pounds of beet-root sugar, their fixed ratio of substitution is ten to eleven; or if a bushel of India wheat can replace a bushel of Dakota wheat, the substitution ratio is unity. In these cases, the fixed ratio is based on the relative capacities of the two commodities to fill a common need, and is quite antecedent to their prices. Ten pounds of cane sugar can replace eleven pounds of beet-root sugar so long as human taste marks no other ratio. India and Dakota wheat have the same desirability or utility because they have the same relation to man's tastes. No change of market conditions,

[1] Substitutes merely in the sense of Gresham's Law that the cheaper will be substituted for the dearer. It does not deny that the metals are differently preferred for different monetary uses. We cannot compare gold and silver to independent commodities as "copper and wheat," or "beef and shoes," but only to some other pair of substitutes, or quasi substitutes, such as iron and steel, cotton and wool, oats and maize, molasses and sorghum, cane and beet-root sugar, India and Dakota wheat.

no change of price, could make a consumer regard one bushel of India wheat as equivalent to two of Dakota. The substitution ratio is fixed by nature, and in turn fixes the price ratio.

In the single case of money, however, there is no fixed ratio of substitution. In one age, ten ounces of silver may circulate as the equivalent of one of gold; in another, twenty ounces. No human taste or need will interfere. We have here to deal, not with relative sweetening power, nor relative nourishing power, nor with any other capacity to satisfy wants — no capacity inherent in the metals and independent of their prices. We have instead to deal only with relative *purchasing* power. We do not reckon a utility in the metal itself, but in the commodities it will buy. We assign their respective desirabilities or utilities to the sugars or the wheats before we know their prices, but we must first inquire the relative circulating value of gold and silver before we can know at what ratio we ourselves prize them. To us the ratio of substitution is identically the price ratio and therefore can have no influence in fixing that ratio. *The case of two forms of money is unique. They are substitutes, but have no natural ratio of substitution*, dependent on consumers' preferences.

The foregoing considerations are emphasized for the reason that they are overlooked by those writers who imagine that a fixed legal ratio is merely superimposed upon a system of supply and demand already determinate, and who seek to prove thereby that such a ratio is foredoomed to failure. This is the monometallist's favorite analogy. It is unsound, though its unsoundness does not necessarily involve the unsoundness of the monometallist's general conclusions. Gold and silver or any other two commodities which serve the purposes of money are not analogous to two ordinary and unrelated articles and are not completely analogous even to two substitutes, because, for two forms of money, there is no consumer's natural ratio of substitution. There seems, therefore, room for an artificial ratio. We shall see, however, that there are limits beyond which an artificial ratio will fail.

§ 2 (TO CHAPTER VII, § 2)

Limits for Ratios within which Bimetallism is Possible

A change of ratio is represented by a reconstruction of our reservoirs in new units, but we can, without the trouble of such a transformation, exhibit on the mechanism as it stands the limiting ratios between which bimetallism is possible. Suppose the film in Figure 7*b* to be forced, firstly to its extreme right limit, and secondly to its extreme left, and in each case permanent equilibrium to be attained. In the one case there is a premium on gold, in the other, a premium on silver. These premiums mark the divergences from the given ratio which are possible without destroying bimetallism. Thus suppose the legal ratio and that for which the mechanism is constructed is 32 of silver to 1 of gold and that, when the film is moved to the left limit, the level of gold will be below *OO* a distance $\frac{7}{8}$ as great as the silver level, while at the right limit it will be $\frac{5}{4}$. Then the ratio 32 to 1 can be varied between the factors $\frac{7}{8}$ of 32 to 1 and $\frac{5}{4}$ of 32 to 1 and bimetallism would succeed at any ratio between $32 \times \frac{7}{8}$ to 1 and $32 \times \frac{5}{4}$ to 1, *i.e.* between 28 to 1 and 40 to 1. A ratio below 28 to 1, such as the famous 16 to 1, would ultimately convert gold monometallism into silver monometallism, but would be inoperative in the opposite direction. A ratio above 40 to 1, such as 50 to 1, would ultimately convert silver monometallism into gold monometallism. A ratio between the two extremes would result in neither sort of monometallism but in bimetallism. The statistical determination of these limits is, of course, a problem which cannot with present knowledge be solved. The figures 28 and 40 are not intended as guesses, but purely as illustrations.

APPENDIX TO CHAPTER VIII

§ 1 (TO CHAPTER VIII, § 6)

Statistics of Turnover at Yale University

The rate of turnover of money varies with the amount of money expended at a given level of prices. In other words, it varies with the volume of trade of the individual. The statistics of turnover among Yale students form two series, the first or earlier showing an average velocity or rate of turnover of 34 per year, the second or later, of 66. The difference is probably due in part to the higher expenditure of the second group of students, although it is probably chiefly accounted for by the fact that the first series were not accurate. Each student in the first series was simply asked to estimate roughly his annual cash expenditure and the average cash on hand. The quotient of the first divided by the second showed his rate of turnover. Estimates were received from 128 men. The average annual expenditure in cash was $514 and the average cash on hand, $15, yielding the quotient 34 times a year as the average rate of turnover. These estimates, being usually little more than guesses, may have been wide of the mark. In order to obtain a more exact estimate the second series was undertåken. The plan was adopted of asking volunteers to keep an exact account for one month of the daily cash expenditures and balances at the beginning and end of each day. It was found from these statistics that for the 113 individuals who contributed these new data, the average annual rate of expenditure was $660 and an average cash on hand was almost exactly $10, giving the quotient 66 times a year. The rougher estimates, the average of which was 34, have so little weight compared with the accurate records, the average of which was 66, that we may place the general average at 60, the nearest round number below 66. Besides the two student series, returns were received from five other persons. One was a stenographer who, during a month, spent at the rate of $435 a year and had an average cash balance of $7.86, making her turnover rate 55 times a year. Another was a young librarian whose cash expenditures, kept carefully for six months, showed a rate of $854 a year and whose average cash balance was $10.41, making a rate of 82 times a year. A third was a lawyer who made a practice of paying all bills in cash, and as these amounted to some $4000 a year, he carried in his pocket an average cash balance estimated at $175. This figure he regarded as correct within $15. His velocity of circulation, on the basis of 4000 divided by 175, shows 23 times a year. The other two cases were of professors. The first, from careful records, found that he turned over his cash 37 times a year and turned over his bank account 52 times a year. The second roughly estimated his rate of cash turnover at 175 and of bank deposits at 25.

Of the total 246 persons whose records were collected, only 116 had kept careful accounts. Of these 116, all except three were students. The reason for believing that the lower velocity of the first series is not wholly accounted for by its being erroneously estimated, but is partly due to the smaller expenditures of that group, is based on the fact that we find a distinct relation between amount of expenditure and rate of turnover within each group. Thus, if we separate the 113 students who gave careful returns into two groups, one, those who spend less than $50 a month and the other those who spend $50 and over, we find the following figures: —

	No. of Cases	Average Annual Rate of Expenditure	Average Cash Balance	Vel. of Circulation
Expending less than $600 a year	72	$ 367	$ 8.60	43
Expending $600 and over a year	41	1175	12.70	93

Here we see that the richer men averaged about three times as great an expenditure as the poorer, but carried only 50 per cent more cash on hand. In consequence, the velocity of the richer was 93 as against 43 for the poorer, or more than double. The progressive relation between expenditure and rate of turnover may be seen by arranging the 113 cases into five groups according to expenditure.

	No. of Cases	Average Expenditure	Vel. of Circulation
Expending less than $300 a year . .	22	179	17
Expending over $300 and under $600 a year	50	450	59
Expending over $600 and under $900 a year	19	781	61
Expending over $900 and under $1200 a year	10	1012	96
Expending over $1200 a year . . .	12	1936	137

The number of cases is small, but the results are uniformly consistent. They show that velocity and expenditure are directly correlated. Even the other series (of rough estimates) show the same general relation. Taking the same classifications for expenditure, we find that the velocities are 22, 30, 44, 88, 32. Here the only exception is the last figure, which, as it is the average of only five individuals, is an exception of little importance. We conclude, therefore, with at least a moderate degree of confidence, that for a given price level, the greater the expenditure the higher the rate of turnover. In other words, persons who spend money faster absolutely than others also spend it faster relatively to the amount kept on hand. The amount kept on hand by the rich, though larger absolutely than that kept on hand by the poor, is smaller relatively to the expenditure.

This law of increasing velocity with increasing expenditure agrees with the general fact that the larger the scale of any business operation, the greater the economy. Small stores have to keep a larger stock relatively to their business than larger stores. Likewise, small banks have to keep a larger reserve in proportion to business transacted. Professor Edgeworth has shown a mathematical basis for the fact that the larger the bank, the smaller relatively the reserve needed. Hence, we need not be surprised to find that the small purchaser finds it well to keep on hand a relatively larger stock of money than the large purchaser.

The data are too meager to state any exact quantitative relation between velocity and expenditure. They show that velocity increases as expenditure increases. But beyond this we cannot safely go. The data seem to point to the conclusion, however, that the velocity increases in a smaller ratio than expenditure.

§ 2 (TO CHAPTER VIII, § 8)

Four Types of Commodities Contrasted

Let us assume four sorts of commodities which we may, for convenience, designate as wine, sugar, beef, and salt. We shall suppose that a reduction in the respective prices of these will have in each case a different effect on the sale. Accordingly we shall witness four possible effects on the general price level, following a reduction in the price of the four commodities respectively.

First, wine. This is assumed to be a commodity of such a sort that a reduction in its price will be accompanied by a *more* than proportionate increase in its sale. Thus the total amount of money expended for wine will be increased. This leaves a less amount with which to buy other commodities. In consequence, the prices of these other commodities, as well as of the wine itself, must fall.

Next, as to sugar. This is assumed to be such a commodity that a reduction in its price will be accompanied by an *exactly* proportionate increase in sales; so that the total money expended upon sugar will be unchanged. Under these circumstances the amount of money to be expended in exchange for other things will be neither increased nor decreased, and other prices will remain unchanged; but the general level of prices, including that of sugar itself, will be slightly lowered because the fall of one commodity, when others do not change, must produce some decrease in the average.

Third, as to beef. This typifies what is called a "necessary." We assume that a reduction in its price will be accompanied by an increase in consumption, but not sufficient to absorb all the money that was previously spent for it. The total expenditure for beef will thus be reduced, and in consequence there will be set free a certain amount of money to be expended for other goods, the prices of which will, therefore, in general, rise slightly. The net effect, however, will be an infinitesimal *fall* of general prices, including beef; for to the slight extent that there has been an increase of the total of goods sold by reason of the increase in the sales of beef, *without any increase in the total amount of money spent*, there must be a fall in the average prices.[1]

Lastly, as to salt. This is assumed to be an "absolute necessary," so that a reduction in its price will not affect the amount sold. The result will be that the general price level will be unaffected, the fall in the price of salt being exactly offset by a compensatory rise in other prices, and the total volume of trade remaining unchanged.

We see then that the degree of fall in price level due to the fall in a single price may be great or small or nothing at all, according to circumstances.

In all of the four foregoing illustrations, it was assumed that the fall in the individual price originated in a change in the supply curve or schedule. If the fall in price originates

[1] The mathematical necessity of this result can be seen from the formulæ in the Appendix to Chapter X, where the right side of the equation of exchange is transformed into the product of two factors, the volume of trade (T) and the price level (P). If their product remains the same, an increase in the volume of trade, however small, must cause a decrease in the price level.

in a change in the demand curve or schedule, there will in general be a *rise* in other prices and in the general price level, for, there being less of the particular commodity bought and that at a less price, there will be less spent upon it and therefore more on other commodities, the price of which will be higher and, as the reduction in the amount bought of the particular commodity will, in general, imply a reduction in the total volume of trade, the general price level will be raised.[1]

[1] See Irving Fisher, "Mathematical Investigations in the Theory of Value and Prices," *Transactions of the Connecticut Academy of Arts and Sciences*, 1892, p. 51.

APPENDIX TO CHAPTER X

§ 1. *Each Form of Index Number for Prices implies a Correlative Form of Index Number for Quantities*

We have seen that the number of possible forms of averages is infinite. Since an index number, as P_1, is an average, it follows that there exists an infinite number of possible forms of index numbers. Forty-four of the simplest and most important forms are given in the table which follows. In this table the subscript "1" relates to any specified year called for convenience "year 1," while the subscript "0" likewise relates to "year 0," called the "base" year. The headings of the columns in the table give the formula for the index number, P_1, for the year 1 relatively to the base year 0. By substituting "2" for "1," each formula could be made to refer to a second year, 2, considered relatively to the base year 0. Likewise, substituting "3," "4," etc., for "1," we have an entire series of index numbers, P_1, P_2, P_3, P_4, etc., for different years, all relative to the same base year 0. Since the formulæ are all alike and differ only in subscripts, it is unnecessary to waste space by expressing P_2, P_3, etc., in the headings. Consequently, in each column heading, only the formula for P_1 is expressed.

Also to save space, the column headings omit the formulæ for T_1, etc., correlative to those for P_1. Each form of price index, P_1, applicable to the equation of exchange, implies a correlative trade index, T_1, such that the product of the two is equal to Σp_1Q_1, the right side of the equation of exchange.

Since $$P_1T_1 = \Sigma p_1Q_1,$$

it follows that $$T_1 = \frac{\Sigma p_1Q_1}{P_1}.$$

Hence, given a particular formula for P_1, we have a resultant and particular formula for T_1. For instance, if P_1 is a simple arithmetic average of $\frac{p_1}{p_0}, \frac{p'_1}{p'_0}, \frac{p''_1}{p''_0}, \ldots \frac{p^{(n)}_1}{p^{(n)}_0}$, *i.e.* if $P_1 = \frac{1}{n} \Sigma \frac{p_1}{p_0}$ (formula 3 of the table), where n is the number of commodities of which the price ratios are included, then the correlative formula for T_1 will evidently be

$$T_1 = \frac{\Sigma p_1 Q_1}{P_1} = \frac{\Sigma p_1 Q_1}{\frac{1}{n} \Sigma \frac{p_1}{p_0}}.$$

Again, if P_1 is the geometric average $\sqrt[n]{\frac{p_1}{p_0} \cdot \frac{p'_1}{p'_0} \cdot \frac{p''_1}{p''_0} \ldots \frac{p^{(n)}_1}{p^{(n)}_0}}$, (formula 7 of the table), then T_1 has the correlative form

$$\frac{\Sigma p_1 Q_1}{\sqrt[n]{\frac{p_1}{p_0} \cdot \frac{p_1}{p'_0} \cdots}}.$$

Conversely any particular formula for T_1 implies a correlative particular formula for P_1. For, since

$$P_1 T_1 = \Sigma p_1 Q_1,$$

it follows that

$$P_1 = \frac{\Sigma p_1 Q_1}{T_1}.$$

By means of this equation, if we have given any particular formula for T_1, we may obtain a resultant particular formula for P_1.

The examples already given of P_1 (the arithmetical and geometric average) illustrate how to obtain the correlative formula for T_1. If we work backward from these somewhat complicated formulæ for T_1, we may in turn derive as the correlative formulæ for P_1 the arithmetic and geometric averages.

As a third example illustrating the derivation of the formula for P_1 from a given formula for T_1, let T_1 be defined as $\Sigma p_0 Q_1$; then

$$P_1 = \frac{\Sigma p_1 Q_1}{T_1} = \frac{\Sigma p_1 Q_1}{\Sigma p_0 Q_1}.$$

(Formula 11 of the table.)

We may consider, then, that each column heading, though stating only the formula for P_1, implies also a corresponding formula for T_1; that is, P_1 and T_1 occur in correlative pairs. P_1 and T_1 are such that if one of them (say P_1) is given independently of the equation, $\Sigma p_1Q_1 = P_1T_1$, the other is then defined by means of that equation.

The two magnitudes P_1 and T_1 are not, however, absolutely symmetrical. There is this important distinction between them: that, while P_1 is an *abstract* number, T_1 is *concrete*, being expressible in dollars and cents.

It thus appears that, although the p's and Q's enter symmetrically into the expression Σp_1Q_1, yet, when this expression is replaced by P_1T_1, the first factor, P_1, represents the p's in a somewhat different manner from that in which the second factor, T_1, represents the Q's. P_1 is a pure number, an average of pure numbers — the ratios the p's bear to the base prices, p_0's, whereas T_1, being $\frac{\Sigma p_1Q_1}{P_1}$, is a concrete number, being a value found by dividing the value Σp_1Q_1 by the pure number P_1.

Thus, while the p's and Q's occur symmetrically in the original formula Σp_1Q_1, the process by which we convert Σp_1Q_1 into P_1T_1 treats them asymmetrically. But evidently we can reverse the asymmetry in their treatment; for, instead of putting Σp_1Q_1 equal to P_1T_1, we may put it equal to $A_1\mathcal{Q}_1$, in which $\mathcal{Q}_1$ is now a *quantity index*, that is, an average of the ratios which the Q_1's bear to the Q_0's or base quantities $\left(i.e.\text{ an average of } \frac{Q_1}{Q_0} \cdot \frac{Q'_1}{Q'_0} \cdot \frac{Q''_1}{Q_0} \cdots\right)$, and A_1, being therefore $\frac{\Sigma p_1Q_1}{\mathcal{Q}_1}$, is the "aggregate price," that is, the *value* found by dividing the value Σp_1Q_1 by the pure number $\mathcal{Q}_1$. Here, if the form of $\mathcal{Q}_1$ is given independently of the equation $\Sigma p_1Q_1 = A_1\mathcal{Q}_1$, the form of A_1 is defined by means of this equation, and conversely.

Thus we may convert Σp_1Q_1 into either P_1T_1 or $A_1\mathcal{Q}_1$. In the first, the p's are represented by a ratio, P_1; in the second, by a value, A_1; in the first, the Q's are represented by a value, T_1; in the second, by a ratio, Q_1. The asymmetry of each of the two formulæ P_1T_1 and A_1Q_1 is the reverse of the other.

Finally we may, if we wish, treat both the p's and Q's *alike* by putting Σp_1Q_1 equal to $(\Sigma p_0Q_0)P_1Q_1$, where P_1 and Q_1 are, both of them, index numbers for the p_1's and Q_1's respectively. That is (as we shall prove), P_1 and Q_1 are *averages* respectively of price ratios like $\frac{p_1}{p_0}$, and of quantity ratios like $\frac{Q_1}{Q_0}$. The equation $\Sigma p_1Q_1 = (\Sigma p_0Q_0)P_1Q_1$ may be said to define either one of the two averages (P_1 and Q_1) in terms of the other. One or the other must be defined irrespective of the equation.

Thus there are three ways of resolving Σp_1Q_1, as follows:—

$$\Sigma p_1Q_1 = P_1T_1 = A_1Q_1 = (\Sigma p_0Q_0)P_1Q_1.$$

The third form becomes, dividing the equation through by Σp_0Q_0,

$$\frac{\Sigma p_1Q_1}{\Sigma p_0Q_0} = P_1Q_1. \qquad (1)$$

We wish now to prove that if either P_1 or Q_1 is first determined in any way conformably to the definition of an average, leaving the other to be determined by the above equation, then the latter also necessarily conforms to the definition of an average. We have to prove that if Q_1 is taken as an average of $\frac{Q'}{Q_0}, \frac{Q'}{Q'_0} \cdots$, then the correlative expression for P_1 derived from (1), viz.:—

$$P_1 = \frac{\frac{\Sigma p_1Q_1}{\Sigma p_0Q_0}}{Q_1} = \frac{\frac{\Sigma p_1Q_1}{\Sigma p_0Q_0}}{\left(\text{Av. } \frac{Q_1}{Q_0}, \frac{Q'_1}{Q'_0} \cdots\right)}. \qquad (2)$$

is an average of $\frac{p_1}{p_0}, \frac{p'_1}{p'_0} \cdots$. It is, therefore, only necessary to show (in accordance with the most general definition of an average as given in the Appendix to Chapter II) that expression (2) shall be equal to k when

$$\frac{p_1}{p_0} = \frac{p'_1}{p'_0} = \cdots = k$$

(and when at the same time

$$\left.\frac{Q_1}{Q_0} = \frac{Q'_1}{Q'_0} = \cdots = k'\right).$$

We therefore suppose that

$$\frac{p_1}{p_0} = \frac{p'_1}{p'_0} = \cdots = k,$$

so that $p_1 = kp_0\,;\; p'_1 = kp'_0;\; \cdots;$

and also that $\dfrac{Q_1}{Q_0} = \dfrac{Q'_1}{Q'_0} = \cdots = k',$

so that $Q_1 = k'Q_0;\; Q'_1 = k'Q'_1;\; \cdots.$

Then $\Sigma p_1Q_1 = \Sigma(kp_0 \times k'Q_0) = kk'\,\Sigma p_0Q_0.$

Now, since $\dfrac{Q_1}{Q_0} = \dfrac{Q'_1}{Q_0} = \cdots = k',$

it follows that $\left(\text{Av. } \dfrac{Q_1}{Q_0}, \dfrac{Q'_1}{Q'_0}, \cdots\right) = k'$

by the definition of an average.

Hence the expression (2) may now be written

$$\frac{\dfrac{kk'\,\Sigma p_0Q_0}{\Sigma p_0Q_0}}{k'}$$

which is evidently equal to k.

Therefore expression (2) is, by definition, an average of $\dfrac{p_1}{p_0}, \dfrac{p'_1}{p'_0}\cdots$. By the same reasoning we may show conversely

that

$$\frac{\dfrac{\Sigma p_1Q_1}{\Sigma p_0Q_0}}{\left(\text{Av. } \dfrac{p_1}{p_0}, \dfrac{p'_1}{p_0}\cdots\right)}$$

is a true average of $\dfrac{Q_1}{Q_0}, \dfrac{Q'_1}{Q'_0}\cdots$. We conclude that if either

P_1 or Q_1 in the formula $P_1Q_1 = \frac{\Sigma p_1Q_1}{\Sigma p_0Q_0}$ is an average of the p or Q ratios respectively, then the other is also an average respectively of the Q or p ratios.

§ 2. *Index Numbers for Prices occur in Antithetical Pairs as also do Index Numbers for Quantities*

We have seen that, given any special form of average for P_1, there results therefrom a correlative form for Q_1 and *vice versa*. Thus if P_1 is the simple arithmetical average $\frac{1}{n}\Sigma\frac{p_1}{p_0}$, then Q_1 is $\frac{\frac{\Sigma p_1Q_1}{\Sigma p_0Q_0}}{\frac{1}{n}\Sigma\frac{p_1}{p_0}}$. Again, if we start with Q_1 as the simple arithmetical average $\frac{1}{n}\Sigma\frac{Q_1}{Q_0}$ then we discover in its correlate a new formula for P_1, viz. $\frac{\frac{\Sigma p_1Q_1}{\Sigma p_0Q_0}}{\frac{1}{n}\Sigma\frac{Q_1}{Q_0}}$. In this way any given formula for P_1 leads to another formula for P_1 which may be called its antithesis. This second formula for P_1 is identical in form with the formula for Q_1 correlative to the first formula for P_1, differing merely in the fact that the p_1's and Q_1's are interchanged.

The four forms and their relations are best seen by placing them in a square, as in the following example:—

$P_1 = \frac{\Sigma\frac{p_1}{p_0}}{n}$	antithetical to	$P_1 = \frac{\frac{\Sigma p_1Q_1}{\Sigma p_0Q_0}}{\frac{1}{n}\Sigma\frac{Q_1}{Q_0}}$
correlative to		correlative to
$Q_1 = \frac{\frac{\Sigma p_1Q_1}{\Sigma p_0Q_0}}{\frac{1}{n}\Sigma\frac{p_1}{p_0}}$	antithetical to	$Q_1 = \frac{\Sigma\frac{Q_1}{Q_0}}{n}$.

The pair of formulæ in the left vertical column express correlative formulæ, one for P_1 and the other for Q_1. The formula diagonally opposite each of these has the p's and Q's interchanged. The right pair thus formed are evidently also *correlates* of each other and each is the *antithesis* of that in the same horizontal line at its left. Since any formula for P_1 involves an antithetical formula for P_1, we have here a means of devising new formulæ from old and also of noting certain unsuspected relationships between formulæ already in use.

In the table of index numbers for P_1 which follows, the antithetical formulæ are in each case placed side by side and joined by a bracket. The two together represent, in each case, the upper half of a square like the above. The omitted lower half, giving the correlative forms for Q_1, can be readily supplied in every case; but, to save space, each column heading in the table only includes the formula for P_1, omitting its correlate for Q_1 as well as the corresponding formulæ for T_1 and A_1. The formula for Q_1 is, as above explained, easily written by interchanging p's and Q's in the formula given in the neighboring (antithetical) columns; that for T_1 is found by dividing Σp_1Q_1 by P_1; that for A_1 by dividing Σp_1Q_1 by Q_1. Practically P_1 and A_1 serve the same purpose, namely, that of indicating price changes; likewise Q_1 and T_1 serve the same purpose, namely, that of indicating quantity changes. For any series of years the numbers for P_1 and for A_1 will be proportional, the only difference being that P_1 is expressed in percentages, the figure for the base year being 100 per cent, whereas A_1 is expressed in dollars, the figure for the base year being the actual exchanges Σp_0Q_0 in that year. Likewise Q_1 and T_1 differ merely as percentage and dollar measurements, the base figure being 100 per cent and Σp_0Q_0 dollars respectively.

§ 3. *General Meanings of p's and Q's*

We may here pause to point out that the whole present discussion relates purely to the *form* of an index number of p's and Q's without reference to the meaning to be assigned to these p's and Q's. These meanings may be far wider than simply the prices and quantities in the equation of exchange. For example, an index number of prices may be constructed with reference to the purchasing power of a workman's wages. In this case, the same formula as before, $\Sigma p_1 Q_1$, may be employed, but the terms have different meanings. The p's now relate to the prices of goods entering into the workmen's budgets, and the Q's to the quantities of workmen's goods entering into their consumption. In this case, the price index, P, indicates the price level of workmen's consumption, and the index, T, means an index for workmen's *real-wages*. Any special form of price index now implies a correlative special form of real-wages index.

Again, if we are studying statistics of capital such as in Giffen's *Growth of Capital*, we have ΣpQ as the value of capital, the p's being the prices of different forms of capital and the Q's, their quantities. For every special form of price index number, P, representing the price level of capital, there will be a correlative special index of *capital* showing the real "growth of capital" as distinct from its mere money value. Such an index seems seldom to have been employed.[1] Yet it is evidently advisable to distinguish between an apparent increase of capital due to inflated prices and a real increase, as would be shown by such an index as here suggested.

[1] See Giffen, *Growth of Capital*, London (George Bell and Sons), 1889, pp. 50–54, where allowance is made for changes in the price level. Index numbers of the *Economist*, of Sauerbeck, and of Soetbeer are cited. Professor J. S. Nicholson has advocated such a capital-standard in the *Journal of the Royal Statistical Association*, March, 1887, pp. 152 ff. This method is discussed by Edgeworth, *Report of the British Association*, 1887, p. 276.

We see, therefore, that wherever prices and quantities are united, we have the requisite conditions for constructing correlative pairs of index numbers, one index in each pair relating to prices, and the other to quantities.

We shall, however, for convenience, continue to employ the magnitude T, rather than Q, and to refer to it as a "trade" index.

§ 4. *Review of 44 Formulæ, heading the Table Columns*

We shall now briefly review the formulæ of the table of selected index numbers. Each even-numbered formula is best regarded as derivable from the odd-numbered formula at its left as its antithesis. The odd formulæ are those constructed directly for the p's without reference to any average for the Q's; the even are constructed indirectly by reference to some average first assumed for the Q's. The latter are what Walsh had in mind under the name of "double weighting."

Formula (1) is simply the ratio of the sums of prices. It may also be considered as the ratio of the averages of prices in the two years considered, as is evident by writing it, —

$$\frac{\frac{\Sigma p_1}{n}}{\frac{\Sigma p_0}{n}},$$ where n is the number of commodities employed.

This formula was used by Dutot in 1738,[1] and has been used recently by Bradstreet,[2] who applied it practically.

Although it is a ratio of average *prices*, it may also be thrown into the form of a weighted arithmetical average of the *price ratios*, $\frac{p_1}{p_0}$, $\frac{p'_1}{p'_0}$, $\frac{p''_1}{p''_0}$, etc., as the following transformation shows: —

[1] See Walsh, *Measurement of General Exchange Value*, New York (Macmillan), 1901, pp. 534, 553.

[2] *Bradstreet's Journal* from 1895.

$$\frac{\Sigma p_1}{\Sigma p_0} = \frac{p_1 + p'_1 + p''_1 + \cdots}{p_0 + p'_0 + p''_0 + \cdots}$$

$$= \frac{p_0\left(\frac{p_1}{p_0}\right) + p'_0\left(\frac{p'_1}{p'_0}\right) + p''_0\left(\frac{p''_1}{p''_0}\right) + \cdots}{p_0 + p'_0 + p''_0 + \cdots}.$$

The formula in this last form is evidently the weighted arithmetical average of the ratios in parenthesis, the weights being the prices p_0, p'_0, p''_0, $\cdots$ of the year 0. A change in the units of quantity for the various goods would change these prices; thus a change from ounces to pounds would multiply the number expressing price by sixteen. Such a change in any price, such as p_0, would entirely change the relative importance of the "weights," p_0, p'_0, etc. Consequently this system of weighting is, as Walsh says, quite accidental or haphazard.[1]

The same formula is also a harmonic average, as the following transformations show: —

$$\frac{\Sigma p_1}{\Sigma p_0} = \frac{p_1 + p'_1 + \cdots}{p_0 + p'_0 + \cdots}$$

$$= \frac{p_1 + p'_1 + \cdots}{p_1\left(\frac{p_0}{p_1}\right) + p'_1\left(\frac{p'_0}{p'_1}\right) + \cdots}$$

$$= \frac{1}{\dfrac{p_1\left(\frac{p_0}{p_1}\right) + p'_1\left(\frac{p'_0}{p'_1}\right) + \cdots}{p_1 + p'_1 + \cdots}}.$$

The last expression is evidently the reciprocal of a weighted arithmetical average of the price ratios in parenthesis. But these price ratios are the reciprocals of $\left(\frac{p_1}{p_0}\right)$, $\left(\frac{p'_1}{p'_0}\right)$, $\left(\frac{p''_1}{p''_0}\right)$, etc. In other words, the formula is the reciprocal of a weighted

[1] Walsh, *op. cit.*, pp. 81 and 82.

arithmetical average of the reciprocals of the ratios $\frac{p_1}{p_0}$, etc. It is therefore the weighted *harmonic* average of these ratios $\frac{p_1}{p_0}$, etc., the weights being p_1, p_1', etc., or the prices of the year 1.

In short, formula (1) is both an arithmetical and a harmonic average of $\frac{p_1}{p_0}$, $\frac{p'_1}{p'_0}$, etc., the weights being, in the first case, the terms of the denominator, and in the second, those of the numerator.

We have seen that formula (1) in the table, although primarily a *ratio of averages of prices*, may be also considered as an *average of ratios of prices* with arbitrary weighting.

Conversely we may, if we choose, regard every average of ratios as a ratio of averages by assuming arbitrary units for measuring commodities. It is evident that, if the unit of measure is increased in any ratio, the number expressing the price is decreased in the inverse ratio. If, therefore, we change the unit of measure of a commodity the price of which is at first expressed by p_1 by dividing by the ratio p_0, this price becomes $\frac{p_1}{p_0}$. Thus $\frac{p_1}{p_0}$ may be considered to be a price as well as a price ratio. Hence an average of $\frac{p_1}{p_0}$, $\frac{p'_1}{p'_0}$, $\frac{p''_1}{p''_0}$, etc., may be regarded as an average of *prices*. The new units, instead of being pounds, yards, etc., are *dollars-worth-in-the-base-year*. With these units, the price in the base year is unity, for dividing the price, p_0, in the original units by the factor p_0, we obtain unity.

Hereafter, however, we shall treat all index numbers as averages of price ratios.

It is interesting to note that the antithesis of Dutot's or Bradstreet's formula (No. 2), found by dividing the fraction $\frac{\Sigma p_1 Q_1}{\Sigma p_0 Q_0}$ by the correlative formula for Q_1, viz., $\frac{\Sigma Q_1}{\Sigma Q_0}$, turns out to be that advocated by Drobisch,[1] and earlier by Sir Rawson-Rawson.[2]

Formula (3)[3] is evidently the familiar simple arithmetical average,—

$$\frac{\Sigma\left(\frac{p_1}{p_0}\right)}{n} \text{ or } \frac{\frac{p_1}{p_0}+\frac{p'_1}{p'_0}+\cdots+\frac{p_1^{(n)}}{p_0^{(n)}}}{n}.$$

Formula (4), the antithesis of formula (3), gives, as the average price ratio, the ratio of total values $\Sigma p_1Q_1 / \Sigma p_0Q_0$ corrected for change in the Q's by division by the arithmetical average ratio of the Q's.

Hereafter the even-numbered formulæ, being antitheses of the preceding odd formulæ, will be passed over unless there is, in any case, special reason for mention.

[1] See M. W. Drobisch, "Ueber Mittelgrössen und die Anwendbarkeit derselben auf die Berechnung des Steigens und Sinkens des Geldwerthes" (*Berichte über die Verhandlungen der Königlich sächsischen Gesellschaft der Wissenschaften zu Leipsig; Mathematisch-physische Classe*, Band XXIII, 1871, pp. 25–48). Also "Ueber die Berechnung der Veränderungen der Waarenpreise und des Geldwerthes" (*Jahrbücher für National-oekonomie und Statistik*, 1871, Band XVI, pp. 143–156); and "Ueber einige Einwürfe gegen die in diesen Jahrbüchern veroffentlichte neue Methode, die Veränderungen der Waarenpreise und des Geldwerthes zu berechnen" (*ibid.*, 1871, Band XVI, pp. 416–427). See also Walsh, *op. cit.*, pp. 97–99, where the method is explained.

[2] See Edgeworth, *Report of the British Association for the Advancement of Science*, 1889, p. 152. Sir Rawson-Rawson's suggestion, as developed by Edgeworth, was to divide the value of exports (or imports) by the tonnage of exports (or imports) and consider the result as an index number of prices of exports (or imports). The suggestion was made not for any theoretical virtues, but because of the practical ease of computation. Edgeworth compares the results of Rawson's rough and ready method with the more exact method of Giffen by actual figures for 1886 compared with 1885, and finds substantial agreement.

[3] For a statement of the history of this formula from Carli to the present, see Walsh, *op. cit.*, p. 534.

Formulæ (5), (7)[1], and (9)[2] are respectively the simple harmonic, simple geometric, and simple median averages. We note that the antithesis of (7), viz. (8), is one proposed by Nicholson and Walsh.[3]

Formula (11)[4] resembles Bradstreet's, except that the introduction of the Q's as multipliers prevents the weighting from being arbitrary; for the weights p_0Q_1, etc., unlike the weights p_0, etc., are uninfluenced by a change in the units of measurement for commodities. Whether an article be measured in pounds or ounces will not affect the value of a given amount of it. The following transformations show that the formula is a weighted arithmetic mean: —

$$\frac{\Sigma p_1Q_1}{\Sigma p_0Q_1} = \frac{p_1Q_1 + p'_1Q'_1 + \cdots}{p_0Q_1 + p'_0Q'_1 + \cdots}$$

$$= \frac{p_0Q_1\left(\frac{p_1}{p_0}\right) + p'_0Q'_1\left(\frac{p'_1}{p'_0}\right) + \cdots}{p_0Q_1 + p'_0Q'_1 + \cdots}$$

The last expression is evidently a weighted arithmetic average of the price ratios in the parentheses, the weights being p_0Q_1, $p'_0Q'_1$, etc., *i.e.* the *values* of the quantities in the year 1 reckoned at the prices of year 0.

But the same formula is also a harmonic average, as may be seen by transforming the denominator instead of the numerator as was done for formula (1). It is a weighted harmonic average, the weights being p_1Q_1, $p'_1Q'_1$, etc., or the values in the year 1.

In short, formula (11) or $\frac{\Sigma p_1Q_1}{\Sigma p_0Q_1}$ is, like formula (1), both a weighted arithmetical and a weighted harmonic average of

[1] See Jevons, *Investigations in Currency and Finance*, London (Macmillan), 1884; Edgeworth, *Reports British Association*, 1887, 8, 9; Walsh, *op. cit.*, pp. 229 ff.

[2] See Edgeworth, *Reports British Association*, 1887, 8, 9, esp. 1888, pp. 206 ff.

[3] Walsh, *op. cit.*, p. 548.

[4] For Formulæ 11 and 12 there exists a large literature. See Walsh, *op. cit.*, esp. pp. 191 ff., and pp. 539 ff.

$\frac{p_1}{p_0}, \frac{p'_1}{p'_0}, \frac{p''_1}{p''_0}$, etc., but the weights are different in the two cases.

(11) has the interesting property that its antithesis (12) is of the same form except that the subscripts for Q are now 0 in place of 1. Similar reasoning shows that this formula (12) is also both an arithmetical and an harmonic average, weighted according to the terms in its denominator and numerator respectively.

These two formulæ, (11) and (12), seem to be the favorites among writers on Index Numbers. Since the shortcomings of one are, in some cases, not shortcomings of the other, there have been many attempts to combine them into some composite. No. (13),[1] for instance, is their simple arithmetical average. The antithesis of (13), viz. (14), turns out to be the simple harmonic average of (11) and (12). Number (15) is the simple geometric average of (11) and (12). This formula (15) has the distinction of being identical with its own antithesis (16). Numbers (17), (19), (21), and (23) are other attempts at combining (11) and (12), not by averaging them, as was the case with (13) and (15), but by averaging their coefficients, viz., Q_1 and Q_0, Q'_1, and Q'_0, etc. Two antitheses of these, namely (18) and (22), turn out to be formulæ proposed by Walsh, and a third (24) to be one proposed by Julius Lehr.[2]

We have seen that the formulæ (11) and (12) considered as arithmetical averages have for weights

p_0Q_1, $p'_0Q'_1$, $p''_0Q''_1$, etc., for No. (11),

and p_0Q_0, $p'_0Q'_0$, $p''_0Q''_0$, etc., for No. (12).

We next use weights

p_1Q_1, $p'_1Q'_1$, $p''_1Q''_1$, etc., for No. (25),

and p_1Q_0, $p'_1Q'_0$, $p''_1Q''_0$, etc., for No. (27),

[1] For references to literature concerning this and many others among the remaining formulæ of the table (col. 13–44), see Walsh, *op. cit.*

[2] *Beiträge zur Statistik der Preise*, Frankfurt-a.-M, 1885 (p. 11 and pp. 37–42 for the method). The method is explained in Walsh, *Measurement of General Exchange-Value*, pp. 386–388.

thus completing the four permutations of the subscripts, 01, 00, 11, 10. Number (29) represents a weighted arithmetical average in which the weights are derived from other considerations than the product of the prices and quantities of the base year (1). An instance is the method employed in some of the tables in the "Aldrich Report,"[1] the weights being the percentage of consumption of various kinds in workingmen's budgets without reference to the base year or any other particular year.

Numbers (31) and (33) are weighted harmonic means in which the weights instead of being

p_1Q_1, etc., as in (11),

or p_1Q_0, etc., as in (12),

are p_0Q_1, etc., for (31),

and p_0Q_0, etc., for (33),

thus completing for harmonic averages the same permutations of subscripts as before for arithmetical averages. We see then that the odd formulæ (11) to (33) inclusive are merely arithmetical averages or harmonic averages of $\frac{p_1}{p_0}$, etc., or else averages or mixtures of such averages.

Numbers (35), (37), (39), (41) are various forms of weighted geometric averages of those price ratios, the weights being

p_1Q_1, etc., for (35).

p_0Q_0, etc., for (37).

p_1Q_0, etc., for (39).

p_0Q_1, etc., for (41).

Number (43) is the ratio of the weighted geometric average of the prices in years 1 and 0, the weights being p_1Q_1, etc., for year 1 and p_0Q_0, etc., for year 0.

[1] *Report on Wholesale Prices*, Senate Report 1394, 2d Session, 52d Congress, 1893.

It will be seen that all of the 44 formulæ selected for the table are based on a few simple principles of averaging. Most are arithmetic, harmonic, or geometric averages or their combinations. Needless to say, numerous other and more complicated forms might be constructed.

§ 5. *Review of Eight Tests, heading the Table Rows*

Having reviewed the headings of the vertical columns of the table, we have next to note the headings of the horizontal rows. These headings are the eight tests of index numbers. The first six tests are arranged in pairs, the odd being expressed in terms of prices and the even in terms of quantities.

THE EIGHT TESTS FOR A GOOD INDEX NUMBER

The eight tests are intended to include all the tests which have been hitherto applied in the study of index numbers and some others. They are:

1. Test of proportionality, as to prices.
2. Test of proportionality, as to trade.
3. Test of determinateness, as to prices.
4. Test of determinateness, as to trade.
5. Test of withdrawal or entry, as to prices.
6. Test of withdrawal or entry, as to trade.
7. Test by shifting base, both as to prices and as to trade.
8. Test by shifting unit of measurement, both as to prices and as to trade.

We shall first define each of these tests in general terms and then proceed to illustrate them by actual applications.

1. *Test of proportionality as to prices.* A formula for the price index should be such that the price index will agree with all individual price ratios when these all agree with each other. Thus, if in 1910 the price of everything is 10 per cent higher than in 1909, the index number should register 10 per cent higher.

2. *Test of proportionality as to trade.* Likewise the correlative formula for the trade index should be such that the trade index will agree with all individual trade ratios when these all agree with each other.

3. *Test of determinateness as to prices.* A price index should not be rendered zero, infinity, or indeterminate by an individual price becoming zero. Thus, if any commodity should in 1910 be a glut on the market, becoming a "free good," that fact ought not to render the index number for 1910 zero.

4. *Test of determinateness as to trade.* The correlative trade index should not be rendered zero, infinity, or indeterminate by an individual quantity becoming zero. Thus, if any commodity should go completely out of use in 1910 so that its quantity exchanged becomes zero, that fact ought not to render the trade index for 1910 indeterminate.

5. *Test of withdrawal or entry as to prices.* A price index should be unaffected by the withdrawal or entry of a price ratio agreeing with the index. Thus, if the price index of a certain number of goods, not including sugar, should be 105 in 1910 as compared with 1900, and the price of sugar itself should be 105 in 1910 as compared with 1900, then the inclusion of sugar in the calculation of the index number ought not to change the index from 105.

6. *Test of withdrawal or entry as to trade.* The correlative trade index should be unaffected by the withdrawal or entry of a quantity ratio agreeing with the index.

7. *Test by changing base.* The ratios between various price indexes (and therefore also, as we shall see, the ratios between the correlative trade indexes) should be unaffected by reversing or changing the base. Thus, if the index number for 1910 is twice that for 1900, when calculated on the basis of 1860, it should remain twice, when calculated on the basis of 1870.

8. *Test by changing unit of measurement.* The ratios between various price indexes (and therefore also, as we shall see, the ratios between the correlative trade indexes) should be unaffected by changing any unit of measurement. Thus, if the index number for 1910 is twice that for 1900 when coal

is measured by the ton, it should remain twice, when coal is measured by the pound.

The statements of tests 7 and 8 are expressed in each case both as to prices and quantities; in these cases it was implied that what holds true of price indexes holds true also of trade indexes, and *vice versa*. To show this reciprocal relation for test 7 (base shifting), let the price index for year 1 in terms of year 0 be designated by $P_{1,0}$ instead of by P_1 as heretofore, in order that the base year may be specifically designated, and let us compare years 1 and 2 by using first year 0 as a base and then (say) year 8. If the base-shifting test is fulfilled for the P's, *i.e.* if $\frac{P_{1,0}}{P_{2,0}} = \frac{P_{1,8}}{P_{2,8}}$, we are to prove that the corresponding relation is also true for the T's, viz. that

$$\frac{T_{1,0}}{T_{2,0}} = \frac{T_{1,8}}{T_{2,8}}.$$

We know that

$$T_{1,0} = \frac{\Sigma p_1 Q_1}{P_{1,0}}. \quad (1)$$

$$T_{2,0} = \frac{\Sigma p_2 Q_2}{P_{2,0}}. \quad (2)$$

$$T_{1,8} = \frac{\Sigma p_1 Q_1}{P_{1,8}}. \quad (3)$$

$$T_{2,8} = \frac{\Sigma p_2 Q_2}{P_{2,8}}. \quad (4)$$

Divide (1) by (2) and (3) by (4). The quotients are

$$\frac{T_{1,0}}{T_{2,0}} = \left(\frac{\Sigma p_1 Q_1}{\Sigma p_2 Q_2}\right)\left(\frac{P_{2,0}}{P_{1,0}}\right),$$

and

$$\frac{T_{1,8}}{T_{2,8}} = \left(\frac{\Sigma p_1 Q_1}{\Sigma p_2 Q_2}\right)\left(\frac{P_{2,8}}{P_{1,8}}\right).$$

Comparing the right sides of these equations, we find that the "Σ" ratios are identical in the two cases, and we know that the P ratios are equal by hypothesis. Consequently the entire right sides of the two equations, and therefore the left sides, are also equal, and this is what was to be proved. The converse reasoning is also evident.

Like the base-shifting test, the unit-shifting test, No. 8, cannot apply to prices without applying also to quantities, and *vice versa*. To show this we employ the equation $T = \frac{\Sigma pQ}{P}$. Evidently the numerator of the right side of this equation is unaffected by a change of unit. For instance, if coal should be measured in ounces instead of tons, thus greatly increasing the number (say Q) representing its quantity, the value (pQ) will not be disturbed, since the number (p) representing the price will be correspondingly diminished. Consequently, if the denominator (P) meets the corresponding test, *i.e.* is likewise unaffected by a change in unit, the quotient (T) must be unaffected. That is, if the unit-shifting test is met for P, it must be met for T. As the converse reasoning also applies, the proposition is proved.

As will have been noted, the first six tests are expressed alternately in terms of *prices* and in terms of quantities. We now wish to point out that those expressed in terms of prices have a significance for quantities also, and that those expressed in terms of quantities have a significance for prices as well. That is, all the tests have significance both as to prices and as to quantities.

To emphasize this fact, which is important, let us note the *price* significance of each test. Since the price significance of tests 1, 3, 5, 7, 8 is evidently expressed in the statement of the test, we have left merely to express the price significance of tests 2, 4, 6.

Test 2 tells us that if all the trade ratios agree, their index should agree with them; that is,

if $$\frac{Q_1}{Q_2} = \frac{Q'_1}{Q'_2} = \frac{Q''_1}{Q''_2} = \cdots = k,$$

then also should $$\frac{T_1}{T_2} = k.$$

The question now before us is, assuming this condition to hold as to the Q's, what condition holds true as to the p's. The answer evidently is:—

$$\frac{P_1}{P_2} = \frac{\frac{\Sigma p_1Q_1}{T_1}}{\frac{\Sigma p_2Q_2}{T_2}} = \frac{\Sigma p_1Q_1}{\Sigma p_2Q_2} \div \frac{T_1}{T_2} = \frac{k\Sigma p_1Q_2}{\Sigma p_2Q_2} \div k$$

[obtained by substituting kQ_2 for Q_1, kQ'_2 for Q_1, etc., and kT_2 for T_1] $= \frac{\Sigma p_1Q_2}{\Sigma p_2Q_2} = \frac{\Sigma p_1Q_1}{\Sigma p_2Q_1}$.

The last form is derived from the next to the last by multiplying both numerator and denominator by k and then substituting Q_1 for kQ_2, Q'_1 for kQ'_2, etc.

The resulting two formulæ for $\frac{P_1}{P_2}$ express test No. 2 in terms of the conditions to which *prices* must conform. These formulæ will be recogniz d as those discussed in § 6 of the Appendix to Chapter II, the significance of which was there explained. It was there shown that a change in M, or a change in V, or a *uniform* change in all the Q's, or any combination of these changes will, through the equation of exchange, affect the price level in the manner expressed by the formula:—

$$\frac{P_1}{P_2} = \frac{\Sigma p_1Q_1}{\Sigma p_2Q_1} = \frac{\Sigma p_1Q_2}{\Sigma p_2Q_2}.$$

Thus the equation of exchange itself prescribes test No. 2; for the fundamental theorems which the equation of exchange has taught us are that prices vary directly as M and as the V's and inversely as the Q's; and the only forms of index numbers which will faithfully reflect these changes, *i.e.* will vary directly with M and inversely with the Q's (assuming that all Q's vary in unison), are those forms of index numbers which conform to test No. 2. Any other form of index number, when M (and M') increased 50 per cent and there was no change in V's or Q's, might register a rise of 49 per cent or 51 per cent. That is, no other forms of index numbers will enable us to say that when the quantity of money changes, the velocity of circulation and the Q's remaining the same, the index number of prices will vary proportionately. No other forms will enable us to state the corresponding theorem as to the effect of a change in velocity or of a (uniform) change in the Q's. But these theorems are fundamental. The very concept of an index number is that it shall replace the divergent individual variations and enable us to state of its proportionate changes the same theorems which hold true when prices all change alike.

Test No. 2 is therefore of such fundamental importance that we may profitably pause a moment to restate it in words. To be concrete, let us suppose two years, 1900 and 1910. Let us assume that the quantity of every kind of goods sold in 1910 is (say) exactly double the quantity sold in 1900. Then the only proper ndex number showing the level of prices in 1910 (year 1) as compared with the level of prices in 1900 (year 0) is the ratio $\frac{\Sigma p_1Q_1}{\Sigma p_0Q_1}$ of the total value of the goods sold in 1910 to what that value would have been at the prices of 1900; or, what amounts to the same thing, it is the ratio $\frac{\Sigma p_1Q_0}{\Sigma p_0Q_0}$ of what the total value of the goods sold in 1900 would have been at the prices of 1910 to what it actually was at the prices of 1900.

Of the 44 formulæ in the table, only the following reduce to the required formula when the Q's change uniformly: (2) of Drobisch, (4), (6), (8), (10), (11), (28), (30), (34), (38), (40). All these are even-numbered except formula 11. Several others will reduce to the required formula, provided one of the years compared is the base year.

The formulæ of the tables which fail to meet test 2 at all would not even allow us to say of $MV+M'V'=PT$ that if all the Q's remain the same, T will remain constant and P will vary as the other side of the equation. For these formulæ T fails as a true index of the Q's, and its error in one direction implies a corresponding error in P in the opposite direction.

Test 2 seems therefore in some respects the most important of all the eight tests for prices; although primarily it was not stated in terms of prices, but in terms of quantities. It is the only test which indicates the kind of *weighting* required. It completely prescribes the conditions which, while permitting any individual changes in prices, however divergent, enable us to say that a change in M or the two V's or in all the Q's in a given ratio will affect prices "on the average" in that same ratio (directly, of course, for the M's and V's and inversely, for the Q's).

Test 2 in fact points out the true form of the index number of prices as prescribed by the equation of exchange under all possible circumstances *except* when the Q's vary in unequal proportions. It also points to the proper weights required. These weights may be said to depend either on the Q_1's or on the Q_0's, interchangeably. The formula suggested by the Q_1's is formula 11; that suggested by the Q_2's is formula 12. Either will be *perfectly* satisfactory when the Q_1's and Q_0's are proportional, while when they are not, their discrepancy is negligible. When the Q's vary unequally, however, there seems to be *no* perfectly satisfactory formula. Under these circumstances the two systems of weights — one in terms of Q_1's, the other in terms of Q_0's — conflict with each other. But the conflict has been shown by Edgeworth[1] to be slight. In fact, the weights are of much less importance in determining an index number of prices than the prices themselves.

The discussion of test 2 will be resumed later when in § 7 we come to compare the various forms of index numbers.

[1] *Report of the British Association for the Advancement of Science* for 1887, pp. 288–292 and for 1888, pp. 197–198, 200, 202, 203, 206. Edgeworth shows in the case specified by him that an "error" in the *weights* only makes an "error" one twentieth as great in the resultant index number, while an "error" in the *prices* themselves makes an "error" in the resultant index number one fourth or fifth as great.

TESTS ALGEBRAICALLY STATED FOR THE GENERAL CASE OF *any* TWO YEARS COMPARED AS TO PRICES AND TRADE. (FOR THE SPECIAL CASE WHEN ONE OF THE TWO YEARS IS A BASE YEAR, SUBSTITUTE "0" FOR "2.")

	GIVEN	THE TEST REQUIRES THAT (as to p's)	(as to Q's)
Test 1, Proportionality as to p's	$\frac{p_1}{p_2}=\frac{p'_1}{p'_2}=\ldots=k$	$\frac{P_1}{P_2}=k$	$\frac{T_1}{T_2}=\frac{\Sigma p_1Q_1}{\Sigma p_1Q_2}=\frac{\Sigma p_2Q_1}{\Sigma p_2Q_2}$
Test 2, Proportionality as to Q's	$\frac{Q_1}{Q_2}=\frac{Q'_1}{Q'_2}=\ldots=k$	$\frac{P_1}{P_2}=\frac{\Sigma p_1Q_1}{\Sigma p_2Q_1}=\frac{\Sigma p_1Q_2}{\Sigma p_2Q_2}$	$\frac{T_1}{T_2}=k$
Test 3, Determinateness as to p's	$p_1=0$ or $p_2=0$, etc.	P_1 and P_2 determinate and not zero nor infinity	T_1 and T_2 determinate and not zero nor infinity
Test 4, Determinateness as to Q's	$Q_1=0$ or $Q_2=0$, etc.	P_1 and P_2 determinate and not zero nor infinity	T_1 and T_2 determinate and not zero nor infinity
Test 5, By withdrawal or entry as to p's	$\frac{p_1}{p_2}=\frac{P_1}{P_2}=k$	$\frac{P'_1}{P'_2}=k$ (Primes signify that p_1, p_2, Q_1, Q_2 are excluded; absence of primes signifies they are included.)	$\frac{T'_1}{T'_2}=\frac{\Sigma p'_1Q'_1}{\Sigma p'_2Q'_2}+\frac{P_1}{P_2}$ (Primes signify p_1, p_2, Q_1, Q_2 are excluded; absence of primes signifies they are included.)
Test 6, By withdrawal or entry as to Q's	$\frac{Q_1}{Q_2}=\frac{T_1}{T_2}=k$	$\frac{P'_1}{P'_2}=\frac{\Sigma p'_1Q'_1}{\Sigma p'_2Q'_2}+\frac{T_1}{T_2}$ (Primes and their absence signify as above.)	$\frac{T'_1}{T'_2}=k$ (Primes and their absence signify as above.)
Test 7, By changing base	Base changed from "0" to "3" changing: $P_{1,0}$ to $P_{1,3}$ $P_{2,0}$ to $P_{2,3}$ $T_{1,0}$ to $T_{1,3}$ $T_{2,0}$ to $T_{2,3}$	$\frac{P_{1,0}}{P_{2,0}}=\frac{P_{1,3}}{P_{2,3}}$	$\frac{T_{1,0}}{T_{2,0}}=\frac{T_{1,3}}{T_{2,3}}$
Test 8, By changing units of measurement	Q_1 and p_1 changed in inverse ratio	$\frac{P_1}{P_2}$ unchanged	$\frac{T_1}{T_2}$ unchanged

As to test 4, this states that if an individual *quantity* becomes zero this fact should not render the quantity or trade-index zero, infinity, or indeterminate. But according as the index does or does not become zero, infinity, or indeterminate, will the price index become or not become infinity, zero, or indeterminate respectively. This is clear from the relation $P_1 = \frac{\Sigma p_1 Q_1}{T_1}$. Hence test 4 possesses a significance as to prices similar to that which it possesses as to quantities.

The price significance of test 6 is more complex and of no apparent importance. Its statement is included in the explanatory table on page 407. In the preceding table of 44 index numbers the "score" for test 6 is bracketed to indicate that it has no important price significance, and is to be omitted in the totals.

Mutatis mutandis, each of the tests expressed in terms of prices (tests 1, 3, 5) has a significance as to quantities also.

The preceding explanatory table exhibits in algebraic terms both hypothesis and conclusion for each of the eight tests with respect both to prices and quantities.

§ 6. *The Interior of the Table; Column 11 in Particular*

We have reviewed briefly the headings of the table, including both those of the vertical columns and those of the horizontal rows. Their relations to each other are contained in the interior of the table. The object of the table is to show the degree of conformity of the 44 various formulæ for P (and their correlates for T) to the eight tests. In spite of all the mathematical ingenuity spent by many writers in devising index numbers, no known formula and apparently no possible formula will meet all eight of the tests.

For each test we note three possible degrees of conformity. It may be fulfilled by any particular formula in three degrees of conformity or nonconformity: (1) completely, (2) partially, or (3) not at all. These three degrees are indicated in the table which follows, by the numbers 1, $\frac{1}{2}$, 0 respectively. A test is completely fulfilled by index numbers for *any two* years whatever (as year 1 and year 2). A test is *partially* fulfilled if it is fulfilled by index numbers for two years, *one of which is the base year* (year 0). Thus the former relates to the general case, the latter to a particular case. Since the general includes the special, if the test is fulfilled in general it is fulfilled in particular; the converse is not necessarily true. But if the test is *not* fulfilled in the particular case, it is not fulfilled in general; the converse of this proposition is not necessarily true. In short, an affirmative answer to the question of complete conformity carries with it an affirmative answer to the question of partial conformity; and a negative answer to the question of partial conformity carries with it a negative answer to the question of complete conformity. These two rules save much labor in working out the figures in the table.

Our next task is to illustrate the eight tests by applying them to a particular formula for P_1 and the correlative formula for T_1. We select for this illustration the pair of formulæ numbered (11) in the table, namely $P_1 = \frac{\Sigma p_1 Q_1}{\Sigma p_0 Q_1}$ and $T_1 = \Sigma p_0 Q_1$, and we seek to know how far this pair of formulæ conform to the eight tests.

TEST 1. *Proportionality as to prices.* — We shall begin with "the particular case" where one of the two years compared is the base year. In concrete terms, this test means that, if all prices for the year 1 are any given number of times (k times) the prices for the base year 0, then the index number for the year 1 (in terms of the year 0) should be the same number k.

The test is best expressed in algebraic language as follows: —

If $$\frac{p_1}{p_0} = \frac{p'_1}{p'_0} = \frac{p''_1}{p''_0} = \cdots = k,$$

i.e. if $p_1 = kp_0;\ p'_1 = kp'_0;\ p''_1 = kp''_0 \cdots$, k being the given constant price ratio, then also should

$$\frac{P_1}{P_0} = k,$$

that is (since $P_0 = 1$), $\qquad P_1 = k.$

It is easy to apply this test to our given pair of formulæ.

The formulæ for year 1 are $P_1 = \frac{\Sigma p_1 Q_1}{\Sigma p_0 Q_1}$; $T_1 = \Sigma p_0 Q_1$.

The formulæ for year 0 are $\quad P_0 = \frac{\Sigma p_0 Q_0}{\Sigma p_0 Q_0} (= 1)$; $T_0 = \Sigma p_0 Q_0$.

It is evident that $\quad P_1 = \frac{\Sigma p_1 Q_1}{\Sigma p_0 Q_1} = \frac{p_1 Q_1 + p'_1 Q'_1 + \cdots}{\Sigma p_0 Q_1}$

$$= \frac{(kp_0)Q_1 + (kp'_0)Q'_1 + \cdots}{\Sigma p_0 Q_1} = \frac{k(p_0 Q_1 + p'_0 Q'_1 + \cdots)}{\Sigma p_0 Q_1}$$

$$= \frac{k \Sigma p_0 Q_1}{\Sigma p_0 Q_1} = k.$$

Therefore test 1 is fulfilled for the particular case when one of the years is the base year.

But, as we have noted, it does not follow that the test is fulfilled *in general*. For "the general case" of any two years the test may be thus stated: If the price of each good for the year 1 is k times the price of the same good for the year 2, then the index number for the year 1 (in terms of the year 0) should also be k times the index number for the year 2 (in terms of the year 0). That this may be true, the test requires, for the general case, that if

$$\frac{p_1}{p_2} = \frac{p'_1}{p'_2} = \frac{p''_1}{p''_2} = \cdots = k,$$

i.e. if $\qquad p_1 = kp_2,\ p'_1 = kp'_2,\ p''_1 = kp''_2$ etc.,

then must $\qquad \frac{P_1}{P_2} = k.$

This general test, however, will not be fulfilled, as may be seen from the following:—

$$\frac{P_1}{P_2} = \frac{\dfrac{\Sigma p_1 Q_1}{\Sigma p_0 Q_1}}{\dfrac{\Sigma p_2 Q_2}{\Sigma p_0 Q_2}} = \frac{\dfrac{k \Sigma p_2 Q_1}{\Sigma p_0 Q_1}}{\dfrac{\Sigma p_2 Q_2}{\Sigma p_0 Q_2}}.$$

In order that this last expression should reduce to k, it is evident that $\frac{\Sigma p_2 Q_1}{\Sigma p_0 Q_1}$ would have to be equal to $\frac{\Sigma p_2 Q_2}{\Sigma p_0 Q_2}$. But this cannot be assumed to be always true. If this equality should happen to hold true for any particular value of (say) Q_2, it would evidently be disturbed by the slightest deviation from that value. If, for instance, Q_2 should vary, the left side, $\frac{\Sigma p_2 Q_1}{\Sigma p_0 Q_1}$, of the supposed equality would be unaffected, but the first term in the numerator and the first term in the denominator of the right side would vary. Consequently the right fraction $\frac{\Sigma p_2 Q_2}{\Sigma p_0 Q_2}$ would be affected, except when the ratio of the first term, $\frac{p_2 Q_2}{p_0 Q_2}$, happened to be equal to $\frac{\Sigma p_2 Q_2}{\Sigma p_0 Q_2}$, in which case by a well-known principle of proportion (the principle of "composition and division") the size of the terms $p_2 Q_2$ and $p_0 Q_2$ would be immaterial.

The first test, therefore, is fulfilled for the particular case where one of the two years compared is the base year, but is not fulfilled in general. Therefore, following our convention, we assign to formula 11 the number ½ as representing its degree of conformity to test 2.

TEST 2. *Proportionality as to trade.* This test, stated for the *general* case, is: If the quantities of all goods sold in the year 1 is k times the quantities of the corresponding goods sold in the year 2, the index number of trade for the year 1 (in terms of the year 0) should also be k times the index number for the year 2 (n terms of the year 0).

That is, if $$\frac{Q_1}{Q_2} = \frac{Q'_1}{Q'_2} = \frac{Q''_1}{Q''_2} = \dots = k,$$

then should $$\frac{T_1}{T_2} = k.$$

We shall find that this test is fulfilled in the general case, and therefore also in the particular case.

Evidently $$\frac{T_1}{T_2} = \frac{\Sigma p_0 Q_1}{\Sigma p_0 Q_2} = \frac{k \Sigma p_0 Q_2}{\Sigma p_0 Q_2} = k,$$

which was to have been proved. Therefore test 2 is completely fulfilled, and the formula is therefore assigned the full credit, "1," in the table.

TEST 3. *Determinateness as to prices.* This test is also completely fulfilled.

If, in the formula for P_1, namely $\frac{\Sigma p_1 Q_1}{\Sigma p_0 Q_1}$, some but not all of the prices, as p_1, or one of the quantities, as Q_1, should become zero, it is clear that the above expression would still be determinate, and lie between zero and infinity. It will merely happen that some of the numerous terms in the numerator will vanish, but all the other terms will remain.

Since the same reasoning applies to P_2, it follows that $\frac{P_2}{P_1}$ must also be determinate, being the quotient of two finite, non-zero, and determinate numbers. Thus test 3 is completely fulfilled.

TEST 4. *Determinateness as to trade.* The fourth test is analogous to the third, and states that the trade index number must not be rendered indeterminate, zero, or infinity simply because some price or prices should become zero. The formula for T_1 is always $\frac{\Sigma p_1 Q_1}{P_1}$. Since, as neither the numerator nor the denominator of this fraction becomes zero, infinity, or indeterminate by the vanishing of some but not all of the p's or Q's, the quotient must likewise be non-zero, finite, and determinate. Thus, test 4 is completely fulfilled.[1]

[1] It might seem that the simple tests of determinateness would be fulfilled by any formula whatever, but such is not the case. (If it were, the total "score" given in the last column opposite test 4 would be 44 instead of 31.) Thus the simple geometrical average (formula 7) will not conform to test 3 of determinateness as to prices. The simple geometrical average for "n" commodities is $P_1 = \sqrt[n]{\frac{p_1}{p_0} \cdot \frac{p'_1}{p'_0} \ldots}$. Evidently if p_1 becomes 0, the value of the entire

TEST 5. *Withdrawal or entry as to prices.* Suppose that there are 100 specified commodities. If the general price level of one year s k times that of another, and if any good, the price of which in the one year is k times that in the other, be withdrawn from the 100 commodities, leaving 99, then the ratio of the price levels of the two years should remain unchanged.

This is a difficult test to meet, and the formula under discussion meets it only partially, that is, when one of the two years compared is the base year.

If $\frac{\Sigma p_1Q_1}{\Sigma p_0Q_1} = k$, where k is a given ratio,

and if also $\frac{p_1}{p_0} = k$, then we are

to prove that $\frac{\Sigma p'_1Q'_1}{\Sigma p'_0Q'_1} = k$, where

of course $\Sigma p'_1Q'_1 = \qquad p'_1Q'_1 + p''_1Q''_1 + \cdots$

while $\Sigma p_1Q_1 = p_1Q_1 + p'_1Q'_1 + p''_1Q''_1 + \cdots$

so that $\Sigma p'_1Q'_1 = \Sigma p_1Q_1 - p_1Q_1.$

Now we know that,

since $\frac{p_1}{p_0} = k,$

then $\frac{p_1Q_1}{p_0Q_1} = k.$

And, since $\frac{\Sigma p_1Q_1}{\Sigma p_0Q_1} = k$, it follows by the principle of pro-

expression becomes 0. If, therefore, we should depend on the geometric mean for ascertaining price levels, the temporary plethora of any commodity, to the extent of making its price vanish for a single moment, would cause the index number representing the entire price level for that moment to fall to 0. A form of average which in an extreme case is so absurd will *approach* absurdity before the extreme is reached. Thus the geometrical average is unduly affected by prices which are low, even if not actually zero.

portion ("composition and division") that

$$\frac{\Sigma p_1Q_1 - p_1Q_1}{\Sigma p_0Q_1 - p_0Q_1} = k;$$

that is, $\frac{\Sigma p'_1Q'_1}{\Sigma p'_0Q'_0} = k$, which was to have been proved.

If the missing commodity is reëntered, the ratio will evidently be undisturbed, so the rule works both ways, *i.e.* for entry as well as for withdrawal. Therefore, test five is fulfilled for the particular case.

When, however, we consider the general case for price ratios of two years neither of which is the base year, the test will not be fulfilled.

That is, if $$\frac{\frac{\Sigma p_1Q_1}{\Sigma p_0Q_1}}{\frac{\Sigma p_2Q_2}{\Sigma p_0Q_2}} = k,$$

and if also $$\frac{p_1}{p_2} = k,$$

then $$\frac{\frac{\Sigma p'_1Q'_1}{\Sigma p'_0Q'_1}}{\frac{\Sigma p'_2Q'_2}{\Sigma p'_0Q'_2}}$$ will not in general be equal to k.

For, if this expression should happen to be equal to k in any particular instance, a slight change in any base year price, such as p'_0, would disturb the equality, unless the variation in p'_0 should affect the denominators of both numerator and denominator of the last expression in the same proportion. This would mean that the ratio $\frac{\Sigma p'_0Q'_1}{\Sigma p'_0Q'_2}$ would be unaffected by a change in p'_0, which in turn would assume (by the principle of "composition and division") that

$$\frac{p'_0Q'_1}{p'_0Q'_2} = \frac{\Sigma p'_0Q'_1}{\Sigma p'_0Q'_2}.$$

This is not necessarily true, as it is evidently easy to assume values for (say) Q'_1 which would render it untrue. Thus, a doubling of Q'_1 would double the left side but not the right. Therefore test five is only partially met by our formula. This is therefore to be credited only with ½ as its degree of conformity to test 5.

TEST 6. *Withdrawal or entry as to trade.* If the index numbers for trade are in a given ratio, the inclusion or exclusion of a given good, the quantities of which are in the same ratio, ought not to disturb that ratio. This test is completely fulfilled by our formula.

The test requires that if $\frac{Q_1}{Q_2} = k,$

and if $\frac{T_1}{T_2} = \frac{\Sigma p_0Q_1}{\Sigma p_0Q_2} = k,$

then should $\frac{\Sigma p'_0Q'_1}{\Sigma p'_0Q'_2} = k.$

This test is fulfilled; for from

$$\frac{Q_1}{Q_2} = k,$$

it follows that $\frac{p_0Q_1}{p_0Q_2} = k,$

which combined with $\frac{\Sigma p_0Q_1}{\Sigma p_0Q_2} = k,$

by the principles of proportion (*i.e.* by "composition and division") gives $\frac{\Sigma p_0Q_1 - p_0Q_1}{\Sigma p_0Q_2 - p_0Q_2} = k.$

That is, $\frac{\Sigma p'_0Q'_1}{\Sigma p'_0Q'_2} = k,$

which was to have been proved.

TEST 7. *Changing the base.* This test 7 is not fulfilled by our formula even in the particular case. The particular case means here the case of *reversing* the base, as between (say) year 1 and year 0.

In order not to alter and thereby confuse the notation we shall have to use the subscript 0, which indicated the original base year, to indicate that same year, even when, for the moment, it is not considered as the base year; and likewise we shall use the subscript 1 to indicate the year 1, even when it is, for the moment, taken as the base year.

By the formula which we are testing, the price index ratio for year 1 compared to year 0 as the base is $\frac{\Sigma p_1Q_1}{\Sigma p_0Q_1}$. By analogy it is clear that the price index ratio for year 0, compared with year 1 considered as the base, is $\frac{\Sigma p_0Q_0}{\Sigma p_1Q_0}$. If these two expressions are reciprocals of each other, then $\frac{\Sigma p_1Q_1}{\Sigma p_0Q_1}$ should be equal to $\frac{\Sigma p_1Q_0}{\Sigma p_0Q_0}$.

That this is not necessarily true is evident, since there is no necessary relation between the Q_0's and the Q_1's. If the equation should accidentally hold true for a particular set of Q_0's and Q_1's, the change, even in the smallest degree, of a single letter, say Q_0 or Q_1, would evidently disturb the relation. Therefore the test is not fulfilled even for the particular case of reversing the base as between two years, and the formula must therefore be assigned a "0" or complete failure to conform to test 7.

TEST 8. *Changing units of measurement.* If the unit for indicating the price, say of coal, should be changed from a ton to a pound, the index number ought not to be affected thereby. We shall find that this test is met by formula (11).

Evidently a change of unit, say from a ton to a pound, applied to any particular goods (the prices of which are p_1, p'_1, p''_1, the corresponding quantities being Q_1, Q'_1, Q''_1) will magnify all the Q's 2000 times, but, on the other hand, will reduce all the p's in the reciprocal ratio $(\frac{1}{2000})$. Consequently, the products p_1Q_1, $p'_1Q'_1$, $p''_1Q''_1$, will be unaffected.

Hence the sum of such products constituting the numerator and denominator of the right side of the equation

$$\frac{P_1}{P_2}=\frac{\dfrac{\Sigma p_1Q_1}{\Sigma p_0Q_1}}{\dfrac{\Sigma p_2Q_2}{\Sigma p_0Q_2}}$$

will likewise be unaffected. Therefore the ratio of the index numbers $\frac{P_1}{P_2}$ will be unaffected. Hence the test is completely fulfilled.[1]

[1] It might seem that every index number would conform to this unit-shifting test. It is true of 40 formulæ out of the 44. Yet the index number which is perhaps the simplest of all, Bradstreet's, $P_1=\frac{\Sigma p_1}{\Sigma p_0}$, fails to conform.

It is evident that if there is a change in the unit of any one commodity, such as that whose prices are p_1, and p_0, both the numerator and denominator will be affected, but not in the same proportion, except when it happens that

$$\frac{p_1}{p_0}=\frac{\Sigma p_1}{\Sigma p_0}.$$

Consequently, the index number is dependent upon the unit of measurement. Such an index number is entirely arbitrary, and by sufficient manipulation of the units of measurement could be made to favor any particular commodity. The larger the unit of any particular commodity employed, the higher the price for it which enters into the formula, and the more that commodity tends to affect the result.

Bradstreet uses 96 commodities in common use, all of which are measured by the pound. The result is that silver, for instance, dominates over iron, entering at several dollars a pound instead of a few cents. If radium, which recently cost $8,000,000 an ounce, were included, it would absolutely dominate the group, and we would reach the absurd result that since radium has fallen to hundreds of thousands instead of millions of dollars an ounce, the general price level must have fallen several fold in spite of the general impression of rising prices! An index number of this kind is fitly called by Walsh one of accidental or haphazard weighting.

§ 7. *The 44 Formulæ Compared*

We have gone through the reasoning by which the conformity of one pair $(P_1 = \frac{\Sigma p_1 Q_1}{\Sigma p_0 Q_1};\ T_1 = \Sigma p_0 Q_1)$ out of the 44 pairs of index numbers of prices and trade, given in the table, are tested and graded with respect to the eight tests. The table contains for the remaining 43 formulæ the results of similar reasoning. This reasoning is here omitted to save space. The mathematical reader who chooses can verify the results as tabulated. He can also prove the relationship by which it follows that the figure in any column for the odd tests corresponds to that in the neighboring antithetical column for the even tests. In consequence of this relationship the sum of any column for the odd tests equals the sum in the antithetical column for the even tests. In fact, the table is full of correspondences and relationships of many kinds.

The footings give us a means of comparing the merits of the various index numbers. These footings are intended to express, so far as may be, the fitness of the formulæ to serve as index numbers for price levels. Consequently the score for test 6 should be omitted from the footing, as test 6 has no value in regard to *prices*. (If it be desired to compare the scores of the correlative index numbers for quantities or trade, the score of test 6 will be included, but that of test 5 should then be omitted.)

Thus a perfect score would be *seven*. The highest score in the table is $5\frac{1}{2}$, the lowest, 2.

It would, of course, be absurd to compare the merits of index numbers merely by their "score" in the table. This score is more or less arbitrary, and it treats all seven tests as equally important. Yet it affords at least some insight into the comparative characteristics of the 44 formulæ. It is noteworthy that, in general, the simplest formulæ have high scores and the most complicated have low scores. Thus formulæ 1 (Dutot), 7 (simple geometric), 9 (median), 11 and 12 (Scrope) have scores of 5 and $5\frac{1}{2}$. The only others as

high as 5 are "mixtures" of formulæ 11 and 12. The simple arithmetical (3) and simple harmonic (5) have a score of 4, which is fairly high. The more complicated forms which have fairly high scores are in several cases "mixtures," averages, or antitheses of simple formulæ 11 and 12.

The above comparisons treat all the other seven tests as of equal importance. But they are not of equal importance. Since opinions might differ as to the exact relative importance of the various tests, we shall not attempt to "weight" them. Nor will this be necessary in order to decide the question of most importance to us, viz., which of the 44 index numbers meet the tests most completely. Tests 3 and 4 are probably of little practical importance as compared with the remaining tests. Test 2, on the other hand, may be accorded chief importance, for reasons given in section 5 of this Appendix and in Chapter II. In order to select the best index numbers of prices, therefore, let us first rule out of the competition all the 18 formulæ which have "0" for test 2. We have left the following formulæ classified into two groups.

(Omitting test 6), score for formulæ which do not completely fail on test 2,

Formulæ completely fulfilling Test 2		Formulæ partially fulfilling Test 2	
Formulæ	Score	Formulæ	Score
2	4	12	5½
4	3	13	4
6	3	14	4
8	4	15	4½
10	4½	16	4½
11	5	17	5
28	4	18	4½
30	3	20	4
34	3	21	5
38	3	22	4½
		24	4
		26	3½
		32	2½
		36	2½
		42	2½

If, next, we rule out of the competition from among those which completely meet test 2, all except those which have scores of 4½ or above, we have left only formulæ numbers 10 and 11. Among the formulæ which only *partially* meet test 2 we may eliminate all which fail to *exceed* 4½ in total score; for, although those which reach 4½ tie formula 10, yet when all tests are counted as of equal importance, they are inferior in not completely meeting the most important test — test 2. Putting the matter in another way, we may say that if test 2 should be weighted more heavily than the other tests, the scores of those formulæ *half* meeting that test which now tie formulæ *wholly* meeting that test would fail to do so and would therefore drop out of competition with formulæ 10 and 11 in the first column.

Eliminating therefore from the second column all formulæ with scores of 4½ or less, we have as the only rivals of formulæ 10 and 11, formulæ 12, 17, and 21, having scores of 5½, 5, and 5 respectively. Our best formula, therefore, should be found among numbers 10, 11, 12, 17, 21. We shall therefore examine with particular care these five surviving competitors.

These all conform to tests 3, 4, and 8. Comparing them in other respects, we find: —

	10	11	12	17	21
Test 1	0	½	1	½	½
Test 2	1	1	½	½	½
Test 5	0	½	1	½	½
Test 7	½	0	0	½	½
Total	1½	2	2½	2	2

Tests 17 and 21 have scores identical in every instance, and may therefore be said to be *tied*.

Comparing tests 11 with 17 (or 21), we see that 11 excels in respect to the important test 2, and 17 in test 7. As test 2 is regarded as of more importance than test 7, we may safely give the preference to formula 11 over 17 (or 21). We therefore now strike out 17 and 21 from the competition.

We have left formulæ 10, 11, 12; comparing 10 and 11, we note that 10 excels in test 7, while 11 excels in tests 1 and 5. If we may be allowed here to exercise a comparative judgment, we shall say that the superiority in the one test 7 is more than offset by superiority in the two tests, 1 and 5. We therefore eliminate formula 10.

We now have left only the two formulæ, 11 and 12. There is not much to choose between them. While 12 has the higher score when all tests are counted as of equal importance, 11 excels in the most important test 2, and we are therefore inclined to give it the preference.

According to our judgment, therefore, test 11 emerges as the winner in the score contest. It has also the advantage of being among the very simplest formulæ and of having as its correlative formula for T the simplest of all formulæ for T, viz. $T_1 = \Sigma p_0 Q_1$.

In nonmathematical language, the pair of formulæ 11 mean that *the level of prices in any year is found by dividing the total value of the quantities sold in that year by what that value would have been at base prices*, and that the trade index in any year is simply the value of the quantities sold in that year *reckoned at base prices*.

Applying formula 11 to the equation of exchange, we have —

$$MV + M'V' = \Sigma p_1 Q_1 \quad (1)$$

$$= P_1 T \quad (2)$$

$$= \left(\frac{\Sigma p_1 Q_1}{\Sigma p_0 Q_1}\right) \Sigma p_0 Q_1 \quad (3)$$

We wish now to emphasize once more the virtues of this formula 11 in respect to test 2. The equation of exchange, stated above, is intended to show how prices are affected by changes in M, M', V, V' or the Q's. It is evident from the original form (1) of this equation that a proportional change in the M and M' (if the V's and Q's remain unchanged) will affect all the p_1's in exactly the same ratio, or else raise some prices more and others enough less than this ratio to compensate in the sense that the equation of exchange will be preserved. In some sense, therefore, the general *level* of prices varies exactly with M and M'. Form (3) enables us to express this proportionality by formulating the price level as the fraction $\frac{\Sigma p_1 Q_1}{\Sigma p_0 Q_1}$. This varies directly with the M's.

In precisely the same way we are enabled to state that a uniform change in the two V's, or any change in the left side of the equation as a whole, will affect prices in precisely the same ratio (the Q_1's being assumed constant). We may also say that a *uniform* change in the Q_1's will affect T_1 in exactly the same ratio, and P_1 in exactly the inverse ratio (assuming the left side of the equation to be unchanged). In fact, if we use formula 11 to express the average price ratio, we are able to state in all cases (so long only as the Q_1's change in unison or not at all) that prices rise or fall "on the average" directly as the left side of the equation, and inversely as the Q_1's.

As noted, these are the basic theorems for which the equation of exchange stands. We would naturally like to remove the restriction as to the Q_1's changing uniformly. We should consider an index number perfect (so far as needed in the equation of exchange) if we could assert of it the same theorem of proportion as above, without the restriction as to the Q_1's changing uniformly, so that we might substitute an *average* change in the Q's in place of a uniform change. No such index is found in the table, and no such index seems possible. Practically this conclusion does not greatly matter, for we are interested in prices far more than in quantities, the latter being chiefly important as supplying weights for the price indexes. As we have already noted, Edgeworth has shown that considerable variation in weighting is of comparatively little practical importance.

The chief use of index numbers is to compare *successive* years, not years remotely distant from each other. We are not so much interested in comparing the prices of 1909 and 1910 each with those of 1873 as we are in comparing them with each other. In fact, the chief use of 1873 as a base year is to enable us to compare any other two years with each other. But only a few index numbers which afford a true comparison between any year and another year as the base will give a true comparison between any two years, each in terms of a third year as the base. These few index numbers are those which completely meet the base-shifting test 7.[1] In the table the only formulæ which come up to this requirement are formulæ numbered 1, 2, 7, 8, 43, 44, to all of which there are serious objections on other grounds. Formulæ 1 and 2 are very arbitrary, having "haphazard weighting"; formulæ 43 and 44 have the lowest scores in the table; formula 7 has no system of weighting; and formula 8 becomes zero if a single quantity, as Q, should disappear from a year's sales.

The question therefore arises, why should we, as has usually been done, construct our index numbers with reference to a fixed base in terms of which we *indirectly* compare two given years? Why not make the comparison *directly?* The indirect comparison introduces an error in all cases except of those formulæ which conform to test 7. In these cases the indirect comparison cannot, of course, give any better result than the direct comparison, while in all other cases the direct comparison is better.

It seems, therefore, advisable to compare each year with the next, or, in other words, to make each year the base year for the next. Such a procedure has been recommended by Marshall, Edgeworth, and Flux.[2] It largely meets the diffi-

[1] That this test is the most difficult one to meet is shown by the fact that the total "score" as given in the last column opposite test 7 is the lowest in that column, being only 12 out of a possible 44; the next most difficult test to meet is test 5 (or 6), opposite which the total "score" is 13½.

The easiest test to meet is test 8, opposite which the total is 40 out of 44; the next easiest is test 3 (and 4) with 31 out of 44.

[2] "Modes of constructing Index Numbers," *Quarterly Journal of Economics*, August, 1907, pp. 613–631.

culty of non-uniform changes in the Q's, for any inequalities for successive years are relatively small.

Such *successive* index numbers, each on the basis of 100 per cent for the previous year, will, if multiplied together, give a *chain* of index numbers showing the fluctuations from year to year, like any ordinary series, but much more suitable for comparison of neighboring years.

Let us now reëxamine the comparative merits of index numbers on the supposition that they are to be used only for successive years, that is, for comparison between each year and the previous year as a base. In this case we do not need to distinguish between a "partial" and a "complete" fulfillment of the tests. We may therefore now substitute "1" for every "½." Omitting, as before, all formulæ which fail to meet test 2, we have the following results: —

FORMULA	SCORE	FORMULA	SCORE
2	4	20	5
4	3	21	7
6	3	22	6
8	4	24	5
10	4½	26	4
11	6	28	4
12	6	30	3
13	5	32	3
14	5	34	3
15	6	36	3
16	6	38	3
17	7	40	3
18	6	42	3
19	6		

We note that formulæ 11 and 12 have scores of 6 each, while their average 15 (and 16) and their mixture 18 and also 22 have the same score, but that formulæ 17 and 21, which are mixtures of 11 and 12, have perfect scores, 7. Each of these two formulæ uses as weights the average of the weights used in formulæ 11 and 12. Theoretically, therefore, we find two formulæ which fit all tests perfectly so far as year-to-year comparisons of prices are concerned.

Where, therefore, great accuracy is desired and there exist abundant funds to provide for the laborious computations necessary, we may recommend the use of formula 17 or 21. This presupposes that statistics are available for the Q's, which is not usually the case.

Thus far our conclusions therefore are (1) that theoretically formula 11 is the best when each year is expressed in terms of a common base; (2) that (also theoretically) formulæ 17 and 21 are slightly superior when each year is expressed in terms of the preceding year as base, and that these two meet *all* tests for year-to-year comparisons.

§ 8. *Reasons for preferring the Median for Practical Purposes*

Practically, however, there is little if any advantage in 17 and 21 over 11 (or 12, which in the case of year-to-year comparisons amounts to the same thing) because (1) weighting is of little importance; (2) the more perfect weighting contained in formulæ 17 and 21 will seldom differ materially from that of 11 and 12, for any gain of precision would probably be less than the errors in measurement of the Q's, which are never exactly known; (3) the systems of 17 and 21 are practically far more laborious. In the end we must be guided largely by practical considerations except where the great labor and expense of computation may be disregarded. If in a *practical* spirit we examine the merits of the various formulæ, we shall, I believe, reject all formulæ except 9 and 11, and come to the conclusion that the best index number is the *weighted median.* It has no rival in ease of computation. The score of the median in the table (formula 9) is high, although it fails in test 2. Excepting this test it meets, partially or wholly, every other test. It therefore possesses some merit even on the theoretical side.

In passing, we may mention a feature of medians, although I am disposed to regard it as a fault. Edgeworth emphasized the fact that price *dispersion upward* always or usually exceeds the price *dispersion downward.* There is no limit to the former, but the latter is limited by zero. Statistical tests show clearly this asymmetry of dispersion.[1] From this fact it has been argued that the best average should be one from which large deviations above it count no more than small deviations below it. This condition, whether good or ill, is not met by arithmetical averages, but is met by the geometric average and by the median[2] which, in fact, usually closely follows the geometric average. Edgeworth also argues that the median is superior when the variabilities of the various elements averaged are widely different.[3]

Edgeworth concludes that "in the present state of our knowledge, and for the purposes on hand, the median is the proper formula."[4]

As to methods of weighting, theoretical discussion with reference to test 2 shows that the weighting should be made on the basis of values sold in one or the other of the years compared.

It is easy to show that a system of weighting the median by given weights, that is, by counting each price ratio, not only

[1] See Edgeworth, "First Report on Monetary Standard," *Report of the British Association for the Advancement of Science*, 1887, pp. 284–855.

[2] Edgeworth, *ibid.*, pp. 284–286. From the standpoint, however, of the relation of prices to the currency, a large upward variation should count more than a small downward variation; for it requires more currency. In fact, as we have already seen, the arithmetical average complained of is precisely the average needed to fit into the equation of exchange. See § 6 of Appendix to Chapter II and § 7 of this Appendix. As to the asymmetry of price dispersion, see Mitchell, *Gold, Prices, and Wages under the Greenback Standard*, Berkeley (University of California Press), 1908, and reviews of same by Edgeworth, *Journal of the Royal Economic Society*, December, 1908, pp. 578–582; and H. G. Brown, *Yale Review*, May, 1909, pp. 99–101.

[3] Edgeworth, Report, etc., 1887, p. 291, and "On the Choice of Means," *Philosophical Magazine*, September, 1887; see also *Report of the British Association for the Advancement of Science*, 1889, pp. 156–161, and *Journal of the Royal Statistical Society*, June, 1888.

[4] *Ibid.*, p. 191.

once but a certain number of times (that number being the weight) will not affect the relative fulfillments of the tests as met by the simple median 9, which is the only median in the table. Edgeworth has shown that for all practical purposes a very rough system of weighting will suffice.[1] Whether the weighting be according to the values p_0Q_0, etc., or p_1Q_1, etc., or p_0Q_1, etc., or p_1Q_0, etc., is usually of no practical importance whatever. If, then, we subordinate theoretical to practical considerations, the proper procedure would seem to be to select certain constants consisting of simple integers, and as near as may be to the values dealt with in the years considered. These weights need not be changed every year, but should be changed when the values (p_1Q_1) change very greatly.

If it be desired to have a quantity or trade-index number (Q_1, or T_1) as well as a price-index number (P_1), we may likewise select as the form for Q_1 the median. In other words, the indexes for p's and Q's are best selected independently of each other. It is true we thereby abandon any absolute mutual consistency between the two, but we are now speaking of practical, not theoretical, considerations.

One of the great practical advantages of the median is its use in conjunction with "quartiles" or "deciles" to portray *dispersion* as well as averages. This method of showing dispersion about a mean is both easier to calculate, and capable of more detail, if detail be desired, than the method of Karl Pearson of the "Standard Deviation" about an arithmetical mean.

The final *practical* conclusion, therefore, is that the weighted median serves the purposes of a practical barometer of prices, and also of quantities as well as, if not better than, formulæ theoretically superior.

In spite, however, of the peculiar simplicity and ease of

[1] See *Report of the British Association for the Advancement of Science*, 1888, pp. 208–211. Edgeworth compares various means for 21 articles in 1885 and 1873, one being that recommended by the committee of which he was a member, and above referred to in the text of Chapter X, § 4.

computation which characterizes the median, and in spite of Edgeworth's strong indorsement, it remains still almost totally unused, if not unknown. Wesley C. Mitchell[1] has used the median for price indexes more extensively than any one else. Professor Davis R. Dewey has used them for wages in his special Census report on that subject.

§ 9. *Summary*

The conclusions of this Appendix may be briefly stated as follows: —

1. Any sum of products of two factors each, such as ΣpQ, may be converted into any one of three forms: (1) PT, in which P is an average of the ratios of the p's to some base p_0's, and T is the quotient $\frac{\Sigma pQ}{P}$; (2) $A\mathsf{Q}$, in which Q is an average of the ratios of the Q's to some base Q_0's, and A is the quotient $\frac{\Sigma pQ}{\mathsf{Q}}$; (3) $P\mathsf{Q}\Sigma p_0Q_0$.

2. Of the foregoing three formulæ only the last is symmetrical in the sense that the p's and Q's are treated alike.

3. P and T (or P and Q) are said to be *correlative*, and any particular formula for either implies a particular correlative formula for the other.

4. Two correlative formulæ for P and Q are, in general, quite unlike each other. If like formulæ be constructed for P and Q, the correlate of Q constitutes a new formula for P,

[1] *Gold, Prices, and Wages under the Greenback Standard*, Publications of the University of California. Mitchell's use of deciles, however, is of small value, as he employs a common base, 1860, so that his figures for each subsequent year give the dispersion of that year *relatively to* 1860. There is practically no use in knowing the dispersion of prices in 1909 or 1910 as compared with 1860, and this knowledge throws no light on whether prices change uniformly or disperse widely from 1909 to 1910. What is needed is a knowledge of price dispersion from year to year, and this can readily be indicated by drawing three radiating lines from 1909 to 1910, the central one to show the movement of the median, and the other two to show the movements of the two neighboring quartiles.

said to be antithetical to the original formula for P, and *vice versa.*

5. There are an indefinite number of formulæ for P, of which 44 are given in the table; and there are at least 8 important tests to which each formula may conform in one of three degrees (1) *wholly*, or for the ratio of P_1 to P_2, each being relative to a third year as a base; (2) *partially*, or for the ratio P_1 to unity; and (3) *not at all.*

6. The eight tests are of *proportionality* as to prices or quantities (1 and 2); *determinateness* as to prices or quantities (3 and 4); *withdrawal or entry* as to prices and quantities (5 and 6); changing base as to prices and quantities (7); and changing units as to prices and quantities (8).

7. The tests arrange themselves in pairs, one of each pair relating to the p's in the same manner as the other is related to the Q's; but each test has significance both with respect to the p's and the Q's.

8. The formulæ arrange themselves in antithetical pairs.

9. Of any four neighboring compartments in the table, relating to two correlative rows (tests) and two antithetical columns (formulæ), the diagonals will have the same "scores."

10. No known form of index number P conforms perfectly to all the eight tests when a common base year is employed, but several conform well, the best being formula No. 11, $\frac{\Sigma p_1 Q_1}{\Sigma p_0 Q_1}$.

11. But if we are content with year-to-year comparisons, renouncing comparisons in terms of a third year, there are two formulæ which conform perfectly, viz. formulæ 17 and 21.

12. Practically, however, formula 11 is superior to 17 or 21, and formula 7 (median) — when properly "weighted" — is superior to 11.

13. For practical purposes, therefore, unless the expense and labor of computation can be disregarded, the median (with its two neighboring quartiles) is recommended, with a simple system of weights (whole numbers) based on expenditures, and changing from time to time for the sake of making better year-to-year comparisons.

APPENDIX TO CHAPTER XII

§ 1 (TO CHAPTER XII, § 1)

Professor Kemmerer's Calculations

Professor Kemmerer (*Money and Prices*, p. 99) estimates the money in circulation (*M*) by deducting from the money in the United States, as estimated by the Comptroller of the Currency, two items, viz. the money in the United States treasury and that in banks (reported and estimated). He then estimates the velocity of circulation of money as 47 times a year, and assumes, in the absence of any data by which to estimate its variations, that it remains constant. He arrives at the figure 47 as follows: The amount of check transactions he first estimates for 1896, at 143 billions (p. 111). This estimate is based on figures taken from Kinley's investigation, made through the Comptroller of the Currency in 1896. Referring to Kinley's estimate that check transactions are *at least* three times money transactions, he takes one third of 143 billions, or 47.7 billions, as the amount of money transactions. Estimating the amount of money in circulation at 1.025 billions for 1896, he divides 47.7 by 1.025 and obtains (p. 114) 47 times a year as the velocity of circulation of money. This figure, as we shall see, is probably nearly three times too large, the error arising from the fact that Professor Kemmerer does not accept the opinion expressed by Professor Kinley that his (Kinley's) estimate for the percentage of check circulation in 1896 was a "safe minimum," but expressed the contrary opinion that it was rather a safe maximum. We shall give reasons for believing that Kinley was quite right in concluding that the estimate of check transactions at three fourths of total transactions was a "safe minimum." The calculations which we shall presently offer prove nine tenths rather than three fourths to be the probable figure.

Professor Kemmerer, as already indicated, estimates check

transactions (what we have called $M'V'$) at 143 billions in 1896. For other years than 1896, there being no corresponding data, he estimates check transactions by assuming that bank clearings are always 35 per cent thereof (p. 118). He makes no attempt to estimate M' (bank deposits) and V' (their velocity) separately. The volume of trade (T) Professor Kemmerer estimates *relatively* (*i.e.* he estimates what we have called Q in the Appendix to Chapter X). This is confessedly one of the roughest parts of all his estimates. He seeks to get as many indicators as possible of the growth of trade (p. 130), without much regard to their suitability. His indicators are fifteen in number, viz. population, foreign tonnage entered and cleared, exports and imports of merchandise (values), revenues of Post Office Department, gross earnings from operation of railroads in the United States, freight carried by railroads, receipts of Western Union Telegraph Company, consumption of pig iron, bituminous coal, wheat, corn, cotton, wool, wines and liquors, and market value of reported sales on New York Stock Exchange. Representing each of these sets of figures by index numbers, he takes their simple average as the index number of trade for each year in question.

Of course, as Professor Kemmerer well realized, many of these figures are open to more or less serious objections. Population is a poor index of trade when trade per capita is changing. Values are inappropriate unless the prices are supposed constant, which cannot be the case for exports and imports, railroad earnings, or stocks, and can be only partially the case for post office revenues and telegraph receipts.

Having thus computed for 1879–1908 the various elements theoretically determining price levels (viz. $MV+M'V'$ and T), Professor Kemmerer uses these to calculate an index number of prices. The index number thus calculated from the other magnitudes in the equation of exchange, he calls the "relative circulation." He then compares the figures for relative circulation (virtually from the formula $P = (MV + M'V') \div T$) with the actual statistics of price levels.

These directly calculated index numbers of prices he takes as an average of index numbers of wholesale prices (Common's figures and those of the Bureau of Labor, p. 137), wages (those of reports of Bureau of Labor, p. 137), and of the Industrial Commission), and prices of railroad stocks (Industrial Commission and Wall Street Journal), weighting them as follows: wages, 3 per cent; stocks, 8 per cent; wholesale commodities, 89 per cent.

The two sets of figures — "relative circulation" and "general prices" — presented visually by curves (p. 149), show a general agreement.

§ 2 (TO CHAPTER XII, § 2)

Method of Calculating M

The estimates for M, or money in circulation in the United States, are based on the reports of Comptroller of the Currency. The calculations are shown in the following table: —

MONEY IN THE UNITED STATES, ETC. (IN BILLIONS OF DOLLARS)

(1) YEAR	(2) MONEY IN U.S. (OFFICIAL)	(3) MONEY IN U.S. (CORRECTED ESTIMATE)	(4) MONEY IN U.S. TREASURY	(5) MONEY IN BANKS (REPORTED)	(6) UNREPORTED AS ESTIMATED PER CENT OF REPORTED MONEY IN BANKS	(7) MONEY IN BANKS (CORRECTED ESTIMATE)	(8) MONEY IN CIRCULATION EXCLUDING (4) AND (7) FROM (3)
1896 . .	1.80	1.74	.29	.53	8.4%	.58	.87
1897 . .	1.91	1.83	.27	.63	8.4%	.68	.88
1898 . .	2.07	1.94	.24	.69	7.7%	.74	.96
1899 . .	2.19	2.09	.29	.72	6.7%	.77	1.03
1900 . .	2.34	2.25	.28	.75	6.4%	.80	1.17
1901 . .	2.48	2.37	.31	.79	5.4%	.84	1.22
1902 . .	2.56	2.45	.31	.84	5.3%	.88	1.26
1903 . .	2.68	2.59	.32	.85	5.2%	.89	1.38
1904 . .	2.80	2.68	.28	.98	4.5%	1.03	1.37
1905 . .	2.88	2.77	.29	.99	3.9%	1.03	1.45
1906 . .	3.07	2.97	.33	1.01	3.4%	1.05	1.59
1907 . .	3.12	3.12	.34	1.11	4.2%	1.15	1.63
1908 . .	3.38	3.38	.34	1.36	3.8%	1.41	1.63
1909 . .	3.41	3.41	.30	1.44	2.8%	1.48	1.63

Column (2) gives the money in the United States in the middle of each calendar year according to the official estimates of the director of the mint. In 1907 these official estimates were corrected by subtracting an estimated error of $135,000,000 from the gold believed to be in the United States, this correction being made in view of the investigations of Maurice L. Muhleman. The mint corrections were made, however, only for the *ends* of calendar years.[1] In order to make the corrections apply to the *middle* of a given calendar year, the corrected figures for gold in the United States at the beginning and end of it were averaged. The average thus obtained was assumed to be the corrected figure for gold at the middle of the year. This corrected figure was then compared with the official figure for gold for the middle of the year and the difference assumed to be the correction for that date. This correction was then deducted from the figures for money in the United States given in column (2) above. We thus obtain the figures in column (3). Mr. Muhleman has made independent corrections for the middles of the years 1896–1900 inclusive. These are slightly smaller than those calculated from the mint figures as given above, the differences being in successive years, .05, .03, .00, .03, .05. Columns (4) and (5) of our table give the money in the federal treasury and the money *reported* in banks as stated in the annual reports of the Comptroller of the Currency. Column (6) gives the estimated percentage not reported. This estimate is found by assuming that the unreported reserves bear the same ratio to the reported reserves as unreported deposits bear to reported deposits, the latter ratios being calculated from the table given in the next section (§ 3) of this Appendix.

This estimated percentage being calculated and the correction found by it being added to the money in reporting banks, (column 5), we get the total estimated money in banks, (column 7). Column (8) is then found by subtracting from the corrected money in the United States (as given in column 3),

[1] See *Report of the Director of the Mint*, 1907, p. 87.

the sum of the money in treasury (column 4), and estimated money in banks (column 7). These estimates of money in nonreporting banks are of course subject to some error; but even a 50 per cent error in the largest of them would not affect the last column much more than 2 per cent. A more important possible source of error is in column (2), which depends upon hypothetical estimates of gold in the United States. Mr. Muhleman writes me that in his opinion the corrections made by the Mint Bureau are not adequate. The corrections as made by that Bureau and here adopted affect several of the figures in column (8) by as much as 10 per cent. The *errors* in these corrections would presumably be much smaller than this. There are few other sources of error and, taking all things into account, it seems likely that the results are in general trustworthy — subject to a probable error of perhaps 2 or 3 per cent. This is fair accuracy as ordinary statistics go.

§ 3 (TO CHAPTER XII, § 2)

Method of Calculating *M'*

The calculations for obtaining M', or individual deposits subject to check, are shown in the table on page 49.

The figures of column (2) are those of "Individual Deposits" taken from the annual reports of the Comptroller of the Currency (see Report for 1909, pp. 64–66). All of these figures, except that for 1909, include the deposits of savings banks and of trust companies in national banks. The change in method in 1909 was doubtless made in recognition of the fact that these deposits are not true individual deposits. They should be deducted; and this not only in order to make the statistics for other years comparable with those for 1909, but also because such deposits in one bank by other banks are not generally used for commercial purchases, but for banking operations. These deposits, to be deducted from column (2), are given in column (3).

The figures in column (3) for 1900–1909 are the figures of

the third report of national banks for each year and are taken from the Comptroller's Reports. The figures for 1896–1899, on the other hand, are estimates. These estimates are based on the fact that the deposits of savings banks and trust companies in national banks are (whenever comparison is possible, viz. 1900–1908) found to be approximately equal to the deposits of state banks in national banks. As the state bank figures are available for 1896–1899, they are taken in lieu of the missing trust and savings figures. Any error from this procedure could scarcely affect the final column more than 1 or 2 per cent.

INDIVIDUAL DEPOSITS, SUBJECT TO CHECK (in Billions of Dollars)

(1) Year	(2) Individual Deposits	(3) Deposits of Trust Companies and Savings Banks in National Banks	(4) Estimated Unreported Deposits	(5) Deposits in Savings Banks	(6) Exchanges for Clearing House	(7) (2)−(3)+(4)−(5)−(6) Corrected Individual Deposits	(8) % of (7) which are Subject to Check	(9) (7)×(8) Individual Deposits Subject to Check
1896 . . .	4.95	.16	.40	1.91	.11	3.17	85	2.68
1897 . . .	5.10	.21	.41	1.94	.11	3.25	86	2.80
1898 . . .	5.69	.25	.42	2.07	.16	3.63	88	3.19
1899 . . .	6.77	.33	.44	2.23	.27	4.38	89	3.90
1900 . . .	7.24	.23	.45	2.45	.18	4.83	87	4.20
1901 . . .	8.71	.25	.46	2.60	.36	5.96	86	5.13
1902 . . .	9.37	.27	.48	2.75	.36	6.47	84	5.43
1903 . . .	9.81	.26	.50	2.93	.25	6.87	83	5.70
1904 . . .	10.39	.39	.45	3.06	.23	7.16	81	5.80
1905 . . .	11.74	.39	.44	3.26	.36	8.17	80	6.54
1906 . . .	12.57	.35	.41	3.48	.40	8.75	78	6.84
1907 . . .	13.47	.37	.55	3.69	.33	9.63	74	7.13
1908 . . .	13.28	.50	.49	3.66	.29	9.25	71	6.57
1909 . . .	14.01	.00	.39	3.91	.38	10.11	67	6.75

After deducting the correction of column (3), our next step is to add the correction of column (4), the estimated deposits unreported.

The figures for nonreporting banks for 1900 and 1902–1909

are the official estimates of the Comptroller of the Currency. (Those for 1900 and 1902 are entered in the Comptroller's tables under the rubric "reporting capital only" instead of "nonreporting," but I am assured by the Comptroller's office that this is a distinction without a difference.) The figure for 1901 is interpolated between those of 1900 and 1902. The figure for 1896 is estimated by the aid of two assumptions. The first assumption is that the unreported deposits in that year should be larger relatively to all deposits than was the case in 1903, as the table shows that the farther back we go the larger is the percentage of missing deposits. This consideration indicates that the correction exceeds .28. The second assumption is that the correction should be less *absolutely* than in later years; because the total deposits were then much less than later; and because the official figures in column (4), viz. those for 1900 and 1902–1909 show, as we proceed backward in time, that there is a slight tendency for them to grow less in absolute amount. (The chief exception is for 1909, when the special investigation of April 28 reached an unusual degree of accuracy.) This consideration would make the correction less than .50. Therefore, between .28 and .50 we select .40 as a rough mean. The error involved is not likely to affect the final column more than 3 or 4 per cent. The corrections for 1897–1899 are interpolated.

Column (5) gives a correction to be subtracted, viz. the deposits in savings banks. These deposits, by the nature of the case, are not used as a circulating medium, but are nevertheless included in the official "individual deposits" of column (2). The item for 1909 as here given includes, besides the reported figures, an additional item of .20 (*i.e.* $200,000,000), being the savings accounts of the state banks of Illinois. The inclusion of this Illinois item is simply in order to make the figures for 1909 comparable with those of the preceding years in which the same item had always been included (see Comptroller's Report, 1909, pp. 43–44).

Column (6) contains another, though small, subtractive

correction, viz. the "exchanges for clearing house." In general, these exchanges represent checks which have been deposited by the persons receiving them but which have not yet reached the home bank and been charged against the persons who drew them. Any one (except a sharper or a blunderer) will, as soon as he has drawn a check, deduct the amount of it (say $100) from his deposit balance and refrain from drawing against it again. Such a person — say Smith — regards the $100 as transferred to his drawee — say Jones — and no more Smith's than money would be which he had paid out. But it takes time before the bank on which Smith draws knows of this transfer of Smith's deposits to Jones. In the meantime the bank books still include this $100 among Smith's deposits. The total figure for deposits is not disturbed by the inclusion of the $100 in Smith's account provided it is not included in Jones's account also. But when Jones deposits the check in his bank, this (Jones's) bank adds $100 to Jones's account *before Smith's bank can deduct it from Smith's account.* That is, the $100 is temporarily counted as both Smith's and Jones's. If both sides of this transfer were recorded at the same time, there would be no double counting. But until the check reaches Smith's bank the only record of the deduction which should be made from Smith's account is in the "exchanges for clearing house" which, accordingly, we must deduct in our statistics.

These figures, however, have to be estimated. Only for April 28, 1909, are they given for *all* banks, the figures being those of the special Report of the Monetary Commission already referred to. Of this amount, four fifths are of national banks; and as national banks report annually their exchanges against clearing houses, we assume that the total each year is five fourths of that reported by the national banks (see Comptroller's Report, 1908, pp. 514–522). The whole correction is so small that any error in this assumed ratio is quite negligible in the final result.

Column (7) is derived by applying to column (2) the above mentioned corrections, — deduction of items in column (3), addition of those of column (4), deduction of column (5), and deduction of column (6).

But even yet we have not reached the desired item,—deposit currency, or deposits subject to check. The net individual deposits which we have estimated include, not only current accounts, but deposits on certificate and other deposits which are considered investments rather than media of exchange. The first published attempt to give the true *deposits subject to check* is that of the National Monetary Commission. In their valuable special Report as of April 28, 1909, constructed through the Comptroller of the Currency, the checkable deposits are given as 6.94 billions.[1] This 6.94 is subject to an addition for "nonreporting banks" and a deduction for "exchange against clearing house." The unreported deposits of all kinds are estimated for 1909 in the table at .39, of which, by proportion, only $\frac{6.94}{14.01}$ of .39 or .19, is probably checkable. The .38 exchanges against clearing houses must be assumed to be almost wholly against deposits subject to check. The *net* corrected figure is therefore 6.94 + .19 − .38 or 6.75 billions as the checkable deposits in 1909. These constitute about 67 per cent of the "net individual deposits" of column (7).

This figure for checkable deposits in 1909 is found at the bottom of column (9) in the table. As it is only 67 per cent of the net individual deposits, and as it could not be assumed that the same ratio obtained for other years, I was unwilling to guess at the deposits subject to check for these other years without further light. Accordingly I wrote to Mr. A. Piatt Andrew, then Director of the Mint, and asked him whether, in his capacity as advisor to the Monetary Commission, he could not have a search made among the Comptroller's records for 1896 and a few other years in order to obtain the

[1] See Senate Document, 225, 61st Congress, 2d Session, *Special Report from Banks of the United States*, April 28, 1909, p. 261; also *Report of Comptroller of the Currency*, 1909, p. 835. The figures are exclusive of Hawaii, Porto Rico, and the Philippines, although the sum thus excluded is scarcely appreciable.

corresponding ratio for such years. Through his kindness and that of the Commission and Comptroller, in acceding to my request, it has been made possible to work out the corresponding ratio for 1896 as 85 per cent; for 1899 as 89 per cent; and for 1906 as 78 per cent.

Mr. Andrew gives 4.97 billions as the total (uncorrected) deposits of all banks as of July 14, 1896. This figure is slightly more complete than what I had already used from the Comptroller's Report (viz. 4.95), doubtless because, for this particular inquiry, a larger number of banks were included than had originally been used in the Comptroller's tables. Mr. Andrew gives the checkable deposits as 2.59 billions. This figure is subject to two corrections: one to account for unreporting banks, and one to account for exchanges for clearing house. We have estimated the deposits of nonreporting banks at .40; and, since Mr. Andrew has discovered in such banks .02 more *total* deposits (4.97) than the Comptroller reported, we must assume that there are .02 less unreported deposits in his figures than in the Comptroller's. This would make the estimated unreported deposits for Andrew's figures .38 instead of .40 which we assumed for the Comptroller's. The part of this ascribable to the deposits subject to check (2.59) is $\frac{2.59}{4.97} \times .38$ or .20. This is the first (and additive) correction. The second (and subtractive) correction is the exchanges for clearing house, viz. .11. The final corrected figure is therefore $2.59 + .20 - .11$ or 2.68. The ratio of this to the "net deposits" is $\frac{2.68}{3.17}$ or 85 per cent.

For 1899, Andrew's figures for total net deposits are 4.38 and for checkable deposits 4.09. His figures for total deposits (7.07) are .30 completer than those of the Comptroller employed in the first column of the above table, and thus reduce the estimate for nonreporting banks applicable to Andrew's figures from .44 to .14, of which $\frac{4.09}{7.07} \times .14$ or .08 are ascribable to the deposits subject to check. The correction consisting of exchanges for clearing house is .27. The figures for checkable deposits are therefore 4.09 + .08 − .27 or 3.90, which is 89 per cent of the "net deposits" (4.38).

For 1906 Andrew's figures for total net deposits are 8.75 and for checkable deposits, 6.90. His figures for total deposits (12.37) are less complete than those of the Comptroller, thus increasing the estimate for unreporting banks applicable to his figures from .41 to .61, of which $\frac{6.90}{12.37} \times .61$ or .34 are ascribable to the deposits subject to check. The exchanges for clearing house were .40. The figures for checkable deposits are therefore 6.90 + .34 − .40 or 6.84, which is 78 per cent of the "net deposits" 8.75) We thus have figures for column (9) and column (8) for the years 1896, 1899, 1906, 1909.

If now, for intervening years, we interpolate evenly between these percentage figures for the years 1896, 1899, 1906, 1909, we shall have column (8) of the preceding table.

Column (9) may next be formed for the remaining years by applying the percentages in column (8) to the net individual deposits in column (7). Thus the table is made complete.

The results are of course subject to a probable error which, however, is believed to be only some 2 or 3 per cent for the years 1896, 1899, 1906, 1909, and perhaps double as much for years midway in the intervals between these four years.

It seems strange, since so much has been said of the relative importance of check and money circulation, that no attempt has previously been made to estimate or record the volume of the currency which circulates by check. This currency and its circulation are of many times the statistical importance of money and its circulation. Our wonder is the greater when we consider that "deposits subject to check" have been regularly reported by individual banks to the Comptroller of the Currency. The published figures began in the '60's to omit this category and lump all "individual deposits" together, and subsequent reports have simply followed the precedent thus established. The present Comptroller states that he intends, hereafter, to separate the item of deposits subject to check; so that we may hope from now on to have annual returns of the checkable deposits. We shall then know each year the magnitude of that item in our circulatory medium which, as we shall see, does nine tenths of the exchange work of the country.

§ 4 (TO CHAPTER XII, § 3)

Method of Calculating $M'V'$ for 1896 and 1909

According to the Comptroller's Report for 1896, the total sum (money and checks) deposited in all reporting banks on the settling day nearest July 1, 1896, was 303 millions. Professor Kemmerer's allowance for nonreporting banks (*op. cit.*, pp. 110–111) brings the figures up to 506 millions. The proportion of checks found in all deposits reported was 92.5 per cent, which, if applied to the estimated 506 millions of total deposits, will give 468 millions as the total checks deposited in one day. But July 1, being a first day of the month, would show exceptionally large deposits. In order to determine how much allowance to make for this fact, I have obtained, through the kindness of Mr. Gilpin of the New York clearing house, the figures for the New York clearings of July 2, 1896. July 2 was selected because the checks deposited in New York July 1 would appear in the clearing house statistics of July 2. The clearings for July 2 amounted to 157 millions, while the daily average for 1896 was only 95 millions or 60 per cent as much. Thus, the excessive clearings of July 2 have to be corrected by multiplying by .60 in order to reach a true average for the year. It is perhaps fair to assume that the deposits made on July 1 *in New York* require substantially the same correction. If we could assume that the abnormality of the day's deposits in the rest of the country were exactly like that of New York, requiring the same correction factor (.60), then this correction factor would apply to the whole country. But this assumption we cannot make. Doubtless .60 is too small an estimate of the true multiplier for the whole country outside of New York. The departure from the average was probably somewhat less than in New York City.

That this is the case appears likely for various reasons. In the first place New York is more sensitive to the variations in business activity than the country generally. Consistently with this view, we find that the percentage fluctuation in clearings from year to year is much greater in New York than in the rest of the country. By comparing each year with the next, we find this to be true of all except five of the twenty-seven years from 1883 to 1909 [1] inclusive.

Again, the quarterly and semiannual dividends would cut a larger figure in a financial center like New York than in other places, in many of which few or no dividends are received.

Finally, in large cities like New York, checks are deposited more systematically and promptly, so that a fuller proportion of the first-of-the-month checks received on July 1 would be deposited on that day than in a smaller community. In the smaller community these checks straggle along to banks through several days after being received, thus tending to even up the daily flow and in particular to diminish the excess on and about July 1. We conclude that .60 is a *minimum* estimate for our multiplier for 1896.

Having obtained .60 as a minimum estimate, we next proceed to ascertain a maximum estimate. We may be reasonably sure that deposits outside of New York are so far subject to the influence of quarterly dividends, first-of-the-month payments, etc., that the volume of checks deposited outside of New York must to *some* extent exceed the average in 1896. We need to know to *what* extent we are safe in assuming that this outside volume of checks deposited on the day chosen exceeded the average. We can best reach such a

[1] See *Financial Review* (the Annual of the *Commercial and Financial Chronicle*), 1906, p. 26 and 1910, p. 33.

safe estimate by means of some data on clearing houses in the Finance Report for 1896 (p. 493, Comptroller's Report). It is there shown that on July 1, or "the settling day nearest July 1," 66 out of the 78 clearing houses of the country had $228,000,000 of clearings. We are safe in assuming that the country's total clearings on that day were larger than this, because the returns as given include only 66 out of the 78 clearing houses of the country; and that on the following day they were larger still,[1] because it was then that occurred the bulk of the heavy July 1 deposits of checks. If the $228,000,000 clearings on July 1, 1896, were representative for each day of 1896, we could, simply by multiplying by the number of settling days of 1896, 305 days, find the total clearings of the country. But the result of this multiplication is 67.1 billions, whereas the actual clearings of the country for 1896 were only 51.2 billions. This is conclusive evidence that the clearings on July 1, and presumably still more those of July 2, exceeded the daily average and need to be reduced *at least* in the ratio $\frac{51.2}{67.1}$ or .76.

Hence the true correction factor must lie between .60 and .76. Splitting the difference we have .68 as an estimate which cannot be far from the correct figures on either side; especially as .60 and .76 are so very safe or extreme limits. Figures very near either of them are improbable. The *probable* error is simply set at 5 or 6 per cent.

We turn now to similar calculations for 1909. At my request Professor Weston of the University of Illinois, through the kindness of Professor Kinley, has used substantially the same method for estimating the check circula-

[1] Convincing proof that the clearings on July 2 exceeded those on July 1 is afforded by the fact that whereas the New York state clearings for July 1, 1896, were $140,000,000, as given in the Comptroller's Report for 1896 (p. 494), the New York *City* clearings alone on July 2 were $157,000,000.

For New York City the clearings, as Mr. Gilpin of the New York clearing house has informed me, were far larger on July 2, 1896, than on July 1, the two figures being 157 and 138 millions respectively.

tion of 1909 based on Kinley's investigation [1] of that year for March 16. Professor Weston estimates the total check deposits of March 16, 1909, at 1.02 billions. This is below the daily average. A proof of this is found in the clearings of the New York clearing house on March 17, which reflect the deposits made in New York banks on the previous day; these were 268 millions, which was not representative of the year, as the average daily clearings were much greater, being 342 millions, or 28 per cent greater than those of March 17. 1.28 is therefore the correction multiplier we would apply if we could trust New York clearings to be a faithful barometer for the whole country. But since, as we have seen, New York is especially sensitive to speculative and other variations in banking operations, and as a part is usually more variable than the whole, it is reasonable to assume that the abnormality we find in New York of the deposits on March 16 exaggerates the abnormality of that day for the country at large, and that the correction multiplier should be less than 1.28. In order to set a safe lower limit, we may see what figure would result from the extreme assumption that outside of New York the day's deposits on March 16, 1909, were exactly the same as the daily average for the year. We can make a fairly good estimate of the resulting correction factor from the table on page 59.

This table is constructed from data taken from Kinley's report to the Monetary Commission on Credit Instruments (pp. 182, 186) together with the estimated corrections for the whole country's check deposits made by Professor Weston.

The figure for deposits in New York City is given for March 16, 1909. Deducting these figures from those estimated by Weston for the entire country, we have the deposits (786) outside New York. But the daily average in New York has been shown to be probably 28 per cent higher, or 306. These figures, added to those for deposits outside New York (786),

[1] Kinley, *The Use of Credit Instruments in Payments in the United States*, National Monetary Commission, 61st Congress, 2d Session, Doc. No. 399, 1910.

give the daily average for the entire country, on the assumption that only New York City was abnormal on the day selected. The result (1092), compared with the actual deposits on the day selected (1025), shows the correction factor on the assumption that only New York was abnormal. This factor is 1.07. This furnishes a lower limit for the correction factor we are seeking.

CHECKS DEPOSITED (IN MILLIONS)

(1)	(2) NEW YORK CITY	(3) OUTSIDE NEW YORK CITY	(4) TOTAL U.S.
March 16, 1909	239	786	1025
Daily average if New York were alone abnormal	306	786	1092
Ratio average to actual $= \frac{1092}{1025} = 1.07$			

Splitting the difference between our extreme limits, 1.07 and 1.28, we get, as our estimate of the correction factors, 1.17 in 1909 as compared with .68 for 1896. The range of *possible* error on either side is about 10 for 1909 and 8 for 1896. As the limits are all very extreme, the *probable* error must be much less — perhaps half as much. We may judge that the correction factors, .68 and 1.17, are probably correct within 5 or 6 per cent.

We conclude, then, that the 468 millions estimated as the *actual* check deposits made on July 1, 1896, must be multiplied by .68 in order to obtain the estimated *average* daily deposits in 1896. The result is 318 millions; which, multiplied by the 305 (settling days), gives 97.0 billions as our estimate for the check transactions in the United States for the year 1896.

Likewise, multiplying the estimated volume of *actual* check transactions in the United States on March 16, 1909 (viz. 1025 millions), by the correction factor, 1.17, we obtain

1.20 billions as the estimated daily *average* check deposits and transactions. Multiplying this by 303 (the number of clearing days of the New York clearing house and presumably the average number of banking days in the country), we obtain 364 billions as our estimate of the check transactions in the United States in 1909.

§ 5 (TO CHAPTER XII, § 3)

Method of Calculating $M'V'$ for 1897–1908

Although New York clearings constitute two thirds of all clearings for the country, it cannot be imagined that the check transactions in and about New York form two thirds of the check transactions of the United States. We have already seen that the reported check deposits in New York on March 16, 1909, amounted to 239 millions. This figure, being for New York, is probably nearly complete and indicates, as we have seen, an estimated average for the daily deposits in New York City in 1909 of 306 millions. This gives 306 × 303 or 93 billions for New York City, for the entire year. Our estimate for the entire country was 364 billions, leaving 271 billions outside of New York City. Let us compare these estimated figures for checks deposited with the figures for clearings. The New York clearings in 1909 amounted to 104 billions and those outside New York, to 62 billions.

The New York clearings (104) thus exceed the New York check deposits (93), probably because the clearings on account of outside banks include clearings representing banking transactions as distinguished from commercial transactions, since New York City is the chief central reserve city. The New York City deposits were thus only $\frac{93}{104}$ or about 90 per cent of the New York clearings. Outside of New York, on the other hand, the deposits far exceeded the clearings, being in the ratio $\frac{271}{62}$ or 4.4. These ratios between check transactions and clearings, viz. .90 for New York and 4.4 for "outside," would indicate that the published figures for clearings should be weighted in the ratio of 4.4 to .9 or about 5 to 1. That is, on the basis of 1909 figures, five times the outside clearings plus once the New York clearings should be a good barometer of check transactions.

Of 1896, unfortunately, we lack the figures for New York City deposits. We have, however, figures for the deposits in New York state in both 1896 and 1909; and a study of these figures indicates that the ratio of weighting for 1896 should be something over 3 to 1. Not to put too fine a point upon it, we shall use the weighting 5 to 1 for all the years. The difference in the results between this system of 5 to 1 and a system of 3 to 1, or any intermediate system, will be small. but 5 to 1 is chosen because (1) the data for 1896 on which the number 3 is based are less certain than those for 1909, and (2) the New York clearings are not as good a representative of New York deposits as the outside clearings are of outside deposits; the New York clearings being somewhat vitiated by an element extraneous to New York and especially by the banking transactions connected with adjustments of bank reserves. We prefer, therefore, to give as much weight as possible to the "outside" clearings.

Having obtained our "barometer" of check transactions, viz. New York clearings plus five times outside clearings, we merely need to multiply this by the proper ratio in order to obtain the check transactions themselves. Absolute knowledge of this ratio of check transactions to the barometer exists only for 1896 and 1909, in which years we know the check transactions as well as the barometer. These ratios are .69 and .88. But we cannot err greatly in assuming that the intermediate years have intermediate ratios, varying regularly each year. The result is the following table: —

CLEARINGS AS BAROMETER OF CHECK TRANSACTIONS

(1) Year	(2) New York Clearings	(3) Outside Clearings	(4) Barometer (2) + 5 × (3)	(5) Ratio of Check Transaction to Barometer	(6) M'V' Check Transactions (4) × (5)	(7) V' Velocity of Circu. of Deposits (V') (6) ÷ M'
1896 .	28.9	22.4	140.9	.69	97	36.2
1897 .	33.4	23.8	152.4	.70	106	37.9
1898 .	42.0	26.9	176.5	.72	127	39.8
1899 .	60.8	33.3	227.3	.73	166	42.6
1900 .	52.6	33.4	219.6	.75	165	39.3
1901 .	79.4	39.0	274.4	.76	208	40.6
1902 .	76.3	41.7	284.8	.78	222	40.9
1903 .	66.0	43.2	282.0	.79	223	39.1
1904 .	68.6	43.9	288.1	.81	233	40.2
1905 .	93.8	50.0	343.8	.82	282	43.1
1906 .	104.7	55.2	380.7	.84	320	46.8
1907 .	87.2	57.8	376.2	.85	320	44.9
1908 .	79.3	53.1	344.8	.87	300	45.7
1909 .	103.6	62.0	413.6	.88	364	53.9

As already indicated, only the first and last figures in column (5) are independently calculated, the rest being interpolated.

The other figures in the table explain themselves. The last column gives the very important magnitude which we have called the velocity of circulation of bank deposits subject to check, or the "activity" of checkable accounts. The probable errors of the last column are believed to range between about 5 and 10 per cent.

§ 6 (TO CHAPTER XII, § 4)

General Practical Formula for Calculating *V*

I. *An Approximate Formula*

For the purpose of tracing the circulation of money, and measuring it by bank records, we may classify the persons who use money in purchase of goods into three groups: —

1. Commercial depositors, *i.e.* all engaged in business — firms, companies, and others — who have bank deposits mainly or wholly apart from personal accounts.

2. All other depositors, chiefly private persons.

3. All who, like most wage earners, are not depositors at all.

These three classes we shall distinguish as "Commercial depositors," "Other depositors," and "Nondepositors," or *C*, *O*, and *N*. The money in the possession of "Commercial depositors" we shall call "till money," and the rest "pocket money."

The three groups necessarily include all in the community who circulate money. By circulating money is meant expending it in exchange, not for some other circulating medium, as checks, but for goods.

The nature of these three groups of people must now occupy our attention. In countries advanced in the art of banking, "Commercial depositors" include practically all business establishments, and little else; "Other depositors" include most persons in the professional and salaried classes and proprietors, and little else; while the class of "Nondepositors" is almost coterminous with wage earners.

It is true that these characterizations of the three classes are not quite complete. "Commercial depositors," for instance, do not include some small business dealers, like street vendors, for these usually have no bank accounts. But the number of such is comparatively small in comparison with the number of business men or corporations who do have accounts, and, what is more to the point, the business they do is still smaller. It follows that the money they handle is negligible. In the United States, at least, excepting those rural parts of the South and a few other places where the money expenditures are very small, the custom of having bank accounts is practically universal among business men, firms, and corporations.

To keep a bank account is, in fact, a practical necessity of business. Without such an account a business man practically deprives himself of three of the most essential aids in modern business: the use of circulating credit; the use of remittance by mail; and the use of time credit.

Unless a dealer is obliged to pay "spot cash" or prefers to do so — and such cases are both few in number and insignificant in the amounts of money involved — he will almost invariably find it easier to make payment by check. Moreover, the very fact that most other business men use banking facilities creates in his mind the desire to have an account himself, both because he dislikes to appear "different," and because, when others pay him by checks, he finds it necessary to cash these checks, — a procedure which is always more trouble than to deposit them.

Cash payments are especially inconvenient when business is done at a distance. Remitting money by post, express, or personal delivery is troublesome, risky, and expensive as compared with posting a letter containing a check. Even a post-office money order is a clumsy and expensive substitute, and its use proclaims the user an insignificant financial factor.

Again, a business man without a bank account cannot usually obtain time credit, either from dealers or from banks. In the United States a bank likes to lend only to its own depositors. A business man who asks for a bank loan usually meets with the request to open an account. If he should seek a loan from another dealer, as for instance, his supply house, the absence of a bank account would arouse suspicions as to his business standing, and might lead to a refusal.

These facts, confirmed by observation and inquiry, have led to the belief that practically all business transactions in the United States, certainly over 99 per cent (measured, not by their number, but by their aggregate size), make some use of bank accounts. Even in localities where there are no banks, traders usually like to have a bank account in the nearest town, in order to facilitate their dealings as purchasers. We conclude, therefore, that the category of "Commercial depositors" coincides for all practical purposes with the category of business establishments.

"Other depositors" include most proprietors, professional, and salaried persons. Almost no wage earners are included, and almost no business establishments or business men in a business capacity. When a single individual conducts a business, he usually separates carefully his business self from his personal self. John Smith, the individual, and the John Smith Shop are distinct. The pocket money of the one and the till money of the other are not often confused. Where payments of money are made from one to the other, the transaction is regarded as of the same nature as the payments between the shop and any other person. Originally, and under primitive conditions, it is of course true that no such distinction was observed, and even to-day the differentiation is sometimes unmarked, *e.g.* in the case of hucksters, peddlers, fruit-stand dealers, and small country shopkeepers. But, as we have seen, these persons are not usually depositors anyway. Moreover, their number is small; and since by the nature of the case the money they handle is also small, their classification is, for practical purposes, a matter of indifference. It is true that occasional cases exist of ordinary business men who have the exclusive ownership of a business and do not take care to separate clearly their business and their personal accounts. Yet we may, in such cases, perform the separation in thought. When such a person withdraws money from his till and puts it in his pocket, we may say his business self has paid his personal self some dividends of the business. Likewise, his checks drawn are usually distinguishable as between his business or his personal expenses, even though he himself fails to keep two separate bank accounts. But such cases are rare and unimportant, because modern business of size is usually conducted by partnerships and corporations, where a strict separation of accounts is necessary to safeguard conflicting interests.

So much for the line of demarcation between "Other depositors" and "Commercial depositors." As to the line separating "Other depositors" and "Nondepositors," it should be observed that, although "Other depositors" include most proprietors and professional and salaried persons, yet some proprietors and professional men, especially in rural communities, and some salaried persons, chiefly small clerks, are "Nondepositors."

Finally, "Nondepositors" consist chiefly of those who are classed in statistics as wage earners. While there are some wage earners who are depositors,[1] they are rare; and while there are some "Nondepositors" who are not wage earners, especially (as just indicated) the agricultural proprietors (farmers) and small clerks, the amount of money circulated by them is small in comparison with the total circulation. While the line separating wages and salaries is not definitely marked in theory, it is usually easily recognized in practice.

Children under, say, twelve years need not be included in any of the three categories, as they are not handlers of money; at least, not to a sufficient degree to have any appreciable influence on the total circulation.

We may now picture concretely the main currents of the monetary flow, including the circulation of money in exchange for goods. Figure 18 illustrates the three principal types.

The corners of the triangle, C, O and N, represent the three groups of "Commercial depositors," "Other depositors," and "Nondepositors," and the B's represent banks. The arrows represent the flow of money from each of these four categories to the others. Thus B_o represents the annual withdrawals from banks by "Other depositors," O_c the spending of this withdrawn money by "Other depositors" among "Commercial depositors," and C_b the return of the money from the "Commercial depositiors" to the banks. This circuit ($B_oO_cC_b$) of three links is very common. A second type of circuit is represented by a chain of four arrows ($B_oO_nN_cC_b$). It is illustrated by private depositors drawing money (B_o), and paying wages (O_n) to servants who in turn spend the money (N_c) among tradesmen who finally deposit it (C_b). A third type of circuit, also fourfold, is represented by the arrows $B_cC_nN_cC_b$. It is illustrated by commercial firms cashing their checks at banks (B_c) for pay

[1] The term "depositors," as here used, does not, of course, include savings bank depositors. A savings bank is not a true bank of deposit, providing circulating credit.

rolls, with the cash so obtained paying wages (C_n) to workmen who spend it (N_c) among other tradesmen who redeposit it in banks (C_b). These three types are not the only ones, but they are so much more important than any others that they merit our undivided attention before a completer study is undertaken. Figure 18 has been constructed for the purpose of exhibiting them uncomplicated by other details.

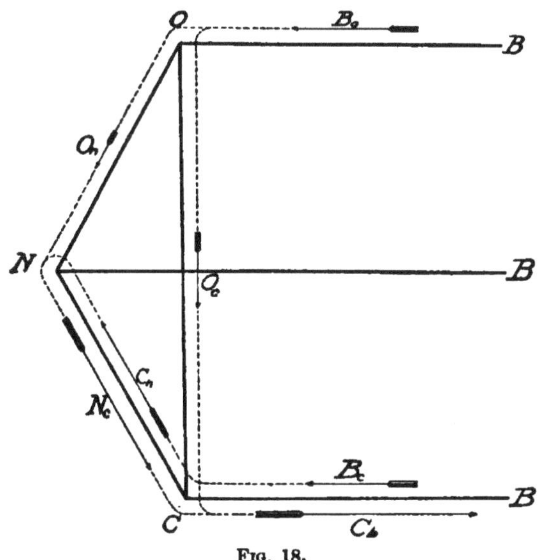

FIG. 18.

It will be noted that not all of the flows described are examples of the *circulation* of money. As already indicated, money may be said to circulate only when it passes in exchange for *goods*. Its entrance into and exit from banks is a flow, but not a circulation against goods. In the diagram the horizontal arrows represent such mere banking operations, not true circulation. On the other hand, the arrows along the sides of the triangle represent actual circulation. The diagram shows four such arrows, representing the four chief types of circulation: O_c payments of money from "Other depositors" to "Commercial depositors" in the purchase of goods; O_n payments from "Other depositors" to "Nondepositors," as when a housewife pays wages; C_n payments from "Commercial depositors" to "Nondepositors," as when a firm pays wages; and N_c payments from "Nondepositors" to "Commercial depositors," as when a wage earner buys goods of a merchant.

These four types of circulation of money occur in the three circuits already described, being sandwiched between the flows from and to the banks. The first, O_c, is contained within the circuit $B_oO_cC_b$, and, since no "Nondepositors" intervene, represents money changing hands *once* between its withdrawal from bank and its re-deposit there. The remaining types (O_n, C_n, and N_c) are contained within the two other circuits ($B_oO_nN_cC_b$ and $B_cC_nN_cC_b$), and, owing to the fact that "Nondepositors" intervene, represent money circulating *twice* between withdrawal and re-deposit.

In short, one of the three circuits ($B_oO_cC_b$) shows money circulating *once* out of bank. Both the others pass through N, and show money circulating *twice* out of bank. The diagram, then, represents all circulating money as springing from and returning to the banks; all of it as circulating *at least once* in the interim; and that portion handled by "Nondepositors" as circulating *once in addition*. Therefore, the total circulation exceeds the total flow from and to banks by the amount flowing through "Nondepositors." In other words, the total circulation in the diagram is simply the sum of the annual money flowing from and to banks and the money handled by "Nondepositors." The quotient of this sum divided by the amount of money in circulation will give approximately the velocity of circulation of money.

II. *The Complete Formula*

We have, however, still to consider the correction to be made for the less important forms of monetary circulation excluded from Figure 18.

In order to estimate the degree of accuracy of the first approximation just made for the circulation of money, we need to compare this approximation with a complete formula framed to include all possible transfers of money against goods.[1] There are nine possible kinds of transfers, three being respectively *within* each one of the three groups C, O, and N, and six being *between* each pair of these three, in either direction.

The exchanges possible within a class are (1) those between one "Commercial depositor" and another "Commercial depositor"; (2) those between one "Other depositor" and another; and (3) those between one "Nondepositor" and another. The transfers possible between classes are (4 and 5) those between "Commercial depositors" and "Other depositors" in either direction; (6 and 7) those between "Other depositors" and "Nondepositors" in either direction; and (8 and 9) those between "Nondepositors" and "Commercial depositors" in either direction. Thus there are three intraclass kinds and six interclass kinds of transfers of money against goods.

Figure 19 gives a complete picture of all these nine flows of money in exchange for goods; that is, of the entire "circulation of money." The nine flows are represented in the diagram by the nine arrows about the triangle, six being along the three sides of the triangle and representing interclass circulation, and three (c, o, and n) at the corners to represent intraclass circulation. The remaining six arrows on the horizontal lines represent, of course, mere banking operations. The total circulation or monetary flow (F) in exchange for

[1] That is, all transfers *within* the community considered. If it is desired to include as part of a community's circulation the sums exported or imported in foreign trade, these may most conveniently be added at the end. But even if they be included, they will be of trifling significance, partly because foreign trade is usually very small compared with domestic, and partly because money is so little used in foreign trade, especially if we exclude bullion from the category of money.

goods is, therefore, the sum of the magnitudes represented by these nine arrows, viz.

$$F = O_c + C_o + N_c + C_n + O_n + N_o + c + o + n. \qquad (1)$$

This is an exact formula for the circulation of money. We shall now compare it with the inexact first approximation,

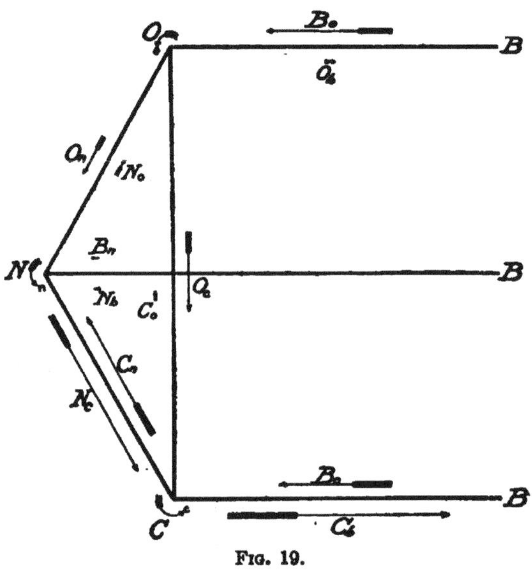

FIG. 19.

namely, "money deposited plus expenditures of 'Nondepositors.'" This comparison will express the error of the first approximation, and will suggest a method of transforming the exact formula (1) into a shape more suitable for statistical application. First, we need to express algebraically the first approximation. This may easily be done by inspecting Figure 19. The total money deposited is $C_b + O_b + N_b$, while the total expenditure of "Nondepositors" is $N_c + N_o$. The sum of these two expressions we shall call F'. It is:—

$$F' = C_b + O_b + N_b + N_c + N_o, \qquad (2)$$

which is, therefore, the algebraic expression for the first approximation.

To obtain the difference, $F - F'$, between the exact and the approximate formula, we subtract (2) from (1), canceling N_c and N_o and placing the negative terms first. We thus obtain for a remainder (r) the following: —

$$r = F - F' = -C_b - O_b - N_b + O_c + C_o + C_n + O_n + c + o + n. \quad (3)$$

That the value of $F - F'$ is small may be seen clearly by transforming (3). We shall transform it by means of another equation (4) given below. In order to derive this new equation (4), we shall need to make a digression. This new equation is merely a special application of the general principle that the net outflow (*i.e.* outflow minus inflow) from the contents of any reservoir must equal the net decrease in its contents during the same time, or (algebraically expressed) that the net outflow (positive or negative) plus the net increase in contents (negative or positive) must be zero. We may apply this principle to any reservoir or store of money, but shall here find it most helpful to apply it to the reservoir of money contained among the "*Commercial depositors*" *and* "*Nondepositors*" *taken together as one group.* Let us designate the combination of these two as the "*CN* group." The total outflow indicated in the diagram from this "*CN* group" is evidently $C_b + C_o + N_b + N_o$, and the total inflow $B_c + O_c + B_n + O_n$. Hence, the net outflow, *so far as the diagram shows us*, is: —

$$C_b + C_o + N_b + N_o - B_c - O_c - B_n - O_n.$$

This, plus the net outflow *not* shown in the diagram, is the true net outflow. Since the diagram was constructed to show only flows against goods (monetary circulation), and flows to or from banks, we have still to take account of money flowing in the community in exchange for something else than goods, and that flowing without any exchange at all, as well as any net outflow *outside* of the community.

We have thus to take account of three undiagramed flows.

The first is the net outflow of money from the "CN group" to the "C group," which, though in exchange, is not in exchange for goods. This means simply cashed checks, for, according to the classification we are here using, "goods" are taken to include anything exchangeable, not either money or checks. Our first correction is, therefore, the net outflow of money from the "CN group" for cashing checks, *i.e.* the difference between the checks cashed by the "CN group" for the "O group" and those cashed in the opposite direction.

It will be understood that we have nothing to do here with the cashing of checks at banks, for this is included in the diagram (B_o, B_n, and B_c). Moreover, we have nothing to do here with cashing of checks *within* the "CN group," as when a storekeeper cashes a check presented by a "Nondepositor." We have only to do with the net outflow for cashed checks from CN to O. This net outflow (which may be positive, negative, or zero) we shall designate by the letter a, to stand for "accommodation" checks.

For the second correction, we have to designate the net outflow of money *given away* by the "CN group" in gifts, taxes, thefts, etc., for which no specific goods are received in return. This net outflow may be designated by g.

We have, thirdly and lastly, the net outflow of money with respect to the "CN group" outside of the community, *i.e.* the net amount of money which is lost to the country by export, fire, shipwreck, melting, etc., in excess of that imported, minted, etc. This net outflow may be designated by e, to stand for "external" outflow. Adding the net undiagramed outflow $(a + g + e)$ to the net diagramed outflow, we have, for the total net outflow,

$$C_b + C_o + N_b + N_o - B_c - O_c - B_n - O_n + a + g + e.$$

Now, on the reservoir principle already explained, the algebraic sum of this net outflow from the "CN group" and the net increase of the money in that group must be zero. That is, representing this net increase by i, we have

$$0 = C_b + C_o + N_b + N_o - B_c - O_c - B_n - O_n + a + g + e + i. \quad (4)$$

We now place this new equation (4) under the old equation (3), giving the value of $r = F - F'$ in the following manner: —

$$r = -(C_b) - O_b - (N_b) \qquad + (O_c) + C_o + C_n + (O_n) + c + o + n$$
$$o = \quad (C_b) + C_o + (N_b) + N_o - B_c - (O_c) - B_n \qquad - (O_n) + a + g + e + i.$$

Adding and canceling the terms of (3) and (4) indicated in parentheses, and rearranging the remaining terms, we have

$$r = F - F' = (C_o + C_n - B_c) + (C_o + N_o - O_b) + (c + o + n) + (a + g + e) + i - B_n. \qquad (3)'$$

The letters are grouped in parentheses forming six terms, arranged, as far as can be judged, in the order of descending importance.

By using the expression just obtained for r, the complete formula (1) for the circulation of money may now be put in a form suitable for statistical application. Since $r = F - F'$, then $F = F' + r$. Substituting for F' and r the expression already given in equations (2) and (3)', we have, as a transformation of (1),

$$F = F' + r$$
$$= (C_b + O_b + N_b) + (N_c + N_o)$$
$$+ (C_o + C_n - B_c) + (C_o + N_o - O_b) + (c + o + n) + (a + g + e) + i - B_n \qquad (1)'$$

= (1) all money deposited
+ (2) money expenditures of "Nondepositors"
+ (3) C's money expenditures from tills (*i.e.* money expenditures in excess of money withdrawn from bank)
+ (4) O's money receipts pocketed (*i.e.* money receipts in excess of money deposited in bank)
+ (5) intraclass monetary circulation
+ (6) CN's undiagramed net outflow of money
+ (7) CN's net increase of money on hand
− (8) N's withdrawals of money from bank.

This is a complete and universal formula for the circulation of money in any community. Its first two terms constitute the first approximation, and the other six terms constitute r, which may be called the "remainder term."

The first and second terms are by far the most important. The last three terms — sixth, seventh and eighth — are doubtless quite negligible under all circumstances actually met with. I am also reasonably confident that, in the United States, the 3d, 4th, and 5th terms amount to less than 10 per cent of the total and probably less than 5 per cent. Therefore, the complete omission of all except the first two terms would still give us a fairly good figure for the total F; for any one familiar with the inaccuracies of statistics knows that 5 or 10 per cent is a small error, especially for a magnitude which has hitherto eluded any attempt at measurement.

We may, therefore, distinguish three successive stages in our approximations. The first approximation comprises only the first two terms, viz. money deposited plus expenditures of "Nondepositors"; the second includes, in addition, terms (3), (4), and (5), viz. till-paid money expenditures of C, pocketed money receipts of O, and intraclass circulation; while the third is rendered absolutely complete by including terms (6), (7), and (8), none of which has practical importance. The complete formula is presented in the hope of arousing discussion and investigation which will disclose in particular to what extent it may be applied in countries where data exist for the first two terms, viz. money deposited and expenditures of "Nondepositors." The former is to a large extent a matter of daily record in most civilized countries, and the latter consists chiefly of wages, a magnitude which has for long been a favorite subject for statistical estimate.

§ 7 (TO CHAPTER XII, § 4)

Application of Formula to Calculation of V for 1896 and 1909

We shall now exemplify the use of our formula by means of actual figures for the United States. The Report of the

Comptroller of the Currency for 1896, already referred to, and the special report of the National Monetary Commission for 1909, give a basis for estimating the first term $(C_b + O_b + N_b)$, the annual money deposited in banks in those years. Both reports were made under the direction of Professor David Kinley of the University of Illinois. We shall consider first the figures for 1896. The total money deposited in banks on the settling day nearest July 1, 1896, was 7.4 per cent of the total deposits of all kinds. This total for all reporting banks was 303 millions, of which 7.4 per cent would make $22,400,000. It was made up of over $16,200,000 from 3474 national banks, and the remainder from 2056 other banks. There were, all together, according to the Comptroller's Report, about 13,000 banks in the country at that time. On the basis of these figures, the Comptroller attempts to estimate the (retail) deposits of all kinds for all these 13,000 banks, assuming that the average deposit was the same as for the country banks replying. This average was $2375 for banks in places of 12,000 inhabitants or less. Applying this average to the unreporting banks, we would increase the retail deposits (which were $26,500,000) by an additional $17,800,000.

If we assume the same ratio of increase for the total *money* deposits, the sum of 22.4 millions would be increased by 15.0 millions, making a total of 37.4 millions, as the amount of money deposited in banks on the settling day nearest July 1, 1896. This figure represents at least a rough approximation to the inflow of cash into, and, therefore, also the outflow of cash from, the banks of the country. Multiplying by 305 settling days for the year, we obtain 11.4 billions as the total annual amounts deposited. The figures, being for the settling day nearest the first of July, are probably above the daily average for the year. Thus 11.4 is an *upper limit* rather than an estimate. Later we shall also set a lower limit.

The preceding figures relate to the year 1896. Similar calculations for 1909 have been made by Professor David

Kinley[1] with the assistance of Professor Weston. The resulting figure for money deposited in 1909 is 19.1 billions.[2]

But if it is necessary to adjust the figures for deposits of *checks* in 1896 and 1909 because the days selected are exceptional (see § 4 of this Appendix), it is also necessary to adjust the figures for the deposits of *money*. On July 1, 1896, many June bills must have been paid by cash as well as by check and on March 16, 1909, the middle of a month, there must have been slackness of settlements by cash as well as by check. Consequently, like the total deposits of checks, the total deposits of money made on July 1, 1896, were in all probability above the daily average for 1896, and on March 16, 1909, they were below the daily average for 1909. In other words, without adjustment for the abnormality of the days selected, the figure expressing monetary circulation for 1896 would be too large, and that for 1909, too small. That is, without such adjustment our calculations merely set an upper limit in 1896 and a lower limit in 1909.

But we may easily set the opposite limits. We may be reasonably sure that deviations from the average are less for money deposits than for check deposits. It cannot be expected that daily money deposits fluctuate as greatly as

[1] See "Note on Professor Fisher's Formula for Estimated Velocity of Circulation of Money." *Publications American Statistical Association*, March, 1910. The calculations are based on data taken from Professor Kinley's valuable monograph on "Credit Instruments," 61st Congress, 2d Session, Doc. No. 399 in *Reports of National Monetary Commission*.

[2] Professor Kinley gives 18.3. The difference is due to the fact that Professor Kinley, while estimating the daily deposits as 62.9 millions, calls this in round numbers 60 millions. It seems preferable to use the estimate as it stands and make any allowances for errors at the end rather than the beginning. Professor Kinley also takes 305 settling days for the year, this being the number used by Professor Kemmerer for 1896. But Mr. Gilpin of the New York clearing house tells me that the clearing house business days, though 305 in 1896, were 303 in 1909. I have therefore used 303 as the number of settling days in 1909. The product 62.9 millions, times 303, is 19.1 billions.

daily check deposits. Practically all check payments are influenced by the periodicity in receipts of checks by the depositors (as of their salary, interest, or dividend checks), or by the periodicity of credit extended to them (as of the tradesmen who render them monthly bills). While the fluctuations to which money payments are subject are more or less similar, they are much less in extent for two reasons: First, the payment or credit cycles which influence the fluctuations of money deposits are usually shorter than those which influence the fluctuations of check deposits; the wage earner usually gets his money weekly as against the salaried man who receives his check monthly, or the stockholder who receives his dividends quarterly. Secondly, unlike check payments, many, if not most, money payments have no payment or credit cycle. There is no credit cycle in what are called "cash" payments, for they imply that no credit is given. The receipts at "cash stores," the smaller receipts at all stores, the receipts of tramway, railway, and steamship offices, the receipts at theaters and many miscellaneous establishments are almost wholly on a cash basis and result in daily and fairly steady money deposits made by these establishments. These are facts of every-day experience and are confirmed by inquiry of bankers, who state that their money deposits are far steadier day by day than their check deposits. Confirmatory and conclusive evidence is also obtainable from Kinley's investigation in the Comptroller's Report for 1896 (p. 95). If check and money deposits were to fluctuate in perfect sympathy with each other, the percentage of the total which consists of checks would remain constant. But if, as we shall endeavor to show, the excess or abnormality of check deposits on July 1 is greater than the excess or abnormality of money deposits on that date, then we ought to find that the percentage of check deposits is greater on July 1 than usual. The figures of the Comptroller's Report indicate that this is the case. They show that the percentage of checks *received* (unfortunately not quite synonymous with "deposits") was on September 17, 1890, 91.0 per cent and on July 1 of the same year, 92.5 per cent, or 1½ per cent higher. Again, comparing July 1, 1896, with the nearest available date for another season of the year, namely, September 15, 1892, we find the figures to be as follows: for September 15, 1892, check receipts, 90.6 per cent; for July 1, 1896, check deposits, 92.5 per cent, or 1.9 per cent higher. The excess would have been still greater if both the figures were for receipts instead of one of them being for deposits; for, as the Comptroller says, the inclusion of other receipts than deposits tends to exaggerate the percentage of checks. That July 1 has a far larger proportion of checks than June 30 is indicated by the figures for retail deposits for June 30, 1894, and July 1, 1896, the former being 58.5 per cent and the latter 67.6 per cent, or 9.1 per cent higher. We should be cautious, however, in drawing any quantitative conclusion from this difference, since the investigations for 1894 and 1896 were conducted somewhat differently. But the difference, as we find it, harmonizes with all the facts at hand. Similar confirmation may be drawn from the absence of any contrast between the figures for June 30 and September 17, 1881, as compared with the sharp contrast already noted between July 1 and September 17, 1890. The credit receipts in 1881 on June 30 and September 17 were 91.77 per cent and 91.85 per cent, respectively, which figures are substantially equal, while, as above noted, for July 1 and September 17, 1890, we find a difference of 1½ per cent.

We feel, therefore, safe in concluding that check deposits are subject to greater fluctuations or abnormalities than money deposits. Consequently the deposits of money on July 1, 1896, while they may have exceeded the daily average, were probably not so far above the daily average as were the deposits of checks; also on March 16, 1909, the deposits of money were probably not so far below the average daily deposits of money as were the deposits of checks.

Now, if this were not true, — if the money deposits fluctuated exactly parallel with check deposits, — we should need to assume the same correction-factors for money as for checks, viz. .68 in 1896 and 1.17 in 1909, with the results given in column (1) of the following table: —

		ESTIMATED MONEY DEPOSITS OF YEAR		
(1)	(2) MONEY DEPOSITED ON DAY SELECTED (IN MILLIONS)	(3) ASSUMING DAY AN AVERAGE ONE (IN BILLIONS)	(4) ASSUMING CORRECTION FACTORS EQUAL TO THOSE FOR CHECK DEPOSITS	(5) MEAN BETWEEN TWO PRECEDING COLUMNS
1896 . .	37.4	11.4	7.8	9.6
1909 . .	62.9	19.1	22.3	20.7

We see that the true value of the money deposited in banks in 1896 must in all probability lie between 7.8 and 11.4 billions, and in 1909, between 19.1 and 22.3 billions. If, in each case, we split the difference, the estimates become for 1896, 9.6, and for 1909, 20.7. The truth cannot be far from these figures, for there are only narrow limits on either side. The probable error, judged roughly from the calculated limits and from the character of the estimates of these limits, is placed at about 1 billion in each case. It will be noted, of course, that this error is larger proportionally in 1896 than in 1909.

We have now estimated the first term (total deposits) of the formula for the total circulation of money.

The next term (N_c+N_o) is the expenditure of the "Non-depositors" made to other classes. This is practically the expenditure of wage earners. The Census gives the average wages in manufacturing industries as $430. Mr. William C. Hunt of the Census Bureau, in an unofficial memorandum which he has kindly allowed me to see, has estimated that the laborers in the United States number about 18,400,000. Let us assume, as a reasonable approximation, that their average wages are the same as the average in manufacturing industries, namely, $430. We first apply this to the 8.5 millions of people which Mr. Hunt estimates are engaged in manufacturing and mechanical pursuits and trade and transportation. These persons, therefore, receive about 3.7 billions of dollars in wages.

The remaining classes of laborers are domestic servants and agricultural laborers. These, however, receive board and lodging as part pay. Since food and rent form about 60 per-cent of workingmen's budgets, we may assume that the actual money paid to domestic and agricultural workers is only about 40 per cent of that paid to manufacturing laborers, *i.e.* about $170. Mr. Hunt estimates the number of domestic and agricultural laborers at 9 9 millions. Hence the total money they handle in a year is probably about 1.7 billions. This, added to the previous 3.7 billions, gives 5.4 billions as the total money paid in wages in the United States All these figures relate to the year 1900, while the figures for our first term relate to 1896. In the interim both the number of laborers and their wages doubtless increased somewhat and we must, therefore, make a correction for each. We shall assume that the number of laborers increased in the same ratio as population, and that population increased between 1896 and 1900 at the same rate per annum as between 1890 and 1900. This would reduce the 5.4 billions to 5.0 billions. If, instead of population, we use the number of employees in manufacturing and mechanical pursuits as given by the Bureau of Labor,[1] the result is lower, viz. 4.6. The truth probably lies between, since agricultural labor, for which we have no statistics, has probably not increased as fast as manufacturing labor, and, therefore, even if labor as a whole increased in the same ratio as population, the relative increase of manufacturing labor, as compared with agricultural labor, would mean a greater payment of *money* wages. We may select 4.8 billions as close to the truth. As to the rate of wages, the index numbers of the Bureau of Labor[2] for 1896 and 1900 are 99.5 and 104.1 respectively. On this account, therefore, we should still further reduce our estimate of money

[1] *Bulletin of the Bureau of Labor*, No. 77, July, 1908, p. 7.
[2] *Ibid.*, p. 7.

wages paid in 1896,—in the ratio of 104.1 to 99.5 or from 4.8 billions to 4.6 billions. Furthermore, a small fraction of these laborers are prosperous enough to have bank accounts, and the expenditures of these should not be included among the expenditures of "Nondepositors." About 4½ billions is probably as close to the truth as we can expect to get.

But we must now *add* to this an allowance for "Nondepositors" other than wage earners. Some of the 2.1 million clerks and 8.6 million proprietors and professional men in Mr. Hunt's estimates, though not laborers, are nevertheless "Nondepositors." As to the clerks, it is said by business men that most clerks who receive over $100 a month, and some who receive less, have bank accounts. Probably, the great bulk of the 2 millions of persons estimated as clerks are far below $100 a month, and many are doubtless included who, like office boys, have less than what are ordinarily called wages. To make a guess sure to be large enough, let us say that three-fourths of the clerks have no bank account and average $60 a month. Even then the total cash-paid clerk hire would scarcely exceed a billion.

Among the proprietors and professional men, the only group we need to consider is agricultural proprietors (5.7 millions). The remainder consists of classes among which bank accounts are practically universal. Of these agricultural proprietors, those who have no bank accounts are doubtless smaller ones, living in districts where little money changes hands. Their number could certainly not exceed four millions, which would be over two thirds of the whole. The problem is, What cash do these farmers pay to depositors, commercial and other? Practically, this means, What do they pay to country storekeepers? Their payments to laborers or other farmers are payments to other "Nondepositors" and do not concern us here. For rent, food, or such farm supplies as they can raise themselves, they pay little or nothing. Thus, the hay crop of the nation is said to exceed in value the wheat crop; but so little hay is marketed that it is seldom quoted or thought of as a market commodity. Even the trade of these farmers with the storekeeper is conducted largely by barter or book credit. Their expenditures in actual money may be conjectured to average less than $250 a year for each farmer, making less than a billion dollars at most (even if the number of such farmers be counted at 4 millions).

It seems safe to say, then, after allowing a billion for clerks and a billion for farmers, that the total expenditures of "Nondepositors" cannot exceed $4\frac{1}{2} + 1 + 1 = 6\frac{1}{2}$ billions.

On the other hand, it can scarcely be less than 5 billions. To reduce it to this figure would require us practically to ignore the existence of "Nondepositors" other than wage earners, or to assume a large error in the estimate of wages.

We conclude that for 1896 the second term lies somewhere between 5 and 6½ billions. Placing it midway, we obtain approximately 5.7 billions with a possible error of .7 or. 8. Similar calculations for 1909 show 13.1 billions for the second term with a possible error of 1.0. To quote from Professor Kinley's article already referred to:[1] —

"The second term of the formula is the money payments of 'Nondepositors,' made up principally, as Professor Fisher thinks, of the wages of working people. The following table shows an estimate of the increase from 1900 to 1909 in certain pursuits on the basis of the percentage of increase from 1890 to 1900 and on census and railroad returns since 1900. As far as possible salaried officers are eliminated.

	1890	1900	Increase Per Cent	Estimate 1909
Agricultural pursuits	8,565,926	10,381,765	21.2	12,362,605
Domestic and personal service	4,220,812	5,580,657	32.2	7,377,628
Total				19,740,233
Trade and transportation	1,977,491	2,617,479	35.2	4,275,913
Manufacturing and mechanism	4,251,613	5,208,406		6,935,113
Total				11,211,026

[1] *Publications of the American Statistical Association*, March, 1910.

"A rough calculation based on the figures of *Census Bulletin* No. 93 gives us about $550 as the average yearly wages of people in manufacturing. If we should include mechanical pursuits, probably the average should be raised a little. Very likely $600 would be more nearly correct for this class.

"Again the Report of the Interstate Commerce Commission for 1907 gives figures from which it appears that the average yearly wage is about $640. It is more difficult to get a ground for making an estimate of the money wages of those engaged in agricultural and domestic pursuits. Doubtless it is more than, at first thought, might be believed. The money wages of domestic servants at present probably will average not less than $250 a year. Agricultural laborers are certainly receiving a good deal more than formerly, and $300 or $350 probably will not be too large a sum to assign to these. Accordingly, we may recapitulate as follows: —

Trade and transportation	4.3 millions at $640	$2,752 millions
Manufacturing and mechanical pursuits .	6.9 millions at $550	$3,790 millions
Agricultural pursuits . .	12.4 millions at $300	$3,720 millions
Domestic and personal service	7.4 millions at $250	$1,850 millions
Clerks, etc., having no bank account		$1,000 millions
Total		$13,112 millions

"This gives us the second term of the formula."

We have now estimated the first two terms (constituting together what has been called the first approximation) for both 1896 and 1909.

To this first approximation must be added the remainder, r, consisting of the many terms already explained, most of which are not known with exactness, but all of which are known to be small. The term "small" is always relative, and in this case a term is small for 1896 which is small compared to 16 billions. For instance, 160 millions is a mere trifle, being only 1 per cent of 16 billions, while 16 millions is only one tenth of 1 per cent. For purposes of comparison we do not need exact statistics for the various terms of which

r is composed. All we need to know is that r is small and that it varies approximately as the rest of circulation varies. Under these circumstances a large mistake in estimating it will make a small error in comparisons. Only in case r were at once large and variable relatively to the other terms could a mistake in its estimation greatly affect the comparisons. Our attempt to estimate r has been made, not so much for the purpose of obtaining its absolute value, as to set for it wide and safe limits.

The magnitude r consists of all the five terms of our formula beyond the second. We shall take these up in order.

The third term of the formula is $(C_o + C_n - B_c)$. This represents the till-paid commercial expenditures, or the excess of the money paid out by "Commercial depositors" over the money withdrawn by them from banks. Personal inquiry shows that the great bulk of the money withdrawn by "Commercial depositors" from the banks is drawn for the purpose of paying wages; also that the great bulk of the actual money expended by "Commercial depositors" is expended for wages. In other words, C_o is very small compared with C_n, and the sum of the two is nearly the same as B_c. Hence the difference $(C_o + C_n - B_c)$, or till-paid expenses, is nearly zero. Till-paid expenses, being mostly wages and, as all observation shows, only a small part of total wages (4½ billions) — certainly not over one tenth — can be set down as less than half a billion in 1896 and less than a billion in 1909.

The fourth term $(C_o + N_o - O_b)$ is O's money receipts which are pocketed instead of being deposited. Now O's money receipts, $C_o + N_o$, are small in the first place, for O, being depositors, usually receive their dividends, interest, and salaries by check. The chief exception is found in the rents and the professional fees paid by workingmen to landlords, physicians, etc., payments which constitute most of N_o. But these rents and fees paid by workingmen to private individuals are only a part of total rents and fees of workingmen, and the total rents and fees themselves are known by statistics of workingmen's budgets to be only about 20 per cent of wages. From this and other clews, we may safely set half a billion as an upper limit for the fourth term in 1896. Professor Kinley places .8 billion as the upper limit in 1909.

The fifth term $(c + o + n)$ is the circulation within each of the three groups. Obviously only in trifling cases does money circulate between one "Commercial depositor" and another, between two "Other depositors," or between two "Nondepositors." Half a billion is put as an extreme upper limit for the total for 1896 and .8 by Professor Kinley for 1909. This would mean that about one dollar out of every thirty-five expended is passed on to other persons who are within the class to which the expender belongs. In fact, the universal testimony of such few representatives of c, o, and n as I have been able to interrogate personally is that the true ratio is less than this.

The remaining three terms are even more insignificant. In the normal state of equilibrium for the "*CN* group" it is evident that the sixth and seventh terms would both be substantially zero. The eighth term, withdrawals from banks by people who have no bank accounts, represents very exceptional conditions, such as where workmen cash checks at banks. Workmen seldom have checks to cash and, when they have, usually cash them in stores or saloons.

We shall summarize the estimates for each of the eight terms in the following table. Each term is placed midway between upper and lower limits estimated as safe, and the possible variation in either direction is indicated after a " ± ". Thus, \$300,000,000 ± \$300,000,000 means simply that, though \$300,000,000 is assigned as the estimate, the true value may be more or less by an amount not exceeding \$300,000,000, in other words, that the truth lies between \$600,000,000 and zero. Instead of half billions we have used in the table \$600,000,000 as being more easily divisible by two. The results for both years are given in the following table, in which generous estimates are given for the "probable error" in each case. In fact most of these "probable" errors are improbably large.

	1896	1909
1. Money deposited $(C_b + O_b + N)$	9.6 ± 1.5	20.7 ± 1.5
2. Expenditure of "Nondepositors" $(N_c + N_o)$ . .	5.7 ± .7	13.1 ± 1.0
3. C's expenditure, till paid . $(C_o + C_n - B_c)$	0.3 ± .3	0.5 ± .5
4. O's receipts, pocketed $(C_o + N_o - O_b)$	0.3 ± .3	0.4 ± .4
5. Intraclass circulation $(c + o + n)$	0.3 ± .3	0.4 ± .4
6. Net undiagramed outflow from CN $(a + g + e)$.	0.0 ± .1	0.0 ± .2
7. Net increase of money of CN (i)	0.0 ± .1	0.0 ± .2
8. Money withdrawn from banks by "Nondepositors" $(-B_n)$	−0.001 ± .001	−0.001 ± .001
	16.2 ± 2	35.1 ± 2

The first two terms (F') constitute the great bulk of the total. The remaining six terms (r) make up less than a billion more for either year. The total reaches about 16 billions as the estimated circulation of money in the United States in 1896. This estimate is subject to error, but not as much as the total of the possible errors of individual terms, which is over 3 billions. Even if each of the possible errors indicated were as likely as not to occur, the chance that in all eight cases they should all simultaneously occur in the same direction is $(\frac{1}{2})^8$, or one chance in 256. We may, therefore, "trust to luck" that the errors will, to some extent, offset each other. In fact, the chance of the error reaching the sum of those of the first three terms, or 3 billions, is less than a half. The "probable error" can therefore be placed with some confidence as less than 2 billions.

Dividing the figures we have obtained for the total circulation of money by the figures for the amount of money in circulation, we obtain figures for the velocity of circulation. These are 18.6 in 1896 and 21.5 in 1909, which show remarkably little change.

Reverting now to the remark with which we began the discussion of money velocity, namely, that it circulates but seldom outside of banks, let us picture our statistical results in the light of this fact.

Evidently, if all money circulated once only, then the bank record for 1896, showing about 9½ billions annually flowing into and out of the banks, would also exactly indicate the volume of the intervening work done. This would then be 9½ billions. But the true figure is, as we have shown, probably about 16 billions, and consequently we infer that some of the 9½ billions emanating from banks changes hands more than once before it returns.

Next let us suppose that all of the 9½ billions circulate once, except the part passing through the hands of "Nondepositors" (6 billions), and that the latter circulates twice. Then 3½ billions circulate once only. Under this assumption we can account for $3\frac{1}{2} + 2 \times 6 = 15\frac{1}{2}$ billions of exchange work. But we have found in fact 16 billions. The difference of about half a billion is chiefly due to the existence of some money which circulates more than twice outside of banks.

The entire 16 billions may be roughly accounted for by dividing the 9½ billions flowing from banks into three streams; 3½ billions circulating once and once only; 5½ billions, twice and twice only; and ½ billion, three times. This makes $3\frac{1}{2} + 2 \times 5\frac{1}{2} + 3 \times \frac{1}{2} = 16$ billions. Of the three parts, the first (3½ billions) is mainly the spending money drawn by "Other depositors," the second (5½ billions) is money withdrawn from bank for wages and other payments to "Nondepositors," and the third (½ billion) is the small amount not otherwise accounted for. This is only a rough scheme of division. A very small part circulates oftener than three times.[1]

[1] It may avoid some confusion to remind the reader that we are dealing with sums of money expended for goods, not with individual coins. Many coins remain "in circulation" a long time without returning to bank, because used "in change." But money used in change enters as a subtractive term in monetary expenditures. When $10 are given for an $8 purchase, and $2 are received back in change, $12 have changed hands, but only $8 of monetary circulation against goods have been effected.

Similarly, for 1909, of the 21 billions flowing into and out of the banks, the 13 billions passing through the hands of "Nondepositors" must have circulated twice or more and thus have accounted for 26 billions or more of the total circulation (35 billions), leaving 21 − 13, or 8, to have circulated only once. This would account for 26 + 8 or 34 billions. The entire 35 billions may be accounted for by supposing the 21 billions flowing from banks to be divided into the following three streams: —

8 billions circulating once, making 8 billions,
12 billions circulating twice, making 24 billions,
1 billion circulating three times, making 3 billions.

The whole 21 billions, bank outflow, perform 35 billions of circulation before returning to bank.

The first two terms of the formula for the monetary circulation evidently give 15½ billions out of our estimated total of 16 billions for 1896, and 34 out of 35 for 1909; showing that the remainder, unless it has been greatly underestimated, is relatively small. The significance of this fact is that the terms most difficult to estimate statistically are least important. Of the two terms constituting the "first approximation," the first and most important is susceptible of the most accurate determination of all, while the second is made up chiefly of wages, which also are susceptible of statistical determination, or seem destined to become so.

In fact, if we should, as a statistical makeshift for the first approximation, merely add the amount of money annually withdrawn from bank to the annual money wages, we should, as to the year 1896, account for 9½ + 4½ or 14 out of 16 billions, leaving only 2 billions to be otherwise accounted for. In other words, this makeshift — the part most adapted to statistical measurement — accounts for about 88 per cent of the total circulation, leaving only 12 per cent for the part which can only be determined within wide limits. For 1909, deposits plus wages make up about 32 billions out of 35, or over 90 per cent. A still simpler makeshift is to add the deposits to the *total* wages without attempting to ascertain the part which is paid in money. This makeshift might be justified on the ground that total wages are more exactly ascertainable than the part paid in money, and that presumably the money part will maintain a fairly constant ratio to the total wages from year to year. The two parts here indicated may be distinguished as the *measurable* part (comprising the first term of our formula (1)′ and most of the second term), and the *conjectural* part, comprising the remainder of the second term and the other six terms. Even if the allowance for the conjectural part should prove to be but half the truth, the measurable part would still constitute the great bulk of the total. The measurable part would therefore still be a safe practical index, or barometer of changes in the volume of circulation. Any excess of variation in the conjectural part, as compared with the measurable part, would, when spread over the whole, produce a disturbance only one fourth as great. It is reasonable to suppose that the conjectural and measurable parts will ordinarily vary together. If the measurable part varies 10 per cent, it is natural to suppose that the conjectural part, and therefore also the total of both, will vary likewise. But suppose this assumption erroneous and that, while the measurable part varies 10 per cent, the conjectural part really varies 14 per cent or 6 per cent. The difference between these and 10 per cent, *i.e.* 4 per cent, representing a supposed excess or deficiency of variation of the conjectural part, would produce a difference of only 1 per cent in the total! That is, the total, instead of varying 10 per cent, would vary 11 per cent or 9 per cent. Evidently, therefore, any unknown variation in the conjectural part can cause only a trifling variation in the result. In other words, the measurable part will always be a good index of the total — a reliable barometer of circulation. If we divide this by the quantity of money in circulation, we obtain a figure indicating the relative velocity of circulation of money from year to year. We conclude, therefore, that *money deposits plus wages, divided by money in circulation,* will always afford a good barometer of the velocity of circulation.

It is not always the absolute value of any magnitude we find most useful, but its relative value under different conditions. We may compare the relative length of two ships by measuring their water lines, although this method omits the overhang at either end. Such a comparison will apply roughly to any two vessels, and with great exactness to two ships of the same build. Similarly, our proposed barometer will afford rough comparisons for any two countries using banking facilities in comparable degrees, and will afford fairly exact comparisons for two successive years in the same country.

The proper statistical procedure would, therefore, seem to be to provide for the conjectural part by an estimated percentage correction, to be applied to the measurable part as a constant factor. Different correction factors will presumably apply in different countries, as, let us say, 10 per cent in the United States, 20 per cent in England, 30 per cent in France, etc. The chief value of such conjectural corrections would be to enable us to compare roughly the circulations and velocities of different countries. For comparisons in the same country at different times it would be almost immaterial what percentage correction were adopted or whether none at all were employed.

By means of the method which has been explained, it is believed that some interesting and valuable results can in the future be obtained, if statisticians in various lands will obtain (1) the total money deposited each year in banks (except by other banks), or, what is normally the same thing, the total money withdrawn from banks (except by other banks); (2) the total wages expended, or, what is practically the same thing, the total wages received; (3) if desired, a conjectural percentage addition to allow for the remaining and less known part of our formula; (4) the total money in circulation. The sum each year of (1) and (2) corrected by (3) and divided by (4) will be a very accurate barometer of the velocity relatively considered, as well as a fair approximation to its absolute value. The omission of (3) will not invalidate the results for purposes of relative comparison.

The importance of such accurate determinations can scarcely be overestimated, as the remarks on the subject by Jevons, Landry, and others have shown. When we know statistically the velocity of circulation of money, we are in a position to study inductively the "quantity theory" of money, and to discover the significance of that velocity in reference to crises, accumulation of wealth, density of population, rapid transit, and communication, as well as many other conditions. In fact a new realm in monetary statistics is laid open.

§ 8 (TO CHAPTER XII, § 4)

Interpolating Values of *V* for 1897–1908

To interpolate values for V we split the difference between two extreme hypotheses: the one of extreme steadiness; the other of extreme variability.

The first of these hypotheses is that V changes in a steady progression from its value of 18.6 in 1896 to its value of 21.5 in 1909. This would imply a perfectly steady growth with time, with no temporary fluctuations. But it seems unlikely that the velocity of circulation of money should not fluctuate somewhat from year to year. We have seen that, theoretically, there is a tendency under normal conditions for money expenditures (MV) to keep pace with check expenditures ($M'V'$). If this correspondence were perfect, we should have the ratio of MV to $M'V'$, if not constant, at least changing in a perfectly even manner with time. Now this ratio for 1896 is 16.7 per cent and in 1909, 9.6 per cent. If we were to assume a perfectly steady change in this ratio during the intervening 13 years, the resulting value for V would have to vary considerably. This assumption is our second hypothesis of extreme variability. The following table shows the results of the two extreme hypotheses. It will be seen that in general there is no great difference between them.

YEAR	(1) HYPOTHESIS OF EXTREME STEADINESS	(2) HYPOTHESIS OF EXTREME VARIABILITY V VARYING AS NEEDED TO PRESERVE EVENLY CHANGING RATIO OF MV TO $M'V'$	(3) MEAN OF TWO PRECEDING
1896	18.6	18.6	18.6
1897	18.8	19.4	19.1
1898	19.0	20.6	19.8
1899	19.3	24.4	21.9
1900	19.5	20.4	20.0
1901	19.7	23.9	21.8
1902	19.9	23.6	21.8
1903	20.2	20.9	20.6
1904	20.4	20.9	20.7
1905	20.6	23.0	21.8
1906	20.8	22.5	21.7
1907	21.1	21.0	21.1
1908	21.3	18.6	20.0
1909	21.5	21.4	21.5

A supplementary calculation reveals the interesting fact that the "hypothesis of extreme variability" would make money velocity fluctuate approximately with deposit velocity. Splitting the difference between the two extreme hypotheses, —that of extreme steadiness and that of extreme variability, —we have what would seem to be an approximately correct estimate of actual velocity. It is probably correct in most cases for the first two digits. We cannot assume even for 1896 and 1909 that the third digit, that beyond the decimal, is correct, much less can we assume this to be true for the intervening years. But it is sometimes advisable to carry out the calculations to one digit beyond "the last significant figure."

§ 9 (TO CHAPTER XII, § 5)

Method of Calculating T

The table in the text is taken from the final column of the following more complete table:—

INDEX NUMBERS OF VOLUME OF TRADE

Direct Indices and Calendar Years					Indirect Indices and Fiscal Years			Calendar Years		
(1) Year	(2) Internal Commerce	(3) Exports and Imports	(4) Sales of Stocks	(5) Weighted Average of Three Preceding $\frac{20\times(2)+3\times(3)+1\times(4)}{24}$	(6) R. R. tons Carried	(7) P. O. Letters Carried	(8) Weighted average of two preceding $\frac{2\times(6)+1\times(7)}{3}$	(9) (8) Reduced to Calendar Years	(10) Relative Trade Weighted average $\frac{2\times(5)+1+(9)}{3}$	(11) Absolute Trade (T) $(10)\times\frac{399}{155}$
1896 . .	89	76	55	86	77	—	72	73	81	209
1897 . .	103	87	77	100	79	63	74	78	93	239
1898 . .	111	96	113	109	91	68	83	86	101	260
1899 . .	111	100	176	112	98	72	89	93	106	273
1900 . .	111	101	138	111	107	78	97	99	107	275
1901 . .	125	107	266	129	108	85	100	105	121	311
1902 . .	119	102	189	120	119	92	110	115	118	304
1903 . .	139	101	161	135	130	101	120	120	130	335
1904 . .	125	101	187	125	127	105	120	126	126	324
1905 . .	149	109	263	149	144	111	133	141	147	378
1906 . .	152	114	284	153	161	128	150	155	154	396
1907 . .	167	117	196	162	172	137	160	154	160	412
1908 . .	148	110	197	145	152	142	149	154	148	381
1909 . .	153	125	215	152	—	152	160	—	155	399

This table is constructed as follows: —

Column (2) is constructed for 1900–1909 from monthly figures on Internal Commerce published in the *Monthly Summary of Commerce and Finance of the United States.* By taking the monthly figures it was possible to obtain results for calendar years. This column is an average of separate indices for 44 articles so far as records were available. The original figures give the quantities of each article brought into the principal cities of the United States. These quantities were each multiplied by an assumed price which remained as a constant multiplier for every year. The products were then added together and the figures thus obtained taken to represent the total trade in these 44 commodities, and to be a barometer of the *relative* internal commerce in the United States.

The 44 articles referred to, and the dates for which data were used (as well as the price factors employed as explained below) are as follows: —

ARTICLES	PRICE	DATES
Cotton	$45.00 bale	Jan., 1900–1909
Rice	5.00 sack	Aug., 1900–1909
Fruit	1000.00 car	Feb., 1900–1909
Lumber (Shipments from South and Southwest)	.02 ft.	Feb., 1900–1909
Boots and Shoes .	80.00 case	Mar., 1900–1909
Anthracite Coal .	4.74 ton	Jan., 1900–1909
Bituminous Coal .	2.74 ton	Jan., 1900–1909
Pig iron, coke, and anthracite . .	19.40 gross ton	July, 1902–1909
Petroleum (Shipments by water from Texas) . .	1.80 bbl.	Nov., 1901–1909
Cattle (Receipts at five cities) . .	55.00 head	Jan., 1900–Dec., 1903
Cattle (Receipts at seven cities) . .	55.00 head	Jan., 1900–1909
Hogs (Receipts at five cities) . .	18.00 head	Jan., 1900–Dec., 1903

Articles	Price	Dates
Hogs (Receipts at seven cities) . .	$18.00 head	Jan., 1900–1909
Sheep (Receipts at five cities) . .	4.00 head	Jan., 1900–Dec., 1903
Sheep (Receipts at seven cities) . .	4.00 head	Jan., 1900–1909
Wheat (Receipts at eleven cities) .	1.00 bu.	June, 1903
Wheat (Receipts at twelve cities) .	1.00 bu.	Apr., 1903–Dec., 1903
Wheat (Receipts at fourteen cities) .	1.00 bu.	May, 1904–1909
Wheat (Receipts at fourteen cities) .	1.00 bu.	May, 1904–1909
Wheat (Receipts at fifteen cities) .	1.00 bu.	Apr., 1903–1909
Corn (Receipts at twelve cities) .	.75 bu.	Apr., 1903–Dec., 1903
Corn (Receipts at fourteen cities) .	.75 bu.	Jan., 1904–1909
Corn (Receipts at thirteen cities) .	.75 bu.	Feb., 1906–Feb., 1907
Corn (Receipts at fifteen cities) .	.75 bu.	Apr., 1903–1909
Oats (Receipts at twelve cities) .	.53 bu.	Apr., 1903–Dec., 1903
Oats (Receipts at fourteen cities) .	.53 bu.	Feb., 1906–Feb., 1907
Oats (Receipts at fifteen cities) .	.53 bu.	Apr., 1903–1909
Barley (Receipts at nine cities) . .	.70 bu.	June, 1903–Aug., 1908
Barley (Receipts at ten cities) . .	.70 bu.	Apr., 1903–May, 1908
Barley (Receipts at eleven cities) .	.70 bu.	Sept., 1903–June, 1908
Barley (Receipts at twelve cities) .	.70 bu.	Feb., 1906–Sept., 1908
Barley (Receipts at thirteen cities) .	.70 bu.	Feb., 1904–1909
Barley (Receipts at fourteen cities) .	.70 bu.	Apr., 1903–1909
Rye (Receipts at eleven cities) .	.80 bu.	Apr., 1903–June, 1906
Rye (Receipts at twelve cities) .	.80 bu.	Jan., 1905–Aug., 1908
Rye (Receipts at thirteen cities) .	.80 bu.	Apr., 1904–1909
Rye (Receipts at fourteen cities) .	.80 bu.	Apr., 1903–1909

ARTICLES	PRICE	DATES
Flaxseed (Receipts at four cities) .	$1.50 bu.	Feb., 1905–1909
Flaxseed (Receipts at five cities) .	1.50 bu.	Jan., 1904–1909
Flaxseed (Receipts at six cities) . .	1.50 bu.	Jan., 1904–1909
Flour (Receipts at ten cities) . . .	4.80 bbl.	Apr., 1903–1909
Flour (Receipts at eleven cities) .	4.80 bbl.	Jan., 1904–1909
Flour (Receipts at twelve cities) .	4.80 bbl.	Mar., 1904–1909
Flour (Receipts at thirteen cities) .	4.80 bbl.	Apr., 1903–1909
Petroleum (Shipments by Pipe-lines — Reg. Deliveries. App. Field	1.80 bbl.	Jan., 1901–1909

These articles are representative for the trade of the country and may well serve as a barometer of that trade. Yet the amount of trade, actually consisting of the sales of these 44 articles in the few cities concerned, constitutes of course only a very small part (probably less than one tenth of 1 per cent) of the total trade of the country.

The actual figures first obtained were all divided by two before being entered in column (2) in order to bring them down to a scale more comparable with the figures of column (3). Since not all of the 44 commodities were quoted in all the years, the table had to be "pieced out" for the defective years by the principles of proportion as already exemplified. As the statistics of the *Monthly Summary* go back only to 1900, the table had to be "pieced" back to 1896. This was done by using data from the statistical abstract of the United States and the abstract of the United States Census for 1900. The only figures obtainable for important articles in internal trade were those for grain, received during calendar years at fifteen principal primary markets, and for the estimated national consumption during fiscal years of the following articles, chiefly, or largely, of domestic production: cotton, wool, bituminous coal, pig iron, iron and steel railroad bars, and "distilled spirits, wines, and malt liquors."

The fiscal year figures were taken from 1896 to 1901 inclusive and reduced to calendar years on the assumption, for instance, that the true figure for the calendar year 1896 is the average of those for the two fiscal years ending June 30, 1896, and June 30, 1897. In this way we get hypothetical calendar year figures for 1896 to 1900. These figures and those for grains, which were already for calendar years, were then reduced by a factor so that each was made to be 111 for 1900, the number for that year found by the calculations involving the 44 articles in the series, 1900–1909. The figures thus found were then averaged with weights selected to correspond with the estimates of their respective importance as judged from the estimates of their national consumption values and from the fact that some of them are indicators of large related businesses. The weights chosen were: for grains (including wheat, wheat flour, corn, rye, oats, barley, malt, and pease [1]), 20; for bituminous coal, iron and steel, liquors, and cotton, 5 each; and for pig iron and wool, 1 each.

The data for 1896–1899 are far inferior to those for 1900–1909 taken from the *Monthly Summary*, and this for three reasons: (1) because they are so few in number; (2) because all except the grains are for fiscal years and the hypothetical correction to calendar years is subject to error; and (3) because all except the grains are very rough estimates of consumption, not based on shipments or receipts, but based on estimated production, corrected for exports and imports, which three elements are all subject to error.

We should not be surprised, therefore, to find larger errors in the resulting figures for 1896–1899 than for 1900–1909. In fact, we shall see that such is probably the case.

For carrying out the laborious operations involved in ascertaining the index numbers from 1900 to 1908, I am in-

[1] See *Statistical Abstract of United States*, 1908, p. 523.

debted to one of my undergraduate students, Mr. Robert N. Griswold, and for bringing them down to 1909, to one of my graduate students, Mr. W. Y. Smiley.

Column (3) is also based on laborious calculations which were performed by Mr. Griswold. The materials were also taken from the *Monthly Summary of Finance and Commerce* and covered 23 staple articles of import and 25 for export. The quantities of each were multiplied by a uniform price, and the sum of the resulting figures for important exports was taken. The articles of imports (with the price multipliers used) were: —

IMPORTS OF THE UNITED STATES 1896–1909

(*Bulletin of Bureau of Commerce and Statistics*)

Article	Price	Article	Price
Cocoa	.13 lb.	Raw silk	.04 lb.
Tea	.16 lb.	Hides and skins (other than fur skins)	.11 lb.
Coffee	.07 lb.	Raw wool	.13 lb.
Sugar	.02 lb.	India rubber	.78 lb.
Lemons	.04 lb.	Boards and sawed lumber	18.00 M. ft.
Bananas	1.60 bunch	Coal (anthracite & bituminous)	2.60 per t.
Cheese	.17 lb.	Tin	.28 lb.
Distilled spirits (imported)	5.00 gal.	Copper (pigs, bar, ingots, old, unmanufactured)	.17 lb.
Sparkling wines (Champagne)	29.00 doz. qts.	Pig iron	23.00 per t.
Leaf tobacco	1.00 lb.	Sodium nitrate	38.00 per t.
Cotton (mfg. cloth)	.09 sq. yd.		
Linens (mfg. flax, hemp, or ramie)	.50 sq. yd.		
Woolen dress goods	.21 sq. yd.		

The articles of exports were: —

EXPORTS OF THE UNITED STATES 1896–1909

(*Bulletin of Bureau of Commerce and Statistics*)

Article	Price	Article	Price
Cattle	55.00 head	Wheat	1.00 bu.
Hams	.11 lb.	Flour	4.80 bu.
Salt pork	.09 lb.	Tobacco leaf	.10 lb.
Fresh beef	.10 lb.	Sawed lumber	23.00 M. ft.
Canned beef	.11 lb.	Wood pulp	.015 lb.
Bacon	.11 lb.	Linseed oil (cake)	.014 lb.
Lard	.11 lb.	Refined illuminating oil	.07 gal.
Butter	.21 lb.	Cottonseed oil	.40 gal.
Sole leather	.21 lb.	Coal	3.70 ton
Boots and shoes	2.75 pr.	Copper	.17 lb.
Raw cotton	.48 bale	Steel rails	31.60 ton
Cotton cloth	.09 yd.	Sheet steel	.0135 ton
Corn	.60 bu.		

The statistics of exports and imports are probably fifty times as full as those of internal commerce and therefore (on the principle that probable errors vary inversely as the square root of the fullness of returns) some seven times as accurate. But, on the other hand, exports and imports represent less than 1 per cent as much trade as the internal commerce of the United States, and, by the principles already explained in previous chapters, should count in the equation of exchange only at half its value, one of the parties in the exchange being a foreigner. In spite, however, of the diminutive character of external commerce, it is to some extent an index of internal commerce; since a vast amount of internal business is a preliminary to exports and a sequel to imports, while perhaps a still larger amount is in other ways indirectly related to such commerce. By balancing these and other considerations, the relative weights to be assigned to the external and internal trade were selected as given in column (5).

Column (4) gives the sales of stocks according to the ordinary figures as given, for instance, in the *Financial Review*. These figures are, of course, not for values, but for amounts.

Column (6) gives the figures for tons of freight carried by railroads according to Poor's *Railroad Manual* for fiscal years.

Column (7) gives the figures for pieces of first-class mail matter carried in fiscal years. These figures were kindly supplied by the Post Office Department. They are lacking for 1896.

We have still to describe the method employed for combining columns (2), (3), (4), (6), (7).

The first three are regarded as constituting a group by themselves, representing *direct* indices of trade: and the last two are regarded as constituting another group of *indirect* indices.

The direct indices are combined by weighting the internal commerce, *twenty*, the exports and imports, *three*, and sales of stocks, *one*. These weights are, of course, merely matters of opinion, but, as is well known, wide differences in systems of weighting make only slight differences in the final averages.

In this way, column (5) is found.

As to the relative weights to be given to the railroad and post office statistics, the former were weighted as *two* and the latter as *one*. Railway tonnage represents almost every conceivable commodity in commerce and comes far closer to actual trade than post office letters.

After railroad and post office indexes are thus combined, the transition from fiscal to calendar years is made on the assumption that the figures for a calendar year are the mean of the figures for the fiscal years ending June 30 of that year and June 30 of the next year.

In this way column (9) is obtained.

From columns (5) and (9) column (10) is obtained by weighting (5) *two*, and (9) *one*.

Finally, column (11) is found by magnifying the figure of column (10) in the ratio $\frac{399}{155}$ in order to make the figure for the base year, 1909, equal to 399 billions of dollars, — the total value of the left side of the equation $(MV + M'V')$.

The probable errors in the values of T which have been calculated are believed to be some 5 to 10 per cent for the years 1900–1909 and 10 to 15 per cent for the years 1896–1900.

§ 10 (TO CHAPTER XII, § 5)

Method of Calculating P

The table in the text for index numbers of prices is taken from the last column of the table on page 103.

Column (2) gives the index numbers of the United States Labor Bureau (No. 81, March, 1909, p. 204).

I am under obligations to the Commissioner of Labor, Mr. Neill, for his courtesy in supplying me with the figure for 1909 in advance of publication.

Column (3) is taken from the *Bulletin of the Bureau of Labor*, July, 1908, p. 7.

Column (4) is from "The Prices of American Stocks, 1890–1909," by Wesley C. Mitchell, *Journal of Political Economy*,

May, 1910. These figures are doubtless the best yet available in this difficult subject.

INDEX NUMBERS OF PRICES

(1) YEAR	(2) WHOLESALE, 258 COMMODITIES	(3) WAGES PER HOUR	(4) FORTY STOCKS	(5) WEIGHTED AVERAGE $\frac{30\times(2)+1\times(3)+3\times(4)}{34}$	(6) COLUMN (5) REDUCED TO BASIS OF 100 IN 1909
1896 . . .	90	100	77	89	63.3
1897 . . .	90	100	84	90	63.7
1898 . . .	93	100	94	93	66.2
1899 . . .	102	102	128	104	73.8
1900 . . .	111	105	134	113	80.2
1901 . . .	109	108	211	118	83.7
1902 . . .	113	112	250	125	88.7
1903 . . .	114	116	201	122	86.5
1904 . . .	113	117	192	120	85.1
1905 . . .	116	119	250	128	90.8
1906 . . .	123	124	267	136	96.5
1907 . . .	130	129	204	137	97.2
1908 . . .	123	—	201	130	92.2
1909 . . .	127	—	277	141	100.0

The general index number in column (5) is a weighted average of the figures in the three preceding columns, the weights being essentially the same as those used by Professor Kemmerer and for the same reasons.[1] For ease in computation the weights are taken in integers, viz. 30 for column (2), 1 for column (3) and 3 for column (4). This calculation brings the table down through 1907. As column (3) is defective for 1908–1909, these years and 1907 are worked out as averages of columns (2) and (4), the weights being the same as already mentioned. The result is two series of figures, one for all three columns ending in 1907, and the other for two columns beginning in 1907. As in this case it happens that both series have the same figure (137) for 1907, no corrections need be made in 1908 and 1909. The probable errors in the figures for P may be placed as about 5 to 10 per cent.

[1] See *Money and Credit Instruments*, New York (Holt), 1909, p. 139.

§ 11 (TO CHAPTER XII, § 7)

Mutual Adjustments of Calculated Values of M, M', V, V', P, T

There are various methods of calculating the best adjustments, involving the theory of least squares. But the problem may be greatly simplified by dividing the process into a few separate steps. First, we ascertain the best adjustments of the calculated values of each side of the equation of exchange considered as a whole. We shall need to exercise judgment in deciding the relative errancy of the two sides, but the total adjustments are so small that differences in judgment could not make much difference in the results.

After a careful weighing of all the evidence, it is believed that the errors in the right side (PT) are liable to be about double those in the left ($MV + M'V'$). Accordingly, the discrepancy between the two sides is corrected by changing PT twice as much as $MV + M'V'$; that is, by applying to PT a correction equal to two thirds of the total discrepancy, and by applying the remaining one third to $MV + M'V'$, the two corrections being, of course, opposite and such as to bring the two sides into agreement. Thus, for 1899, the total discrepancy is 5 per cent, of which we assign about a third, say 2 per cent, to $MV + M'V'$, and the remaining 3 per cent to PT. That is, we propose to increase the calculated figures for $MV + M'V'$ by 2 per cent and decrease those of PT by 3 per cent. The result will bring them nearly into agreement at 185 billions. Sometimes the results will not exactly agree, as this method of adding and subtracting percentage corrections is only approximately correct; but any remaining slight discrepancies are readily adjusted by slight empirical changes in the factors. The result is shown in the Figure 20, which gives $MV + M'V'$ and PT (reduced by dividing by 1.11) as originally calculated, and a mean (dotted) curve which is the revised estimate of both $MV + M'V'$ and PT.

The corrections which are thus made in $MV + M'V'$ and PT, by which they are brought into mutual agreement, are small; but the corrections necessary in the individual factors, M, V, M', V', P, T, are smaller still. We assume, for simplicity, that the percentage corrections to be made in M and M' are equal to each other and also that the corrections to be made in V and V' are equal to each other. This is a reasonable assumption; but even if some other assumption were made, the final results would be scarcely changed.

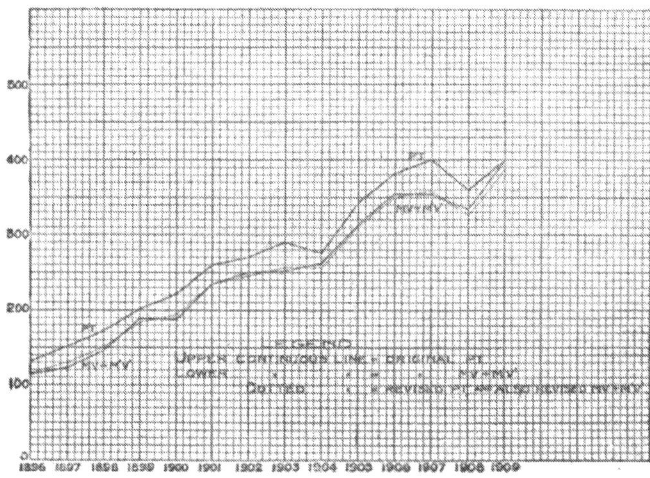

FIG. 20.

A correction of 1 per cent simultaneously in M and M' will produce a correction of 1 per cent in $MV + M'V'$. Likewise a correction of 1 per cent simultaneously in V and V' will produce a correction of 1 per cent in $MV + M'V'$. We may then regard the correction of $MV + M'V'$ as practically consisting of two parts: one, the correction of M and M'; and the other, the correction of V and V'. As the M's are more accurately ascertained than the V's, their correction should be smaller. Thus, for 1897, the total correction assigned to $MV + M'V'$ is 3 per cent, of which we assign 1 per cent to M and M', and the remaining 2 per cent to V

and V'. That is, we increase the calculated values of M and M' by 1 per cent and those of V and V' by 2 per cent, thus effecting (approximately) the desired increase of 3 per cent in $MV+M'V'$. In like manner the total correction assigned to PT is distributed over P and T, assigning the major part to T. By thus distributing the corrections over (1) M and M', (2) V and V', (3) P, and (4) T, we find that only very slight individual corrections are needed, the maximum being only 5 per cent and the vast majority (50 out of 56 cases) not exceeding 2 per cent. In fact, a decided majority (35 out of 56 cases) are within 1 per cent. It is really astonishing to think that a correction of only 2 per cent or less is usually required in our calculated values of M, M', V, V', P, T, in order to make them conform perfectly to the equation of exchange. In fact, 2 per cent is less than what might naturally be considered the probable error in most of the figures as calculated. This fact justifies confidence in the general correctness of our results.

Having thus corrected, by mutual adjustment, all the factors in the equation of exchange, we are left with a figure for P which is not 100 per cent for any one year. As we prefer to call 1909 the unit year, the figures for P are adjusted on that basis and the figures for T accordingly. This change disturbs the system of corrections as measured relatively to the original figures. It reduces to zero the correction of P for 1909. In general, it makes smaller the corrections for P and T for years near 1909 and makes correspondingly larger those for years remote from 1909. But, even so, the corrections never exceed 10 per cent for T nor 6 per cent for P. As the entire scheme of corrections thus outlined is a matter of judgment and each figure was frankly "doctored" on its own individual merits in view of all the circumstances in the case, it seems inadvisable to burden these pages by any fuller statement of the voluminous details of the process. The results as shown in Figures 13, 14, 15, and 16, already given in the text, speak for themselves.

§ 12 (TO CHAPTER XII, § 17)

Credit and Cash Transactions. Comparison with Kinley's Estimates

These figures agree surprisingly well with what might be expected from a rougher calculation from Kinley's investigations. For July 1, 1896, he found that money deposits constituted 7.4 per cent of all deposits and, on March 16, 1909, 5.9 per cent. Both of these figures are too low to represent the percentage of money *transactions*, for the reason that money often circulates more than once before being deposited, whereas checks in general circulate but once. The figure for 1896, especially, is too low, because of the excessive amounts of checks deposited on July 1. In fact, it was largely because the 1896 figures had been criticized in this respect that Kinley made the 1909 investigation. He did not, of course, take the figures of deposits as indicating exactly the ratios of check and money transactions. He recognized the fact that these would give too low a ratio for money and too high a ratio for checks. He expressed the belief that a safe minimum for check transactions in 1896 was 75 per cent[1] and in 1909, 88 per cent, implying that 20 per cent and 12 per cent were safe maxima for monetary circulation. Professor Kinley's purpose seems to be to establish safe maxima rather than to attempt exact estimates. Tabulating Kinley's figures, we have for money transactions expressed in percentage of all transactions: —

(1)	(2)	(3)	(4)	(5)
Year	Maximum (Kinley's estimate)	Minimum (as indicated by deposits)	Mean of two preceding	Present estimate
1896	25	7.4	16¼	14
1909	12	5.9	9	9

[1] His original estimate for a safe minimum was 80 per cent. But in the *Journal of Political Economy*, Vol. V, p. 172, and in "Money," p. 44, and pp. 108, 14, he takes 75 per cent as safer.

According to this table, if we take the percentage of money in bank deposits as a lower limit of the percentage of money transactions, and if we take Kinley's estimates as a safe upper limit, and if we split the difference between these two limits, we shall reach almost[1] the same results as already reached by the more exact calculations in this book, which results are given, for comparison, in the last column. Thus the results of this book strikingly confirm those of Professor Kinley. They also agree remarkably well with the prevailing impression among business men that about 90 per cent of trade is now performed by means of checks.

[1] If we take Kinley's original "safe minimum" for checks of 80 per cent, and consequently the "safe maximum" for cash as 20 per cent, we shall obtain in the above table 14 per cent, instead of the figure 16½, which would make the last two columns agree absolutely.

INDEX

D

E

Q

R

S

T

Y

Z

An Introduction to Public Finance

By CARL C. PLEHN, Ph D.

Third edition, enlarged and partly rewritten, $1.75 net

"The book as it first appeared was an excellent one; in the present form its usefulness has been greatly enhanced," says the *Journal of Political Economy*. "At present the best text on public finance for general use." —*Political Science Quarterly.*

Public Finance

By C. F. BASTABLE, M.A., LL.D., Professor of Political Economy in the University of Dublin.
Published in London, 1892. Third edition, 1903.

Cloth, 8vo, 780 pages, $4.25 net

Practical Problems in Banking and Currency

Being a number of selected addresses delivered in recent years by prominent bankers, financiers, and economists. Edited by WALTER HENRY HULL With an Introduction by the Hon. C. F. PHILLIPS, of New York.
Published in New York, 1907. *Cloth, 8vo, 596 pages, $3.50 net*

A compilation of addresses delivered since 1900 before associations of bankers throughout the country. The addresses are grouped under the following heads: General Banking; Banking Reform and Currency; Trust Companies.

The Distribution of Wealth

By THOMAS NIXON CARVER, Professor of Political Economy in Harvard University.
Published in New York, 1904. *Cloth, 12mo, 290 pages, $1.50 net*

An explanation of the valuation of the services of the factors of production made by means of an analytical study of the motives which govern men in business and industrial life.

Money

A Study of the Theory of the Medium of Exchange. By DAVID KINLEY, Professor of Economics and Dean of the College of Literature and Arts in the University of Illinois.
Published in New York, 1904.

Half leather, 12mo, 415 pages, $1.25 net

The purpose of this book is to give a systematic account of the principles of the monetary system of exchange, and especially to present a consistent theory of the value of money. New points of view are taken in the statement of the functions of money, the distribution of the precious metals, the quantity of money in relation to its value, and the standard of deferred payments.

PUBLISHED BY

THE MACMILLAN COMPANY

64-66 Fifth Avenue, New York

CPSIA information can be obtained
at www.ICGtesting.com
Printed in the USA
LVHW051158051222
734562LV00028B/656